PART-TIME PROSPECTS

This book presents a wide-ranging survey of the major issues concerning the recent growth of part-time work in industrialised economies. It examines many of the debates and analyses the different circumstances in the United States, Japan and Europe. Chapters deal with questions such as, why is part-time work growing more in some countries than others? What is the nature of part-time work in the United States and how does it compare to the situation in Australia, Britain or the rest of Europe? Who can afford to work in this way? When do men work part-time?

The recent change of government in Britain has brought the whole subject of part-time work to the forefront; the recent signing of the Labour government to the Social Chapter is intended to improve employment rights and there are plans to introduce a minimum wage which will affect low-paid part-time workers. Issues such as the effect of this on unemployment or the risk of social welfare operating as a disincentive to taking up any kind of work must now be addressed.

Part-time Prospects brings together sociologists and economists to provide an up-to-date debate on the changing organisation of work and time, giving for the first time a detailed analysis of this controversial and current issue.

Jacqueline O'Reilly is Senior Research Fellow at the Wissenschaftszentrum Berlin für Sozialforschung and also teaches at the Royal Holloway School of Management, London University. She is currently co-ordinating a comparative research programme on employment in Europe funded by the Targeted Socio-Economic Research Programme from DGXII of the European Commission.

Colette Fagan is Lecturer in Sociology at the University of Liverpool and an Honorary Research Fellow at the European Work and Employment Centre, at UMIST. Her research focuses on gender relations in labour markets, working time and the organisation of domestic life, with a particular interest in international comparisons.

PART-TIME PROSPECTS

An international comparison of part-time
work in Europe, North America
and the Pacific Rim

*Edited by Jacqueline O'Reilly
and Colette Fagan*

London and New York

First published 1998
by Routledge
11 New Fetter Lane, London EC4P 4EE

Simultaneously published in the USA and Canada
by Routledge
29 West 35th Street, New York, NY 10001

© 1998 selection and editorial matter, Jacqueline O'Reilly and
Colette Fagan; individual chapters, the contributors

Typeset in Goudy by Florencetype Ltd, Stoodleigh, Devon
Printed and bound in Great Britain by
Creative Print and Design (Wales) Ebbw Vale

British Library Cataloguing in Publication Data
A catalogue record for this book is available
from the British Library

Library of Congress Cataloguing in Publication Data
A catalogue record for this book has been requested

ISBN 0–415–156696 (hbk)
ISBN 0–415–15670–X (pbk)

TO SUNNY DAYS AND THE PLEASURES
OF COLLABORATION

CONTENTS

CONTENTS

ILLUSTRATIONS

FIGURES

ILLUSTRATIONS

TABLES

BOX

CONTRIBUTORS

Sara Arber is Professor and Head of the Department of Sociology at the University of Surrey. Her research is in the areas of gender and ageing, inequalities in health, and women's employment across the life course. Her publications with Jay Ginn include *Gender and Later Life* (Sage, 1991) and *Connecting Gender and Ageing* (Open University Press, 1995), and, with Nigel Gilbert, *Women's Working Lives* (Macmillan, 1992).

Haesun Bae is a lecturer in economics at the Pukyong National University, South Korea. She conducted a comparative study of Nagoya University Japan from 1991 to 1996. She is currently interested in the female labour market in fisheries and is working as a special researcher at the Fishery Research Institute.

Janeen Baxter is Senior Lecturer in Sociology at the University of Tasmania. Her research has focused on gender inequality at work, particularly the links between paid and unpaid work. Her publications include *Work at Home: The Domestic Division of Labour* (University of Queensland Press, 1993) and *Class Analysis and Contemporary Australia* (Macmillan, 1991) as well as numerous articles on cross-national differences in women's access to authority in paid work, domestic labour patterns and attitudes to gender roles. She is currently working on a comparative project examining the impact of post-industrialism on work and inequality in Australia, the United States and Sweden, as well as a longitudinal study of men's and women's employment patterns in Australia over the lifecourse.

Angela Dale is Director of the Cathie Marsh Centre for Census and Survey Research, and Professor of Quantitative Social Research, at the University of Manchester. Her research includes women's employment and occupational attainment and its relationship to domestic and family life. She has also published on secondary analysis of survey and census data and directs the ESRC-funded support and access programme for the UK Samples of Anonymised Records from the 1991 Census.

Anne-Marie Daune-Richard is a researcher in sociology at the CNRS (National Centre for Scientific Research), Laboratoire d'Economie et Sociologie du Travail (LEST, Aix-en-Provence, France). Her research focuses on theoretical considerations on gender relations and female labour with respect to paid and unpaid work, labour markets and family policy. She has contributed to various publications: 'Gender relations and female labour: a consideration of sociological categories' in J. Jenson, E. Hagen and C. Reddy *Feminization of the Labour Force: Paradoxes and Promises* (Polity Press, 1988); (with M.-Cl. Hurtig) 'Catégories et représentations de sexe: un débat loin d'être clos' in Ephesia *La place des femmes* (La Découverte, 1995), and 'Travail et citoyenneté: un enjeu sexué hier et aujourd'hui' in P. Bouffartigue and H. Eckert *Le travail à l'épreuve du salariat* (L'harmattan, 1997).

Lei Delsen is Assistant Professor at the Department of Applied Economics of the University of Nijmegen, the Netherlands. His present research deals with a number of topical European labour market problems and issues, including international comparative research of new forms of work, labour market institutions and performance, and employment opportunities for disabled people. He is author of *Atypical Employment: An International Perspective* (Wolters-Noordhoff, 1995), co-editor (with Geneviève Reday-Mulvey) of *Gradual Retirement in the OECD Countries* (Dartmouth, 1996) and co-editor (with Eelke de Jong) of *The German and Dutch Economies: Who Follows Whom?* (Physica-Verlag, 1998).

Marco Doudeijns has been working for the Social Policy Division in OECD since 1994. Previously, he worked as a consultant for the EU and as a British civil servant. Now, he is employed at OECD as a microsimulation modeller of taxes and benefits. His recent research has focused on part-time work and financial work incentives. He is interested in practical issues related to the growing importance of atypical employment and its impact on the social welfare state in an international context.

Colette Fagan is a lecturer in sociology at the University of Liverpool, and an Honorary Research Fellow at the European Work and Employment Research Centre at UMIST. Her research focuses on gender relations in labour markets, working time and the organisation of domestic life, with a particular interest in international comparisons. Her most recent relevant publications include 'Gendered time schedules: paid work in Great Britain' (*Social Politics*, Spring 1996); 'The salience of the part-time divide in the European Union' (*European Sociological Review*, December 1996) with Jill Rubery; and *Women and European Employment* (Routledge, 1997) with Jill Rubery, Mark Smith and Damian Grimshaw.

Jay Ginn is employed as Research Fellow in the Sociology Department of the University of Surrey, investigating the gender impact of change in the British mix of state and private pensions. She was previously employed for five years in the department researching gender differences in the economic and health resources of elderly people and subsequently the employment of women in mid-life. Her publications focus on gender, employment and pensions and have included cross-national comparisons. She co-authored *Gender and Later Life* (Sage, 1991) and co-edited *Connecting Gender and Ageing* (Open University Press, 1995), both with Sara Arber.

Maria do Pilar González is Assistant Professor at the Faculty of Economics of the University of Porto, Portugal, teaching labour economics and economic history. She is a member of CETE (Research Centre of Labour and Industrial Economics). Her research interests are essentially on female participation in the labour market and on family organisation models. She is the Portuguese member of the European Commission's Network of Experts on Gender and Employment.

Clare Holdsworth is a Research Fellow at the Centre for Census and Survey research, University of Manchester. Her research interests focus on the inter-relationship between employment and family formation, particularly from a comparative perspective. Her recent research has also included women's occupational health in the nineteenth century.

Susan Houseman is a senior economist at the W.E. Upjohn Institute for Employment Research in the United States. Prior to going to the Upjohn Institute, she was Associate Professor at the School of Public Affairs, University of Maryland, and a visiting scholar at the Brookings Institution. Her research has focused on comparative labour market studies in the United States, Japan and Europe. She has written extensively on job security and labour adjustment and on atypical employment.

Jacqueline O'Reilly has been Senior Researcher at the Wissenschaftszentrum Berlin (WZB) since 1994. She previously taught HRM and organisational theory at London University. Her research has looked at organisational change and labour flexibility in the British, French and German banking sector. She has published *Banking on Flexibility* (Avebury, 1994) and has edited the *International Handbook of Labour Market Policy and Evaluation* with Günther Schmid and Klaus Schömann (Edward Elgar, 1996). She is interested in methodological and theoretical issues related to cross-national comparisons, working time and female employment.

Machiko Osawa is Professor of Economics at Japan Women's University. Her research focuses on the role of women in the Japanese economy, demo-graphic change and corporate restructuring in comparative perspective. Her recent research includes papers co-authored with Susan Houseman including 'Part-time and temporary employment in Japan' (*Monthly Labor Review*, October 1995). Her monographs in Japanese include *Economic Change and*

Women Workers: A US–Japan Comparison (1993) and *Women in the Japanese Economy: The Shifting Paradigm in the 21st Century* (1997).

Birgit Pfau-Effinger is Senior Lecturer in Sociology at the University of Bremen, Germany. She has published widely on theoretical and methodological issues with respect to labour markets, family structures, welfare state policies and gender relations in cross-national perspective. She is one of the co-ordinators of the European Network 'Gender Inequality and the Regions' of the European Research Foundation.

Jill Rubery is Professor of Comparative Employment Systems at Manchester School of Management, UMIST. She has published widely on labour market regulation policies; new forms of work and flexibility; women's employment and pay; employers' working time policies; and international comparative labour market analyses. She is co-editor of the journal, *Gender, Work and Organization*, director of the European Work and Employment Research Centre and from 1991–6 was co-ordinator of the European Commission's Network of Experts on the Situation of Women in the Labour Market.

Margarida Ruivo is Assistant Professor in Labour Economics at the Faculty of Economics of the University of Porto, Portugal. She is a member of CETE (Research Centre of Labour and Industrial Economics). She is interested in local labour markets under globalisation, working time and women's employment.

Mark Smith is a research associate at the European Work and Employment Research Centre at UMIST. He worked as a member of the co-ordinating team of the European Commission's Network of Experts on the Situation of Women in the Labour Market. His research has included atypical work and working time, occupational segregation, the employment rate and the prospects for women's employment. He has also carried out research for the ILO and the ESRC.

José M. Varejão is a teaching assistant at the Faculty of Economics of the University of Porto, Portugal, and a member of CETE (Research Centre of Labour and Industrial Economics). His research focuses on working time and work sharing related issues. Currently, he is working on the dynamic theory of labour demand and the evaluation of the effects of job security policies at the firm level.

Akira Wakisaka is a professor at Okayama University, Japan. His research focuses on women's labour in Japan. He has published two books in Japanese about career formation among Japanese woman. He has also written (in English) 'Woman at work' for the edited book by Mari Sako and Hiroki Sato, *Japanese Labour and Management in Transition* (Routledge, 1997).

Ulrich Walwei is Senior Researcher at the Institute for Employment Research (Institut für Arbeitsmarkt und Berufsforschung, IAB) in Nuremberg,

Germany. He is head of the IAB department dealing with medium-term and long-term labour market projections. He has published widely on labour market regulation policies, non-standard forms of employment such as part-time work or fixed-term contracts, active labour market policies (particularly job placement) and various international comparative labour market analyses. He has also carried out research for several international organisations including the European Commission and the ILO.

ACKNOWLEDGEMENTS

The idea for this book developed from a discussion on a sunny afternoon in Berlin in 1994. We were remarking that although much had been written about part-time work in a variety of journals and reports, there were hardly any books on the subject which examined the wide range of issues that affect part-timers from a comparative, theoretical and empirically informed perspective. We started to develop a structure for an edited collection with the criteria that each contribution would be comparative and together would cover the key issues of debate.

Extremely helpful comments on initial drafts of the proposal were made by Professor Eileen Applebaum (Economic Policy Institute, Washington), Professor Günther Schmid (WZB and Technical University, Berlin), Dr Christel Lane (St John's College, Cambridge University) and Dr Christoph Büchtemann (Rand). Françoise Coré (OECD), Dr Mari Sako (Oxford University) and Professor Sara Arber (Surrey University) also made useful suggestions when we were identifying authors for the proposed chapters. We appreciate the encouragement and support they have given us in the process of putting this volume together, and especially to Günther Schmid for inviting Colette to work at the WZB as a visiting research fellow on two occasions during 1994–5.

We would also really like to thank all the authors in this volume both for the excellent work they delivered (on time!) and the enthusiastic and informative discussions we were able to have over the first draft of the chapters at a workshop held in Berlin in September 1996. We were also very pleased that our editor Mari Shullaw from Routledge was able to attend this meeting, and help keep us on course as to what was realistic and viable. We are grateful to Dr Jürgen Schupp (German Economic Institute, Berlin), Silke Bothfeld (Dip. Soz.) (WZB) Dr Karin Schulz-Buschoff (WZB) and Professor Günther Schmid (WZB), who were lively and provocative discussants at the workshop. Hannelore Minzlaff, Christoph Albrecht and Karin Reinsch at the WZB were a great help, with their usual efficiency and humour, in managing the finances and administration of the project.

We were fortunate enough to receive funding from the Fritz Thyssen Stiftung and the WZB to pay for participants' travel costs and expenses to attend the workshop. Funds from the European Commission's Targeted Socio-Economic Research Programme (DGXII) contributed to research conducted for Chapter 1 and allowed us to travel between Berlin and Manchester to be able to write and edit together and fill the gaps that e-mail can never quite reach.

We would also like to thank Roxy Walsh for allowing us to use her work 'Coal fire quilt' for the cover of this book.

We have both really enjoyed working on this book together and feel we have learnt much from the process; however, we are finally responsible for any errors or gaps which remain.

Jacqueline O'Reilly and Colette Fagan
Berlin and Liverpool

1

CONCEPTUALISING PART-TIME WORK

The value of an integrated comparative perspective

Colette Fagan and Jacqueline O'Reilly

INTRODUCTION

Part-time work is a particularly apposite issue for cross-national comparison as it highlights many of the controversies in comparative research, such as whether or not there are universal laws of convergence in social development. These debates were revived by the convergence thesis of industrialism (Kerr *et al.* 1960) and the subsequent rejoinders which give more salience to the diversity of industrial and political development (e.g. Goldthorpe 1985; Przeworski and Teune 1973; Maurice *et al.* 1982; Inkeles and Sasaki 1996). Universal trends in part-time work can be seen across countries: it is primarily performed by women; it is often associated with marginal employment; its expansion has coincided with a period of industrial restructuring and a growing presence of women in the labour market. From this vantage point, part-time work appears to be emerging as a universal modification to the existing sexual division of labour.

Nevertheless, comparative research indicates considerable differences between countries in the extent and form of part-time work between men and women and over the life cycle. Employment conditions in terms of hours, wages and associated benefits also vary significantly. Researchers are therefore faced with several related theoretical questions. Why is part-time work universally gendered and under what conditions will this change? What social processes account for the variation in different countries and will these differences persist or converge? And finally, will change be in the direction of marginalised or more integrated forms of part-time work? Our aim is not to look *only* at similarities or *only* at differences across countries; instead, we are, as Siltanen proposes (1994: 1), in 'pursuit of the twin objectives of recognising diversity and isolating major processes' to understand what the phenomenon of part-time employment means in countries with different institutional settings.

1

Cross-national theoretical approaches which seek to account for both similarities and differences in women's employment patterns have developed rapidly since the 1980s. Many of these studies focus on the conditions under which women are available for full- or part-time work ('labour supply'), while others pay more attention to how firms use part-timers ('labour demand'). What they all do, however, is demonstrate that analyses which attempt to reduce explanations to one or two explanatory variables, such as child care provisions or employers' flexibility strategies, are often inadequate in accounting for cross-national variation in the use of part-time work.

Our aim in this introductory chapter is to outline and critically discuss the various theoretical approaches used to analyse part-time employment. We start by reviewing the sociological and economic debates related to labour supply and demand; we then focus on approaches which have sought to develop a framework that can be applied to cross-national comparative research.[1] We argue that the value of an integrated comparative perspective is that it attempts to encompass the insights gained from these specific debates and apply them to different societal contexts, avoiding over-deterministic or reductionist explanations. This allows us to understand how the behaviour of collective actors and individuals, located within particular institutional systems, construct, reproduce and change gender relations. We conclude this chapter by assessing whether or not the emergence of part-time employment can be understood as a particular form of 'gender contract' or compromise. On the basis of this discussion we draw out the implications for a re-conceptualisation of part-time employment and policy directions.

HOW DOES THE GENDER DIVISION OF LABOUR IN THE HOME AFFECT THE 'CHOICE' TO WORK PART-TIME?

The separation and relationship between the sphere of economic market production and domestic reproduction has formed the analytic basis underlying explanations of women's availability for part-time work. Industrialisation modified the pre-existing gender division of labour within families as the dominant means of gaining a living became waged labour located in workplaces away from the home. This commodification of women's and men's labour retained a gender division. Men's labour became increasingly associated with waged work and market production, while women remained responsible for combining household work with any paid employment which they undertook (Humphries 1977; Tilly and Scott 1987; Hudson and Lee 1990). It is not only that distinct tasks are located in these two sites, but also the principles of orientating and justifying behaviour in them vary. Weber (1978) argued that the public sphere is organised through a legal regulatory framework of capitalist accounting, the labour contract and bureaucratic principles of organisation based on achieved

characteristics. This is distinct from the private family arena, where the organising principle is ascribed kinship relations, even where legally regulated, such
as in the marriage contract. Later in this chapter we will argue that the growth
in female labour market participation brings these two organising principles
into conflict, providing one stimulus for social change. Our immediate concern,
however, is to discuss how the gender division in responsibilities within the
home makes women more available for part-time work than men.

One type of explanation for women's involvement in part-time work is that
this is universally functional or efficient for the household and society.
Functionalist theory distinguishes between men's 'instrumental' role as wage-
earners and women's 'expressive' role where waged work takes second place to
the responsibilities for caring for children and providing men with emotional
support and respite from the pressures of public life (Parsons 1943). Parsons
argued that this gender division was found in most societies, and that the existence of this universal pattern was evidence that it was a functional arrangement
for the maintenance of social order, for example, by fulfilling the necessary
tasks of socialising children (Parsons and Bales 1956). Becker's (1981) 'household economics' approach also claims to be universally applicable in market
economies. The argument is that women anticipate future labour market interruptions associated with raising children and running a home, and on this basis
make particular types of 'human capital' investment in education and training,
while men prepare for a more continuous and intense labour market involvement in their role as household breadwinner. At the point of setting up home
together it is economically rational for men to specialise in waged work, and
for women to do most of the child-raising and other unpaid household tasks;
their tendency to gravitate towards the part-time market work allows for a
compromise which does not disrupt this division of labour. Thus, while Parsons
distinguishes between instrumental and expressive roles, Becker attempts to
differentiate between economic rationality in relation to the market and 'altru-
istic' motives for resource allocation within the household. Both, however,
provide a theoretical explanation which suggests that women's part-time
employment is an optimal arrangement for families, at least when two parents
are present.

Both of these theories have been heavily criticised, although Becker's thesis
has received the most attention in contemporary labour market debates. The
first point of criticism is that these theoretical approaches are teleological:
essentially the sexual division of labour is argued to be a functional or efficient
arrangement on the basis that it would not continue otherwise. Second, both
approaches are also largely premised on a consensual understanding of household decision-making, thus neglecting conflict and unequal power relations
between household members. A further criticism specifically directed at Becker's
work is that supply-side 'human capital' arguments are insufficient to account
for gender differences in wages; discriminatory labour market processes have
a major impact on the acquisition of human capital and its rewards (e.g.

Humphries and Rubery 1984; Gittins 1985; Walby 1988; Morris 1989). Finally, even within its own criteria of individuals making rational responses to wage differences, claims that such a division of labour is 'efficient' are shown to be flawed when analysed from a lifetime rather than a cross-sectional perspective (Owen 1987; Fagan and Rubery 1996b).

More recently, debates around household labour supply decisions have taken a further turn in response to Hakim's explanation for why women work part-time (1991, 1995, 1996a: 103–20, 1997). Unlike the 'functional family' and the 'household economics' approaches, the emphasis is upon women's aspirations and decisions rather than upon what is beneficial to the family division of labour. She suggests that women can be broadly divided into 'self-made women' committed to an employment career and 'grateful slaves' who prefer a more traditional homemaker role. For this latter group of home-centred women, employment has a secondary and subordinate role in their life compared to other interests. Working part-time is argued to be a proxy indicator for this 'qualitatively different' labour market involvement of home-centred women.

Hakim's thesis challenges labour market researchers to take more account of the heterogeneity in women's work orientations than often occurs. However, there are some problems with her argument. The first is the explanatory role attributed to work orientations, and the conceptualisation of these orientations. She claims that social scientists overemphasise structural constraints in explanations of women's employment patterns, such as a lack of child care services. In contrast, she prioritises differences in work orientations as the primary explanatory factor for the diverging labour market behaviour among women, even though she acknowledges that preferences do not determine outcomes (Hakim 1996a: 202–15). This emphasis on preferences and choices leads to a voluntaristic account of women's behaviour which neglects the structural constraints which women act within (Devine 1994; Crompton with Le Feuvre 1996; Ginn et al. 1996). Partly as a result, preferences are discussed in a simplified and essentially static way, suggesting that women's attitudes remain largely constant as they move from adolescence through their lives and that women can be divided into discrete categories. Little attention is given to the literature which explores how attitudes are at least partly dependent on environmental factors, and develop over time in an adaptive process, responding to opportunities and experiences (Dex 1988). For example, qualitative research has shown how young women's labour market aspirations and their training plans are lowered if they perceive that they have few labour market prospects (Rees 1992).

The second problem is that there are dangers in using information on labour market behaviour as a proxy for inferences about preferences. For example, a study of women who left employment at the end of maternity leave in Britain revealed that one group of women was following their preferences to look after their children themselves, and another group had quit because they could not find child care (McRae 1991). Such studies provide a strong caution against replacing a structural analysis with an overly voluntaristic emphasis on women's choices.

International comparisons of women's employment patterns throw both of these problems into particularly stark relief. Indeed, it was the evidence from cross-national comparisons which led Hakim to revise her initial suggestion that working part-time provides a suitable proxy measure for work orientations in cross-national research (1991) to one where she excludes some forms of part-time work (Hakim 1997). This is because comparative work reveals that women's involvement in paid work, and particularly the extent to which motherhood involves a shift into part-time work, varies markedly between countries (e.g. Dex and Shaw 1986; Rubery 1988; Crompton et al. 1990; Dale and Glover 1990; Dex et al. 1993; O'Reilly 1994; Fagan and Rubery 1996a; see also contributions to this volume). Even if it is accepted that this reflects national differences in women's work orientations, we are left with the task of accounting for this cultural variation (see Pfau-Effinger, Chapter 9, this volume).

Differences in social structures therefore have a central role in the production of satisfactory accounts for international variations in part-time work among women. Researchers have for some time pointed to differences in social policies, such as child care provision, as important societal features which structure women's labour supply. The debate has been widened by developments in the comparative analysis of Welfare State regimes, opened by Esping-Andersen (1990). His typology of Welfare States rests on the concept of 'de-commodification', which refers to the extent of state intervention in the class system so that 'a person can maintain a livelihood without reliance on the market' (Esping-Andersen 1990: 21–2). He argues that these different Welfare State regimes are 'unique configurations' which refute both Marxist and Modernisation theses on convergence. Furthermore, these regimes have a differential effect on the position of women in the labour market. For example, social-democratic states (e.g. Sweden) have a stronger commitment to providing public child care services than a liberal state (e.g. the US and UK), and in doing so create a larger demand for women's labour as public sector employees.[2] Esping-Andersen's analysis has drawn attention to critical differences in Welfare State regimes, and in the process has inspired debate and criticism. Feminists have criticised his analysis for ignoring women's unpaid domestic labour in his concept of 'de-commodification', and argue that Welfare State regimes have to be gendered. Orloff (1993), for example, has suggested than Esping-Andersen's model needs to be re-formulated to examine how far the state guarantees women's access to paid work or the 'right to be commodified', and how far the state enables women to form autonomous households. In a similar vein, Lewis (1992) has proposed a typology of 'strong', 'moderate' and 'weak' breadwinner states according to whether state policies reinforce or begin to dismantle the traditional breadwinner model of family life.

So while 'human capital' and 'work orientations' theories have the merit of drawing attention to the effect of differences in women's market resources and plans on their labour supply, it is critically important that this behaviour is located and interpreted within the incentive structure created by state policies

5

and other institutional arrangements. This is clearly demonstrated by international evidence of the influence of education on women's behaviour. The 'educational lever' (Crompton and Sanderson 1990) has proved to be a universally powerful predictor of women's labour market behaviour. Highly qualified women maintain a higher and more continuous labour market involvement during motherhood than women without educational capital in Europe and North America (Dex 1985; Crompton et al. 1990; McRae 1991; Dale and Egerton 1995; Rubery et al. 1995; Spain and Bianchi 1996: 67). This is because education increases women's aspirations and access to the better-paid professional jobs. High qualification levels are also associated with an attitudinal shift in favour of more egalitarian gender roles among younger generations of both sexes, and even signs of some minor adjustments to the unequal gender division of housework (Dale and Egerton 1995). Thus, education reduces the constraint which motherhood makes on women's labour and hence the type of compromise they make about the gender division of labour. Yet even when mothers' qualification levels are taken into account, marked national differences persist in their involvement in full-time and part-time employment (Fagan and Rubery 1996a). These differences arise because the influence of supply-side characteristics is mediated by state policies and other institutions which affect both the conditions under which women supply their labour and the organisation of labour demand.

Finally, it is through an examination of the household division of labour in relation to Welfare State regimes and labour market conditions that we can begin to identify the circumstances which are contributing to the growth of part-time work among men in some countries. Essentially a part-time wage is insufficient to provide an acceptable standard of living in all but the most highly paid occupations (Rubery, Chapter 7, this volume). So part-time work for either sex results in economic hardship unless there is recourse to additional income transfers through family relationships or Welfare State entitlements. Most male part-timers are students, other young labour market entrants and older men approaching retirement (Delsen, Chapter 3, this volume). Their wages are supplemented by student grants or pensions plus some inter-generational transfers within the family. Although the expansion of part-time work is frequently mooted as one way of tackling unemployment (Walwei, Chapter 5, this volume), this is unlikely to happen without social security reforms to remove the financial disincentive for those with unemployment benefit entitlements to enter part-time work (Doudeijns, Chapter 6, this volume). Therefore, the growth in the supply of men for part-time work in some countries is due to the compositional effect of an expansion of education (Blossfeld et al. 1995) and Welfare State restructuring. This restructuring may make men more available for part-time work through a process of impoverishment, whereby the basic income standards guaranteed by the state are driven down, or a process of flexible reform so that social security systems accommodate rather than penalise part-time work (Doudeijns, Chapter 6, Ginn and Arber, Chapter 8, this volume).

In this section we have considered how, on one hand, the gender division of labour within the home makes women more available for part-time work than men, and, on the other hand, how labour supply plans and behaviour are structured through state policies. The next section examines the role of firms and their demand for part-time workers.

WHY DO FIRMS WANT PART-TIMERS?

Attempts to explain the use of part-time employment from a demand-side perspective has largely been found in the literature on dual and segmented labour markets. These theories have developed as a critique to neo-liberal economic theories of labour market inequalities, such as those associated with the school of 'household economics'. Early versions of these theories suggested that the division between primary and secondary labour markets was primarily associated with firm size (Averitt 1968): large firms offered primary employment and smaller firms used disadvantaged secondary forms of labour. This approach was developed by Doeringer and Piore (1971) to show that employers segmented the workforce within the firm through the creation of internal and external labour markets. In internal labour markets employees have access to relatively superior employment conditions, including training and career ladders. Jobs in the secondary labour market are inferior, lower paid and more precarious. This approach accounted for labour market divisions in terms of employer behaviour, in contrast to the neo-classical emphasis on the differential effects created by individual workers' 'human capital', and part-time work was essentially conceptualised as a secondary form of employment.

A range of motives has been suggested for why employers segment labour markets. The reasons for retaining certain employees via internal labour markets include investments in technology and the associated requirement for specialised operational skills (Berger and Piore 1980), the retention of skills which are firm-specific or otherwise in short supply, and more generally the gain in productivity and employee commitment in certain production processes. Others have emphasised the way these divisions are created by different forms of managerial control (Edwards 1979; Gordon et al. 1982), or distinctions created by legal regulation (Berger and Piore 1980; Michon 1981; Boyer 1986), and the influence of trade unions in protecting their members against outsiders (Rubery 1978). It is not our aim to repeat the critical debates on these theories, as they have been discussed in more depth elsewhere (MacInnes 1987; Rogers and Rogers 1989; Rosenberg 1989; Pollert 1991; O'Reilly 1994). Instead we will focus here on their relevance to the analysis of part-time employment. The main issue of debate in explanations for firms' use of part-timers focuses on whether this is a marginalisation or integration strategy: are part-timers mainly concentrated in secondary forms of employment, or is this a strategy to integrate or retain certain groups of workers?

Subsequent developments in segmentation theory were made in the debates on labour market flexibility and restructuring and rising unemployment in the 1970s and 1980s (Atkinson and Meager 1986; Rosenberg 1989). It is in this economic context that part-time employment largely emerged, although in some countries it had begun to expand in response to labour shortages in the post-war period of full employment (see Dale and Holdsworth, Chapter 4, this volume). Flexibility can mean a number of things, at both the labour market and enterprise level (OECD 1986). On one hand, functional flexibility, flexible specialisation or polyvalence has been associated with a broadening of tasks and skills which qualitatively improve the competence of workers and the organisation of work within firms (Piore and Sable 1984). This is associated with a reaction against Taylorist and Fordist principles, and the spreading influence of Human Resource Management and Japanese examples of 'best practice'. Often this reorganisation of tasks is accompanied by job loss, to create a smaller primary segment of employees. In some circumstances, this has encouraged outsourcing and the displacement of tasks once performed by employees within the firm, so that sub-contractors bear the costs of market uncertainty. On the other hand, 'numerical' and 'working-time flexibility' entail matching labour input to peaks and troughs in production, and it is with these dimensions to flexibility that the issue of part-time work is usually connected. As with earlier formulations in segmentation theory, part-time employees and other numerically flexible workers belong to a peripheral ring, distinct from core employees. A considerable amount of research took place in the 1980s and 1990s which examined the extent to which part-time employment demonstrates secondary labour market or numerically flexible characteristics.[3] The key issues of debate in these studies examine whether part-time work represents a marginalised form of cheap labour and precariousness employment, or whether it is a 'bridge' either allowing women to enter paid employment, or maintain continuous participation, albeit on reduced hours.

A major reason why part-time work represents a marginalised, secondary form of employment is because it provides employers with a source of cheap labour. The main reason for the lower hourly pay for part-timers is that they are segregated into low-paid jobs and low-pay sectors (Rubery and Fagan 1993, 1994; Rubery, Chapter 7, and Baxter, Chapter 14, this volume). Where part-timers and full-timers are found in similar jobs they are more likely to receive pro-rata pay, although thresholds of hours and/or pay (as in Germany) can serve to exclude them from extra pay entitlements, such as overtime premia or social insurance and employment protection (see O'Reilly 1996b; Rubery et al. 1995; Schoer 1987). Minimum wage systems play an important part in closing the wage gap between full-timers and part-timers in some countries, and in reducing the scope of employers to use part-timers as a cheap labour force. Büchtemann and Quack (1990) and Quack (1993) argue that in West Germany it is not part-time work per se that is a secondary form of employment but it is the accumulation of disadvantage associated with remaining in this type of employment. For example, missing out on training and promotion pushes these workers into a peripheral labour market in terms of qualifications and income, or lower lifetime accumulation of pension entitlements (see Baxter, Chapter 14, and Ginn and Arber, Chapter 8, this volume).

Whether part-time work is a precarious form of employment is related to the issue of job security and social security entitlements. Part-time workers may be more vulnerable to losing their jobs because they have poorer terms of employment protection than those in the full-time core workforce. This is largely dependent upon statutory employment protection regulations. Part-timers with earnings or hours below a certain threshold may be less protected, such as marginal part-timers in Germany (*'geringfuge Beschaftige'*) or those working less than eight hours in the UK. In many other countries, such as Sweden, France, Belgium and the Netherlands, equality of treatment between full- and part-timers is enforced in labour law (Maier 1994; Fagan *et al.* 1995; O'Reilly 1996b). However, even where equal treatment is ensured by regulation, part-time jobs may still be more vulnerable due to being concentrated in certain parts of the production system where there is a heavy reliance on numerical flexibility through seasonal and cyclical lay-offs, or the use of temporary contracts (see Smith *et al.*, Chapter 2, this volume). This vulnerability in many cases is associated with lower entitlements to unemployment benefits in social insurance systems which are still largely based on the presumption of lifelong, full-time employment.

One of the key assumptions in segmentation theory is that there is little mobility from the secondary into the primary labour market. This has resulted in a relative neglect of the possibility of part-time work being used as an integration strategy or a transitional stage. The emphasis of segmentation theory has tended to focus on static cross-sectional pictures of occupants of particular labour market segments. However, research on labour market transitions has pointed to the different role that part-time work plays over the life cycle. The common gender pattern is that part-time work is generally triggered by motherhood, whereas for men it is more likely to occur at the point of labour market entry or exit (see Delsen, Chapter 3, this volume; Quack 1993; Blossfeld *et al.* 1995; Hakim 1996b; Blossfeld and Hakim 1997). At the same time there are important national variations in the extent of full-time, part-time and non-employment among mothers, as well as in the role of part-time work in the youth and older labour market. Furthermore, transitions into part-time employment may be associated with job changes or employment interruptions, while others occur through a reduction in hours within the existing job, for example, as a result of leave arrangements and other 'family-oriented' employment policies. Arrangements to enable employees to adjust their working time vary nationally, but there is also evidence of occupational and sectoral differences. Across Europe, for example, provisions seem to be more developed in the public sector rather than the private sector (Fagan and Rubery 1996b). This latter form of working time transition may actually serve to keep employees in the primary sector, or to make the barriers between 'core' full-time and 'secondary' part-time more permeable for at least some groups of workers. For other women, however, the switch to part-time employment involves downward occupational mobility, and a perhaps permanent demotion to the secondary labour market. Finally, for the unemployed or new labour market entrants, part-time employment may be the only employment option in slack labour markets and where employers are developing flexibility strategies (see Walwei, Chapter 5, this volume); in some countries, however, such as the UK, the benefits system makes it difficult for the unemployed to take up these low-paid jobs (see Doudeijns, Chapter 6, this volume; Gregg and Wadsworth 1995). Thus for the young, and those with few qualifications, the main transitions may be a round-about of part-time peripheral employment, unemployment and inactivity.

Finally, Beechey and Perkins (1987) have argued that flexibility is essentially gendered: where the labour force is predominantly female, employers are more likely to introduce part-time work, in contrast to the use of other means of acquiring flexibility from men, such as overtime and shift-work. The flexibility debates have not specified this sufficiently clearly so that the neutral conceptualisation of part-time work as 'non-standard' or 'atypical' is held up in contrast to the implicit gender-blind norm of (male) full-time employment patterns. As feminists have pointed out, part-time work is typical for women in many countries, and in some service sectors it approaches the standard employment form. Indeed, this may indicate the substitution of cheaper part-time labour in place of full-time workers within the female workforce in some societal contexts (see Rubery, Chapter 7, and Houseman and Osawa, Chapter 12, this volume).

While segmentation theory is clearly useful for highlighting labour market inequalities, the conceptualisation of part-time work as a secondary form of employment does not explain why some forms of part-time work may integrate some employees and marginalise others. These differences would suggest that further distinctions need to be made between the category of part-time employment. We need to be able to identify where employers use part-time work as a strategy of marginalisation or where it is used to retain employees (Tilly 1992); this also needs to be tied to the distinction between short or long hour part-time jobs (Fagan 1996; Plantenga 1996). Another important consideration is the particular role of the state, not just as a regulator of employment conditions, but as a major employer of women (Schmid 1991). Public sector employment conditions vary markedly between countries (Meyer 1994), and current public sector restructuring in many countries can be expected to impact unevenly on different groups of workers. In the UK, for example, privatisation has had particularly negative consequences for the conditions in part-time jobs. Further we need to integrate an analysis of employer behaviour with employee characteristics. For example, are there differences between the experience of low- and high-qualified women who work part-time, and is part-time employment part of a continuous or interrupted pattern of labour market participation?

Such distinctions highlight how part-time work embraces a number of characteristics, not all of which fall within the secondary or 'atypical' category.

Segmentation theories and the flexibility debate must also be broadened beyond the focus on the production sphere to improve our understanding of why women are prepared to take up part-time employment, even when it is a disadvantaged form of employment. For example, policies which promote part-time employment as part of work-sharing or equal opportunities policies neglect that most of these jobs can only provide a 'component wage' (Siltanen 1994), so that the only people who can afford to work part-time are those with another source of household income, from either family members or state transfers. The state's full role in structuring women's labour supply is also usually neglected by studies which have concentrated on the economic sphere of production and the narrower influence of state labour market regulations and unemployment policies. Thus, the availability of workers to fill part-time jobs is affected by the interaction between household circumstances, firms' behaviour, labour market policies and regulation as well as the wider Welfare State regime. These aspects can be examined in terms of the interaction between three components – households, firms and the state – as the basic elements of an integrated approach which we would argue is essential for cross-national comparisons.

COMPARATIVE FRAMEWORKS FOR EXAMINING PART-TIME WORK

In contrast to convergence or universalist theories which emphasise global, common trends and pressures – such as market forces, or technological change – theoretical approaches concerned with the persistence of difference pay more attention to the influence of distinct societal features. Comparative frameworks of analysis can be broadly divided between institutional and ideational approaches (O'Reilly 1996a). Ideational approaches stress the importance of culture, namely the beliefs, values and normative practices or 'way of life' in a society. The problem with explaining societal differences simply in terms of cultural differences is that it is ultimately tautological and provides little insight into the material and historical origin of cultural variation and change. Some of these problems are overcome by an institutional 'societal' approach. First, cultural domination or hegemonic power is at least partly embodied in social and economic institutions. Second, these institutions create different material and ideological constraints and resources for social action.

An institutional approach, therefore, reduces some of the problems involved in defining and operationalising abstract notions of 'national culture'. At the same time, most institutional theorists would accept that culture is not totally subsumed within institutions, and that even dominant cultural values may move out of step from those embodied in certain institutions, for example, in periods of rapid economic or political change. (The events leading up to the Wende in East Germany are a particularly poignant example of this.) A minimalist stance adds cultural dimensions to institutional explanations in passing, through reference to 'tradition' or 'individual attitudes'. Others argue for a greater role for cultural values, on the basis that they are partially independent of institutional structures, with which they interact (e.g. Dore 1973; Gallie 1978). More recently, Sorge (1994) has also argued for the integration of an ideational dimension into institutional analyses. Thus, despite its advantages, an institutional approach does not fully capture the values and beliefs of social actors, which we will return to below.

Institutional approaches to the cross-national analysis of employment have developed in two broadly parallel strands of literature. The first is the 'societal employment systems' approach, rooted in industrial sociology and in economic theories of labour market segmentation. The primary focus is economic production and industrial organisation, and the relationship between capital and labour. Some theorists have elaborated this approach to integrate gender divisions; however, many studies within this theoretical framework remain 'gender-blind'. The second approach encompasses feminist theories which explicitly set out to theorise differences in gender relations. Common to both the 'societal employment systems' and the 'gender systems' approaches to understanding cross-national differences in women's employment is a concern to identify the salient institutional arrangements and the interactive processes between these different structures, or sites of action, which create and re-create sexual divisions in society.

Societal employment systems

A key contribution to the development of the 'societal employment systems' framework was made by the cross-national work on the 'societal effect' by Maurice et al. (1982). They argue that national institutions influence the organisation of work at the level of the firm, with their empirical work paying particular attention to the relationship between the educational system, the industrial relations system and the industrial structure. Each institutional system is argued to have a degree of autonomy within an interdependent macro structure. Social behaviour is institutionally embedded, and in turn institutions are modified through social action. No one part of the system, therefore, such as the level and form of part-time work, can be understood in isolation from the societal context. This means that rather than conducting a term-for-term comparison, a particular phenomenon needs to be examined in relation to other institutions in the given society (see Daune-Richard, Chapter 11, this volume). This type of institutional approach is echoed in other more recent institutional approaches, such as the Business Systems perspective (Whitley 1992).

The 'societal effect' approach has made theoretical and methodological progress through providing a distinct material basis for the analysis of cross-national differences in the organisation of work. However, it has been criticised for the functionalist and static nature of the analysis, which, particularly in the early periods of this work, emphasises institutional coherence. As a result there is little theory of social change or indeed the causal nature of the relationship between different institutions, and social action is given only a limited theoretical role (Rose 1985; Lane 1989). Finally, gender relations and heterogeneity within nation state societies are largely ignored (O'Reilly 1996a: 11). Some of these criticisms have been accepted by Maurice (1995), who argues for the need to include historical data, elaborate the articulation between macro and micro levels, and identify a 'new' flexible societal coherence.

The second important contribution to the 'societal employment systems' literature has been made by the development of labour market segmentation theory. The central theoretical goal of this work is to understand how labour market divisions are developed and maintained through the action of employers, organised labour and the intervention of the state in response to changing economic conditions (Rubery 1978; Wilkinson 1981). Initially, particularly in the early dual labour market theories, an inadequate conceptualisation of gender was used (see Beechey and Perkins 1985, 1987; Dex 1985; Walby 1988). Gender mainly appeared in connection with the division of labour in the household, whereby women supply their labour under different conditions to men. Women were largely treated as an undifferentiated group, with gender-specific household roles treated as exogenous. The role of male resistance and exclusionary mechanisms against women workers, as well as wider cultural and normative prescriptions concerning gender roles, were virtually ignored by these theories. However, as segmentation theory has developed, the construction of gender relations has been theoretically refined through arguments about the 'relative autonomy' of the sphere of social reproduction (Humphries and Rubery 1984), the contribution of class struggles around the notion of a 'family wage' to the maintenance of a sexual division of labour within the household (Humphries 1977), male exclusionary tactics at the workplace (Rubery 1978; Cockburn 1991) and the role of the Welfare State in constructing men's and women's labour supply (Picchio del Mercato 1981).

Within this tradition of segmentation theory, Rubery (1988) has explicitly sought to develop a framework which is capable of accounting for cross-national differences in gender relations, by drawing upon the 'societal effect' approach of the LEST school (Maurice et al. 1982), as well as emphasising the effect of cultural values. She argues that to apply a societal perspective to women's employment

> means that we need to understand the way in which the system of industrial, labour market and family organisation interrelate and the role of the society's political and social values in maintaining these relationships before we could expect to make sense of the differences between countries in the position of women.
>
> (Rubery 1988: 253)

Furthermore, these national variations in the position of women are not simply of interest to those studying gender relations. Gender-blind studies miss the crucial point that the characteristics and organisation of employment and the production system are influenced by the structure of the sphere of social reproduction (Rubery 1994). Subsequently, Rubery and Fagan (1994, 1995) have identified a set of institutional structures which are pertinent components of a holistic and systemic framework for cross-national comparisons of women's integration into full-time and part-time work. These include the organisation and industrial structure of the production system; labour market conditions and regulations; the training and education system; and dominant social attitudes and values, including those concerned with gender roles. To develop this framework a more detailed understanding of the influence of wider social institutions, such as Welfare State policies and social attitudes, help to structure gender roles. The social reproduction of gender roles has been directly addressed by writers who have set out to theorise changing relations between men and women which we now examine.

Gender systems

An early contribution to the English-language debate was made by Connell (1987), who outlined a framework for a dynamic approach which can be applied to understanding gender relations across societies and over time. A central premise is that actors are both affected by the structural relations in which they live, while at the same time they have a capacity to act to change these relations.

Connell argues that gender relations are produced through the interrelationship of the 'gender order' and different 'gender regimes'. The 'gender order' refers to the way that power relations, and definitions of femininity and masculinity, have been historically constructed in societies through three interrelated structures of gender relations. These are: the division of labour; power relations and the connection of authority with masculinity; and cathexis, which refers to emotionally charged social relations, particularly between the sexes. These constituent structures have independent effects which may conflict with each other. The concept of 'gender regime' describes the way that these power relations and identities are shaped in specific practices at the institutional level, such as in the labour market. Thus the 'gender order' is institutionalised through social practices, ranging, for example, from state regulation at the national level down to localised peer group pressures in daily encounters. Tensions and struggles for change in the existing gender regime arise when social actors have interests in challenging cyclical or routinised practices (Connell 1987: 141), perhaps in response to changes elsewhere within the gender order. An example of such a dynamic is young women entering the labour market with higher qualifications and career aspirations due to expanding educational opportunities. Thus, there is not necessarily a functional fit between the practices in different institutional regimes. Connell's model therefore identifies the way in which social action can bring about change in gender relations. It also allows us to compare the particular gender orders found in different societies, and to begin to locate the emergence of divergent practices in different national contexts.

An empirical application and adaptation of Connell's approach can be found in Pfau-Effinger's (1993, and Chapter 9, this volume) historical analysis of national differences in women's integration into full-time and part-time employment. Her theoretical model is of a 'gender arrangement' which adds the concept of 'gender culture' to Connell's 'gender order'. By 'gender culture' she means the nationally specific, dominant norms about gender relations, and inter-generational responsibilities found in every society. This gender culture is institutionalised and so is relatively constant over time, although variations by region or position in the social strata can occur.

Her thesis is that the 'gender culture' influences individual and collective practices in different social settings and institutional sites. The employment system, the Welfare State and the family and household system are specified as the key institutional settings which affect the particular form of women's economic integration. Through her cross-national application she is able to test the relevance of a range of institutional features. From this she draws the crucial point that national differences in the 'gender culture' are rooted in the different processes of transformation from agrarian to industrial society, and the relative power of different social groups during this transition. She is also able to explore the varying role that part-time employment has played in the modernisation of the family model in different societies (Pfau-Effinger 1993). Her thesis is corroborated by other historical analyses of women's employment which stressed the lasting impact of national differences in the transition to industrial society and later periods of rapid economic change on the contemporary employment position of women (Tilly and Scott 1987; Hantrais 1990; Crompton *et al.* 1990).

Strong parallels can be found in Hirdmann's (1988) theoretical model of 'gender systems' and 'gender contracts', which has been developed in relation to women's position in Swedish society. Rantalaiho (1993) provides an English-language summary of this approach. The gender system rests on two basic principles. First, that differences in virtually all areas of life are divided into male and female categories, such as through segregated work, or identities of masculinity and femininity. Second, this difference is organised hierarchically, on the basis of the primacy or cultural prestige of the male norm. The gender system is maintained and reproduced on three levels: the cultural sphere, social institutions and the direct learning of gender roles through socialisation. The most important departure which distinguishes this framework from Connell's is that Hirdmann employs the concept of a 'gender contract'. This exposes the specific historical or geographical form which the gender system takes, and refers to

> unspoken rules, mutual obligations and rights which define the relations between women and men, between genders and generations, and finally between the areas of production and reproduction.
>
> (Rantalaiho 1993: 2)

This contract has two inherent tensions, which rest upon the different organisational principles and legal contractual frameworks found in the public and private spheres, first identified by Weber (1978). The public sphere is organised on the principle of individual political citizenship and employment contracts. Women's entry into waged employment produces a growing 'contradiction of equality' as they are increasingly involved in competitive relations based on the principle of individual merit and citizenship, which is largely defined with reference to institutionalised male norms. The 'conflict of difference' arises because women realise that this individualised, public role stands in sharp contradiction to the family responsibilities and dependencies in the sphere of social reproduction. A similar argument about the inherent tension between the sexual division of labour and the development of individual political citizenship is made by Stockman et al. (1995). These tensions produce a 'renegotiation' of the gender contract, which is more to do with changes in social practices and particular institutional reform rather than explicit and open political negotiation. Thus in her analysis of Sweden, Hirdmann argues that economic and political pressures eroded the 'housewife contract', which was replaced by the 'equality contract' of the 1960s. This contract normalised women's employment through institutional reform and the expansion of the Welfare State. However, the contradictions between the organisation of production and reproduction were still experienced by women through their day-to-day involvement in paid and unpaid care work. This produced new political pressures and by the 1980s a new transitional phase had emerged in the direction of an 'equal status contract' which coincides with competing economic pressures of recession and restructuring (Duncan 1994, 1995).

This 'gender systems' approach has several merits. First, referring to a systems approach does not imply implicit functionalism because the unity between the different elements of a system are 'always imperfect and under construction' (Connell 1987:116). The speed of change may be more rapid in one set of institutions than in another; similarly, institutional arrangements may be out of step with contemporary social values. The tensions which result can provide a catalyst for change by challenging the status quo. As a result a new gender contract may emerge in the subsequent process of negotiation and compromise. Second, it emphasises women's capacity to resist and change the existing order through a variety of actions, overcoming some of the problems identified with those theories (e.g. Walby 1990) which focus on the universal dominance of patriarchy (Duncan 1995; Pollert 1996). Finally, it emphasises the necessity of analysing the dynamics of change. Hirdmann, for example, stresses the inherent contradictions of equality and difference as women are integrated into the public political and economic spheres. The constellation of conditions which challenged the existing gender relations in the 1960s and 1970s included the availability of more reliable contraception, expansion of women's access to higher education, the tension between the 'rhetoric of equality and the practice of sexual oppression' experienced by women involved in the civil rights movements (Connell 1987: 160). Certain groups will have more resources and incentives to rebel against the dominant gender culture. This may be seen at the individual level, where professional qualifications raise women's employment aspirations and opportunities. Similarly, the resources to rebel may come via collective action with other women and coalitions with supportive men, for example, when implementing equal opportunities at the workplace (Cockburn 1991), and in the development of trade union policies in connection with part-time employment.

In this review of comparative frameworks we have shown that gender relations have become an increasingly important component of segmentation theories and the 'societal employment systems' perspective. Furthermore, gender is increasingly conceptualised as a process which permeates institutions and social relations throughout the employment system when this theoretical approach is applied to analyse women's labour market situation. However, gender-blind analyses still predominate when women are not the self-evident focus of the research. The *gender systems* approach takes as its starting point the examination of relations between men and women, and how these are structured through a variety of social institutions, work being just one of them. The value of these comparative frameworks, on one hand, is that they identify how a range of universal components structure gender arrangements related to paid and unpaid work. At the same time these frameworks can be applied to understand how these institutional configurations vary both between societies and over time. They also allow us to identify processes and actors of change within different institutional settings.

One of the aims of this book is to explore the organisation of part-time employment in different institutional settings. With this purpose in mind we asked all authors to make comparisons between at least two countries (with the exception of Chapter 4, which focuses on ethnic differences in the UK). Many of the chapters show how comparative analysis needs to take account of the relationship between the sphere of economic production and social reproduction and the intermediary role played by regulation. Further, not only does such a framework need to examine the role of institutional incentives and disincentives for part-time work, but it also needs to incorporate an analysis of embedded societal values associated with work and the family, both at the individual level and in the form of organised interests and the way these are changing.

STRUCTURE OF THE BOOK

The contributions to this book are organised into two sections. In the first section, authors examine the debates which seek to account for the growth and development of part-time work. The first two chapters, by Smith *et al.* and Delsen, provide an overview of international trends in the expansion of part-time employment and the processes which account for this development. Smith *et al.* show that part-time jobs accounted for most of the net job creation in Europe since the 1980s, although marked national differences persist in the incidence of part-time work. Most of this increase in part-time work resulted from employers changing their labour-use strategies – albeit in a limited range of service sector jobs – rather than simply because of an expansion of the service sector, a result which is corroborated by the analysis by Walwei in Chapter 5. Although there has been some growth of part-time work in higher-level jobs in some countries, overall part-time work remains female-dominated and disproportionately concentrated in low-paid, low-status jobs such as sales, catering and cleaning.

National differences in the levels of part-time work among women and men are explored in more detail by Delsen using OECD data. He argues that the differential rate of expansion in part-time work across countries since the mid-1980s is evidence of a gradual convergence in national rates of part-time work. He also shows that part-time work has expanded rapidly for men in some countries, mainly among young men and those approaching retirement. Nevertheless, male rates of part-time employment remain markedly lower than those for women. Both Smith *et al.* and Delsen identify similar institutional features which influence the amount and quality of part-time jobs which employers create, and the different availability of women and men for these jobs. These societal features include tax, child care and social security policies, labour costs and regulations, government and trade union working-time policies. Their analysis also points to the need for a gender dimension as an integral element in analyses of developments in part-time work.

It is important not to employ the concept 'gender' as a way of simply dividing women and men into opposing and homogeneous groups. There are significant differences among women in their propensity to work part-time, as there are among men, which may be lost sight of when comparing averages. In Chapter 4, Dale and Holdsworth demonstrate this clearly with their analysis of ethnic variations in rates of part-time work among women in the UK. They show that while part-time employment is the norm for white mothers, this is not the case for black and Asian mothers. Thus within the same state regulatory and institutional framework quite different models of maternal employment exist. Similarly, lines of differentiation among women could be found along with other characteristics, such as lone parenthood, educational level or region. They argue that the differentiation by ethnic group is due to differences in past historical processes of immigration and labour market entry, current economic circumstances and cultural norms; and the way that these factors interact with labour market institutions.

Preoccupation with unemployment and the potential for part-time work to solve labour market problems is examined by Walwei in Chapter 5. He demonstrates that even consistently high rates of economic growth will be insufficient to produce a significant decline in unemployment without policy intervention to promote a more employment-intensive pattern of growth. The promotion of part-time work is frequently put forward as a solution in policy debates across Europe, but Walwei is cautious about the efficacy of this strategy for reducing *unemployment* as opposed to *non-employment*. This is because most of the part-time jobs created since 1970 have been taken by women and young people entering or re-entering the labour market rather than the unemployed. Thus he predicts that in countries with low female labour force participation rates any expansion of part-time work will encourage women to enter the labour market and will do little to reduce recorded levels of unemployment.

The last three chapters in Part I focus on part-time work in relation to the wage and social security systems. The starting point for Rubery's chapter (Chapter 7) is that part-time jobs do not just involve shorter hours but constitute a different employment form which is organised on different principles, terms and conditions to full-time work and potentially undermines the norms and standards which organised labour has established for full-time jobs. She argues that this threat to standards is reduced where wage and other labour market regulations have been extended to incorporate part-time jobs, such as in Scandinavian countries and to a large extent the Netherlands. Minimum wage protection is particularly important given that part-time jobs are largely concentrated in low-paying sectors, organisations and occupations.

Picking up on Walwei's point that few part-time jobs are taken by the unemployed, Doudeijns (Chapter 6) uses the recently established OECD tax and benefit database to examine the financial incentives for entering part-time work faced by women and men living as couples. He shows that there are few incentives for someone in receipt of unemployment insurance to take part-time work in most countries. In contrast the incentives are greater for someone who has no benefit entitlement providing their partner is employed or in receipt of unemployment insurance. However, once unemployment insurance is exhausted and is replaced by means-tested social assistance there are few financial incentives for either partner to work part-time. These incentive structures appear to have an actual impact on work decisions: in countries where the disincentives against part-time work are high the incidence of this form of employment is low and the proportion of 'jobless' households is high. Thus the inability of most national unemployment benefit systems to accommodate part-time work appears to be contributing to employment polarisation between households in Europe.

The inability of most current Welfare State regimes to accommodate rather than penalise part-time work is exposed further in Ginn and Arber's analysis of the pension implications of part-time work (Chapter 8). Despite the *Bilka-Kaufhaus* ruling in 1986 many part-timers are still excluded from state or occupational pension schemes in many countries. Thus the proportion of working life in which a person is employed full-time profoundly affects their eventual pension entitlement. At the same time, the pension penalty incurred from part-time work is mediated by the Welfare State regime, as well as the timing and duration of part-time employment. Part-timers fare best where there is a basic, individual entitlement based on citizenship rights rather than life-time employment, yet the trend in most countries is to cut basic guarantees and to tighten the link to lifetime earnings.

Taken together, five themes emerge from the chapters in Part I. First, that where part-time employment is expanding it is still largely female-dominated and concentrated in certain service sector jobs. Second, that the expansion of part-time work has as yet done little to reduce recorded unemployment. Third, labour regulations have to be extended to integrate part-time work in order to stop standards being reduced for all workers and make it more attractive for men. Fourth, that the unemployment and pension systems in most countries are out of step with the growth of part-time work, creating disincentives for the unemployed to take part-time jobs and pension penalties for those who work less than full-time. Finally, the level and quality of part-time work vary across countries and between different groups of women.

Debate surrounding these questions provides the context to the chapters in Part II, where authors make comparisons between specific countries. Chapters 9–11 look at these in the European context; chapters 12–14 in the North American and Pacific Rim regions. The aim of these chapters is to examine part-time work within the context of particular national frameworks. We wanted to avoid simply putting together a collection of national reports on the situa-tion of part-time work in each country; instead we were interested in drawing out the questions and difficulties associated with making direct comparisons, both theoretically and methodologically. Each of these chapters sets out the rationale for the comparison: what do these countries have in common and what makes them different? Would we expect to find similar or divergent patterns of part-time employment? And if so why? The authors provide basic descriptive data on trends in part-time employment relating to supply- and demand-side characteristics, which are discussed more broadly in the earlier chapters by Smith *et al.* and Delsen in Part I. These trends and characteristics are then examined in relation to institutional and in some cases cultural factors shaping part-time employment.

The effect of cultural attitudes to child-rearing and the domestic division of labour, as well as institutional structures in the differing use of part-time employ-ment, is examined by Pfau-Effinger (Chapter 9), who develops an approach in terms of 'gender arrangements' for three North European countries. She argues that the traditional breadwinner family model plays a central role affecting the desirability of part-time employment and the cultural construction of mother-hood employment in West Germany and the Netherlands, whereas in a more modern egalitarian model, as found in Finland, part-time employment is negligible.

The relatively low use of part-time work is also examined in Chapter 10 by Ruivo *et al.* for Southern Europe, looking particularly at Spain and Portugal. They compare the historical stages of female integration into paid employment, economic development and the nature of employment regulation in these two societies which provides little incentive for employers or employees to take up part-time employment. While the prospects of increasing part-time work are higher in Spain than in Portugal, so are the possibilities of this becoming a marginalised form of employment.

The relationship between high levels of female participation and the role of part-time work is examined by Daune-Richard in Chapter 11. She shows that whereas French women have tended to have a full-time pattern of employment, British and Swedish women are more likely to work part-time, albeit associated with very different employment conditions. She argues in favour of adapting the societal effect approach so that it takes a closer account of gender relations from historical and institutional perspectives and the construction of relations between the public and private sphere as an explanation for these differences.

√ The last three chapters in this volume focus on part-time employment in North America and the Pacific Rim. Houseman and Osawa's comparison of Japan and the US (Chapter 12) highlights how despite similar rates of part-time employment the demographic and industrial patterns are quite different. They argue that human capital theory cannot explain the wage and benefits gap between full- and part-timers found in both countries. They show that while there is support for the theory that some workers voluntarily choose shorter hours, this choice needs to be seen within the context of a lack of adequate child care, and particularly in Japan the forms of segmentation created by the tax and employment system, which effectively reinforce the status of the male breadwinner family model. The growth in part-time work, especially in Japan, has largely been demand driven, as Japanese employers have maintained the status of full-time employees at the expense of lowering their costs through the use of part-timers. American employers have not used this strategy to the same extent because the demarcation in status is not so entrenched. Despite the growing demand among some women for full-time work, the prospects for part-time employees have largely been associated with the growth of low-quality jobs and a lack of benefits, or trying to string together two or more part-time jobs.

The unique status of Japanese part-timers is not found in other Asian countries, as can be seen from the chapter by Wakisaka and Bae (Chapter 13), who examine why part-time work is more prevalent in Japan than in South Korea. They show how despite converging trends to similar levels of female activity part-time work is more closely associated with precarious employment and a higher degree of dissatisfaction in South Korea. Although Japanese part-timers already work considerably longer hours than their equivalents in other countries, the striking incentives created by the Japanese tax system to encourage both employees and employers to reduce their hours do not exist in South Korea. The prospects for further increases in part-time work need to be seen in the context that Korean part-timers tend to be more polarised than in Japan both in terms of age and educational attainment.

Finally, in Chapter 14, Baxter looks at Australia and New Zealand which have among the highest rates of part-time employment in the OECD countries. She argues that the comparatively good conditions for part-timers, in terms of the relative wage gap with full-timers, has been achieved through centralised wage bargaining and the relative success of 'femocrats', especially in Australia. However, these gains are being potentially undermined by employment deregulation, declining support for the trade unions and occupational segregation. An increasing casualisation of the labour market makes marginalisation of these jobs more likely, together with the fact that increased female labour force participation has not significantly changed the domestic division of labour. The prospects for part-time work are likely to be an increasing polarisation between marginalised and protected jobs.

CONCLUSIONS AND PROSPECTS

In this introductory chapter we have argued that two of the key features of cross-national research have been to emphasise trends towards convergence and to argue that differences will persist. This dichotomy is rather artificial, for similar pressures and social processes may be identified across societies, but differences in the particular constellation of events and actors means that the outcome is not predetermined. We have outlined two frameworks which have been used for cross-national analyses of women's employment and which accommodate and explain diversity: the 'employment systems' and the 'gender systems' approaches. These systemic models incorporate similar key actors and institutional structures, but with different emphases. We argued that a 'gender systems' approach which incorporated the detailed labour market focus of the 'employment systems' framework is the most appropriate for analysing cross-national similarities and differences in the pattern of part-time employment.

The key points we have identified in these debates are how particular institutional arrangements and 'gender contracts' give rise to particular forms of gender relations, and how the inherent tensions can be identified within a given society. Part of the dynamic comes simply from women and men responding to economic restructuring and changes in their material conditions; carving out their way of life in light of their resources, values, and the constraints that they face. But another important dynamic in modern states is organised political action premised on notions of citizenship, so that gender relations in any society are a form of 'gender compromise' in the sense that they have resulted from coalitions of interests supporting, or opposing, a more equal treatment of men and women in the workplace and the household, at particular historical periods. Particularly important parts of this have been the different intersections of the feminist movement and the traditional labour movement. For example, Jenson (1991) argues that in Sweden, the strong commitment of women to involvement in political parties and trade unions enabled them to widen the scope of thinking on equality beyond the labour market and into the private domain of family life. In contrast the absence of any link between the feminist movement and political power or even the trade unions in France means that demands for equality remained more confined to the productive system (Daune-Richard 1988). These different forms of political alliances have had a marked impact on the Welfare State regime which emerged (Mósesdóttir 1995).

Part-time work is essentially a similar gender compromise across national boundaries: women are able to enter the labour market and meet the particular labour requirements of service sector employers without disrupting men's traditional 'breadwinner' status at the workplace or at home. But, as the contributions to this book show, this apparently universal rule can be broken under certain conditions.

First, the quality of part-time work is improved when it is integrated alongside full-time work in labour law, employment regulations and income replacement entitlements. This prevents the marginalisation of part-time work as a cheap labour source and helps to prevent the driving down of standards in full-time jobs. Instead, it provides the basic conditions to encourage firms to use part-time work as a means to gain competitive advantages from hours scheduling or as a means of retaining workers who want reduced working hours (Tilly 1992). Integration requires the dismantling of hours or earnings thresholds for employment-related benefits which encourage employers to develop short, marginalised jobs at the expense of part-time jobs with longer hours and higher wages. And in order to reduce the inequalities arising from the segregation of part-timers into low-paying parts of the economy, national minimum wage standards are required. Finally, income replacement systems, such as unemployment benefits or pensions, have to be modernised if they are to accommodate rather than penalise part-time workers. Such reforms will improve the quality of part-time work for women, and will also make this form of employment more attractive to men.

Second, when part-time work is developed within a formalised political renegotiation of the 'gender contract' which encompasses home life as well as the workplace, it may develop as a bridge which helps to reconcile the demands of private care work and public waged work. This, as Hirdmann argued, may even provide a springboard to a further transformation of the gender contract because, on the one hand, maternal employment becomes normalised while, on the other hand, the tensions between the organisational logic of the public and private spheres are thrown into sharper relief. A wider range of policies to do with part-time work is connected with an explicit concern to renegotiate the gender contract. These include increased parental rights to reduce their hours in order to manage paid and unpaid responsibilities, such as part-time or short-hour parental leave, and incentives targeted at men to take up their entitlements. Public resourcing of child care services is a necessary complement to enable parents to develop their preferred way of managing employment and care work.

What are the prospects for part-time work? Where deregulation is occurring in response to high levels of unemployment and the political quest for more flexible labour markets, part-time employment is likely to be marginalised, even if full-time standards are also reduced. Those women and men who are able to do so will avoid this form of employment, contributing to a polarisation of employment conditions and standards of living between the sexes and between households. Alternatively, where policies are being developed to modernise rather than dilute labour market standards as an explicit response to accommodate or encourage part-time work, the quality of part-time work is likely to increase. This will contribute to reducing gender inequality in the labour market by raising women's conditions. It may also make part-time work more attractive to men, thus helping to promote a more equal time-involvement of parents in raising young children plus participation in part-time jobs as part of work-sharing policies.

To test if, or where, these competing predictions materialise, it is necessary to monitor international developments in part-time work. Yet many contributors to this volume have indicated that current labour market indicators are inadequate. Not only are there methodological problems in developing systematic and comparable international data on the levels of part-time work when definitions of part-time work vary across countries, there is also an increasing recognition that distinctions between casualised and more secure forms of part-time employment need to be made. This is partly connected to international differences in the various types of legal and social protection guarantee for part-timers. It is also partly to do with occupational inequalities and employers' labour-use strategies: women who are well qualified, or who have certain skills which are in market demand, are in a better position to negotiate their working-time arrangements than women in lower-status manual jobs. On this basis Tilly (1992) has argued that it is important to distinguish between part-time jobs created as part of employers' strategies to retain certain groups of workers, and the creation of low-paid and casualised part-time jobs.

How then do we develop suitable indicators to track the quality of part-time work and draw international comparisons? Blossfeld and Hakim (1997) suggest that a distinction should be made on the basis of hours, so that jobs which average 15 hours a week or less are classified as 'marginal', those between 15 and 29 hours are treated as 'half-time', and part-time jobs with longer hours are defined as 'reduced hours'. These distinctions are useful for some questions, particularly when comparisons are being made about the actual volume of work undertaken, although we would be inclined to use a threshold of 25 hours to distinguish between 'reduced' and 'half-time' hours. However, the Japanese case shows that the divide between part-timers and full-timers is not drawn along the dimension of the volume of hours worked, but simply on status. This suggests that additional indicators of the social and economic distance between part-time and full-time work also need to be developed. A basic step in this direction is to improve the collection of pay data so that average pay ratios between part-time and full-time work can be computed. In many countries this data is partial or simply not available (Rubery and Fagan 1994). Another important distinction may be to use relative rather than absolute hours thresholds for 'marginal' part-time work to capture country specific thresholds for coverage by labour law and social protection. Similarly, given that full-time hours vary markedly across countries, for specific questions about proportioning the volume of work done by full-time and part-time workers it may be useful to express part-time hours as a fraction of full-time hours. Finally, it would be useful in standard series of employment statistics to distinguish those people who are taking advantage of statutory or occupational schemes to reduce their hours.

In sum, a range of indicators is needed, depending on the aspect of part-time work which is being addressed. While an hours distinction can be useful and is quite simple to collect, other indicators are required to analyse the relational role of part-time work within the employment system. Furthermore, an important direction for future research is to examine international comparisons of the extent and form of transitions in and out of part-time work over the life cycle. Studies already indicate that marked differences exist between countries (e.g. Quack 1993; O'Reilly and Bothfeld 1996; Blossfeld and Hakim 1997; Rubery et al. 1997). We need to know in what institutional settings a spell of part-time work provides a bridge which facilitates entry or if re-entry to employment and an eventual stepping stone into full-time work, or if it becomes part of a labour market trap of flows between casualised employment and spells of unemployment. It is only from this life-course perspective that we get a full understanding of the processes of marginalisation and inclusion. This volume of contributions seeks to show how the prospects for part-time work are likely to remain high on the agenda of policy-makers and households, and raises questions for the future development of theoretical debates in cross-national employment research and gender.

NOTES

1 Duncan (1995) cautions against a 'fetishism of the nation state' in comparative research. He argues that regional variation in gender relations within countries can be attributed to varying economic conditions, localised discourses and practices around gender divisions of labour which are beyond the direct influence of national-level state intervention. Furthermore, the relevance of comparisons along national boundaries is being questioned by the increasingly international division of labour and by the emergence of supra-national political and economic institutions. While we would agree that there are distinct benefits to be obtained from localised and supra-national studies, nevertheless, our rationale for cross-national comparisons is based on the argument that the nation state still remains a powerful structural influence on labour market and household structures, often mediating the influence of supra-national legislative bodies such as the European Union and the impact of an increasingly global economy.

2   This influence of the Welfare State regime on women's employment is predicted to create 'new axes of social conflict'. For example, he argues that as a result of pressures for wage moderation in Sweden 'one might easily imagine a war between (largely) male workers in the private sector and (largely) female workers in the Welfare State' (p.227). For Germany he envisages conflicts between insiders (job-holders) and outsiders (the jobless and inactive), and in the US 'class differences will crystallize more sharply within the various minority groups. As some women become yuppies and some blacks become bourgeois, the women and blacks left behind will experience much more keenly the phenomenon of relative deprivation' (pp.228–9).

3   See e.g. Büchtemann and Quack (1990) and Quack (1993) for West Germany; O'Reilly (1995) for East and West Germany; Schoer (1987) for Britain and Germany; Sundström (1987) for Sweden; Beechey and Perkins (1987) for the UK; Gregory (1987), Letablier *et al.* (1986) and O'Reilly (1994) for Britain and France; Fagan *et al.* (1995) for Britain and the Netherlands; Ellingsaeter (1992) for the Nordic countries; Delsen (1995) for OECD countries; Meulders *et al.* (1993) and Rubery *et al.* (1995) for the European Union.

BIBLIOGRAPHY

Atkinson, J. and Meager, N. (1986) 'Is flexibility a flash in the pan?', *Personnel Management* 18, 9.

Averritt, R. T. (1968) *The Dual Economy: The Dynamics of American Industry Structure*. New York: W. W. Norton.

Becker, G. (1981) *A Treatise on the Family*. Cambridge, MA: Harvard University Press.

Beechey, V. and Perkins, T. (1985) 'Conceptualising part-time work' in C. Roberts, R. Finnegan and D. Gallie (eds) *New Approaches to Economic Life*. Manchester: Manchester University Press.

Beechey, V. and Perkins, T. (1987) *A Matter of Hours: Women, Part-time Work and the Labour Market*. Cambridge: Polity Press.

Berger, S. and Piore, M. (1980) *Dualism and Discontinuity in Industrial Societies*. Cambridge: Cambridge University Press.

Blossfeld, H.-P. and Hakim, C. (1997) *Between Equalisation and Marginalisation: Women Working Part-time in Europe and the USA*. Oxford: Oxford University Press.

Blossfield, H.-P., DeRose, A., Hoem, J. and Rohwer, G. (1995) 'Education, modernization and the risk of marriage disruption in Sweden, West Germany, and Italy' in K. O. Mason and A. M. Jensen (eds) *Gender and Family Change in Industrialized Countries*. Oxford: Clarendon Press.

Boyer, R. (1986) *La flexibilité du travail en Europe*. Paris: Editions La Découverte. Translated (1988) as *The Search for Labour Market Flexibility: The European Economies in Transition*. Oxford: Clarendon Press.

Büchtemann, C. and Quack, S. (1990) 'How precarious is non-standard employment?', *Cambridge Journal of Economics* 14: 315–29.

Cockburn. C. (1991) *In the Way of Women: Men's Resistance to Sex Equality in Organizations*. London: Macmillan.

Connell, R. W. (1987) *Gender and Power*. Cambridge: Polity Press.

Crompton, R. with LeFeuvre, N. (1996) 'Paid employment and the changing system of gender relations: a cross-national comparison', *Sociology* 30, 3: 427–45.

Crompton, R. and Sanderson, K. (1990) *Gendered Jobs and Social Change*. London: Unwin Hyman.

Crompton, R., Hantrais, L. and Walters, P. (1990) 'Gender relations and employment',

British Journal of Sociology 4, 3: 329–49.

Dale, A. and Egerton, M. (1995) *Highly Educated Women: Evidence from the National Child Development Study*. London: Report to the Employment Department.

Dale, A. and Glover, J. (1990) *An Analysis of Women's Employment Patterns in the UK, France and the USA: The Value of Survey Based Comparisons*. London: Department of Employment Research Paper no. 75, DE.

Daune-Richard, A.-M. (1988) 'A consideration of sociological categories' in J. Jensen, E. Hagen and C. Reddy (eds) *Feminization of the Labour Force: Paradoxes and Promises*. Cambridge: Polity Press.

Daune-Richard, A-M. (1995) 'Women's employment and different societal effects in France, Sweden and the UK', *International Journal of Sociology* 25, 2: 39–65.

Delsen, L. (1995) *Atypical Employment: An International Perspective, Causes, Consequences and Policy*. Groningen: Wolters-Noard hoff.

Devine, F. (1994) 'Segregation and supply: preferences and plans among 'self-made' women', *Gender, Work and Organization* 1, 2: 94–109.

Dex, S. (1985) *The Sexual Division of Work: Conceptual Revolutions in the Social Sciences*. Sussex: Wheatsheaf Books.

Dex, S. (1988) *Women's Attitudes towards Work*. London: Macmillan.

Dex, S. and Shaw, L. (1986) *British and American Women at Work: Do Equal Opportunities Policies Matter?* London: Macmillan.

Dex, S. and Walters, P. (1989) 'Women's occupational status in Britain, France and the USA: explaining the difference', *Industrial Relations Journal* 20, 3: 203–12.

Dex, S., Walters, P. and Alden, D. M. (1993) *French and British Mothers at Work*. Basingstoke: Macmillan.

Doeringer, P. and Piore, M. (1971) *Internal Labor Market and Manpower Analysis*. Lexington, MA: Heath Lexington Books.

Dore, R. (1973) *British Factory – Japanese Factory. The Origins of National Diversity in Industrial Relations*. London: Allen & Unwin.

Duncan, S. (1994) 'Theorising differences in patriarchy', *Environment and Planning A* 26: 1177–94

Duncan, S. (1995) 'Theorizing European gender systems', *Journal of European Social Policy* 5, 4: 263–84.

Edwards, R. (1979) *Contested Terrain: The Transformation of the Workplace in the Twentieth Century*. London: Heinemann.

Einhorn, B. (1993) *Cinderella Goes to Market: Citizenship, Gender and Women's Movements in East and Central Europe*. London: Verso.

Ellingsaeter, A.-L.(1992) *Part-time Work in European Welfare States: Denmark, Germany, Norway and the United Kingdom Compared*, Report 92:10. Oslo: Institute for Social Research.

Escott, K. and Whitfield, D. (1995) *The Gender Impact of CCT in Local Government*. Manchester: Equal Opportunities Commission.

Esping-Andersen, G. (1990) *The Three Worlds of Welfare Capitalism*. London: Polity Press.

Fagan, C. (1996) 'Gendered time schedules: paid work in Great Britain', *Social Politics: International Studies in Gender, State and Society* 3, 1: 72–106.

Fagan, C. and Rubery, J. (1996a) 'The salience of the part-time divide in the European Union', *European Sociological Review*, December: 348–78.

Fagan, C. and Rubery, J. (1996b) 'Transitions between family formation and paid employment' in G. Schmid, J. O'Reilly and K. Schömann *International Handbook of Labour Market Policy and Evaluation*. Cheltenham: Edward Elgar.

Fagan, C., Plantenga, J. and Rubery, J. (1995) *Does Part-time Work Promote Sex Equality? A Comparative Analysis of the Netherlands and the UK*, WZB discussion paper FS I 95–203. Berlin: WZB.

Finch, J. (1993) 'Conceptualising gender' in D. Morgan and L. Stanley (eds) *Debates in Sociology*. Manchester: Manchester University Press.

Gallie, D. (1978) *In Search of the New Working Class: Automation and Social Integration within the Capitalist Enterprise*. Cambridge: Cambridge University Press.

Ginn, J., Arber, S., Brannen, J., Dale, A., Dex, S., Elias, P., Moss, P., Pahl, J., Roberts, C. and Rubery, J. (1996) 'Feminist fallacies: a reply to Hakim on women's employment', *British Journal of Sociology* 47, 1: 167–74.

Gittins, D. (1985) *The Family in Question: Changing Households and Familiar Ideologies*. London: Macmillan.

Goldthorpe, J. (1985) 'The end of convergence: corporatist and dualist tendencies in modern western societies' in B. Roberts, R. Finnegan and D. Gallie (eds) *New Approaches to Economic Life*. Manchester: Manchester University Press.

Gordon, D. M., Edwards, R. and Reich, M. (1982) *Segmented Work, Divided Workers: The Historical Transformation of Labor in the United States*. Cambridge: Cambridge University Press.

Gregg, P. and Wadsworth, J. (1995) 'Gender, households and access to employment' in J. Humphries and J. Rubery (eds) *The Economics of Equal Opportunities*. Manchester: Equal Opportunities Commission.

Gregory, A. (1987) 'Le travail à temps partiel en France et en Grande-Bretagne: temps imposé ou temps choisi?', *Revue Française des Affaires Sociales* 3: 53–60.

Hakim, C. (1991) 'Grateful slaves and self-made women: fact and fantasy in women's work orientations', *European Sociological Review* 7, 2: 101–21.

Hakim, C. (1995) 'Five feminist myths about women's employment', *British Journal of Sociology* 46, 3: 429–55.

Hakim, C. (1996a) *Key Issues in Women's Work: Female Heterogeneity and the Polarisation of Women's Employment*. London: Athlone.

Hakim, C. (1996b) 'Labour mobility and employment stability: rhetoric and reality on the sex differential in labour market behaviour', *European Sociological Review* 12, 1: 1–31.

Hakim, C. (1997) 'A sociological perspective on part-time work' in H. Blossfeld and C. Hakim (eds) *Between Equalisation and Marginalisation: Women Working Part-time in Europe and the USA*. Oxford: Oxford University Press.

Hantrais, L. (1990) *Managing Professional and Family Life: A Comparative Study of British and French Mothers*. Dartmouth: Aldershot/Vermont.

Hirdmann, Y. (1988) 'Genussystemet -reflexioner kring kvinnors sociala underordning', *Kvinnovetenskaplig Tidskrift* 3: 49–63.

Hudson, P. and Lee, W. R. (1990) *Women's Work and the Family Economy in Historical Perspectives*. Manchester: Manchester University Press.

Humphries, J. (1977) 'Class struggle and the persistence of the working class family', *Cambridge Journal of Economics*, September: 241–58.

Humphries, J. and Rubery, J. (1984) 'The reconstitution of the supply side of the labour market: the relative autonomy of social reproduction', *Cambridge Journal of Economics* 8, 4: 331–46.

Inkeles, A. and Sasaki, M. (1996) *Comparing Nations and Cultures: Readings in a Cross-disciplinary Perspective*. Englewood Cliffs, NJ: Prentice-Hall.

Jenson, J. (1991) *Making Claims: Social Policy and Gender Relations in Post-war Sweden and France*. Annual meeting of the Canadian Sociology and Anthropology Association, mimeo cited in Daune-Richard (1995: 29)

Kerr, C., Dunlop, J. T., Harbison, F. H. and Myers, C. A. (1960) *Industrialism and Industrial Man: The Problems of Labor and Management in Economic Growth*. London: Heinemann.

Lane, C. (1989) *Management and Labour in Europe: The Industrial Enterprise in Germany, Britain and France*. Cheltenham: Edward Elgar.

Lane, C. (1993) 'Gender and the labour market in Europe: Britain, Germany and France compared', *The Sociological Review* 41, 2: 274–301.

Letablier, M.-T. (1986) 'Les dynamiques de diffusion du travail à temps partiel aux Etats-Unis et en France', *Travail et Emploi* 30: 19.

Lewis, J. (1992) 'Gender and the development of welfare regimes', *Journal of European Social Policy* 2, 3: 159–73.

Lewis, J. (1993) *Women and Social Policies in Europe*. Cheltenham: Edward Elgar.

MacInnes, J. (1987) 'The question of flexibility', *Research Paper* no.5. Department of Social and Economic Research, University of Glasgow.

McRae, S. (1991) *Maternity Rights in Britain*. London: Policy Studies Institute.

Maier, F. (1994) 'Institutional regimes of part-time working' in G. Schmid (ed.) *Labour Market Institutions in Europe*. New York: M. E. Sharpe.

Maurice, M. (1995) 'Convergence and/or societal effect for the Europe of the future?' in P. Cressey and B. Jones (eds) *Work and Employment in Europe: A New Convergence?* London and New York: Routledge.

Maurice, M., Sellier, F. and Silvestre, J.-J. (1982) *Politique d'éducation et organisation industrielle en France et en Allemagne*. Paris: Presses Universitaires de France. Translated (1986) as *The Social Foundations of Industrial Power: A Comparison of France and Germany*. Cambridge, MA: MIT Press.

Meulders, D., Plasman, R. and Vander Stricht, V. (1993) *Position of Women on the Labour Market in the European Community*. Aldershot: Dartmouth Publishing.

Meyer, T. (1994) *The German and British Welfare States as Employers: Emancipatory or Patriarchal?*, WZB discussion paper FS I 94–211. Berlin: WZB.

Michon, F. (1981) 'Dualism and the French labour market: business strategy, non-standard job forms and secondary jobs' in F. Wilkinson (ed.) *The Dynamics of Labour Market Segmentation*. London: Academic Press.

Morris, L. (1989) 'Household strategies: the individual, the collectivity and the labour market – the case of married couples', *Work, Employment and Society* 3, 4: 447–64.

Mósesdóttir, L. (1995) 'The state and the egalitarian, eccesiastical and liberal regimes of gender relations', *British Journal of Sociology*, December: 623–42.

OECD (1986) *Labour Market Flexibility*. Report by a high-level group of experts to the Secretary General. Paris: OECD.

O'Reilly, J. (1994) *Banking on Flexibility: A Comparison of Flexible Employment Strategies in Britain and France*. Aldershot: Avebury.

O'Reilly, J. (1995) 'Le travail à temps partiel en Allemagne de l'Est et en Allemagne de l'Ouest: Vers un "modèle sociétal sexué"', *Cahiers des MAGE* (Marché du Travail et Genre) 1, 2: 77–88.

O'Reilly, J. (1996a) 'Theoretical considerations in cross-national employment research', *Sociological Review Online* 1, 1: http:\\www.soc.surrey.ac.uk.

O'Reilly, J. (1996b) 'Labour force adjustments through part-time work' in G. Schmid et al. (eds) *International Handbook of Labour Market Policy and Evaluation*. Cheltenham: Edward Elgar.

O'Reilly, J. and Bothfeld, S. (1996) 'Labour Market Transitions and Part-time Work', *InfoMISEP* no. 54, Summer (DGV European Commission: Brussels).

Orloff, A. S. (1993) 'Gender and the social rights of citizenship: the comparative analysis of gender relations and welfare states', *American Sociological Review* 58, 3: 303–8.

Owen, S. (1987) 'Household production and economic efficiency: arguments for and against domestic specialisation', *Work, Employment and Society* 1, 2: 157–78.

Parsons, T. (1943) 'The kinship system of the United States', *American Anthropologist* 45: 22–38.

Parsons, T. (1966) *Societies: Evolutionary and Comparative Perspectives*. Englewood Cliffs, NJ: Prentice-Hall.

Parsons, T. and Bales, R. F. (eds) (1956) *Family, Socialisation, and Interaction Process*. London: Routledge & Kegan Paul.

Pfau-Effinger, B. (1993), 'Modernisation, culture and part-time employment: the example of Finland and West Germany', *Work, Employment and Society* 7, 3: 383–410.

Pfau-Effinger, B. (1996) *Theorising Cross-national Differences in the Labour Force Participation of Women*. Paper presented to the Seminar on Gender Relations, Employment and Occupational Segregation: A Cross-national Study. University of Leicester, 23–4 February.

Picchio del Mercato, A. (1981) 'Social reproduction and the basic structure of labour markets' in F. Wilkinson (ed.) (1981) *European Business Systems: Firms and Markets in Their National Contexts*. London: Sage.

Piore, M. and Sabel, C. (1984) *The Second Industrial Divide: Possibilities for Prosperity*. New York: Basic Books.

Plantenga, J. (1996) 'For women only? The rise of part-time work in the Netherlands', *Social Politics: International Studies in Gender, State and Society* 3, 1: 57–71.

Pollert, A. (1996) 'Gender and class revisited; or the poverty of "patriarchy"', *Sociology* 30, 4: 639–59.

Pollert, A. (ed.) (1991) *Farewell to Flexibility?* Oxford: Blackwell.

Przeworski, A. and Teune, H. (1973) 'Equivalence in cross-national research' in D. Warwick and S. Osherson (eds) *Comparative Research Methods*. Englewood Cliffs, NJ: Prentice-Hall.

Quack, S. (1993) *Dynamik der Teilzeitarbeit*. Berlin: editions sigma.

Quack, S. and Maier, F. (1994) 'From state socialism to market economy – women's employment in East Germany', *Environment and Planning A* 26, 8: 1171–328.

Rantalaihio, L. (1993) 'The gender contract' in H. Vasa (ed.) *Shaping Structural Change in Finland: The Role of Women*. Helsinki: Ministry of Social Affairs and Health (Equality Publications).

Rees, T. (1992) *Women and the Labour Market*. London: Routledge.

Rodgers, G. and Rodgers, J. (eds) (1989) *Precarious Jobs in Labour Market Regulation: The Growth of Atypical Employment in Western Europe*. Geneva: International Labour Organisation.

Rose, M. (1985) 'Universalism, culturalism and the Aix group: promise and problems of the societal approach to economic institutions', *European Sociological Review* 1, 1: 65–83.

Rosenberg, S. (1989) 'From segmentation to flexibility', *Labour and Society* 14, 4: 17–36.

Rubery, J. (1978) 'Structured labour markets, worker organisation and low pay', *Cambridge Journal of Economics*, 2, March: 17–36.

Rubery, J. (ed.) (1988) *Women and Recession*. London: Routledge & Kegan Paul.

Rubery, J. (1994) 'The British production regime', *Economy and Society* 23, 3: 335–54.

Rubery, J. and Fagan, C. (1993) 'Occupational segregation of women and men in the European Community' (*Social Europe* Supplement 3/93). Luxembourg: Official Publications of the European Community.

Rubery, J. and Fagan, C. (1994) 'Wage determination and sex segregation in the European Community' (*Social Europe* Supplement 4/94). Luxembourg: Official Publications of the European Community.

Rubery, J. and Fagan, C. (1995) 'Gender segregation in societal context', *Work, Employment and Society* 9, 2: 213–40.

Rubery, J., Fagan, C. and Smith, M. (1995) *Changing Patterns of Work and Working-time in the European Union and the Impact on Gender Relations*. V/6203/95-EN. Brussels: European Commission (DGV-Equal Opportunities Unit).

Rubery, J., Smith, M., Fagan, C. and Grimshaw, D. (1997) *Women and European Employment*. London: Routledge.

Schmid, G. (1991) *Women in the Public Sector*. OECD working paper no. OECD/GD (91)213. Paris: OECD.

Schmid, G., O'Reilly, J. and Schömann, K. (1996) *International Handbook of Labour Market Policy and Evaluation*. Cheltenham: Edward Elgar.

Schoer, K. (1987) 'Part-time employment: Britain and W. Germany', *Cambridge Journal of Economics* 11: 83–94.

Siltanen, J. (1994) *Locating Gender*. London: University College London Press.

Sorge, A. (1994) *Actors, Systems, Societal Effects and Culture: Conceptualising Variations in Cross-national Personnel and Organisations*, Paper presented to the EMOT Group 1 Workshop, Humbolt University, Berlin, 22–4 March.

Spain, D. and Bianchi, S. M. (1996) *Balancing Act: Motherhood, Marriage and Employment among American Women*. New York: Russell Sage.

Stockman, N., Bonney, N. and Xuewen, S. (1995) *Women's Work in East and West: The Dual Burden of Employment and Family Life*. London: University College London Press.

Sundstrom, M. (1987) *A Study in the Growth of Part-time Work in Sweden*. Stockholm: Swedish Centre for Working Life and Almqvist & Wicksell International.

Tilly, C. (1992) 'Two faces of part-time work: good and bad part-time jobs in US service industries' in B. Warme, K. Lundy and L. Lundy (eds) *Working Part-time: Risks and Opportunities*. New York: Praeger.

Tilly, L. and Scott, J. (1987) *Les femmes, le travail et la famille*. Marseilles: Editions Rivages.

Walby, S. (1986) *Patriarchy at Work*. Cambridge: Polity Press.

Walby, S. (ed.) (1988) *Gender Segregation at Work*. Milton Keynes: Open University Press.

Walby, S. (1989) 'Theorising patriarchy', *Sociology* 23, 2: 213–34.

Walby, S. (1990) *Theorising Patriarchy*. Oxford: Blackwell.

Walby, S. (1994) 'Methodological and theoretical issues in the comparative analysis of gender relations in Western Europe', *Environment and Planning A* 26: 1339–54.

Walters, M. (1989) 'Patriarchy and viriarchy: an exploration and reconstruction of concepts of masculine domination', *Sociology* 23, 2: 193–211.

Warme, B., Lundy, K. and Lundy, L. (eds) (1992) *Working Part-time: Risks and Opportunities*. London: Praeger.

Weber, M. (1978) *Economy and Society: An Outline of Interpretive Sociology*, vol. 1, edited by G. Roth and C. Wittich. Berkeley, CA: University of California Press.

Whitley, R. (1992) *European Business Systems: Firms and Markets in Their National Contexts*. London: Sage.

Wilkinson, F. (ed.) (1981) *The Dynamics of Labour Market Segmentation*. London: Academic Press.

Young, I. (1981) 'Beyond the unhappy marriage: a critique of dual systems theory' in L. Sargent (ed.) *Women and Revolution: The Unhappy Marriage of Marxism and Feminism*. London: Pluto Press.

Part I

WHO WANTS PART-TIME WORK AND ON WHAT CONDITIONS?

2

WHERE AND WHY IS PART-TIME WORK GROWING IN EUROPE?

Mark Smith, Colette Fagan and Jill Rubery

INTRODUCTION

Since the 1970s, and particularly in the 1980s, there has been a rapid expansion of part-time employment in almost all OECD countries. Initially the growth of part-time jobs in many Northern European countries occurred as a means of encouraging married women to take jobs in the expanding service sector in a period of labour shortages. This development was premised upon such women being second income earners within a 'male breadwinner' model of family life, in which women combine employment with their primary responsibility for unpaid domestic labour in the household (Beechey and Perkins 1987; Marshall 1989; Maier 1994). More recently, part-time work has been suggested as a method of reducing mass unemployment across Europe and increasing the overall employment rate (CEC 1993; Delsen 1993). However, the evidence suggests that part-time employment serves mainly to increase the overall size of the labour force rather than reduce measured unemployment (Rubery *et al.* 1997a; Walwei 1995, and Chapter 5, this volume). Such policy prescriptions to tackle unemployment neglect the gendered nature of part-time employment (Meulders 1995). The only people who can usually work for a part-time wage are those with recourse to other income sources, for example, from a partner or other household member employed full-time, or other financial transfers such as a student grant or pension. Part-time work is therefore not a viable option for many of the unemployed within the existing structure of social protection systems in most countries (see Doudeijns, Chapter 6, this volume).

This chapter examines the expansion of part-time employment in recent years in the European Union, paying attention to both the commonalities and national variations in the expansion, extent and quality of this form of employment. The first part considers the levels and growth of part-time employment across the different member states and identifies the role of the sectoral and occupational segregation of part-time employment and the associated role of structural change. The second part examines how different institutional, regulatory and social factors have affected the use and expansion of part-time employment.[1]

GENDER AND THE EXPANSION OF PART-TIME WORK

There are two basic features common to the pattern of part-time work across the European Union, both of which are mirrored in other OECD countries more generally. First, since the early 1980s there has been a general expansion in the rate of part-time work in every EU country except Greece and Denmark where rates have fallen slightly.[2] Second, the rate of part-time employment is much higher for women than men in every country. In 1994 women accounted for 70 per cent of part-timers in twelve of the fifteen member states, and between 59 and 67 per cent in the other three countries (Portugal, Finland, Greece). Thus, the gender dimension is a key concept for understanding the expansion of part-time work.

These commonalities coexist with national differences in the level and trends in part-time work, particularly among women. In 1994, rates of part-time work for employed women in the EU ranged from over 40 per cent in the Netherlands, Sweden and the UK, to around one-third in Denmark and Germany and down to 12 per cent or less in Finland, Italy, Portugal and Greece. For men the levels range from under 5 per cent in most countries to 10 per cent or more in Denmark and the Netherlands. Trends in the expansion of part-time work also vary across countries. Between 1983 and 1994 the increase in the rate of part-time work for employed women ranged from three percentage points or less in four countries to at least eight percentage points in three countries. The largest increase occurred in the Netherlands, but interpretation of this expansion must be tempered by the awareness that this is partly a statistical artefact resulting from a change in the definition of part-time work used in the Dutch Labour Force Survey.[3] During the same period, the rate of part-time work for employed women fell in four countries: by 6–10 per cent in Denmark and Sweden from a relatively high rate of 45 per cent in 1983, and by 3 per cent or less in Greece and Finland which already had among the lowest rates of part-time work in the EU. Male rates of part-time work rose everywhere, but at a far more modest pace than for women (see also Delsen, Chapter 3, this volume).

This differential expansion in the level of part-time work for women has no simple relation with the integration of women into the labour market, for high levels of part-time work are neither necessary nor sufficient to ensure high levels of female employment among women with family responsibilities (Rubery et al. 1995a). This is demonstrated in Figure 2.1, which shows the marked variation in levels of both full-time and part-time employment for mothers with young children. Particularly high rates of maternal employment are found in

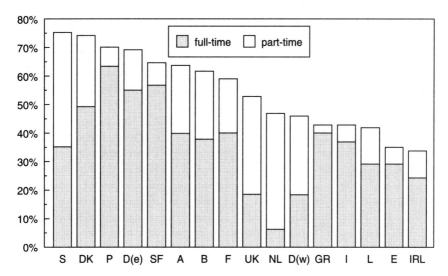

Figure 2.1 Employment rates of mothers with a child aged 10 or under by full- and
part-time status, 1993
Note: mothers aged 20 to 39.
Source: EC Childcare Network (1996)

countries where part-time employment is common (Sweden and Denmark) but
also where it is rare (Portugal, former East Germany, Finland).

Overall, a significant proportion of net job increase since the early 1980s
has been through the expansion of part-time employment. In many countries
this compensated for falling full-time work, particularly among men (Rubery
et al. 1997a). More than four-fifths of net job creation in the European Union
(E10) was part-time in the period 1983 to 1994. Disaggregated by sex, part-
time jobs accounted for 62 per cent of the net employment growth for women
and 20 per cent for men. The prevalence of part-time jobs in the overall level
of job creation has meant that measures of employment performance are
distorted when a simple headcount statistic is used. When employment growth
is estimated using measures of full-time equivalence this exposes a much weaker
record of job creation in all countries (except Denmark and Greece), but particularly in France, the Netherlands and the UK (Rubery and Smith 1996).

In sum the expansion of part-time employment has largely been a female
phenomenon, but this common pattern coexists with national variations such
as in patterns of maternal employment and the overall level of job creation in
the economy. Thus, a framework which incorporates societal features which
influence the organisation of production and the labour market, and the 'gender
order' more generally, is required for the analysis of trends in part-time employment (see Fagan and O'Reilly, Chapter 1, and Pfau-Effinger, Chapter 9, this
volume). This is discussed more fully in section 4, but first we take a closer
look at the sectors and occupations in which part-time work is found.

GENDER SEGREGATION, PART-TIME WORK AND ECONOMIC RESTRUCTURING

In most countries part-time jobs are disproportionately concentrated in the service sector at the lower occupational levels, such as in sales work, catering, cleaning and related personal services (Meulders *et al.* 1993; OECD 1994). Such jobs generally attract the lowest pay and status in society. In some countries, such as Denmark and Sweden, part-time work is more integrated across the job hierarchy and there are more opportunities for part-time work in higher-level occupations. However, part-time work still tends to be clustered in certain areas, mainly public sector professional jobs where the workforce is predominantly female (Rubery and Fagan 1993; Fagan and Rubery 1996).

Part-time work adds an extra layer to sex-segregated employment patterns. Women and men in part-time jobs are less segregated from each other than those in full-time work (Rubery *et al.* 1997b), but at the same time most part-time jobs are found in female-dominated job areas and are done by women. Women in part-time jobs are, therefore, even more segregated from male workers than women who are employed full-time (Rubery and Fagan 1993; Rubery *et al.* 1995b). This is illustrated in Figure 2.2, which shows that part-time work is more common in occupational groups where there is also a high presence of female full-timers. Particularly large incidences of part-time work are found in the two highly feminised categories of clerical and service and sales jobs, as well as in the low-status elementary occupations.[4] In these three occupational categories at least one-fifth of the jobs are held by women or men in part-time jobs. Within countries this occupational effect largely persists: the highest rates of part-time work are found in service and elementary occupations while

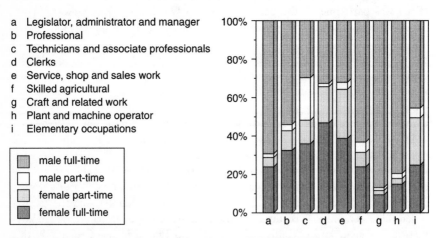

a   Legislator, administrator and manager
b   Professional
c   Technicians and associate professionals
d   Clerks
e   Service, shop and sales work
f   Skilled agricultural
g   Craft and related work
h   Plant and machine operator
i   Elementary occupations

male full-time
male part-time
female part-time
female full-time

Figure 2.2 The female and male share of major ISCO 88 (COM) occupational group by full- and part-time in the European Union (E12), 1994
    Source: Rubery *et al.* (1997b) (European Labour Force Survey)

rates of part-time work are much lower in the male-dominated job areas of management, craft workers, plant and machine operatives and the armed forces (Rubery *et al.* 1997b).

Although part-time employment is highly concentrated in certain occupations there is no simple and systematic explanation of the female share of occupations based on the distribution of part-time work. Clerical work provides one such example. This occupation is highly feminised in France and Denmark due to a large share of these jobs being held by women full-timers *and* part-timers. This is in contrast to the Dutch situation where high levels of female part-time work combine with very low shares of female full-timers, possibly reflecting a substitution of part-time workers for full-timers over time.

Overall, in 1994 84 per cent of European (E12) part-time workers were employed in the service sector. The concentration was higher for women than for men (85 per cent compared to 73 per cent), and for employees (88 per cent and 78 per cent). This high concentration in the service sector is found across the EU, but is lower in the southern countries of Greece, Portugal and Italy due to high levels of agricultural part-time work. This is illustrated in Table 2.1 for the twelve member states in 1994, which lists the industrial groups that account for the three largest concentrations of female and male part-timers in each country. Overall, the wholesale and retail sector accounts for the highest share of female and male part-timers, at around one-fifth of each. Health and education hold the second and third highest concentrations of women part-timers, while for men it is manufacturing and agriculture. At the national level the wholesale and retail sector appears in the top three sectors for both women and men in every country except France and Portugal. In eight countries the health sector appears in the top three for women, but this sector does not employ significant proportions of male part-timers in any country. The education sector is also an important source of part-time jobs for both women and men across countries, appearing in the top three sectors in six countries in both cases. Manufacturing is one of the three most important sources of part-time jobs for men in seven countries, but only in four countries for women (Denmark, Germany, Italy and Portugal). Agriculture also appears in the top three sectors in Greece, Italy and Portugal for both sexes, as well as in Spain, Ireland and France for men.

Most of the national variation in part-time rates is due to differences in the use of part-time work within sectors and not simply differences in the distribution of employment between sectors and the relative importance of the service sector (Rubery *et al.* 1995a). However, the high concentration of part-time work in particular industries and occupations raises the question of whether the recent growth of part-time work is possibly the result of economic change and restructuring, or whether it is the result of changing employment practices within existing firms. We shall explore this issue using shift-share analysis[5] in two ways, first by looking at the effect of industrial change and, second, by examining the available data on occupational change.

Table 2.1 Sectors accounting for the three highest concentrations of male and female part-timers, 1994 (%)

	Female part-timers			Male part-timers		
	1st	2nd	3rd	1st	2nd	3rd
Belgium	N (26)	G (19)	M (15)	G (15)	M (15)	D (12)
Denmark	N (37)	G (15)	D (9)	G (24)	D (13)	K (11)
France	N (17)	G (14)	L (11)	A (11)	K (11)	L+M (11)
Luxembourg	N (15)	G (13)	P (11)	M (15)	D (12)	G+K(11)
Netherlands	N (30)	G (18)	M (9)	D (18)	G (18)	K (15)
United Kingdom	G (23)	N (22)	M (12)	G (28)	H (12)	M (12)
East Germany	G (36)	M (14)	L (11)	G (19)	L (14)	D (14)
West Germany	G (33)	D (14)	N (11)	G (27)	D (15)	M (12)
Ireland	G (21)	N (18)	H (14)	G (16)	A (13)	F (11)
Italy	G (19)	D (15)	A (12)	A (24)	G (15)	F (11)
Portugal	A (29)	P (16)	D (15)	A (43)	G (12)	D (8)
Greece	A (39)	G (14)	M (11)	A (35)	F (19)	G (10)
Spain	P (24)	G (17)	M (11)	A (17)	G (16)	M (12)
E12	G (23)	N (17)	M (10)	G (20)	D (12)	A (10)

Source: Eurostat (1994)

Note: Industry groups

A Agriculture	J Financial Intermediation
B Fishing	K Real estate
C Mining	L Public administration
D Manufacture	M Education
E Electricity, gas and water	N Health
F Construction	O Other community
G Wholesale and retail	P Private households
H Hotels	Q Extra terrestrial organisations
I Transport	

Employment data by industrial sector (NACE 1-digit) is available for nine countries (no data for Italy, Spain or Portugal) which permits country changes in part-time employment between 1983 and 1992 to be decomposed into the change resulting from shifts in the structure of employment (sector effect) and the changes resulting from increased or decreased use of part-time employment within different sectors (share effect).

Table 2.2 shows that between 1983 and 1992 the European (E9) part-time rate increased by 3.2 percentage points from 13.4 per cent to 16.6 per cent. More than one-third of this total expansion (1.3 percentage points) resulted from the increased use of female part-timers within sectors (female share effect) and just under another percentage point increase resulted from the male share effect. The changing industrial structure of female employment only accounted for 0.9 of a percentage point increase in the part-time rate, while changes in the male employment structure had a slight negative effect (–0.1).

At the national level the pattern was more diverse. The impact of the changing use of female part-timers within sectors ranged from a 4.6 percentage

Table 2.2 Decomposition of the change in the part-time rate, 1983 to 1992 (%)

	Male sector effect	Female sector effect	Male share effect	Female share effect	Interaction term	Change in part-time rates
Belgium	−0.08	1.19	0.11	2.80	0.37	4.4
Denmark	0.08	0.47	1.61	−3.65	−0.30	−1.8
Germany (w)	−0.04	0.70	0.87	1.87	0.17	3.6
Greece	−0.20	0.28	−0.30	−0.94	−0.21	−1.4
France	−0.02	0.51	0.62	1.74	0.28	3.1
Ireland	−0.13	0.22	0.71	1.14	0.56	2.5
Luxembourg	−0.02	0.69	−0.01	−0.39	−0.16	0.1
Netherlands	−0.28	3.09	5.28	4.58	0.49	13.2
UK	0.00	1.52	1.43	1.09	0.14	4.2
E9	−0.07	0.91	0.95	1.29	0.11	3.2

Source: European Labour Force Surveys 1983 to 1992 (Eurostat 1992)
Note: Sector effect is the impact of the changing structure of male/female employment by sector; share effect is the impact of the increased use of male/female part-timers within sectors.

point increase in the Netherlands to a 3.7 percentage point fall in Denmark. The female share effect was positive in six of the nine countries while the male share effect was positive in all countries except Greece. In all countries the changing structure of female employment had a positive impact on the national part-time rate but the contributions were less than a percentage point in all but three countries (the Netherlands, UK and Belgium). In the UK this sector effect for women was more significant as a result of the large-scale shift to service sector employment in the 1980s. The impact of the sector effect for men was small and very slightly negative in nearly all countries, as was the interaction term.

These results clearly show that it is the diffusion of part-time employment within industrial groups which explains much of the increase in part-time employment over the 1980s (see also Walwei, Chapter 5, this volume), although there has been a slight positive role for the shifts in the structural composition of female employment reflecting the further concentration of employment in the service sector. Similar results have been shown for other European and OECD countries between 1973 and 1990 (Walwei 1995). This positive sector effect for women reflects the way that women were net beneficiaries of employment restructuring over this period as a result of their concentration in clerical and non-manual jobs, but there is now increased insecurity in some feminised parts of the service sector as a result of a new wave of restructuring, such as in banking (Rubery and Fagan 1994; Rubery 1996).

That part-time work is increasing over and above changes in the industrial structure of economies does not imply a more desegregated labour market either by gender or by working time (Rubery 1988). Much of the increased utilisation of part-time work (share effect) that has boosted the overall level of part-time employment was the result of increased levels of part-time work for both women and men in just two sectors: distributive trades and other services.[6] Between 1983 and 1992 these two sectors accounted for 70 per cent of all new part-time jobs and for 73 per cent and 60 per cent of new female and male part-time jobs respectively (Rubery et al. 1997a: 99–101). Analysis of part-time growth by detailed industrial group over the 1980s showed that the largest increases in female part-time employment were found in sub-sectors such as hotels and catering, sanitary services and recreational services (Meulders and Plasman 1993). Changes in the level of part-time work within industrial sectors is also linked to the long-term trend away from blue-collar male-dominated occupations to white-collar occupations, which also helps explain the positive effect of the female sector effect while the male effect was mainly negative.

The analysis of the impact and role of occupational change over the 1980s on part-time employment trends is more limited due to the constraints of the data (see Rubery and Fagan 1993: 124–8). This analysis is restricted to the period between 1983 and 1990 for just six countries and for ten countries for the period 1987 to 1990. However, as with the analysis of the role of industrial restructuring, we see that changes in the occupational composition of employment were less important than the increasing incidence of part-time rates within occupations (Table 2.3). Between 1983 and 1990 the E6 part-time rate rose by just over three percentage points and more than two percentage points were the result of the female (1.2) and male (1.0) share effects. Most of the remaining growth was due to a shift in the occupational structure of female employment (0.8 percentage points). However, data for ten member states for the shorter period 1987 to 1990 shows only a very slight rise in the part-time rate from 14.3 per cent to 15 per cent, and here the main component is the occupational effect for women (0.38 percentage points) which exceeded the female and the male share effects (0.24 and 0.16 percentage points), while the male occupation effect exerted a slight negative effect.

Examination of the trends in the national occupational data provides more insight than the aggregate European data. In five of the six countries for which there are data between 1983 and 1990 there were increases in the part-time rate. In Greece and Luxembourg the female share effect was negative but only in Greece was it sufficient to cause a fall in the overall rate. In the UK the male share effect was actually greater than the female share effect but the change in the female occupational structure was larger, making the female contribution to the overall rate the greater. For the period 1987 to 1990 part-time rates actually fell in four countries and where the rates rose, the increased use of female part-time was once again the most important factor, except in the UK where the female occupational effect and the male share effect were more significant (Table 2.3). In all countries changes in the male occupational structure had a small and negative effect. The male share effect was negative in three countries but only exceeded half a percentage point in the UK and the Netherlands. The nature of the occupational data limits the extent to

Table 2.3 Decomposition of the change in the part-time rate, 1983 to 1990 (%)

a) 1987 to 1990

	Male occupation effect	Female occupation effect	Male share effect	Female share effect	Interaction term	Change in part-time rates
Germany (w)	−0.03	0.23	0.12	1.40	0.07	1.8
France	−0.03	0.06	−0.12	0.26	0.02	0.2
Netherlands	−0.06	1.09	0.93	1.38	0.12	3.4
Belgium	−0.03	0.44	0.05	0.57	0.04	1.1
Luxembourg	−0.01	−0.22	0.18	−0.06	−0.02	−0.1
UK	−0.05	0.97	0.81	−0.09	−0.01	1.6
Ireland	−0.04	0.15	0.23	0.57	0.01	0.9
Greece	−0.08	0.03	−0.29	−1.02	0.01	−1.3
Portugal	−0.18	−0.06	0.12	−0.18	−0.06	−0.4
Spain	−0.09	0.11	−0.41	−0.36	0.00	−0.7
E10	−0.05	0.38	0.16	0.24	0.03	0.8

b) 1983 to 1990

	Male occupation effect	Female occupation effect	Male share effect	Female share effect	Interaction term	Change in part-time rates
France	−0.05	0.27	0.47	1.42	0.20	2.3
Belgium	0.01	0.61	0.00	2.13	0.13	2.9
Luxembourg	−0.04	0.11	0.57	−0.32	−0.01	0.3
UK	−0.06	1.51	1.98	1.13	0.04	4.6
Ireland	−0.06	0.15	0.40	0.73	0.22	1.4
Greece	−0.22	0.22	−0.92	−1.38	−0.01	−2.3
E6	−0.07	0.84	1.01	1.17	0.15	3.1

Source: European Labour Force Surveys 1983 to 1990 (Eurostat 1992)
Notes: Occupation effect is the impact of the changing structure of male/female employment by occupation and the share effect is the impact of the increased use of male/female part-timers within occupations. E10 excludes Italy and Denmark. E6 excludes Italy, Denmark, Spain, Portugal, Germany and the Netherlands.

which the conclusions can be generalised but the share effect for both men and women was a significant factor in the increasing part-time rates, with the UK the only exception.

The first part of this chapter has outlined the recent growth in part-time employment and explained the variety of experiences between both countries and the sexes. Increased use of part-timers within sectors and occupations has been the key factor in the growth of part-time job opportunities rather than the rate of industrial restructuring. It is therefore the rate of diffusion of part-time employment within the labour market that is important in understanding the variety of experiences over the 1980s and early 1990s. The rest of the chapter considers the institutional, societal and regulatory factors that have led both to variations in the use of part-time employment and to its recent expansion.

THE DEMAND FOR AND USE OF PART-TIME EMPLOYMENT

The analysis so far suggests that part-time work is mainly expanding because employers are changing their labour use strategies – albeit mainly in a limited range of service sector jobs – rather than simply as a result of service sector expansion. Employers' decisions about whether to organise employment on a full-time or part-time basis depends upon the legal, social and economic environments in which they find themselves. These different environments influence the scope for manoeuvring and managerial prerogative (Maier 1994; Marshall 1989; Fagan et al. 1995). Thus, while certain sectors and occupations have greater requirements than others for flexible working time practices to meet the variable demands of the production system, there is a variety of ways in which employers can achieve such flexibility. For example, working-time flexibility can be provided by full-timers on shift-work or overtime or by part-timers employed specifically to cover additional or antisocial hours. Thus, there are a number of factors that influence the decision to create part-time jobs over full-time work. Box 2.1 groups these factors into five broad areas: the production system; competitive conditions in the product market; labour regulation; government and union activity; and labour market conditions. These factors interact to produce both national and sectoral variations in the extent and type of part-time employment.

The *production system* affects the need for work schedules to be organised to meet regular and irregular peaks in labour demand and to cover extended operating hours. Part-time work is one way of providing this labour. Part-time work also allows the intensity of work to be increased to improve productivity where the work is tiring or intense. A survey of establishments in eight EU countries found that managers consistently ranked making the firm more competitive and covering peak workloads as either the first or second most important factors for employing part-timers (except in the UK) (Bielenski 1994: 89). In Denmark, for example, twice the number of part-timers than full-timers had schedules that vary from week to week (Boje 1994). Production in the service sector is more labour intensive and labour costs account for a higher proportion of total production costs than in manufacturing (Bosch 1995). Thus there are relatively greater productivity gains to be made from a closer matching of work time to peaks in service demand.

Box 2.1 Factors influencing employers' demand for and use of part-timers

Production system requires non-standard or flexible hours
- To extend operating hours beyond the standard week.
- To schedule hours to meet regular, period peaks in production on a daily, weekly or annual basis, such as lunchtime cover.
- To cover irregular and temporary changes in labour demands, for example, to substitute for absent employees or to meet unexpected orders.
- To extract more effort per hour in jobs where productivity is increased through short and intense work periods.

Competitive conditions in the product market
- The extent of competitive pressures to adopt flexible practices in order to compete on product price or extended service hours, for example, between large and small retail firms in relation to opening hours.
- Variation in the volume of labour hours required in times of economic boom versus recession.

Labour regulations (statutory and collectively bargained)
(a) Working time system
- Statutory and collective working-time restrictions on the use of full-timers to provide flexibility through overtime, shift patterns and other variable hours schedules.
- Regulations relating to the use of part-time work.
- Workplace custom and practice creates inertia.

(b) Wage and social protection system
- Regulations concerning working time premia for shifts, overtime or antisocial hours.
- The structure of non-wage costs for employers, such as hours or earnings thresholds for social insurance contributions or other conditions of employment.

Government and trade union activity
- Work-sharing policies to reduce unemployment.
- Policies to enable parents to reconcile work and family life.
- Government's personnel policies in the public sector.

Labour market conditions

(a) Labour supply

- Family responsibilities within the household and the Welfare State system influence labour supply according to the relations of gender and generation. For example, a strong 'male breadwinner' model of family life encourages women to work part-time rather than full-time.

(b) Labour demand

- The type of flexibility practices implemented by employers are 'gendered' because they are contingent on the sex of the current or desired workforce, so part-time schedules are more usually available in feminised areas than in male-dominated jobs.
- Employment shortages encourage people who want full-time work to accept part-time work.

Source: adapted from Fagan *et al.* (1995)

The high concentrations of part-timers in the service sector in Table 2.1 clearly illustrate how part-time work helps to deal with the demands of the service sector. However, part-time work is not the only way of securing working-time flexibility. For example, examination of working-time patterns in the catering and distribution sectors has revealed two modes of work organisation, with some countries using short hours schedules, particularly in Northern Europe, while other countries in the South use standard or long full-time hours, with only the UK using a combination of the two (Rubery *et al.* 1995a). Similar requirements for flexibility in the transport sector are typically achieved through the use of shifts and overtime rather than part-time work. This is connected with gender-related conditions in labour supply and demand, discussed below.

The organisation of the production system in a particular sector or market will also be influenced by the *competitive conditions* within which the firm operates. In highly competitive product markets firms may face particularly strong pressures to increase the flexibility of working time practices in response to changing consumption patterns or the behaviour of rival firms. In certain product markets firms may, for example, gain significant competitive advantages from extended opening hours, or extended operating times to improve utilisation of machinery in capital-intensive production systems, both of which may involve working-time reforms or innovations. An increased use of part-timers is one possible component of the firm's competitive strategy

(Bosch et al. 1994). Retailing is a good example of where there are growing pressures for firms to extend opening hours in many countries. Traditionally, shop opening hours have been strictly regulated, in part to protect smaller firms from 'ruinous' competition driven by large retailers, as well as because of religious and other cultural norms (Bosch 1995). Large retailers are successfully exerting pressure for an extension to opening hours in many national markets, even where the service sector is dominated by small firms, such as in Italy (Bettio and Villa 1994). Consumer pressure is another important factor in many national debates about removing statutory restrictions on retail hours, for example, in the Netherlands (Plantenga and van Velzen 1994). The extension of Sunday opening hours in the UK retail sector has resulted in increased requirements for weekend cover, and part-timers are often employed specifically for Sunday work (Rubery 1994: 133; IDS 1995: 10). Pressures for longer operating times in other sectors are also leading to a greater use of part-timers (see below), as well as shift and overtime work.

Labour regulations in connection with working-time and wages have a major effect on the extent and type of part-time work which develops (Marshall 1989; Maier 1994). Thus, in countries where the standard full-time week is highly protected and there are many restrictions on the flexibility of full-timers, employers may make a greater effort to create non-standard jobs compared to countries with few regulations on working-time (Rodgers and Rodgers 1989). However, there is also an influence for social norms and expectations, so that in these societies atypical employment may be less acceptable than in more deregulated environments. There is a variety of systems of national working-time regulation across the EU. In some countries, such as Germany and France, there are strict limits on daily and weekly hours set by legislation or collective bargaining, in contrast to the weaker regulations operating in the UK (Bosch et al. 1994; Rubery et al. 1995a). Working-time regulations, including those which are specifically concerned with part-time work, are being reformed in many countries. For example, in France and Belgium statutory limits on the variability of part-time hours on a weekly or annual basis have recently been revoked (Meulders et al. 1994; Silvera et al. 1994). Strong regulation on the use of part-time workers in Southern countries, such as Spain, has been one of the factors that has limited the expansion of part-time employment (Cousins 1994), and the recent deregulation of the laws affecting part-timers in Spain has led to an expansion of part-time work (Ruivo et al. 1996). The evidence suggests that this increase is employer led and that Spanish women are still mainly seeking full-time work.

Related to the issue of working-time regulations is that of labour costs. The wage and social insurance system in some countries provides inferior entitlements for part-timers, making such workers a cheaper labour source relative to full-timers. To start with, premia for antisocial or overtime hours have historically been established with reference to the full-time standard week (Bosch et al. 1994). Part-timers are frequently excluded from such elements of wage systems, making them a cheaper source of cover for variable or antisocial hours relative to using full-timers. For example, surveys in the Netherlands and the UK showed that part-timers were expected to work a full-time week before any premia were paid in 53 per cent and 78 per cent of cases respectively (Plantenga and van Velzen 1994; Rubery 1994: 133). In contrast, part-timers in Luxembourg and France are entitled to premia pay once hours exceed contracted hours or a particular threshold (Plasman 1994: 55; Silvera et al. 1994: 92).

Over time there has been a gradual extension of employment rights to part-timers in most countries through a combination of rulings established using the European sex discrimination legislation combined with collective bargaining (Maier 1994). For example, minimum wage protection in the Netherlands has been extended to part-timers, and in the UK a recent legal ruling extended employment protection to all part-timers working at least 8 hours a week. Nevertheless, hours or earnings thresholds still operate for entry into the social insurance system in Germany and the UK, whereas in countries such as Denmark or France the contributions made by employers are unaffected by such thresholds. Since employers do not have to pay social insurance contributions for employees who fall below these thresholds this creates a strong financial incentive to construct these marginalised part-time jobs. This differential treatment in regulations has stimulated the creation of short or marginal part-time jobs in some countries, most notably the UK (Schoer 1987; Marshall 1989). A similar process may emerge in Spain, where recent legislation has reduced social protection payments for part-time workers working short hours (Ruivo et al. 1996). Furthermore, the recent relaxation of shop opening hours in Germany is expected to increase the demand for marginal part-time workers who can work outside the social security net and are thus cheaper to employ (IDS 1996: 6).

The form and content of labour regulations, and hence the promotion or discouragement of part-time work is obviously driven by the activity of *social partners*. In recent years several governments have actively sought to encourage the expansion of part-time work as a form of work-sharing in response to high unemployment rates. For example, policies have been developed in Belgium, France and Germany to encourage the unemployed to enter part-time jobs, or early retirement on a part-time basis (see Delsen, Chapter 3, this volume). Depending on how the schemes are designed this can create divisions between part-timers on the basis of wage and social protection entitlements according to whether they entered part-time work by reducing their hours within an existing job, from unemployment or from inactivity (see Rubery, Chapter 7, this volume). The Dutch government has been the strongest advocate of part-time work as a way to reduce unemployment and this can be dated back to the 1970s (de Lange and van Maanen 1995: 173). The overall policy approach in the Netherlands has been a combination of removing disincentives for part-time work for employers and employees and the integration of part-timers into the employment system on the basis of equal treatment (Fagan et al. 1995).

Part-time work has also been actively promoted as a way for parents to combine work and family life to avoid total labour market withdrawal or occupational downgrading. In Sweden, individuals have the right to work part-time at 75 per cent of usual hours or more for up to eight years after the birth of a child without any loss of income and then have the right to transfer back to full-time work (Gonäs and Spânt 1996). In France, women have been able to choose to work long full-time hours in the public sector as a way to reconcile work and family life and often choose to take time off in the week such as on Wednesday afternoons when schools are closed (Silvera et al. 1994: 34). The role of government as an employer also has to be considered; for example, in Belgium, Ireland, Germany and Italy part-time posts have increasingly been created in the public services, accounting for many of the new jobs in the public sector (Meulders and Plasman 1993).

Trade unions have often tried to restrict the spread of part-time jobs, fearing that this will undermine full-time standards. Paradoxically, where unions have viewed part-time work negatively it has expanded without protection and has been further marginalised (Marshall 1989; Maier 1994). Unions have tended to concentrate on the traditional full-time employee despite the expansion of other forms of employment, and this has resulted in the alienation of 'modern' groups of employees such as white-collar workers, women and the young (Mückenberger 1995: 160). However, union attitudes and policies towards part-time work have changed over time, reflected in current policy developments within the European Trade Union Confederation (Hoffmann and Lapeyre 1995), and there is a growing awareness of the need to protect part-timers' interests. For example, collective bargaining in France has limited the scope and spread of very short part-time jobs in retail, while the weaker union presence in the UK has enabled employers to create very short-hour jobs which avoid the costs of providing employees with breaks (Gregory and O'Reilly 1995). In Germany, although part-timers working less than 8 hours are excluded from social protection, many part-timers, particularly those working at least 15 hours, are entitled to the same collectively negotiated conditions as full-timers on a pro rata basis (Maier et al. 1996: 78). And in the Netherlands, many trade unions have begun to look more favourably upon part-time jobs which offer 'long' rather than 'short' hours, such as 20 or more hours a week (de Lange and van Maanen 1995: 179). However, evidence from many unions elsewhere in Europe suggests that part-time work is still regarded as a temporary measure to avoid redundancy rather than a means to share work (Mückenberger 1995: 171).

The final factor which affects employers' use of part-time work is *labour market conditions*, in other words a supply of people who are prepared to work less than full-time and are judged suitable for the available jobs. Membership of this pool of labour is heavily influenced by the organisation of family responsibilities within households and the Welfare State system. Women are an important source of part-time labour in societies where a 'male breadwinner' model of family life dominates, for in this context women are presumed to place employment second to their primary domestic responsibilities. Thus, the expansion of part-time employment has largely been premised on an available supply of married women with children who are unable or unwilling to work full-time. Limited child care services and a tradition of labour market withdrawal around childbirth has helped to create a buoyant supply of mothers for part-time work in some countries such as Ireland and the UK, whereas in other countries different family policies and employment opportunities contribute to a greater degree of full-time employment for mothers (see Figure 2.1 above; EC Childcare Network 1996; Rubery *et al.* 1997a). There are signs that younger, more educated generations of mothers may become a declining source of labour for part-time jobs, particularly in countries where maternal employment is an established norm. Thus, recently in Denmark and the USA there has been a fall in the female rate of part-time employment as fewer women move from full-time to part-time jobs at the birth of a child (Williams 1995; Boje 1996). One reason for this changing labour market behaviour in Denmark is that younger and more educated generations of women have a stronger commitment to a labour market career (Boje 1995: 36). Similar factors account for the 'normalisation' of maternal full-time employment over time in the USA, as well as the growing economic pressures on households as men's earnings stagnated or declined from the mid-1970s onwards (Spain and Bianchi 1996: 110–11; see also Houseman and Osawa, Chapter 12, this volume).

However, the lack of full-time jobs may oblige some women to take part-time work on an involuntary basis, for the incidence of involuntary part-time work has increased over time in many countries, correlated with recession and increased unemployment (OECD 1995: 74). Even when women express a preference for part-time rather than full-time employment, as in the UK, they may still be underemployed due to labour market conditions: in many instances they have moved into lower occupational levels in order to find part-time work (Dex 1987), and more than one in five would like to work longer part-time hours (Fagan 1996). Persistent unemployment and stagnating or declining sources of unearned income are also contributing to the increasing supply of men for part-time jobs, particularly among students and the semi-retired, but also from the pool of unemployed in response to various new policies (see Duodeijns, Chapter 6, Delsen, Chapter 3, this volume). Indeed, this increase in the male supply has, in some countries, partly compensated for falling female rates of part-time work.

Gender relations and norms affect labour demand as well as labour supply. The type of flexibility adopted in companies is gendered, for the sex of the current or prospective workforce influences the type of working-time arrangement used by employers (Beechey and Perkins 1987; Horrell and Rubery 1991; Hunter *et al.* 1993; Plantenga and van Velzen 1994). Thus, part-time jobs are more likely to be created in job areas where employers rely on women, students or others who are available for part-time work, whereas similar requirements for flexibility in male-dominated workforces are usually covered by full-timers working overtime or different shift systems, such as in transport. Indeed, the prevalence of the full-time breadwinner ethos in male-dominated jobs may create greater expectations concerning premia pay for extra or antisocial hours and a greater resistance to the introduction of part-time work. Compensation may even be offered where part-time work is introduced into male-dominated sectors as a result. For example, in Greece and Spain new part-time weekend contracts in manufacturing are treated as full-timers in all aspects including social security and unemployment insurance (Cavouriasis *et al.* 1994; Moltó 1994; Rubery, Chapter 7, this volume). Gender relations within the workplace can clearly have a strong impact on the use of part-time employment that may be more entrenched than the explicit regulatory regime.

CONCLUSIONS

Part-time employment is expanding in most European countries. While this tendency is common for both sexes, part-time work is still female-dominated and in every country women's rates of part-time work vastly exceed those for men. This pattern of employment cannot be presumed to correspond to women's working-time preferences in any simple way. Significant proportions of women in part-time jobs would prefer longer hours of work, including full-time jobs (Fagan 1996; Fagan and Rubery 1996), while others have adjusted their aspirations in light of child care constraints and high unemployment levels (Dex 1985).

This expansion of part-time work has not produced an even outcome across countries or sectors. It is still much more common in certain Northern European member states than elsewhere in the EU, and in particular occupations and sectors. Overall, part-time jobs are disproportionately concentrated in low-paid, low-status occupations such as sales, catering and cleaning. Most of these jobs are found in the service sector, particularly in distribution services, but also health and education.

This chapter has shown that most of the increase in part-time employment in the EU over the 1980s resulted from a diffusion in the use of part-time workers within sectors and occupations and not simply because of changes in the structural composition of the economy due to the expansion of service activities which already make high use of part-timers. Nevertheless, the increased use of part-timers in sectors where such jobs were already common such as distribution and public services accounted for the majority of the increase in part-time employment. So far, therefore, there is little evidence that the process of diffusion in the use of part-timers is sufficient for part-time work to spread evenly across the economy. Instead, it is still predominantly a highly segregated and female-dominated form of service work.

Part-timers offer many advantages to employers, including increased productivity and intensity of work, a closer relation between paid time and work time, the opportunity to cover unsociable hours and short shifts as well as cost advantages from reduced basic pay and premia (Delsen 1993; Maier 1994). However, a number of other factors influence the work practices and flexibility strategies developed by employers, including labour regulations, government and trade union working-time policies, and conditions in both the product and labour markets. These institutional arrangements and conditions vary across countries, influencing the extent and quality of part-time work which has developed. But the common cross-national tendency is that part-time work has primarily been adopted in female-dominated job areas while male-dominated workplaces rely on overtime and new shift patterns for working-time flexibility. This indicates that across Europe employers' flexibility practices are still heavily gendered. Thus, while continued high levels of unemployment may create a context in which certain groups of men become more willing to accept part-time employment, it is likely to remain feminised for some time to come.

NOTES

1 The chapter draws on the work carried out for the European Commission's Network of Experts on the Situation of Women in the Labour Market (see Rubery and Fagan 1993, 1994; Rubery et al. 1995a, 1997a, 1997b). Much of the data used in this chapter for the twelve member states of the EU in 1994 are taken from special tabulations of the European Labour Force Survey (ELFS) provided by Eurostat. The definition of part-time adopted in the ELFS is based on respondents' perceptions of whether they have full- or part-time employment (Eurostat 1988, 1992).

2 There was also a slight fall of half a percentage point in the part-time rate in Sweden between 1983 and 1994 but this fall occurred between 1993 and 1994 and was not a general trend over the whole period.

3 The large increase in the Dutch part-time rate is somewhat distorted by changes in the Dutch labour force survey that have affected the European Labour Force Survey data. The survey design of the Dutch national labour force survey was changed in 1987 and again in 1992, altering the recorded level of part-time employment. The latter change has been adjusted for in the Eurostat data but the former saw the part-time rate rise sharply with the inclusion of many more short part-time jobs (see Rubery et al. 1997a).

4 Elementary occupations in the ISCO-88 (COM) classification include sales and service work, such as vendors, cleaners and porters, and labourers in agriculture and industry (see Eurostat 1992).

5 Shift share analysis decomposes the change in the part-time rate by holding sector or occupation specific part-time rates constant while allowing the structure of employment to change (male and female sector of occupation effects). Holding the structure of employment constant and allowing the sector or occupation specific part-time rates to change produces male and female share effects. The interaction of these effects is the interaction term.

6 Other services in the NACE 1-digit classification include public administration, education, sanitary services and personal and domestic services (see Eurostat 1988).

BIBLIOGRAPHY

Beechy, V. and Perkins, T. (1987) A Matter of Hours. Cambridge: Polity Press.

Bettio, F. and Villa, P. (1994) 'Changing Patterns of Work and Working Time for Men and Women: Italy'. Report for the European Commission's Network of Experts on the Situation of Women in the Labour Market. Manchester School of Management, UMIST.

Bettio, F., Rubery, J. and Smith, M. (1996) 'Gender, Flexibility and New Employment Relations'. Paper presented to the European Seminar on Women and Work; integration between labour polices and equal opportunities. ILO Training Centre, Turin, Italy, April.

Bielinski, H. (1994) 'New Forms of Work and Activity: A Survey of Experience at Establishment Level in Eight European Countries'. Dublin: European Foundation for the Improvement of Living and Working Conditions.

Boje, T. (1994) 'Changing Patterns of Work and Working-time for Men and Women. Towards the Integration or the Segmentation of the Labour Market: Denmark'. Report for the European Commission's Network of Experts on the Situation of Women in the Labour Market. Manchester School of Management, UMIST.

Boje. T. (1995) 'Women and the European Employment Rate: The Causes and Consequences of Variations in Female Activity and Employment: National Report for Denmark.' Report for the European Commission's Network of Experts on the Situation of Women in the Labour Market. Manchester School of Management, UMIST.

Boje, T. (1996) 'Trends and Prospects for Women in Employment in Denmark in the 1990s'. Report for the European Commission's Network of Experts on the Situation of Women in the Labour Market. Manchester School of Management, UMIST.

Bosch, G. (1995) 'Synthesis Report' in OECD (1995) Flexible Working Time; Collective Bargaining and Government Intervention. Paris: OECD.

Bosch, G., Dawkins, P. and Michon, F. (1994) 'Working Time in 14 Industrialised Countries: An Overview' in G. Bosch, P. Dawkins and F. Michon (eds) Times Are a Changing. International Institute for Labour Studies, Geneva: ILO.

Cavouriasis, M., Karamessini, M. and Symeonidou, H. (1994) 'Changing Patterns of Work and Working-time for Men and Women. Towards the Integration or the Segmentation of the Labour Market: Greece.' Report for the European Commission's Network of Experts on the Situation of Women in the Labour Market. Manchester School of Management, UMIST.

CEC (1993) Growth, Competitiveness and Employment. Brussels: Commission of the European Communities.

Cousins, C. (1994) 'A Comparison of the Labour Market Prospects of Women in Spain and the UK with Reference to the "Flexible" Labour Debate', Work Employment and Society 8, 1: 45–68.

Delsen, L. (1993) 'Part-time Employment and the Utilisation of Labour Resources', Labour 7, 3: 73–91.

Dex, S. (1985) Sexual Division of Work. Brighton: Harvester Press.

Dex, S. (1987) Women's Occupational Mobility: A Lifetimes Perspective. London: Macmillan.

EC Childcare Network (1996) Review of Children's Services. Report to the Equal Opportunities Unit of the European Commission, DG-V. Brussels: European Commission.

Eurostat (1998) Labour Force Survey: Methods and Definitions. Luxembourg: Eurostat.

Eurostat (1992) Labour Force Survey: Methods and Definitions. Luxembourg: Eurostat.

Fagan, C. (1996) 'Gendered Time Schedules: Paid Work in Great Britain', *Social Politics: International Studies in Gender, State and Society* (special issue 'Gender Inequalities in Global Restructuring') 3, 1: 72–106.

Fagan, C. and Rubery, J. (1996) 'The Salience of the Part-time Divide in the European Union', *European Sociological Review* 12, 3: 227–50.

Fagan, C., Plantenga, J. and Rubery, J. (1995) 'Part-time Work and Inequality? Lessons from the Netherlands and the UK' in J. Lapeyre and R. Hoffman (eds) *A Time for Working – A Time for Living*. Brussels: European Trade Union Institute/Labour Research Department.

Gonäs, L. and Spânt, A. (1996) 'Trends and Prospects for Women's Employment in the 1990s in Sweden'. Report for the European Commission's Network of Experts on the Situation of Women in the Labour Market. Manchester School of Management, UMIST.

Gregory, A. and O'Reilly, J. (1995) 'Checking Out and Cashing Up' in R. Crompton (ed.) *Changing Forms of Employment: Organisation, Skills and Gender*. London: Routledge.

Hoffman, R. and Lapeyre, J. (eds) (1995) *A Time for Working – A Time for Living*. Brussels: European Trade Union Institute/Labour Research Department.

Horrell, S. and Rubery, J. (1991) 'Gender and Working-time Divisions', *Cambridge Journal of Economics* 15, 4: 373–92.

Hunter, L., McGregor, A., MacInnes, J. and Sproull, A. (1993) 'The Flexible Firm: Strategy and Segmentation', *British Journal of Industrial Relations* 31, 3: 383–408.

IDS (1995) 'ASDA Cuts Sunday Overtime Rates', *Employment Europe* 407: 10.

IDS (1996) 'Hours Deregulation Hobbles Retails Pay Talks', *Employment Europe* 416: 6.

Lange, W. de and van Maanen, D. (1995) 'The Netherlands: The Case of Health' in OECD *Flexible Working Time: Collective Bargaining and Government Intervention*. Paris: OECD.

Maier, F. (1994) 'Institutional Regimes of Part-time Working' in G. Schmid (ed.) *Labour Market Institutions in Europe*. New York: Sharpe.

Maier, F. Quack, S., Martschink, A. and Rapp, Z. (1996) 'Trends and Prospects for Women's Employment in Germany in the 1990s.' Report for the European Commission's Network of Experts on the Situation of Women in the Labour Market. Manchester School of Management, UMIST.

Marshall, A. (1989) 'The Sequel of Unemployment: The Changing Role of Part-time and Temporary Work in Western Europe' in J. Rodgers and G. Rodgers (eds) *Precarious Jobs in Labour Market Regulation: The Growth of Atypical Employment in Western Europe*. International Institute for Labour Studies, Geneva: ILO.

Meulders, D. (1995) 'Reorganisation of Work' in J. Rubery (ed.) *Equal Opportunities for Women and Men: Follow-up to the White Paper in Growth, Competitiveness and Employment*. Brussels: Report for the Employment Task Force of the European Commission, DG-V. V/5532/95-EN.

Meulders, D. and Plasman, R. (1993) 'Part-time Work in EEC Countries: Evolution during the 1980s', *Labour* 7, 3: 49–71.

Meulders, D., Hecq, C. and Ruz Torres, R. (1994) 'Changing Patterns of Work and Working-time for Men and Women. Towards the Integration or the Segmentation of the Labour Market: Belgium'. Report for the European Commission's Network of Experts on the Situation of Women in the Labour Market. Manchester School of Management, UMIST.

Meulders, D., Plasman, R. and Vander Strict, V. (1993) *The Position of Women on the Labour Market in the European Community*. Aldershot: Dartmouth Publishing Company.

Moltó, M. L. (1994) 'Changing Patterns of Work and Working-time for Men and Women. Towards the Integration or the Segmentation of the Labour Market: Spain.' Report for the European Commission's Network of Experts on the Situation of Women in the Labour Market. Manchester School of Management, UMIST.

Mückenberger, U. (1995) 'Working Time and a Modernised Trade Union Policy' in J. Lapeyre and R. Hoffman (eds) *A Time for Working – A Time for Living*. Brussels: European Trade Union Institute/Labour Research Department.

OECD (1994) *Women and Structural Change*. Paris: OECD.

OECD (1995) *Flexible Working Time; Collective Bargaining and Government Intervention*. Paris: OECD.

Plantenga, J. and van Velzen, S. (1994) 'Changing Patterns of Work and Working-time for Men and Women. Towards the Integration or the Segmentation of the Labour Market: Netherlands'. Report for the European Commission's Network of Experts on the Situation of Women in the Labour Market. Manchester School of Management, UMIST.

Plasman, R. (1994) 'Changing Patterns of Work and Working-time for Men and Women. Towards the Integration or the Segmentation of the Labour Market: Luxembourg'. Report for the European Commission's Network of Experts on the Situation of Women in the Labour Market. Manchester School of Management, UMIST.

Rodgers, J. and Rodgers, G. (1989) *Precarious Jobs in Labour Market Regulation: The Growth of Atypical Employment in Western Europe*. International Institute for Labour Studies, Geneva: ILO.

Rubery, J. (1988) *Women and Recession*. London: Routledge & Kegan Paul.

Rubery, J. (1994) 'Changing Patterns of Work and Working-time for Men and Women. Towards the Integration or the Segmentation of the Labour Market in the UK'. Report for the European Commission's Network of Experts on the Situation of Women in the Labour Market, Equal Opportunities Unit of the European Commission, DG-V.

Rubery, J. (1996) 'Trends and Prospects for Women's Employment in UK in the 1990s'. Report for the European Commission's Network of Experts on the Situation of Women in the Labour Market. Manchester School of Management, UMIST.

Rubery, J. and Fagan, C. (1993) *Occupational Segregation of Women and Men in the European Union*. Social Europe, 3/93.

Rubery, J. and Fagan, C. (1994) 'Does Feminisation mean a Flexible Labour Force?' in R. Hyman and A. Ferner (eds) *New Frontiers in European Industrial Relations*. Oxford: Blackwell.

Rubery, J. and Smith, M, (1996) 'Factors Influencing the Integration of Women into the Economy'. Paper presented to the European Seminar on Women and Work; integration between labour polices and equal opportunities. ILO Training Centre, Turin, Italy, April.

Rubery, J., Fagan, C. and Smith, M. (1995a) 'Changing Patterns of Work and Working Time in the European Union'. Brussels: Report for the Equal Opportunities Unit of the European Commission DG-V. V/6203/95-EN.

Rubery, J., Smith, M. and Fagan, C. (1995b) 'Occupational Segregation of Men and Women and Atypical Work in the European Union'. Brussels: Report for the Equal Opportunities Unit of the European Commission DG-V. V/5619/95-EN

Rubery, J., Smith, M., Fagan, C. and Grimshaw, D. (1997a) *Women and the European Employment Rate*. London: Routledge.

Rubery, J., Smith, M. and Fagan, C. (1997b) 'Trends and Prospects for Women's Employment in the European Union'. Brussels: Report for the Equal Opportunities Unit of the European Commission DG-V.

Ruivo, M., Pilar, G. and Varejao, J. (1996) 'Part-time work in Portugal and Spain'. Paper presented to the Eighteenth Conference of the International Working Party on Labour Market Segmentation, Tampere, Finland.

Schoer, K. (1987) 'Part-time Employment: Britain and West Germany', *Cambridge Journal of Economics* 11, 1: 83–94.

Silvera, R., Gauvin, A. and Granie, R. (1994) 'The Evolution of Employment Forms and Working-time among Men and Women. Towards the Integration or the Segmentation of the Labour Market: France'. Brussels: Report for the European Commission's Network of Experts on the Situation of Women in the Labour Market, Equal Opportunities Unit of the European Commission, DG-V.

Spain, D. and Bianchi, S. (1996) *Balancing Act: Motherhood, Marriage and Employment among American Women.* New York: Russell Sage Foundation.

Walwei, U. (1995) 'The Growth of Part-time Employment; Demand Side versus Supply Side Explanations'. Paper Presented to the Seventh Conference of the European Association of Labour Economists, Lyon, France.

Williams, D. R. (1995) 'Women's Part-time Employment: A Gross Flow Analysis', *Monthly Labour Review* 118, 4: 36–44.

3

WHEN DO MEN WORK PART-TIME?

Lei Delsen[1]

INTRODUCTION

The expansion of part-time work over the past two decades has varied cross-nationally, but a common characteristic is that up to now it has been an almost exclusively female phenomenon. This chapter tries to unravel why and where part-time work is still dominated by women and asks when do men work part-time? It will assess whether male part-time employment is likely to expand and, if so, where. In the first part of this chapter data on the international differences in the overall level and development of part-time employment are presented. Special attention is paid to the gender dimension. Next, the variation in the patterns and in the growth rates of part-time employment between countries and between different groups of workers is explained. Relevant factors include (changes in) employee preferences, the sectoral distribution of employment, transition rates, personnel policy, the business cycle, wages and non-wage cost and trade union and government policy. The chapter concludes with a summary and an outlook on the prospects for part-timers.

THE DEVELOPMENT AND STRUCTURE OF PART-TIME EMPLOYMENT

Change in the volume, age and sex structure of part-time employment in seventeen OECD member countries can be seen from Tables 3.1 and 3.2. The operational definitions of a part-time worker differ substantially across countries. Essentially three approaches can be distinguished (OECD 1996): a classification based on the worker's perception of his/her employment situation; a cut-off (generally 30 or 35 hours) based on normal working hours, with persons usually working less than this cut-off being considered part-timers; and a comparable cut-off based on actual hours worked during the reference week. A criterion based on actual hours will generally yield a part-time rate higher

Table 3.1 Proportion of part-time employment by age and sex in selected OECD countries, 1986

	Males								Females						
	All persons	All males	15–19 years	20–24 years	25–54 years	55–59 years	60–64 years	65+ years	All females	15–19 years	20–24 years	25–54 years	55–59 years	60–64 years	65+ years
Australia	20.0	7.4	30.8	8.8	3.7	6.4	13.6	35.0	39.2	43.5	20.3	45.5	44.2	48.6	58.3
Belgium	9.4	2.1	13.7	3.8	1.3	1.7	5.7	20.9	22.6	26.6	19.8	23.0	20.3	23.0	33.8
Canada	15.2	7.6	55.0	11.6	2.1	4.9		27.6	25.3	65.4	20.5	20.9	28.2		47.2
Denmark	23.7	8.7	47.6	9.0	2.7	2.9	10.5	30.6	41.9	62.1	21.6	40.2	55.4	64.8	66.5
France	11.8	3.4	20.6	7.0	1.7	4.8	9.1	35.8	23.2	37.3	21.7	22.0	28.7	33.2	43.4
Germany	12.9	2.1	1.8	4.6	1.6	1.7	5.5	39.9	29.8	3.6	8.3	36.5	36.2	42.4	58.4
Greece	5.8	3.4	9.8	4.9	2.1	3.0	5.2	18.0	10.4	11.4	8.2	9.3	10.3	12.4	32.3
Ireland	6.2	2.5	9.2	3.5	1.7	2.0	2.3	5.7	14.2	11.8	4.8	17.2	25.6	24.7	23.5
Italy	5.0	2.8	5.9	4.7	1.7	3.5	6.3	20.5	9.5	8.8	8.6	8.9	12.0	18.1	27.6
Japan	16.6	7.3	18.2	8.9	4.0	7.6	18.1	35.2	30.5	25.0	11.4	30.9	33.7	42.1	53.3
Luxembourg	6.6	1.8	23.8	2.6	0.3	–	–	16.7	15.4	22.0	5.7	17.4	19.0	14.3	–
Netherlands	25.3	10.1	33.2	10.5	8.3	10.4	17.8	51.7	55.2	43.3	28.7	63.8	70.9	70.8	64.5
Norway	23.1	7.9	46.2	8.8	3.9		10.5	40.9	45.0	63.5	25.8	41.8	55.2		75.0
Portugal	6.0	3.4	4.4	3.1	1.8	4.4	5.9	23.3	10.0	8.0	7.5	8.9	16.5	14.9	25.4
Sweden	25.2	6.7	28.4	7.3	3.9	5.1	24.7	–	45.1	51.5	27.7	45.2	51.3	63.1	–
United Kingdom	21.6	4.6	21.4	4.3	1.5	3.1	7.3	66.2	45.0	32.8	14.6	49.8	56.2	71.7	80.7
United States	17.3	10.2	59.6	16.8	4.0	6.1	12.1	46.2	26.1	66.6	25.6	21.0	24.3	32.2	59.4

Source: calculated from OECD data
Note: The data refer to 1985 for the Netherlands and 1987 for Australia, Canada, Japan, Sweden and the United States.

Table 3.2 Proportion of part-time employment by age and sex in selected OECD countries, 1995

	All persons	Males							Females						
		All males	15–19 years	20–24 years	25–39 years	40–54 years	55–64 years	65+ years	All females	15–19 years	20–24 years	25–39 years	40–54 years	55–64 years	65+ years
Australia	24.8	11.1	49.4	16.0	6.1	5.3	14.0	43.5	42.7	72.3	29.8	41.3	40.4	49.5	66.6
Belgium	13.6	2.8	27.9	5.8	2.4	1.6	3.6	22.4	29.8	28.9	22.2	30.9	30.5	28.6	23.2
Canada	18.6	10.6	66.7	23.3	4.9	4.1	9.6	34.5	28.2	76.5	35.5	22.6	22.4	32.6	58.7
Denmark	21.6	10.4	61.5	19.3	4.6	2.1	9.1	40.7	35.5	76.4	35.5	25.6	34.5	44.3	74.5
France	15.6	5.0	18.7	12.5	4.0	3.0	9.6	39.1	28.9	41.9	34.5	28.2	26.8	35.3	44.7
Germany	16.3	3.6	5.5	4.4	3.7	2.3	3.8	40.8	33.8	8.0	10.4	35.2	46.1	49.9	60.6
Greece	4.8	2.8	11.1	5.1	2.1	1.4	3.1	12.9	8.4	17.3	8.9	7.2	6.2	12.7	26.1
Ireland*	11.3	5.1	21.7	7.2	3.7	3.9	4.7	10.8	21.7	35.2	11.4	16.9	33.5	33.3	28.6
Italy	6.4	2.9	5.9	4.8	2.6	1.8	3.8	15.3	12.7	11.3	13.0	13.4	11.7	12.0	15.9
Japan	20.1	10.1	–	–	–	–	–	–	34.9	–	–	–	–	–	–
Luxembourg	7.9	1.1	17.5	2.8	0.7	0.4	1.1	11.0	20.3	20.9	9.8	18.8	26.4	24.4	18.8
Netherlands	37.4	16.8	81.8	35.1	9.3	22.8	75.1	67.2	89.0	49.0	62.3	76.2	81.7	83.8	
Norway	21.2	9.4	64.7	17.6	6.9	3.9	7.8	38.5	46.6	81.8	47.7	41.4	44.5	56.1	66.7
Portugal	7.5	4.3	6.8	3.6	1.5	1.9	7.1	27.3	11.6	9.1	7.9	8.0	11.1	20.1	38.7
Sweden	24.3	9.4	50.5	6.2	4.9	21.1	–	40.3	73.3	40.9	39.5	35.2	50.6	–	
United Kingdom	24.1	7.7	45.6	9.8	2.9	2.9	11.2	66.5	44.3	56.0	21.2	41.0	46.8	60.0	87.5
United States	18.6	11.0	62.7	20.9	4.8	10.9	49.5	27.4	74.4	33.5	22.1	20.1	28.4	65.6	

Source: calculated from OECD data
Note:* Ireland's category data are for 1994.

than one based on normal hours. The impact on the part-time rate of a classification based on a worker's perception relative to the one based on a fixed cut-off is not entirely clear. In France, the 1982 change from actual hours cutoff to one based on a respondent's perception resulted in slightly higher estimates. In Canada, Japan and the United States seasonal and casual part-time workers are included in the statistics, implying a (considerable) increase in the level of part-time employment (see Wakisaka and Bae, Chapter 13, and Houseman and Osawa, Chapter 12, this volume). In the European Labour Force Sample Survey, on the other hand, the respondents indicate both the number of hours usually worked by their colleagues and the number they themselves actually worked during the reference week. If the actual hours are fewer than the usual hours worked by their colleagues they are counted as part-time workers, even if they describe themselves as full-time workers. The fact that there is no single cut-off point yields lower estimates than using a cut-off definition (de Neubourg 1985). In some countries, the hours cut-off is based on hours for the main job, in others on total hours for all jobs. This is why data on part-time employment may not always give a coherent picture of country-to-country differences, and hence comparisons of levels or proportions between countries require some caution. However, trends within countries and comparisons of trends between them are probably meaningful. Bearing this reservation in mind, five main points can be mentioned relating to the volume and structure of part-time employment.

First, there is a great divergence in the importance of part-time employment between countries (see Smith *et al.*, Chapter 2, this volume). In 1995 the share of part-time work in total employment varied from 5 per cent in Greece and 6–8 per cent in Italy, Portugal and Spain to more than 20 per cent in Australia, Denmark, Japan, Norway, Sweden and the United Kingdom, and over 37 per cent in the Netherlands. In the United States the proportion was around 18 per cent in 1995. These differences seem likely to be real despite the problems of comparability. Second, for men, part-time work is less significant than for women (in 1995). Third, among females the proportions of part-time employment show larger inter-country variation. In 1995, among males the proportion ranged from 1 per cent in Luxembourg, 3–4 per cent in Belgium, Germany and Greece, to 10–11 per cent in Australia, Canada, Denmark, Japan and the United States and almost 17 per cent in the Netherlands. The proportions of part-time work for employed women ranged from 8 per cent in Greece, 12–13 per cent in Italy and Portugal to over 40 per cent in Australia, Norway, Sweden and the United Kingdom, and to over 67 per cent in the Netherlands. Fourth, the proportion of part-time employment in total employment has increased considerably in most OECD countries over the past ten years. High increases in the proportion of part-time employment were recorded in Australia, Belgium, France, Ireland and the Netherlands. A number of these countries started with relatively low proportions. Modest increases were recorded in Canada, Italy, Japan, Luxembourg, the United

Kingdom and the United States. In contrast, the level of PTW fell in Denmark, Norway and Sweden. A number of these countries with modest increases or declines in PTW already had high levels of part-time employment. This would seem to suggest that there is a trend towards convergence in the part-time rates between countries as in countries with high rates growth has declined or stagnated, while countries with more modest levels have increased in recent years. Fifth, the proportions of male and female part-time employment show a similar development, increasing in most countries over the past decade. Decreases were recorded for males in Greece and Luxembourg and for females in Denmark, Greece, Sweden and the United Kingdom. Furthermore, the United States shows a decreasing trend in women's part-time employment (see Williams 1995). The percentage increases in the low male rates were considerable in a number of countries, notably in Australia and most European countries, but were modest in Italy, Norway and the United States. In 1995, 5 per cent of men in the EU as a whole worked part-time, compared with 4 per cent in 1991. If part-time working were to continue to expand at this rate, then in ten years' time an average of around 10 per cent of all men in employment would be working part-time in the EU (EC 1996). The relatively high proportions of female part-time employment show only modest percentage increases in most of the countries over the past ten years. It may be concluded that the male and female part-time rates show some signs of convergence. However, the overwhelming majority of all part-time workers are still women, most of whom are married, except in Finland (see de Neubourg 1985; Blank 1994; Delsen 1995; Houseman and Osawa 1995; Nätti 1995).

The age distribution of part-time workers reveals a divergence in the patterns for men and women (see Tables 3.1 and 3.2). The profile for the male part-time rate by age has a U-shape. Male part-time work is typical of either end of the age spectrum (see also Baxter, Chapter 14, this volume). With few exceptions, above-average proportions of employed men work part-time in the 15 to 24 and 55 and over age groups. There are, however, rather large cross-country differences in the proportion of young and older workers in part-time employment. Table 3.1 shows that, among males, the rate of part-time work tends to be highest in the older age groups in Europe and Japan (see also Meulders and Plasman 1993; Maier 1994; Houseman and Osawa 1995). On the other hand, in Canada, the United States and Australia the majority of male part-time workers are concentrated among the young. Among male teenagers in 1986, it ranged from about 60 per cent in the United States to as low as about 2 per cent in Germany. Among men aged 65 and over, it is as much as two-thirds in the United Kingdom and as little as 6 per cent in Ireland. These older employed men are generally more likely, sometimes considerably so, to work part-time than are teenagers, the exceptions being Canada, Denmark, Ireland, Luxembourg, Norway and the United States. However, from a comparison of Tables 3.1 and 3.2 it can be concluded that notably among young and prime-age males the proportions of part-time employment have

61

increased. In fact, in the EU, between 1991 and 1995 the relative number of prime-age men (25 to 49 years) working part-time increased by 50 per cent. Most (60 per cent) of the growth in male part-time employment is attributable to increases among this age group (EC 1996), indicating a convergence between age groups.

Unlike the case for men, female part-time employment tends to be more widely spread across age groups. There are, nevertheless, several common features in the patterns for women and men. As for men, a U-shaped part-time age profile can be detected. Similarly, the proportion of teenage women's employment that is part-time is above the overall female average in most countries. This appears to be especially true in Canada, Denmark, Norway and the United States. In the United States, Canada and Australia, the share of the under-25s in the female part-time workforce is high relative to other countries: in these countries, young females account for 20–35 per cent of total female part-time employment. Whereas in 1986 the part-time proportion among young adult women between the ages of 20 and 24 was below average virtually everywhere, by 1995 this only applied in half of the countries. Between 1986 and 1995 increases in the part-time rate among young females were recorded, although at a lower rate than among young men. Similar to the pattern for older men, the proportion of part-time workers among older women – those of more than 55 years of age – tends to be high, and increases steadily among the three age groups of older workers. In 1986, around two-thirds of older employed women worked part-time in Denmark, Norway, Sweden, the Netherlands and the United Kingdom. Finland is an exception (see Nätti 1995, and Pfau-Effinger, Chapter 9, this volume). Between 1986 and 1995 part-time work became more common for older women in most OECD countries. The proportion of prime-age (25–49 years) employed women working part-time is, in most cases, close to the overall average. Particularly among women in this prime-age group the part-time rate is declining in Australia, Denmark, Greece, Norway, Portugal, Sweden and the United Kingdom, as can be seen from a comparison between Tables 3.1 and 3.2. It is precisely in this age group that an increase in the total number of women active in the labour market is found (Boje and Olsson Hort 1994). So in contrast to males, for females the part-time rate between age groups diverges.

The development of part-time employment has made a significant contribution to employment growth over the 1970s and 1980s and during the first half of the 1990s in many OECD countries (OECD 1994a; Delsen 1995; EC 1995, 1996). In Belgium, Ireland, France, Germany, the Netherlands, New Zealand, Portugal and the United Kingdom part-time employment was the more dominant source of overall job growth; and for a considerable proportion in Australia, Norway and Japan, but less so in the United States. In many OECD countries part-time employment played a dominant role in the growth of female employment but has generally been much less important for male employment growth. However, there have been changes over time. Between 1985 and 1989 in the European Union 25 per cent of the new jobs for males were part-time jobs; for females 40 per cent. Between 1990 and 1994 full-time employment decreased by 5.5 per cent for men and 3.5 per cent for women, while part-time employment grew fastest for men, increasing by 21 per cent, compared with 11 per cent for women. In 1995, 71 per cent of the additional jobs created for men were part-time compared with 85 per cent for women (EC 1995, 1996). In sum, trends in the development of part-time work show signs of convergence across countries and age groups and between men and women.

DETERMINANTS OF PART-TIME EMPLOYMENT

The diverse trends and the wide variation in the relative share of part-time employment across OECD countries suggest that no single factor can explain the growth of part-time work.

Employees' availability for part-time work

The development in part-time employment reflects changes in the demographic composition of the labour force. On the supply side the major factor is associated with growing female participation in the labour market. This trend has been especially noticeable for married women, whose participation rate has increased substantially in all OECD countries. Factors that play a role here are the need to supplement the family income, the reduction in the number of children per family, a higher education, the availability of child care and changing opinions about gender roles. Marital status, combined with the presence of dependent children, is strongly associated with women's decision to work part-time in Europe and Japan. The incidence of part-time employment among women rises when children are present in the family. However, there is no uniform pattern in Europe for combining family and paid work, which depends heavily on child care provisions, regulations for maternity and parental leave, and cultural and social norms. These factors also help explain the large inter-country differences in men's and women's involvement in part-time work (Maier 1994; Delsen 1995; Smith et al., Chapter 2, Pfau-Effinger, Chapter 9, and Daune-Richard, Chapter 11, this volume). The proportion of female part-time employees who are in their prime child-raising years is declining in several OECD countries, and this may indicate that the link between family status (marriage) and part-time employment is loosening. However, most female part-timers still live in households where there is another (usually full-time) earner (see Gregg and Wadsworth 1995; Nätti 1995; and Doudeiins, Chapter 6, this volume).

For teenage and older women, the reasons for the high proportion of part-timers are likely to be the same as for their male counterparts. For younger workers, part-time employment may be a comparatively easy way of gaining entry into the labour market. In the Netherlands, young people are often obliged to take a part-time post as an entry job. It may also offer the opportunity to combine work with school, as seems to be the case in Australia, Canada, Denmark, Norway, the United Kingdom and the United States. Yet, the most important reason why young people work part-time is in order to secure additional income (see Warme *et al.* 1992). There has been an increasing tendency among youth to combine education and part-time employment. This increase can be explained from the spread of training programmes offering part-time employment (OECD 1991) and the reduction in financial support for students, with an increase in student fees financed through loans (Nätti 1995). Planned reductions in financial support in countries like Germany, the Netherlands and the United Kingdom will result in a further increase in the part-time rate among young men and women in the future.

Older workers, notably in Europe and Japan, use part-time work in order to retire gradually. Considerable proportions of older workers in Europe, Japan and the United States prefer part-time employment as a way of easing the transition from work to retirement, thus avoiding the 'pension shock'. Financial considerations also play an important role. For instance, the high proportion of part-time employment among males and females of 65 years and over in the United Kingdom is partly attributable to the level of the full state pension. Moreover, for men between 65 and 70 years of age the pension system provides the opportunity to work less than 12 hours per week and to earn less than about £80 per week. The increasing tendency of males aged over 65 in the United States to engage in part-time work is a response to the fact that pension benefits are subject to an earnings test. Part-time work is often chosen to avoid this earnings test. Furthermore, the planned higher thresholds and the reductions in social security and pension benefits are incentives to work part-time in the future for this group of people. In a number of OECD countries, including France, Germany, Italy, Japan, the Netherlands and the Nordic countries, partial pensions and partial disability benefits are currently considered as alternatives for complete retirement (see Delsen 1996; Delsen and Reday-Mulvey 1996). Policy changes to pension systems also contribute to the increase in the part-time rate among older workers, notably men.

In 1988, in Australia, Europe, Japan and North America the large majority of the individuals who worked part-time did so voluntarily in the sense that they said they did not want full-time work. On an unweighted basis 26 per cent of the part-time employment was involuntary. For males this proportion was 36 per cent and for females 22 per cent.[2] In 1991, between 20 and 30 per cent of all part-timers across the OECD area declared themselves as working part-time involuntarily. Comparison with earlier data shows that the proportions of involuntary part-time work have risen over the past decades in many countries. These increases cannot be attributed to cyclical effects alone; they also reflect the secular increase in the demand for part-time workers (OECD 1994a; Delsen 1995; Walwei, Chapter 5, this volume).

Cultural differences and norms play a role in explaining why relatively few men work part-time. The low status of part-time workers derives from the underlying cultural assumption about what is 'normal and proper' for men and women to do with their lives and time and what is appropriate work for men and women. Men appear to be unwilling to take parental leave and to provide flexibility within the families' time-budgets and men's working lives are rarely affected by family responsibilities (Liff 1991; Maier 1994; Fagan *et al.* 1995). Although the run-down in industrial employment has hit male employment growth harder it is not always feasible for them to take up new jobs in the service sector especially if they are part-time. Earning a wage sufficient to support a family is still of enormous symbolic and material importance even though the number of households solely dependent on such a wage is declining (Liff 1991). Nevertheless, in the EU part-time employment has grown swiftly among prime-age male workers over the past five years, indicating a potential change in culture and a dismantling of the 'breadwinner norm'. There is evidence that there is an increasing demand for part-time jobs from male and female workers in many countries, suggesting a potential for a further development of part-time employment in several OECD countries (OECD 1994b).

Transition rates

Part of the differentials in the levels of the male and female part-time employment rates and the trends in these rates can also be contributed to transition rates. European and American data show that women are more likely to make a transition from full-time to both part-time employment and non-participation in the labour force, and have a lower probability of transition from part-time employment to both full-time employment and unemployment. In addition, the probability of leaving unemployment for a full-time job is higher for men than for women. The opposite is true with respect to part-time employment (see OECD 1995; Williams 1995; O'Reilly and Bothfeld 1996).

Longitudinal analysis in the United States shows that women rarely use part-time work as a transitional labour market state. Most women use part-time work as an alternative for full-time work and return to full-time work after some period, or they enter part-time work from out of the labour market and then leave the labour market again after a part-time spell. Hence, there is little evidence that placing women in part-time jobs will greatly increase their probability of moving into full-time employment over time (Blank 1994). Williams (1995), however, found that the part-time rate for women has been falling in the 1980s in the United States because their rates of transition from full-time employment to both unemployment and non-participation in the labour force are falling, and because their transition rates from part-time work and non-participation in the labour force to full-time employment have been rising. The growth of full-time employment among women is not the result of an increase in the proportion of unemployed women finding full-time employment. It is the joint product of increases in the proportions of women moving from part-time to full-time employment and decreases in the proportion leaving full-time employment when they get there. Further, in Denmark, Finland and Sweden in the 1980s women changed more frequently from part-time to full-time employment, explaining the decreasing trend in the female part-time rate. In the Nordic countries, for most workers, part-time jobs seem to be bridges rather than traps (see Sundström 1991; Boje and Olsson Hort 1994; Nätti 1995).

Service sector employment

The differences in the rate of part-time employment between countries can also partly be explained by differences in the industrial structure of the economy. Shift-share analysis (Walwei and Werner 1995, and Walwei, Chapter 5, this volume) shows that part-time employment to a large degree developed independently of sectoral employment change and changes in the gender-specific composition of employment. However, the bulk of part-time employment is concentrated in the service sector. This sector accounts for more than 80 per cent of part-time employment in Australia, Belgium, Canada, Denmark, Finland, the Netherlands, New Zealand, the United Kingdom and the United States. In Japan almost half of all part-time employment is in the service sector, while in Greece it is the lowest, although still 40 per cent. In contrast, the proportion of part-time employment in industry varies widely across countries but is lower than that found in services, ranging from less than 10 per cent in Canada and the United States to more than 20 per cent in Germany and Italy and almost 30 per cent in Japan (OECD 1983; Delsen 1995). The concentration of part-time jobs in services partly reflects the organisation of production: predictable short-run variations in demand, for example, require part-time workers as a back-up for full-time staff. In general, mass-production and capital-intensive industries rely much more on full-time employees.

The issue of 'gendered flexibility' plays a role (Beechey and Perkins 1987). Many services rely on a female-dominated workforce, while male-dominated sectors have been more resistant to part-time work. These factors explain low rates of part-time work in manufacturing and the construction sector.[3] However, the organisation of work in manufacturing industries is changing in a way that is conducive to the expansion of part-time work. Job growth mainly took place in administrative and professional job functions alongside a trend for manufacturing companies to externalise work which has been classified as services (Boje and Olsson Hort 1994). Service functions are predominant in all types of production activity in the secondary, industrial as well as the primary, agricultural sector. Modern technology has forced the tertiary sector to make radical changes to some of its functioning modes through the introduction of processes which are very close to the capital intensive processes in manufacturing (Giarini and Stahel 1993). In the EU there is some tendency for men's employment to become concentrated in the same sectors as women's (EC 1996). These trends will of course impact upon the male part-time rate.

Personnel policy

Part-timers may be brought in at predictable peak times and to cover regular and anticipated variations in demand, thereby avoiding underemployment of full-time staff during off-peak periods, or overtime payments in busy periods, and to enable establishments to remain open longer, for example, on evenings or weekends (see Delsen 1995). Employers' use of flexible working-time arrangements is 'gendered' in the sense that overtime is often used for full-time workers in male-dominated jobs, whereas part-time work is more common in female-dominated sectors (Maier 1994; Fagan et al. 1995). Evidence from Europe and the United States shows that enterprise policy to achieve flexibility, including the use of part-time working, is marginal, ad hoc and tentative. Short-term cost saving rather than long-term development dominates management thinking. The decision-making over types of employment contracts is not based on detailed cost comparison, but on stereotyping of full-time, part-time and temporary employees and women (Pollert 1991; Hunter et al. 1993). Resistance to part-time work is seldom based on experience. Employers in Europe and the United States seem to overestimate the disadvantage and underestimate the advantages of part-time working (see Hunter et al. 1993; Delsen 1995; O'Reilly 1996).

Part-time employment is mainly located in low-status, low-paid 'dead-end' jobs in most countries (see Smith et al., Chapter 2, this volume). The empirical research, using establishment data, shows common European patterns of explanatory variables for the variation in the part-time rate in Europe. The most significant determinants are the proportion of females in the total workforce, the sector of activity, the average qualification level of the workforce, the turnover rate and the establishment size. The part-time employment rate is inversely related to the qualification level and the firm size. Part-time employment is mainly located in jobs which have few or no formal human capital entry requirements (Delsen 1995; Delsen and Huijgen 1994). This supports what the human capital theory predicts. Team production and fixed employment costs affect the availability and pay of part-time work (Hurd 1993). Because of team work and fixed employment costs, an older worker who wants to reduce his or her hours cannot do that in a career job and will have to change occupation or industry. These jobs will be easy entry jobs that require few specific skills, a rather low level of general skills and minimal search costs because of the short pay-back period, due to high turnover, and low wage rates and no fringe benefits. This explains why part-time employment is under-represented in higher-level jobs and why men are not likely to choose part-time work.

On the other hand, part-time work may be used as a retention strategy, to avoid the loss of investments in human capital and to retain valued employees.

Part-time employment may also be used to attract valued workers. International evidence shows that although part-time employment is concentrated at the lower level, it is increasingly introduced successfully at all levels, including management (DuRivage 1992; Warme *et al.* 1992; Boje and Olsson Hort 1994; Delsen 1995; Fagan *et al.* 1995), indicating a trend away from marginalised part-time employment. An example in this respect is the Netherlands, where most part-timers are women in the service sector and in low-skilled jobs. However, the growth of part-time employment for men in industry and for highly qualified jobs is above average. Part-time employment developed from secondary jobs for married women to fully acceptable jobs for all women and increasing numbers of men (EC 1994).

Business cycle

The business cycle and associated labour market situation also has an influence on the supply of part-time labour. In case of unemployment, workers may be more willing to accept a part-time job. On the other hand, a tight (slack) labour market may induce additional (reduce) supply of labour, notably part-time labour of women (discouraged worker effect) (see OECD 1995 for evidence). Moreover, the slower growth in real earnings over the past few years together with rising unemployment may have contributed to the part-time labour supply (additional worker effect). In part the latter effect may also be the result of part-time employment. Supply of part-time work will result in additional (involuntary) supply of part-time labour, to compensate for reduction in family income (see Marshall 1989 and Clain and Leppel 1996 for evidence). On the other hand, cross-country correlation between the part-time employment share in total employment and the women's (long-term) unemployment rates relative to men's is negative. This may be explained by the fact that part-time employment has been an important source of female employment growth (OECD 1994a).

The labour market situation also influences the quality and quantity of demand for part-time labour. Offering part-time employment may be used as a way to avoid dismissals. During a downturn employers may cut back on the hours of work of the existing workforce and, to the extent that any new hiring is undertaken, it may only be for part-timers, resulting in involuntary part-time employment. Experience in the Netherlands shows that despite the recent recession the number of jobs was stable, due to part-time employment. Part-time employment may also serve to tap additional labour resources and increase the supply of labour. In an upswing part-timers may become full-timers. The latter is illustrated by the Swedish experience. The strong growth of full-time work among women in the 1980s reflects the difficulty in increasing already high participation rates (tight labour market) and changes in Swedish tax policy, resulting in women switching from part-time to full-time jobs (Sundström 1991). In a tight market the 'tap'-motive will prevail, while in a slack market with reduced union strength, the employer-centred flexibility motive, resulting in part-time jobs with variability in working hours, will prevail (see Bruegel and Hegewisch 1992).

Delsen (1995) found no relationship between overall employment growth and the rate of part-time employment in the European Union countries. In addition, the fact that managers have to cope with substantial changes of the workload within the same day, from day to day and/or within a year when organising work, has an insignificant impact on the part-time rate. Bruegel and Hegewisch (1992) also found that in Europe the link between changes in product demand and employment at the enterprise level is not strong. These results not only illustrate the heterogeneity of part-time employment but also that the institutional differences, such as differences in labour law and social security, availability of child care and parental leave, financial incentives, and so on, have an important influence on the way part-time labour is used and affects men's and women's involvement in part-time work (see Maier 1994; Delsen 1995; O'Reilly 1996; Doudeiins, Chapter 6, this volume).

Wages and non-wage cost

Labour cost considerations also appear to be an important influence on firms' use of part-timers. The hourly wage rate for part-time workers in Europe, Japan and the United States is often lower (15–20 per cent) than for *comparable* full-time workers (see DuRivage 1992; Warme *et al.* 1992; Maier 1994; Delsen 1995; Houseman and Osawa 1995).[4] These wage differentials can be explained by fixed employment costs and the requirements of team production. Fixed employment costs must be covered by a substantial number of hours of work and will tend to lower wages for part-time work.

In many OECD countries, especially in Europe, substantial growth in part-time employment has gone hand-in-hand with increases in non-wage labour costs (OECD 1983). Full-time and full-year wage employment is still the standard in business and industry as well as within labour law, collective bargaining and social security and pension systems, resulting in discrimination and exclusion of those workers on part-time contracts. There are many examples of partial coverage existing in Europe, Japan and the United States.[5] This creates, *ceteris paribus*, an incentive for employers to hire part-timers, notably on marginal jobs. Delsen (1995) found a significant positive relationship between perceived hourly cost advantages by managers in Europe, including lower hourly wages and/or lower national insurance contributions and/or fewer fringe benefits and/or other cost advantages and the rate of part-time employment. The most important determinants of short part-time jobs are the cost advantages of part-time workers.

However, changes have occurred over time. For instance, in the Netherlands since the late 1970s part-time jobs are far from marginalised jobs. Surveys show higher hourly wages of female part-timers over female full-timers (Tijdens 1995), indicating a normalisation of part-time work. Also, during the 1980s, the drop in temporary part-time jobs and the fact that the growth in part-time employment was in permanent jobs in Australia, Belgium, Denmark, Germany, the Netherlands, Norway, Sweden and the United Kingdom indicate a normalisation of part-time work. In Finland, France, Luxembourg and Spain a casualisation was recorded (see Delsen 1995; Nätti 1995; Rubery, Chapter 7, this volume).

Trade union and government policy

Trade union policy towards atypical employment contracts has contributed to the development of part-time employment in Europe and Japan as well as in North America. Although attitudes are slowly changing, trade unions in Europe, Japan and North America have generally opposed part-time work as a threat to full-time standards. In all three economic blocks trade unions did not do much to protect and organise these workers. In fact, in Japan trade unions are a major barrier for equal treatment of these workers. This may be an incentive for employers to use atypical employment (see Lapeyre and Hoffman 1994; Delsen 1995). Union preferences may be heavily weighted in favour of older workers (the insiders), and both employers and unions may seek to off-load some of the costs on to third parties (the outsiders, for example, atypical or unemployed workers) who are not represented at the bargaining table. The insider–outsider theory explains why part-time employment or job-sharing is not a pervasive response to involuntary unemployment in Europe (Lindbeck and Snower 1988).

Three models of analyses are available to explain the gender bias in bargaining outcomes on working hours (Tijdens 1995). First, *the workforce model*: male workers opposed part-time jobs for two reasons: to protect wages in full-time jobs, because they feared wage pressing effects of the so-called marginal part-time jobs; on average male breadwinners preferred their wives to remain housewives, because of emotional reasons, because they did not want to spend time on household labour and because they were frightened that the argument that they had to earn a family wage lost its meaning. The married male workers did not intend to work part-time to share household duties. The workforce model shows that part-time work was allowed first in the female-dominated sectors and was followed by the male-dominated sectors.

Second, *the median voter model*: the median union member is a breadwinner and in general breadwinners preferred their wives to remain housewives. Initially, the unions perceived the male breadwinner as being their largest group of union members. The man who works full-time, the median union member, was not willing to work less hours if it would include loss of pay. Part-time work was considered to be marginal work. Therefore, the unions wanted a reduction of the standard working week and were opposed to policies to promote part-time work.

Third, *the representation model*: focusing on the percentage female negotiators. Essentially, the controversy between the reduction of the working week and the promotion of part-time work was a gender conflict. The conflict was won by the female workers, with a little help from the employers (Tijdens 1995).

Measures taken by governments to protect part-timers and initiatives to promote part-time work in order to redistribute employment or to increase labour force participation rates, notably in Europe and Japan in the 1980s, have contributed to the growth of part-time labour supply. It is likely that this policy will continue in order to make economic growth more employment intensive. Certain groups of workers were encouraged to seek or obliged to accept part-time jobs, for example, the 32-hour part-time entry jobs for youth in the Netherlands, partial entitlement to unemployment benefit in Belgium, and part-time exit jobs for the disabled and older workers. In Germany, part-time early retirement, combined with a replacement obligation, has been introduced, while the full early retirement option has been abolished (see Meulders and Plasman 1993; Houseman and Osawa 1995; Delsen and Reday-Mulvey 1996; O'Reilly 1996).

Social security impacts upon the gender differentials in the part-time rate. The posts that have been disappearing have mostly been reasonably well-paid, full-time industrial jobs. Those that have been growing fastest have been part-time and often lower-paid service jobs. Consequently, even though the income replacement ratio for those receiving unemployment benefits may be much less than previous (full-time) earnings, many unemployed will be discouraged from taking the available job opportunities because they would experience a decline in net income. One inference is that it makes no sense for unemployed males to fill part-time job vacancies if this means an income cut, while women coming from outside the labour force are willing to take up such jobs (see Meulders and Plasman 1993), resulting in an unemployment as well as a part-time employment trap. Pension systems also discourage employed people from taking a part-time job, accounting for both the retirement trap as well as male reluctance to work part-time (Delsen 1995, 1996; Delsen and Reday-Mulvey 1996).

Tax policy also has its, sometimes unintended, influence on the supply of part-time labour. Joint taxation and upper limits for social security contributions have impacts on disposable income of a switch of earnings of the husband towards part-time employment by wives (OECD 1990). In Sweden the income tax is fully individualised. Combined with highly progressive tax rates, it favours reallocation of family time towards more market work and less housework for wives and the reverse for men. In the 1980s marginal tax rates were reduced, resulting in a shift from part-time to full-time work by women (see Sundström 1991).

Governments financially support the supply of, and the demand for, part-time employment. An example is France, where there is a reduction of employers' social security contributions by 30 per cent for either newly recruited part-time employees on open-ended contracts (between 19 and 30 hours per week) or at the request of full-time workers. In the Netherlands, 20,000 temporary part-time jobs of on average 32 hours were created in the private sector in 1996 with the use of social assistance benefits as a two-year subsidy. Furthermore, the structure and level of taxation and the method of calculation of social security premiums are of influence on the demand for part-time employment in the private sector (see Maier 1994; Delsen 1995).

Part-time employment has also grown significantly in the public sector where governments in Norway, Sweden and the Netherlands have actively sought to expand part-time jobs, partly for budgetary reasons, but also to create jobs. In the Netherlands between 1995 and 1998, 40,000 regular jobs of on average 32 hours with a structural subsidy in the public sector will be created which will aim to reduce long-term unemployment.

In the Netherlands the number of part-time jobs continues to grow. Considerable proportions of working men and women want to reduce working hours at the same hourly wage rate. This is simulated by change in cultural impediments and reduction in prejudice. There is a growing consensus between social partners on the value of part-time employment (Delsen 1993; EC 1994). Since 1980, the Dutch government has stimulated part-time employment through legal equality and information. Abolition of exclusion from the legal minimum wage in 1993, exemption from pension funds in 1994 and the legal equal treatment of part-time and full-time workers in 1996 confirmed the demand by employees and employers for more part-time employment. It also served to make part-time employment more attractive to male employees. A legal right to part-time work is due to come before the Dutch parliament.

CONCLUSIONS

The growth rates of part-time employment vary across countries as well as over time. Particularly in Europe and Japan the shares of part-time employment in total employment have grown, while in the United States they remained quite stable. For the growth of part-time employment, the supply side of the labour market, that is the quest by (female) employees, is the most important factor. There are signs of a convergence in the part-time rate between countries, in that countries with high rates have seen a stagnation or decline in the growth of part-time work while countries with more modest rates have seen a substantial growth; however, there still remain low-use countries where growth has not increased at all. The variation in the part-time rate suggests that it is affected by the differences in legal and socio-economic setting. Not only in Europe but in Japan and the United States, social security systems, tax systems, pensions systems and labour law have been designed with the full-time worker, that is the male breadwinner, in mind, resulting in discrimination and exclusion of those workers on part-time contracts. This explains to a large extent why part-time jobs are still mainly women's work. Men are unwilling to take part-time jobs and remain working full-time partly because of unequal treatment of part-time work. However, culture differences also play a role in explaining why relatively few men work part-time.

The opportunities for governments in the OECD to promote part-time employment (among men) are still considerable (Delsen 1995). Relevant policy options are offering organisational support to enterprises, legal equal treatment and the promotion of secure and long-term part-time jobs. Notably, equal treatment will make part-time employment more attractive for men. Other options are separate income tax systems to replace joint taxation; thresholds in contributions and high progressive tax rates and the abolition of ceilings to the social security contribution and flat-rate contributions, for they discourage the substitution of earnings of one partner for the earnings of the other. In addition, a right to part-time employment, national legal gradual retirement schemes, child care provisions and legal national schemes for part-time parental leave may significantly contribute to the promotion of part-time work and the redistribution of employment among sexes.

Although part-time employment is still a female phenomenon concentrated in lower functions within the service sector, recent developments point towards convergence of the rates between men and women and a spread of part-time employment towards the industrial sector and higher-level jobs. There is not only growing male involvement in part-time employment, but in a number of countries female involvement shows a decreasing trend. In the literature it is often suggested that, for men, part-time employment is a temporary way of entering and leaving the labour market. Female part-time employment is more widely spread across age groups. For women part-time employment is a more stable way of participating in the labour market (Warme et al. 1992; Maier 1994; Fagan et al. 1995). Thus women and men work on a part-time basis in different stages in the life cycle. For young people it is a bridge into full-time work or for older people a bridge to retirement. For others it is a trap. However, the convergence of the part-time rates goes beyond numerical similarity. From the dramatic increase in male part-time employment across all age groups, notably in the prime-age group in Europe, it may be concluded that the promotion of part-time employment (for men) is an appropriate policy option to advance a more equal sharing of parental duties in households. The Dutch experience moreover shows that it may be an appropriate policy to redistribute employment and hence serve as an alternative for collective working-time reduction. The gendered flexibility is losing ground. Like that for women, male part-time work is at the lower qualification levels. Moreover, they work outside their main line of employment in low-paid, insecure part-time jobs. This is certainly the case for the young and older male workers. However, the above-average growth of part-time employment for men in industry and for highly qualified jobs indicates a normalisation of part-time employment.

73

Taking the Netherlands as a norm, there is considerable potential for part-time work, on both the demand and the supply sides. Due to new technology and changes in the organisation of work, part-time employment is likely to expand in segments of the labour market where the proportion is low: manufacturing, building and transport. Also the ageing of the labour force, increasing female labour market participation rates, the growing service industry, the internationalisation of the economies and increased competition will contribute to the growth of part-time employment. These developments are likely to influence the male-dominated segments of the labour market more than the services, dominated by females. Cross-country differences and gender and age differences in the part-time rates may diminish further.

NOTES

1   The author would like to thank the participants in the workshop, particularly Colette Fagan, Jacqueline O'Reilly and Jürgen Schupp, for their comments on an earlier version of this chapter, and his colleague Iman van Lelyveld for assistance with the tabulation.
2   Involuntary part-time employment comprises three categories of workers: those who normally work full-time but worked fewer hours than normal due to economic reasons; those who normally work part-time but worked fewer hours than usual due to economic reasons; and workers who worked part-time because they could not find full-time work. See also the introductory chapter by Fagan and O'Reilly in this volume for a discussion on choosing part-time work within structural constraints.
3   Japan seems to be the only exception to this.
4   An exception is Australia where part-timers get higher hourly wages than full-timers to compensate for poorer access to fringe benefits.
5   See Meulders and Plasman 1993; Maier 1994; Delsen 1995; and Houseman and Osawa 1995 for more details.

BIBLIOGRAPHY

Beechey, V. and Perkins, T. (1987) *A Matter of Hours: Women, Part-time Work and the Labour Market*. Cambridge: Polity Press.
Blank, R. M. (1989) 'The Role of Part-time Work in Women's Labour Market Choices over Time', *American Economic Review* 78: 295–9.
Blank, R. M. (1994) *The Dynamics of Part-time Work*. Working Paper no. 4911. Cambridge, MA: National Bureau of Economic Research.
Boje, T. P. and Olsson Hort, S. E. (eds) (1994) *Scandinavia in a New Europe*. Oslo: Scandinavian University Press.
Bruegel, I. and Hegewisch, A. (1992) *Flexibilisation and Part-time Work in Europe*. Working Paper SWP 19/92. Bedford: Cranfield School of Management.
Clain, S. H. and Leppel, K. (1996) 'Further Evidence of the Added-worker Effect among White Couples', *The Economist* 144, 3: 473–86.
Delsen, L. (1993) 'Atypical Employment and Industrial Relations in the Netherlands', *Economic and Industrial Democracy* 14, 4: 589–602.

Delsen, L. (1995) *Atypical Employment: An International Perspective. Causes, Consequences and Policy*. Groningen: Wolters-Noordhoff.

Delsen, L. (1996) 'Gradual Retirement: Lessons from the Nordic Countries and the Netherlands', *European Journal of Industrial Relations* 2, 1: 55–66.

Delsen, L. and Huijgen, F. (1994) *Analysis of Part-time and Fixed-term Employment in Europe Using Establishment Data*. Working Paper no. WP94/14/EN. Dublin: European Foundation for the Improvement of Living and Working Conditions.

Delsen, L. and Reday-Mulvey, G. (eds) (1996) *Gradual Retirement in the OECD Countries. Macro and Micro Issues and Policies*. Aldershot: Dartmouth Publishing Company.

DuRivage, V. L. (ed.) (1992) *New Policies for the Part-time and Contingent Workforce*. Washington, DC: Economic Policy Institute.

EC (1994–6) *Employment in Europe*. Luxembourg: European Commission.

Fagan, C., Plantinga, J. and Rubery, J. (1995) *Does Part-time Work Promote Sex Equality? A Comparative Analysis of the Netherlands and the UK*. Discussion Paper FS I 95–203. Berlin: Social Science Research Centre Berlin.

Giarini, O. and Stahel, W. (1993) *The Limits to Certainty*. Dordrecht: Kluwer.

Gregg, P. and Wadsworth, J. (1995) 'Gender, Households and Access to Employment' in J. Humphries and J. Rubery (eds) *The Economics of Equal Opportunities*. Manchester: Equal Opportunities Commission.

Houseman, S. and Osawa, M. (1995) 'Part-time and Temporary Employment in Japan', *Monthly Labor Review* 118, 10: 10–18.

Hunter, L., McGregor, A., MacInnes, J. and Sproull, A. (1993) 'The "Flexible Firm": Strategy and Segmentation', *British Journal of Industrial Relations* 31, 3: 383–407.

Hurd, M. D. (1993) *The Effects of Labor Market Rigidities on the Labor Force Behaviour of Older Workers*. Working Paper 4462. Cambridge: National Bureau of Economic Research.

Lapeyre, J. and Hoffman, R. (eds) (1994) *A Time for Working – A Time for Living*. Brussels: ETUC and ETUI.

Liff, S. (1991) 'Part-time Workers: Current Contradictions and Future Opportunities' in M. J. Davidson and J. Earnshaw (eds) *Vulnerable Workers: Psychosocial and Legal Issues*. Chichester: Wiley & Sons Ltd.

Lindbeck, A. and Snower, D. J. (1988) *The Insider–Outsider Theory of Employment and Unemployment*. Cambridge, MA: MIT Press.

Maier, F. (1994) 'Institutional Regimes of Part-time Working' in G. Schmid (ed.) *Labor Market Institutions in Europe*. New York: M.E. Sharpe.

Marshall, A. (1989) 'The Sequel of Unemployment: The Changing Role of Part-time and Temporary Work in Western Europe' in G. Rodgers and J. Rodgers (eds) *Precarious Jobs in Labour Market Regulation: The Growth of Atypical Employment in Western Europe*. Geneva: International Institute for Labour Studies.

Meulders, D. and Plasman, R. (1993) 'Part-time Work in EEC Countries: Evaluation during the 1980s', *Labour* 7, 3: 49–71.

Nätti, J. (1995) 'Part-time Employment in the Nordic Countries', *Labour* 9, 2: 343–57.

Neubourg, C. de (1985) 'Part-time Work: An International Quantitative Comparison', *International Labour Review* 124, 5: 559–76.

OECD (1983–96) *Employment Outlook*. Paris: Organisation for Economic Co-operation and Development.

OECD (1994a) *The OECD Jobs Study. Evidence and Explanations. Part I Labour Market Trends and Underlying Forces of Change*. Paris: Organisation for Economic Co-operation and Development.

OECD (1994b) *The OECD Jobs Study. Evidence and Explanations. Part II The Adjustment Potential of the Labour Market*. Paris: Organisation for Economic Co-operation and Development.

O'Reilly, J. (1996) 'Labour Adjustments through Part-time Work', in G. Schmid, J. O'Reilly and K. Schömann (eds) *International Handbook of Labour Market Policy and Evaluation*. Cheltenham: Edward Elgar.

O'Reilly, J. and Bothfeld, S. (1996) 'Labour Market Transition and Part-time Work', *inforMISEP* 54: 20–7.

Pollert, A. (ed.) (1991) *Farewell to Flexibility?* Oxford: Blackwell.

Sundström, M. (1991) 'Part-time Work in Sweden: Trends and Equity Effects', *Journal of Economic Issues*, March: 167–78.

Tijdens, K. (1995) *Gender and Labour Market Flexibility: The Case of Working Hours*. Faculty of Economics and Econometrics, University of Amsterdam.

Walwei, U. and Werner, H. (1995) 'Entwicklungen der Teilzeitbeschäftigung im internationalen Vergleich. Ursachen, Arbeidsmarkteffekten und Konsequenzen', *Mitteilungen aus der Arbeidsmarkt- und Berufsforschung* 28, 3: 365–82.

Warme, B. D., Lundy, K. L. P. and Lundy, L. A. (eds) (1992) *Working Part-time. Risks and Opportunities*. New York: Praeger.

Williams, D. R. (1995) 'Women's Part-time Employment: A Gross Flows Analysis', *Monthly Labor Review*, April: 36–44.

4

WHY DON'T MINORITY ETHNIC WOMEN IN BRITAIN WORK PART-TIME?

Angela Dale and Clare Holdsworth

INTRODUCTION

Other chapters in this volume compare part-time working between countries. By contrast, this chapter makes comparisons of part-time working between different ethnic groups within the same country. While countries may be broadly classified on the basis of their 'gender order' (Connell, 1987; O'Reilly, 1996), gender orders will also differ between ethnic groups. Similarly, while the representation of gender relations within a country will depend upon how the gender order is shaped by institutions such as the family, the state and the workplace (Fagan and O'Reilly, Chapter 1, this volume) these institutions will also shape the relationship of gender and ethnicity within the same country (Anthias and Yuval-Davies, 1993). This chapter therefore provides an opportunity to examine differences in women's part-time working between ethnic groups which share the same state policies, and to explore some of the reasons for the observed differences.

Despite an increasing rate of full-time, more continuous employment among younger cohorts of women, part-time work is still the norm for most married mothers in Britain (Martin and Roberts, 1984; McRae, 1993; Bennett *et al.*, 1996; Macran *et al.*, 1996). Britain is distinctive for having a high rate of part-time work, which is concentrated in lower-level occupations or grades. Thus the disparity in occupational level between women in full- and part-time jobs is greater in Britain than in many other European countries (Dale and Joshi, 1992; Rubery *et al.*, 1995). However, cross-national comparative work (Walters and Dex, 1992; Lewis, 1993; Rubery *et al.*, 1995; Hantrais and Letablier, 1996) has shown that historical and current differences in institutional policies and labour market conditions, and cultural expectations about women's roles, are associated with very different levels of part-time working. Part-time work is not, therefore, an inevitable response to combining motherhood with employment.

In Britain, part-time working is much higher among white women than minority ethnic women (Owen, 1994); however, there has been little research on ethnic group differences in employment in relation to life stage and domestic circumstances and the consequences of these differences for women's occupational attainment. In this chapter we use individual level data from the 1991 British Census to establish differences in women's levels of full- and part-time employment by ethnic group and how this varies with the presence of dependent children and a partner. We then relate this to differences in levels of full- and part-time working within occupations. Finally, using individual level census data for 1981 and 1991, we chart the differences between ethnic groups in the extent to which women retain full-time profiles over a ten-year period, and the consequences of this for occupational attainment. First, we consider the emergence of part-time employment in Britain and the public policy framework in which it is located.

THE EMERGENCE OF PART-TIME JOBS: A HISTORICAL PERSPECTIVE

At the beginning of the twentieth century employment opportunities for women were limited, and particularly restrictive for married women. In 1911, 55 per cent of unmarried women in England and Wales were employed by comparison with 10 per cent of married women (1911 Census). Despite the contribution that many working-class women made to their families' financial resources, the dominant ideology of the family located the woman's role within the household as that of homemaker and mother (Rose, 1992). For middle-class women this was reinforced by the 'marriage bar' which operated in many non-manual jobs (for example, teaching, the Civil Service) and compelled women to resign from their jobs on marriage (Walby, 1986).

During the 1914–18 and the 1939–45 World Wars, women in Britain were urged to take on the work of men who were fighting overseas and day nurseries were set up to provide child care (Winter, 1985; Holdsworth, 1988). In the Second World War in particular, part-time working was introduced as an alternative means of enabling women with children to take part in the 'war effort' (McDowell et al., 1989). However, at the end of the war, nurseries closed and women returned to their homes or to 'women's' work (Holdsworth, 1988). In large part this was a response to the influential work of John Bowlby which emphasised the importance of the physical presence of the mother to the well-being and healthy development of her child (Holmes, 1993). All these factors acted to keep married women with young children out of the labour force.

However, the post-war economy of the 1950s needed more workers, in part because of economic growth and reconstruction, but also because of the expansion in services associated with the Welfare State, and a decline in the number of single women available for work (Dale, 1991). During the 1950s much of this labour came through the recruitment of immigrants from the Commonwealth. However, during the 1960s Britain restricted further immigration, and leaders of industry identified an alternative source of labour: the 'reserve army' of married women (Fabian Society, 1966; CBI, 1967). They proposed an increase in part-time jobs that would fit in with what was seen as women's primary responsibility – home and children. Employers, at first reluctantly, were soon persuaded to introduce part-time jobs for married women, particularly in the growing service sector. Thus part-time work was explicitly designed to be undemanding and lacking in responsibility and promotion prospects and was, inevitably, low paid and segregated from the work of men. None the less, there was a ready supply of women eager to take the part-time work offered to them.

While part-time working may have been initially introduced as a way of meeting a labour shortage without challenging traditional assumptions about the domestic division of labour, its continued growth reflects an increase in service sector jobs, and a demand from employers for organisational flexibility and cheaper labour (Dale and Joshi, 1992).

Other European countries faced similar labour shortages in the 1950s and 1960s but adopted different solutions. For example, in France, national policy combined pro-natalism with support for women's full-time employment through the provision of day care and after-school facilities, generous parental leave and flexible work-time arrangements (Hantrais and Letablier, 1996). The Nordic States have also sought to implement policies which encourage maternal employment, primarily through reduced hours and generous parental leave (see Daune-Richard, Chapter 11, this volume). In Britain the provision of affordable child care is limited and the majority of women who work part-time use informal care, usually provided by a partner or mother (Ward et al., 1996) and so avoid the problem of high costs for good-quality care. For many white women part-time working appears to provide a preferred employment option in that it offers some limited financial independence achieved with a relatively modest disruption of domestic roles. However, it also offers low levels of pay (Rubery, Chapter 7, this volume), lower returns than full-time work holding constant other factors (Ermisch and Wright, 1993; Dale and Egerton, 1997), few fringe benefits (Ginn and Arber, Chapter 8, this volume) and little prospect of promotion. Part-time working therefore generates fewer opportunity costs for women with poor employment prospects. This may go some way to explaining the fact that better-qualified women are more likely to work full-time and less qualified women to work part-time, with, overall, a positive relationship between level of qualification and economic activity (Dale and Egerton, 1997).

We have argued that the expansion of part-time jobs in Britain was influenced by assumptions about gender roles drawn from a white British culture. This is in marked contrast with the basis on which immigrant women from the West Indies were employed. The labour shortages of the 1950s gave rise to recruitment campaigns in the West Indies, particularly Barbados, to provide labour for the National Health Service, British Rail and London Transport (Peach, 1996) and included both men and women. Many Black-Caribbean women came to Britain specifically to find employment rather than as dependants, and were quickly recruited, on a full-time basis, into the growing National Health Service (Phizacklea, 1983).

By contrast, South Asian women usually came to Britain as dependants of husbands and fathers already living here. Indian migration was rather later in time than that from the West Indies and largely male led. After the 1962 Immigration Act most migrants were wives, fiancées and children, although from about 1973 there was a 'professionalisation' of Indian immigration, imposed by entry criteria (Robinson, 1996). The expulsion of Indians from East Africa led to further immigration of highly qualified groups during the 1970s. Immigrants from Pakistan and Bangladesh formed the most recent wave, again mainly male led. The largest growth in the Bangladeshi population in Britain occurred during the 1980s when male workers were joined by wives, often much younger than their husbands, and their children (Eade *et al.*, 1996). These women were entering Britain at a very difficult time in terms of employment and few had any formal educational qualifications. The employment patterns of South Asian women, and also West Indian women, have been influenced by the timing of migration and the reasons for migration; and by the nature of the labour market in the areas of settlement, their own qualifications and experience, as well as culturally specific expectations about women's roles. There was, however, no particular reason for immigrant women to take part-time jobs which had been designed to tap white women's labour.

EMPLOYMENT PATTERNS BY ETHNIC GROUP

A stylised set of transitions through the life course[1] for women from different ethnic groups[2] is shown in Figure 4.1, based on data from the 1 per cent Household Sample of Anonymised Records (SARs) from the 1991 Census for Great Britain (Census Microdata Unit, 1994). It is not assumed that all women (or even a majority) move through these stages in sequential fashion; however, they provide a useful presentational device. The graphs also conflate age/life cycle and cohort effects as they are based on cross-sectional data. Thus younger cohorts of women may be expected to record rather higher levels of employment than suggested by the cross-sectional data when they reach later life stages. All analyses are restricted to women aged between 18 and 60 who are usual household residents and not in full-time education.

Each figure distinguishes between: (1) unemployed women and women on a government scheme (the difference between economically active and in work); (2) women in part-time employment (the difference between in work and in full-time work); (3) women in full-time employment. Our discussion focuses on full- and part-time work. In all ethnic groups, women under age 35 without

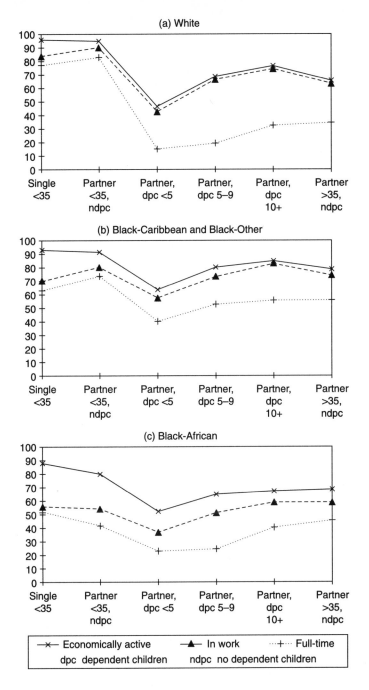

Figure 4.1 Women's economic activity at different life stages by ethnic group. Percentage of all women, 18–60, not in full-time education.

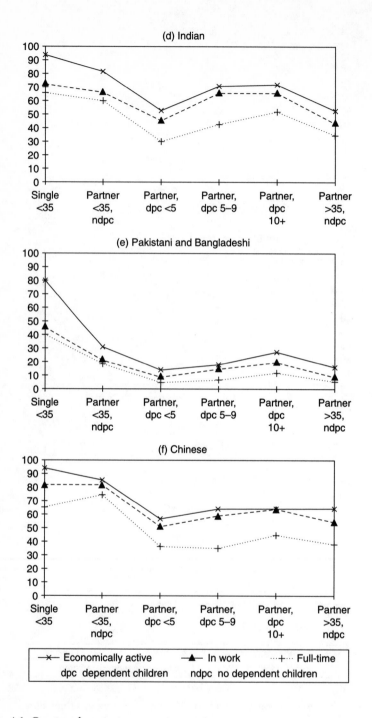

Figure 4.1 Continued

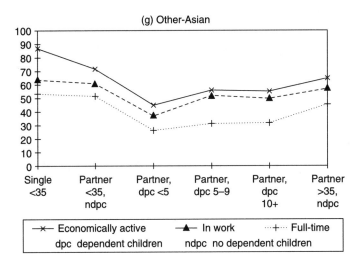

Figure 4.1 Continued

domestic constraints record high levels of economic activity and low levels of part-time working. Lower levels of full-time employment for all minority ethnic women are due to much higher levels of unemployment by comparison with the White group. Full-time working remains high and part-time low in the next life stage – young women with a partner but no child – for all groups except Pakistani and Bangladeshi women where the presence of a partner is associated with much lower levels of economic activity.

As expected, it is among White women with a partner and a dependent child that we see a large drop in economic activity, and particularly full-time working. Among White and Pakistani/Bangladeshi women, levels of full-time employment fall below 20 per cent for partnered women with a child under 10.[3] In all other ethnic groups levels are considerably higher.

Partnered White women with dependent children of all ages are distinctive in their high levels of part-time working (consistently higher than levels of full-time working), by comparison with other ethnic groups.[4] Levels run at least 10 percentage points higher where the youngest child is pre-school and over 20 percentage points higher where the child is aged between 5 and 9.

Women heading one-parent families with a pre-school child (Figure 4.2a) have lower levels of full- and part-time working. The distinctive White pattern is absent, although it reappears where children are aged 5 or over (Figure 4.2b), but at a lower level than among partnered women. Where children are under age 5, Black-Caribbean and Black-African women have particularly high levels of economic activity (47 per cent and 53 per cent respectively) by comparison with White mothers (28 per cent). This suggests that, for White women, there is a relationship between part-time working and the presence of a partner that is much stronger than for other groups.

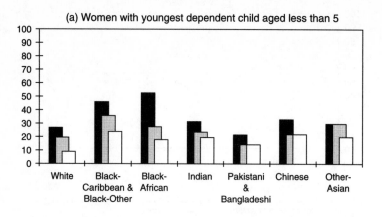

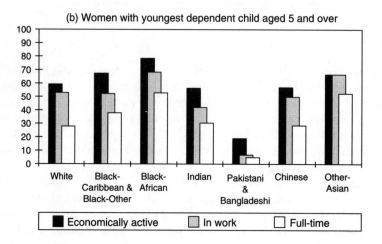

Figure 4.2 Economic activity of women heading one-parent families by ethnic group: (a) youngest child under 5; (b) youngest child 5–9.

It is evident that the major differences between the *minority ethnic* groups relate to levels of economic activity, rather than differences in part-time working. Generally, the likelihood of part-time working for minority women in employment is about half that for White women, controlling for life stage and level of qualifications (Holdsworth and Dale, 1997).

From the above discussion it may not be surprising that minority ethnic women have not adopted part-time working at the same levels as White women. For Black women in particular, there appears to be a greater priority given to economic independence, reinforced by cultural factors and also employment-related reasons for immigration (Stone, 1983; Bruegel, 1989; Mirza, 1992).

First-generation Black-Caribbean women are slightly more likely to be economically active than second generation, after controlling for age, life stage and qualification level (Holdsworth and Dale, 1997), reflecting the selective nature of Black-Caribbean migrant women who came to Britain to find work. By contrast, Pakistani and Bangladeshi women not only have a very different cultural background where Islamic traditions may place constraints on employment outside the home, but came to Britain as dependants, during a period of acute depression in the local labour markets in the areas of settlement. It may therefore be more accurate to see their exclusion from the labour market as beginning on their arrival in Britain, rather than simply as a product of cultural norms (Brah, 1992). For this group, UK-born women are twice as likely to be economically active as those born outside the UK, although educational qualifications and family circumstances are much more important factors (Holdsworth and Dale, 1997).

In general, White women use informal child care (defined as care by family and friends), although use of formal care is much higher where women work full-time and have a child under 5 (Joshi et al., 1995). There is little evidence to suggest that minority ethnic women have easier access to child care than White women. Indeed, we may assume that the relative cost per hour worked will be greater for minority ethnic women, given their lower level of earnings (Bruegel, 1989). Available evidence suggests that minority ethnic women's higher level of full-time working is in spite of difficulty in obtaining child care, rather than through preferential access to it (CRC, 1975; Warrier, 1988).

The number of children in a family will also influence the cost of child care as well as the ease of organising it. There is substantial variation in the family size of different ethnic groups. Fertility figures are only available based on country of birth; these show total period fertility rates of only 1.5 for Caribbean-born women in 1991, by comparison with 3.3 for Bangladeshi- and Pakistani-born women and 1.8 for the country as a whole. Generally, fertility rates for minority ethnic women born overseas have declined steadily over the last twenty years (CSO, 1992).

The gender order (Connell, 1987) may provide a primary basis for differences in gender relations between ethnic groups; for example, between Black-Caribbeans and Pakistanis or Bangladeshis. These differences, based in historical experiences and in religious practices and beliefs, will interact with structural factors in the UK such as the labour market and the education system to generate different gender regimes. Some of these factors (for example, discrimination) are likely to be specific to minority ethnic women while others (the lack of state-provided child care) are common to all women. Both the construction of gender orders and their representation in gender regimes will vary over time and, in particular, may result in employment differences between first- and second-generation women.

RELATIONSHIP BETWEEN ETHNIC SEGREGATION AND PART-TIME SEGREGATION

It is well established that part-time employment is highly segregated (Scott, 1994) and concentrated in particular occupations. There is also considerable occupational segregation by ethnic group. However, while some minority women are over-represented in occupations with high levels of full-time working (for example, Indian, Bangladeshi and Pakistani women in semi-skilled factory work), Black women and Other-Asian women are over-represented in nursing and allied occupations which have relatively high levels of part-time working.

Table 4.1 shows that minority ethnic women's lower levels of part-time work cannot be explained by their occupational distribution. Levels of part-time working are shown within each occupational group, for women with dependent children, by ethnic group. Overall, 57 per cent of White women with dependent children are in part-time jobs by comparison with 28 to 34 per cent of women from other ethnic groups. While part-time working is higher among minority ethnic women in those occupational groups where part-time working is generally high (shop work, other semi-skilled jobs), levels are none the less generally 20 to 30 percentage points lower than for White women. Black women in nursing occupations are also much less likely to be working part-time than White

Table 4.1 Percentage of women working part-time, of those in paid employment and with dependent children, by ethnic group and WES* class, in Great Britain, 1991

WES Class	Ethnic group					
	White	Black-Caribbean and Black-Other	Black-African	Indian	Pakistani and Bangladeshi	Chinese and Other-Asian
Professional and teachers	40	(14)	–	28	–	(23)
Nurses and allied	57	28	(25)	37	–	32
Intermediate	32	11	–	17	(48)	18
Clerical	54	17	(24)	29	(19)	33
Shop assistants	80	(77)	–	54	–	(64)
Skilled	49	21	–	13	–	32
Semi-skilled factory	41	(13)	–	20	(20)	–
Other semi-skilled	82	50	64	47	–	45
All women	57	28	33	28	33	34

Source: © Crown copyright
Note: 1% Household SAR. Usual residents, women in employment aged 18 to 60 with dependent children. All percentages are based on cell totals. Percentages based on cell totals between 20 and 29 are in parentheses. Those below 20 are not shown.
* The occupational class is that used in the Women and Employment Survey (Martin and Roberts, 1984).

women. However, we cannot tell from these data whether minority ethnic women are unable to obtain part-time employment or work full-time through choice.

From a 'white' model of women's employment we would expect increased levels of full-time working to have a beneficial effect in retaining or improving occupational attainment, particularly during family formation. We test this assumption in the next section by using longitudinal data to analyse the role of a full-time employment profile in promoting occupational attainment over the ten-year period 1981 to 1991.

LONGITUDINAL DATA

For British women it is well established that the effect of absence from the labour market and particularly a return to part-time work is likely to be downward occupational mobility (Martin and Roberts, 1984; Dex, 1987; Joshi and Newell, 1987). By contrast, women who retain full-time employment seem to suffer little occupational downgrading associated with family formation (Joshi et al., 1995). McRae (1991) provides more recent information on occupational differences in mobility associated with childbirth. Of those returning to part-time work, women who were managers or administrators, or who were in clerical or secretarial jobs before giving birth, were most likely to move down the occupational structure (29 per cent and 26 per cent respectively). By contrast, only 9 per cent of women in professional occupations who returned to part-time work experienced downward occupational mobility.

The ONS Longitudinal Study (LS) links together census data and vital registration records (including births) from 1971 to 1991 and later (Hattersely and Creeser, 1995). We have used this data source to obtain information on ethnic differences in women's employment status over a ten-year period (1981 to 1991), and the extent to which a full-time profile is associated with occupational stability or upward mobility.

The sample of women used to analyse occupational attainment was restricted to all those in employment at both 1981 and 1991 and aged between 16 and 50 in 1981.[5] In 1981 there were 95,297 women in the LS aged between 16 and 50, not in full-time education and also present in the LS in 1991. Ethnicity, from the 1991 Census, has been collapsed into five categories: White; Black; Indian; Pakistani and Bangladeshi; Chinese and Other-Asian.[6]

Generally, just over one-third of women in this age group were in employment at both time points (37.5 per cent) – slightly more Black women (39.1 per cent) and slightly fewer Indian (31 per cent) and Chinese and Other-Asian women (31 per cent). However, as expected from the cross-sectional analysis, Pakistani and Bangladeshi women are very unlikely to be in employment at both points in time – only 5 per cent.

This longitudinal sample is distinctive in that women from all ethnic groups are more likely to have higher qualifications than the 1981 cross-sectional sample. This is to be expected, given the well-established relationship between continuity in the labour market and level of qualification. Only a minority of women in the longitudinal sample gave birth to a child between 1981 and 1991, although this was lower for White women (19 per cent) than for minority ethnic women (28 per cent) (Table 4.2). Despite the fact that minority ethnic women were more likely to have had a child during the decennial period and to have dependent children in both 1981 and 1991, they were much more likely to be in full-time employment at both time points: 65 per cent by comparison with 33 per cent of White women (Table 4.2). This reflects the findings from the cross-sectional analysis, that women from minority ethnic groups are more likely than White women to be economically active when they have a dependent child. White women demonstrate the expected mobility from full- to part-time work: 52 per cent who had a child between 1981 and 1991 made this change by comparison with 22 per cent for minority ethnic women (Table 4.2).

Previous research on White women leads us to expect that those in higher-level occupations are more likely to retain a full-time profile during family formation. Table 4.3 shows the percentage of women in full-time work at both time points by occupational group in 1981 as a percentage of all those in work in both 1981 and 1991. Among White women in a professional or teaching job in 1981, who had a child between 1981 and 1991 (column 1), 50 per cent remained in full-time work, while only 27 per cent of women in semi- and unskilled jobs in 1981 did so. White women with no child born between 1981 and 1991 (column 2) showed a similar differential, but with rather higher levels of full-time working. Among women from minority ethnic groups (columns 3 and 4), a substantially higher percentage of women in each occupational group were in full-time work in both 1981 and 1991 by comparison with White women, and there is less difference between occupations. Levels are generally higher for women who did not give birth during the 1981–91 period than for those who did, but the difference is much less marked than for White women.

Table 4.2 Women's employment status at 1981 and 1991 by ethnic group and whether child born between 1981 and 1991

Employment col %	White		Minority ethnic	
	Child 1981–91	No child	Child 1981–91	No child
Full-full	33	53	65	76
Part-full	5	19	8	11
Full-part	52	7	22	6
Part-part	10	21	6	8
Total no.	6,340	26,958	348	878
	19.0%		28.4%	

Source: © Crown copyright. ONS Longitudinal Study
Note: All women aged 16 to 50 in 1981 and in employment in 1981 and 1991.

Table 4.3 Percentage of women in full-time work in 1981 and 1991 by 1981 occupation, child born and ethnic group. Base population: all women aged 16–50 in 1981 and in employment in 1981 and 1991

1981 WES occupation	White		Minority ethnic	
	Child 1981–91	No child	Child 1981–91	No child
Professional/teacher	50	68	67	79
Nursing/allied	28	47	49	67
Other intermediate	41	67	77	80
Clerical/secretarial	32	61	66	84
Shop/sales	23	30	(38)*	55
Skilled manual	37	57	71	79
Semi-unskilled	27	35	72	75
All	33	53	65	76

Source: © Crown copyright. ONS Longitudinal Study
Note: All women aged 16 to 50 in 1981 and in employment in 1981 and 1991.
* base number of 16; all other base numbers greater than 30.

For this group, these results accord with McRae (1993), who found that women in higher-level occupations were more likely to retain full-time employment during child-bearing. However, Table 4.3 shows that minority ethnic women in semi- and unskilled occupations are as likely to remain in full-time work as those in professional and teaching jobs. The contrast in the employment profiles of semi- and unskilled women is most striking, with 27 per cent of White women who were working in that occupational group in 1981 remaining in full-time work, against 72 per cent of ethnic minority women. This information for women from minority groups has not been available before.

In summary, ethnic minority women in employment in 1981 and 1991 were much more likely than White women to be working full-time in both years, and showed little variation in full-time working either by occupation or whether they had a child during this period. This suggests that different processes are in operation for White and minority ethnic women. Whereas higher-status employment and higher qualifications appear influential in keeping White women out of part-time work, full-time working seems to be the norm for minority ethnic women, irrespective of occupation. Only in those occupations such as shop work does full-time employment for minority ethnic groups drop as low as 38 per cent. This suggests that assumptions about reasons for retaining full-time work, based on the experiences of White women, may not be generalisable to other ethnic groups. In particular the association of full-time employment with career-orientated occupations and subsequent improvement in occupational attainment may not necessarily hold for the large number of full-time minority ethnic women at the bottom of the occupational hierarchy. In this section we therefore consider occupational mobility for these women who were in employment in both 1981 and 1991.

By cross-tabulating 1981 occupation with 1991 occupation for White and minority ethnic women (Table 4.4) we can see whether the latter group gains from the greater likelihood of having a full-time profile. Table 4.4 contains all women, full- and part-time who were in employment in both 1981 and 1991. We would expect that, if working full-time is advantageous, minority ethnic women would be more likely to retain their occupation or move upwards than White women, because they are more likely to be in full-time work.

Generally, both White and minority groups who were in non-manual occupations in 1981 are equally likely to retain their occupational position or to move up. Only in intermediate jobs are minority ethnic women more likely to move down into manual work – and the numbers are very small. However, minority ethnic women are much more likely to remain in manual occupations (most of which are semi- or unskilled jobs) than White women. Half of all White women in manual jobs in 1981, who were in employment in 1991, had moved into non-manual jobs, with nearly one-fifth going into clerical work. By contrast, three-quarters of minority ethnic women stay in manual jobs.

For White women we are able to examine whether there are differences in mobility by whether they remain in full-time employment, in part-time employment, or move from one to the other of these states. Analysis (not presented here) shows that women in professional, teaching and nursing jobs retain their occupa-

Table 4.4 Comparison of women's WES occupational class in 1981 with WES class in 1991, by ethnic group. All women employed in both 1981 and 1991 (top row represents all white women; bottom row in **bold** represents all non-white women)

1981 WES	Profes- sional/ teacher	Nursing	Inter- mediate	Clerical	Shop	Manual	No.
Professional/	85	2	7	4	1	1	2,820
Teacher	**86**	**3**	**5**	**3**	**–**	**2**	**59**
Nurse	3	83	5	5	2	2	2,710
	1	**90**	**2**	**3**	**2**	**2**	**225**
Intermediate	8	5	54	19	7	5	3,178
	4	**10**	**54**	**15**	**6**	**12**	**82**
Clerical	3	2	19	67	5	4	12,919
	4	**4**	**18**	**67**	**4**	**4**	**341**
Shop	2	5	15	20	49	11	3,216
	2	**6**	**16**	**22**	**43**	**10**	**49**
Manual	2	7	10	19	12	50	8,654
	1	**4**	**11**	**5**	**5**	**74**	**483**

Source: © Crown copyright. ONS Longitudinal Study
Note: All women aged 16 to 50 in 1981, in employment in 1981 and 1991, with valid WES class in both years.

tion irrespective of employment status or whether a child has been born. Women in 'intermediate' jobs do rather better if they remain in full-time employment at both time points and also if they have a child at some time during the period – the latter probably reflecting a self-selection process. Women in clerical and secretarial jobs in 1981 who have a child and either retain full-time employment or move from part- to full-time work are most likely to be in higher-level jobs in 1991 – again reflecting a commitment associated with working full-time with a young child. Women in these employment categories (full-time to full-time or part-time to full-time) are also most likely to move up to higher-level work from shop and sales jobs in 1981. However, among women with manual jobs in 1981, only 39–41 per cent of those who *do not* retain a full-time profile stay in manual jobs, by comparison with 65 per cent who retain a full-time profile.

For minority ethnic women, numbers are too small to support this more detailed analysis. However, we are able to show that 68 per cent of Black women and 80 per cent of Indian women who worked full-time in 1981 and 1991 remained in manual jobs. (Most of the Indian women are in semi-skilled factory work.) Thus, irrespective of ethnic group, a full-time profile does not lead to upward mobility for women in manual work. This probably reflects the lack of promotion prospects in most manual jobs held by women and, in particular, for Indian women doing factory work. The effects of these differences are exaggerated in Table 4.4 because a higher percentage of minority ethnic than White women remain in full-time work.

The mobility recorded for White women conflates a number of different processes. Many White women who move from full-time to part-time employment go into sales jobs or clerical work. These may not be any better paid than the manual jobs which they held before, although the work may be preferable. Older women may move into part-time work as their household finances improve. White women moving from part-time to full-time work are most likely to move into clerical work – probably regaining occupations held before child-bearing.

An important question, which cannot be answered here, is whether women who retain a full-time profile in manual work do so through choice or from economic necessity. Phizacklea and Wolkowitz (1993), in a study of homeworking, suggest that economic necessity is likely to be the main reason for full-time working among South Asian women. South Asian men have lower wage levels and higher rates of unemployment than White men (Jones, 1993) which may require their wives to work full-time, for example, in semi-skilled factory jobs, in spite of difficulties in obtaining child care. Evidence from the Commission for Racial Equality also suggests that, in some cases, employers may offer part-time employment preferentially to White women (CRE, 1991). Minority ethnic women may also have particular difficulty in obtaining full-time jobs in higher-level non-manual work. These reasons can only remain speculative at the moment. They do, however, suggest the need for more detailed research on the relationship between family and work histories for minority ethnic women.

CONCLUSION

Minority ethnic women record lower levels of part-time working than White women, irrespective of life stage and partnership status. With the exception of Pakistani and Bangladeshi women they are also more likely to work full-time, particularly if they have a dependent child. In a wider European context, it is the high part-time rates of White women that are distinctive, rather than the employment patterns of minority ethnic groups.

The experience of minority ethnic women challenges the assumption that, in Britain, women who combine paid work with having children fall into two categories: those who work part-time and use informal child care and those who work full-time in career-orientated jobs and earn enough to pay for high-quality, formal child care. Minority ethnic women with dependent children are more likely than White women to work full-time across all occupational sectors, even in occupations where part-time work predominates. For women in non-manual jobs the consequences of retaining a full-time profile are generally beneficial and similar between ethnic groups. However, in manual jobs, retaining a full-time profile does not appear to lead to upward mobility. Women from all ethnic groups who retain full-time manual work appear trapped, but this effect is much stronger for Indian women in semi-skilled factory work. The effect is amplified for minority ethnic women because they are much more likely to retain full-time employment. White women appear to move more easily from manual into non-manual jobs such as clerical work. Further work is needed, with more detailed work history data, to compare the employment careers of minority ethnic and White women.

From these results it is clear that, within the same state regulatory and institutional framework, there are very considerable differences in part-time working between women from different ethnic groups. These differences can only be understood in terms of the historical, cultural and economic circumstances of each ethnic group (exemplified by the gender order or gender culture (Connell, 1987; Pfau-Effinger, Chapter 9, this volume) and the way in which these interact with the labour market and other institutional structures.

ACKNOWLEDGEMENTS

The research was carried out under ESRC/JISC grant H507255/34 as part of the Census Analysis Programme. The samples of anonymised records have been provided through the Census Microdata Unit at the University of Manchester, with the support of ESRC/JISC. All tables containing SAR and ONS data are reproduced with the permission of the Controller of Her Majesty's Stationery Office and are Crown Copyright. We would also like to thank the LS Support Unit at SSRU, City University, and, in particular Rosemary Creeser, for assistance in obtaining data from the ONS Longitudinal Study. We would like to thank *Work, Employment and Society* for allowing us to reproduce Figures 4.1 and 4.2.

NOTES

1 The hierarchical structure of the 1 per cent SAR allows the construction of an eight-category life stage variable, based on age, the presence of a partner and the presence and age of a dependent child (Holdsworth and Dale, 1995).
The categories of the life stage variable are:

1 No partner, less than age 35, no dependent children
2 With partner, less than age 35, no dependent children
3 With partner, youngest dependent child aged less than 5
4 With partner, youngest dependent child aged 5 to 9
5 With partner, youngest dependent child aged 10 or over
6 With partner, aged 35 and over, no dependent children
7 No partner, dependent child less than 5
8 No partner, dependent child aged 5 or over

A dependent child is defined as a child aged less than 16, or 16 to 18 years old, single and in full-time education. A partner may be either married or cohabiting.
2 The original ten ethnic groups distinguished by the census have been collapsed into seven. They are: White, Black-Caribbean and Black-Other combined; Black-African; Indian; Pakistani and Bangladeshi combined; Chinese; and Other-Asians. A detailed discussion of the construction of the census ethnic groups can be found in Dale and Holdsworth (1996).
3 Qualitative studies (Phizacklea and Wolkowitz, 1993) suggest that data collection exercises such as the census may fail to capture homeworking, particularly among Pakistani and Bangladeshi women.
4 The only other groups where this occurs are Black-African and Pakistani/ Bangladeshi women with a partner and youngest child aged between 5 and 9.
5 While the census (and thus the LS) holds information on last occupation for women with a job in the previous ten years, women who were not in paid work in 1991 could have left employment at any time between a week after the 1981 Census to two weeks before the 1991 Census date. More importantly, there is no information as to whether the date of a 'last' occupation reported in the 1991 Census occurred before or after a child was born. In addition, the 1981 Census did not seek occupational information for women who were categorised as a 'housewife' in 1981, making occupational comparisons impossible between women not working in 1981 and working in 1991. Information on employment comes from census data at two time points; we cannot therefore assume that women employed at both time points were in continuous employment for the ten-year period.
6 Although analysis would, ideally, have used detailed work history information, there are, as yet, no such British data available which can provide adequate distinctions between ethnic groups; for example, the British Household Panel Study, with only 10,000 respondents, cannot support analyses by ethnic group. The Working Lives Survey, conducted by the Department for Education and Employment, will provide work histories for ethnic minorities but this information was not available for academic analysis at the time of writing.

BIBLIOGRAPHY

Anthias, F. and Yuval-Davies, N. (1993) *Racialized Boundaries*, London: Routledge.
Bennett, N., Jarvis, L., Rowlands, O., Singleton, N. and Haselden, L. (1996) *Living in Britain: Results from the 1991 General Household Survey*, London: HMSO.

Brah, A. (1992) 'Women of South Asian origin in Britain: issues and concerns' in P. Braham, A. Rattansi and R. Skellington (eds) *Racism and Antiracism: Inequalities, Opportunities and Policies*, London: Sage.

Bruegel, I. (1989) 'Sex and race in the labour market', *Feminist Review* 32: 49–68.

CBI (1967) *Employing Women: The Employers' View*, London: Confederation of British Industry.

Census Microdata Unit (1994) *User Guide to the SARs*, 2nd edn, Manchester: CMU, Manchester University.

Central Statistical Office (CSO) (1992) *Social Trends 22*, London: HMSO.

Commission for Racial Equality (CRE) (1991) *Annual Report, 1993*, London: CRE.

Community Relations Commission (CRC) (1975) *Who Minds? A Study of Working Mothers and Childminding in Ethnic Minority Communities*, London: CRC.

Connell, R. (1987) *Gender and Power*, London: Polity Press.

Dale, A. (1991) 'Women in the labour market: policy in perspective' in N. Manning (ed.) *Social Policy Review 1990–1*, London: Longman Group.

Dale, A. and Egerton, M. (1997) *Highly Educated Women: Evidence from the National Child Development Study*, DfEE Research studies RS25, London: HMSO.

Dale, A. and Holdsworth, C. (1996) 'Issues in the analysis of ethnicity in the 1991 British census: evidence from microdata', *Ethnic and Racial Studies* 20: 160–81.

Dale, A. and Joshi, H. (1992) 'The social and economic status of women in Britain', in G. Buttler, G. Heileg and G. Schmitt-Rink (eds) *Acta Demographica*, Heidelberg: Physica-Verlag.

Dex, S. (1987) *Women's Occupational Mobility*, Basingstoke: Macmillan.

Eade, J., Vamplew, T. and Peach, C. (1996) 'The Bangladeshis: the encapsulated community' in C. Peach (ed.) *Ethnicity in the 1991 Census: The Ethnic Minority Population of Great Britain*, London: HMSO.

Ermisch, J. F. and Wright, R. E. (1993) 'Wage offers and full-time employment by British Women', *Journal of Human Resources* 28: 2.

Fabian Society (1966) *Womanpower*, Young Fabian Pamphlet no.11, London.

Hantrais, L. and Letablier, M.-T. (1996) *Families and Family Policies in Europe*, London: Longman.

Hattersley, L. and Creeser, R. (1995) *Longitudinal Study 1971–1991: History, Organisation and Quality of Data*, London: HMSO.

Holdsworth, A. (1988) *Out of the Dolls House*, London: British Broadcasting Corporation.

Holdsworth, C. and Dale, A. (1995) *Ethnic Homogeneity and Family Formation: Evidence from the 1991 Household SAR*, CCSR Occasional Paper no. 7.

Holdsworth, C. and Dale, A. (1997) 'Ethnic differences in women's employment', *Work, Employment and Society* 11: 3.

Holmes, J. (1993) *John Bowlby and Attachment Theory*, London: Routledge.

Jones, T. (1993) *Britain's Ethnic Minorities*, London: Policy Studies Institute.

Joshi, H. and Newell, M.-L. (1987) 'Job downgrading after childbearing' in M. Uncles (ed.) *London Papers in Regional Science 18*, London: Pion.

Joshi, H., Dale, A., Davies, H. and Ward, C. (1995) *Dependence and Independence in the Finances of Women Aged 33*, London: Family Policy Studies Centre and the Joseph Rowntree Foundation.

Lewis, J. (ed.) (1993) *Women and Social Policies in Europe*, Aldershot: Edward Elgar.

McDowell, L., Sarre, P. and Hamnett, C. (1989) *Divided Nation: Social & Cultural Change in Britain*, London: Hodder & Stoughton.

McRae, S. (1991) 'Occupational change over childbirth', *Sociology* 25, 4: 589–606.

McRae, S. (1993) 'Returning to work after childbirth: opportunities and inequalities', *European Sociological Review* 9: 125–38.

Macran, S., Joshi, H. and Dex, S. (1996) 'Employment after childbearing: a survival analysis', *Work, Employment and Society* 10, 2: 273–96.

Martin, J. and Roberts, C. (1984) *Women and Employment: A Lifetime Perspective*, London: HMSO.

Mirza, H. S. (1992) *Young, Female and Black*, London: Routledge.

O'Reilly, J. (1996) 'Theortical considerations in cross-national employment research', *Sociological Research Online* 1: 1.

Owen, D. (1994) *Ethnic Minority Women and the Labour Market: Analysis of the 1991 Census*, Manchester: Equal Opportunities Commission.

Peach, C. (1996) 'Black-Caribbeans: class, gender and geography' in C. Peach (ed.) *Ethnicity in the 1991 Census: The Ethnic Minority Population of Great Britain*, London: HMSO.

Phizacklea, A. (1983) 'In the front line' in A. Phizacklea (ed.) *One Way Ticket: Migration and Female Labour*, London: Routledge & Kegan Paul.

Phizacklea, A. and Wolkowitz, C. (1993) *Homeworking Women: Gender, Racism and Class at Work*, London: Sage.

Robinson, V. (1996) 'The Indians: onward and upward' in C. Peach (ed.) *Ethnicity in the 1991 Census: The Ethnic Minority Population of Great Britain*, London: HMSO.

Rose, S. (1992) *Limited Livelihoods: Gender and Class in Nineteenth-century England*, London: Routledge.

Rubery, J., Fagan, C. and Smith, M. (1995) *Changing Patterns of Work and Working Time in the European Union and the Impact of Gender Divisions*, Brussels: Report to the European Commission Equal Opportunities Unit.

Scott, A. (1994) 'Gender segregation and the SCELI research' in A. Scott (ed.) *Gender Segregation and Social Change: Men and Women in Changing Labour Markets*, Oxford: Oxford University Press.

Stone, K. (1983) 'Motherhood and waged work: West Indian, Asian and White mothers compared' in A. Phizacklea (ed.) *One Way Ticket: Migration and Female Labour*, London: Routledge & Kegan Paul.

Walby, S. (1986) *Patriarchy at Work*, Cambridge: Polity Press.

Walters, P. and Dex, S. (1992) 'Feminisation of the labour force in Britain and France' in S. Arber and N. Gilbert (eds) *Women and Working Lives: Divisions and Change*, London: Macmillan.

Ward, C., Dale, A. and Joshi, H. (1996) 'Combining employment with childcare: an escape from dependence', *Social Policy* 25: 2.

Warrier, S. (1988) 'Marriage, maternity and female economic activity: Gujarati mothers in Britain' in S. Westwood and P. Bhachu (eds) *Enterprising Women: Ethnicity, Economy and Gender Relations*, London: Routledge.

Winter, J. (1985) *The Great War and the British People*, London: Macmillan.

5

ARE PART-TIME JOBS BETTER THAN NO JOBS?

Ulrich Walwei

INTRODUCTION

Even if we were to accept the rather optimistic expectations[1] with regard to the future trend of economic growth, the acute unemployment problems of the European countries would not be anywhere near being solved within a foreseeable period. Regardless of the success of national economic policies, the question thus arises, at least in the short and medium terms, what additional possibilities exist for creating more employment? To bring unemployment down to the levels recorded in the US and Japan requires not only strong economic growth but also more employment-intensive growth.[2] The inadequate employment intensity of economic growth is widely considered to be one of the most important reasons for the employment malaise from which Western Europe is suffering. The required increase in the employment intensity of growth can be achieved by more wage and/or more working-time flexibility.

This chapter will deal with one of the most interesting aspects of the flexibilisation debate, namely the consequences of more part-time work for employment and unemployment. The distribution of the working-time available in the national economy to a larger part of the labour force, for example, in the form of more part-time work, might help to keep or get more people into employment and to avoid or reduce unemployment. The growth of this form of employment, which has become evident in the past and can probably be expected to continue in the future, raises a very important question: Are part-time jobs better than no jobs? This question involves both a macro perspective and a micro perspective. From the macro perspective, the main question is whether a labour market situation with more employment opportunities due to increasing part-time work necessarily has to be preferred to an alternative situation with fewer full-time jobs. From the viewpoint of job seekers (i.e. from a micro perspective) we must discuss whether the opportunity for part-time employment is at least in most cases more attractive than the possible alternatives of unemployment or inactivity.

96

Before discussing these aspects in more detail, the chapter begins by assessing the significance of the debate on working-time in general economic terms. The starting point is the analysis of the relationship between economic and employment growth and the associated discussion on so-called 'jobless growth' based on the example of the Federal Republic of Germany. The heart of this chapter is an analysis of the effects of part-time growth on employment and unemployment, based on international comparison.

ECONOMIC GROWTH, EMPLOYMENT AND WORKING HOURS

Developments over time show that the US has experienced a significant increase in employment without an outstanding growth in output. By contrast, a comparable rate of economic growth in Europe has produced very little increase in employment. As a consequence the growing fear is that European industrial nations in particular might again experience an economic upswing with an insufficient rate of job creation. Such a 'jobless growth' would entail massive social problems in light of the existing high levels of unemployment.

In order to learn from recent trends and to illustrate the relationship between economic growth and employment, the case of West Germany is taken as an example. The developments in West Germany are quite representative for the European Union as a whole. Table 5.1 documents the results of several linear regressions. The growth rate of the real gross domestic product was selected as the independent variable; the dependent variables were the trend of gainful employment (headcount of people in paid work) and the volume of work (total hours of paid work). To indicate changes in development over time, a distinction was made between the overall period (1973–94) and two sub-periods (1973–83 and 1983–94). Assessment of the relationship between economic growth and employment is based on the so-called 'employment threshold' because it is at this point that gainful employment and the volume of work increase. The findings indicate that economic growth needs to be almost twice as large to increase the volume of work compared to the level required to create more jobs (2.9 per cent of GDP in 1973–94 compared to 1.5 per cent). Second, the results show that the employment threshold fell during the 1973–94 period. In other words, economic growth has become more employment intensive over time, both in the volume of employment and the number of jobs. The reasons for this development are manifold and difficult to isolate (see below). They have to do with the speed of technological progress, trends in real wages and working hours per employee, and the sectoral composition of employment (for example, the relative weight of low-productivity sectors such as services).

Were one to extrapolate the trend of the more recent sub-period (1983–94), there would perhaps be less reason for concern about the labour market than is apparent in the current public discussion. But three counter-arguments warn

Table 5.1 Economic growth and employment in West Germany, 1973–94

Dependent variable (y)		Independent variable (x)		Regression function (y = a + bx)		Employment threshold level (0 = a + bx)	
GE	1973–94	GDP	1973–94	GE	= −0.72 GDP + 0.47	GDP	= 1.5
GE	1973–83	GDP	1973–83	GE	= −0.91 GDP + 0.35	GDP	= 2.6
GE	1983–93	GDP	1983–93	GE	= −0.84 GDP + 0.68	GDP	= 1.2
GE	1983–94	GDP	1983–94	GE	= −0.89 GDP + 0.61	GDP	= 1.5
VoW	1973–94	GDP	1973–94	VoW	= −1.97 GDP + 0.67	GDP	= 2.9
VoW	1973–83	GDP	1973–83	VoW	= −2.16 GDP + 0.58	GDP	= 3.7
VoW	1983–93	GDP	1983–93	VoW	= −1.40 GDP + 0.54	GDP	= 2.6
VoW	1983–94	GDP	1983–94	VoW	= −2.19 GDP + 0.81	GDP	= 2.7

Source: OECD *Labour Force Statistics* and OECD *National Accounts* (different volumes)
Notes:
GDP = Real Gross Domestic Product (change compared to previous year in %)
GE = Gainfully Employed (change compared to previous year in %)
VoW = Volume of Work (change compared to previous year in %)

against any optimism. First, the employment thresholds are still so high that, even with an economic upswing, a lasting rise in employment and a significant decline in unemployment appear utopian. Second, considering the economic level the European economies have reached, high growth rates (particularly over a longer period) become increasingly difficult to achieve and appear less and less acceptable in the face of the possible negative effects on the environment. Third, there are clear indications that the thresholds for employment have risen most recently and, for the medium term, possibly have to be set at a higher level than at the end of the 1980s and even the beginning of the 1990s. Hof (1995: 1) found higher employment thresholds for the 1983–94 period than for the 1980–92 period using similar regressive estimates.[3] He attributes this to massive rationalisation processes in manufacturing industries plus rapid gains in productivity in the services sector (for example, at banks and insurance companies), and efficiency gains in the public sector. Klauder (1990: 99) has also argued that employment thresholds will increase in the 1990s owing to massive technological advances and the efforts of companies to improve their international competitiveness because of globalisation.

Which factors explain trends in the employment intensity of growth? Essentially, the level of employment (E) is influenced by Gross Domestic Product (Y), average working hours per employed person (H) and productivity per hour (P). This can be expressed formally as:

$$Y = E \times \frac{VoW^{1)}}{E} \times \frac{Y}{VoW^{1)}} \tag{1}$$

$$Y = E \times H \times P \tag{2}$$

VoW = Volume of Work (total hours)

Employment growth may then be expressed as the result of the growth rate in output, average working hours per employed and productivity per hour:

$$Y_1 = E_1 \times H_1 \times P_1 \tag{3}$$
$$Y_0 = E_0 \times H_0 \times P_0$$

$$\frac{Y_1}{Y_0} = \frac{E_1}{E_0} \times \frac{H_1}{H_0} \times \frac{P_1}{P_0} \tag{4}$$

$$\Delta Y = \Delta E \times \Delta H \times \Delta P \tag{5}$$

$$\lambda n(\Delta Y) = \lambda n(\Delta E) + \lambda n(\Delta H) + \lambda(\Delta P) \tag{6}$$

This conditional equation shows that measures to promote economic growth (ΔY) only result in more employment (ΔE) if they are not simultaneously offset by an increase in labour productivity (ΔP) or the hours of work per employed (ΔH). Since the economic growth that can be anticipated in the foreseeable future can probably only make a modest contribution to solving the employment problems, more employment-intensive growth is the order of the day. The equation offers two options in this respect. One option would be to slow down productivity gains, for example, in the form of a smaller increase or even cuts in the cost of labour. Such a strategy only leads to more employment if economic growth is not negatively affected by this and the number of working hours per employed does not increase (for example, through more overtime). The other option to promote employment-intensive growth is a greater flexibilisation of working hours.

Can greater flexibilisation of working-time schedules (for example, through evening, shift and weekend work) and reductions in the duration of individual work hours (for example, part-time work, annualised hours) effectively mitigate labour market problems? The advantage of working-time flexibilisation for companies is that it permits more intensive utilisation of operating capacities and so reduces unit costs (for example, extension of machine operating hours or service opening hours) of the capital for existing capacities. It also permits greater flexibility in the use of labour to meet fluctuations in production and market demand, hence cutting labour costs (see Smith *et al.*, Chapter 2, and Rubery, Chapter 7, this volume).

As a result of reduced unit capital costs and labour costs to companies, the prices of goods and services could fall. Lower product prices would in turn generate additional demand, which would favourably influence economic growth and thus also the employment situation. Whereas the direction of this effect is undisputed, assessments of its possible magnitude differ. This depends on the extent to which a lack of working hour flexibility actually raises product prices. The picture can be very different depending on the situation in the business cycle situation, the industry or the company size. To obtain reliable information, more company case studies on the cost and benefit of measures taken to flexibilise working hours would be desirable.

From the viewpoint of employment policy, however, the relationship between working hour flexibilisation and hours reduction appears most significant. There are indications that working hour flexibilisation creates considerable potential for reduced working hours. Possibilities for reduction would result from the introduction of alternative shift models with respect to weekly hours (for example, four shifts of nine hours each instead of five shifts of eight hours); from the use of annual working-time models offering opportunities to reduce or even eliminate overtime; and from the extension of plant operating times through the creation of new part-time jobs.

Using the equation above, the effects of possible cuts in working hours in regard to employment (ΔE) would be all the greater,

- the more comprehensive the reduction in working-time (ΔH) is;
- the smaller the induced productivity effects (ΔP) are (for example, due to an increase in unit wage costs, more work compression or rationalisation spending);
- the less economic growth (ΔY) is affected negatively by this (for example, if the skills of the newly hired do not sufficiently meet company needs).

However, job creation due to cuts in working hours would not necessarily mean less unemployment if new working-time arrangements stimulate an increase in the supply of labour. For example, more part-time jobs may be taken by persons looking for work for the first time (for example, young people) or again (for example, women returnees) rather than by the unemployed. This relationship between the number of employed persons (E), the size of the working population (WP) and the size of the labour force (LF) can be expressed formally:

$$E = WP \times \frac{LF}{WP} \times \frac{E}{LF} \tag{1}$$

$$E = WP \times LFPR \times (1{-}UR) \tag{2}$$

Employment (E) equals the size of the working-age population (WP) times the labour force participation rate (LFPR) times one minus the unemployment rate (UR), which indicates the employed part of the labour force (see also Houseman 1995: 95). The identity is also valid for the corresponding growth rates:

$$E_1 = WP_1 \times LFPR_1 \times (1{-}UR_1) \tag{3}$$
$$E_0 = WP_0 \times LFPR_1 \times (1{-}UR_0)$$

$$E_1 = WP_1 \times LFPR_1 \times (1{-}UR_1) \tag{4}$$
$$E_0 = WP_0 \times LFPR_1 \times (1{-}UR_0)$$

$$\Delta E = \Delta WP \times \Delta LFPR \times \Delta(1{-}UR) \tag{5}$$

$$\lambda n(\Delta E) = \lambda n(\Delta WP) + \lambda n(\Delta LFPR) + \lambda n(\Delta(1{-}UR)) \tag{6}$$

The extent to which the unemployed or the inactive flow into employment largely depends on two factors:

- the labour force participation rate ($\Delta LFPR$): if the rate is still low, a greater reservoir of available workers exists than if the activity rate is already relatively high – all other conditions being equal;

101

- the type of newly created jobs (ΔE): the more marginal (short part-time) jobs are created the more suppliers will enter the labour market who otherwise would probably remain outside the labour force (as non-active population).

There are a number of ways to reduce working hours, including shorter daily or weekly hours, or increased leave entitlements such as vacations and sabbaticals. In the European working-time discussion, one topic has been at the top of the hit parade of employment policy options for some time: the promotion of part-time work. This is the focus of the next section.

GROWTH OF PART-TIME EMPLOYMENT

The following analyses are based on aggregate data from European and individual national labour force surveys. Although there are some differences in counting between countries, and the counting methods have partly changed over time, the data used provide a sound and recognised basis for international comparisons.[4] The extent and trend of part-time work differs considerably by country (see Delsen, Chapter 3, this volume). There has been a more or less strong rise in the rate of part-time work in most OECD countries since the 1970s. However, as the trend from 1983 to 1994 documents, declining part-time rates (for example, in the USA and Denmark) cannot be ruled out. The rates of part-time work vary nationally. The Mediterranean countries have low levels of part-time work, Germany and France are examples of middle-rank countries, and a higher rate of part-time work is found in the UK. The Netherlands stand out with over 60 per cent of employed women and more than 15 per cent of employed men working part-time. Moreover, this country recorded by far the highest growth of part-time work in the Western world between 1973 and 1994.

From a qualitative viewpoint, part-time employment is a very heterogeneous form of employment. It is essentially a domain of women, but it encompasses both employment with relatively short weekly working hours ('marginal part-time work') and jobs involving longer average weekly hours, in some cases only slightly below full-time hours. Do marginal or longer part-time hours generate higher rates of part-time work? On this point, the European Labour Force Survey (ELFS) offers two interesting results. First, higher rates of part-time work are associated with lower average part-time hours (see Walwei 1996). This suggests that high levels of part-time work occur mainly through marginal/short hours jobs. For countries with low rates of part-time employment rates, therefore, the question is whether the potential for expanding part-time employment is more likely to be found in the area of part-time work involving only few weekly hours. However, the available survey results on hours preferences appear to contradict this, at least in the Federal Republic of

Germany, since demand is mainly for part-time jobs offering clearly more than half-time work, for example, two-thirds or three-quarter jobs (Kohler and Spitznagel 1995: 350; for discussion of other evidence see Fagan and O'Reilly, Chapter 1, this volume). Second, the ELFS shows the UK has the longest average working week for full-time employees and the shortest weekly working hours for part-time employees. Bell and Freeman (1995) get similar results for the USA. They explain the polarisation as the consequence of deregulated labour markets, which seem to generate marginal part-time jobs alongside long full-time hours. Due to the drop in real wages in the USA in the 1980s, many employees are said to be dependent on long working hours (including over-time). In addition, a deregulated regime favours the spread of precarious employment (for example, jobs with short hours). The polarisation may also occur along gender lines (long hours for men and short hours for women) or skill shortages and human capital usage due to inadequate initial training and inadequate public adult training programmes.

It is of interest to compare not only different levels of part-time work but also the development over time and the reasons behind the dynamics. There are essentially two factors which may explain the growth of part-time employment (Meulders et al. 1994; Delsen 1995): on the one hand, structural shifts, for example, in respect of the sectoral distribution or the gender-specific composition of employment, and, on the other hand, changes in the preferences of the players in the labour market in respect of the choice of part-time work either as a recruiting alternative or an employment alternative. Shift-share analysis can be used to explore whether structural or behavioural aspects are the more important (see Walwei and Werner 1995 on details of method).

We start with an analysis of sectoral structural change. The analysis questions whether the development of part-time employment is due more to sectoral changes in employment between agriculture, manufacturing and services (structural effect) or to the penetration of part-time work into some or all sectors (diffusion effect). Mathematically, the structural effect is calculated by assuming that the part-time rates per sector remain unchanged over time. In contrast, to compute the diffusion effect, the sectoral shares of the reference year are kept constant and multiplied by the current part-time rates. Normally, a small quantity remains which results from combining both effects (so-called inter-action term).

The analysis presented in Figure 5.1 shows that the major driving force behind the rise in the rate of part-time work is the diffusion effect. Independent of sectoral shifts, companies are using part-time work more frequently (but less frequently in Denmark and the USA), indicating a change in attitude among employers and/or unions. Although a positive structural effect can be noted as well, it is relatively minor. The UK is exceptional for its significant structural effect of about one-third, which is due to the strong growth of the part-time intensive service sector and the rapid decline of the predominantly full-time manufacturing sector. A positive structural effect prevented an even stronger

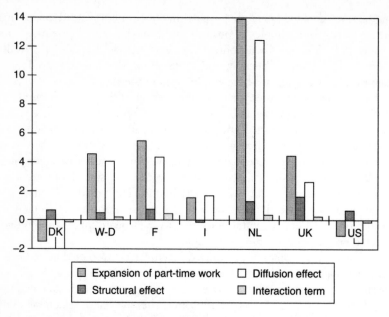

Figure 5.1 Sectoral shifts and the dynamics of part-time work (shift-share analysis), 1983–93

decline in the rate of part-time work in Denmark and the USA (see also Smith *et al.*, Chapter 2, this volume, for complementary results).

Shift-share analyses also help to determine the effect of changes in the gender composition of employment on the increase in rates of part-time employment. The question in this context is whether growth in part-time work results more from changes in the female proportion of the total labour force (structural effect) or more from the changing rates of part-time work for both sexes (diffusion effect). The results of these analyses again indicate that it is the diffusion effect that is mainly responsible for the growth of the part-time rate (Figure 5.2). This means that, even if the female proportion of employment had remained unchanged over time, part-time work would have developed as it did to almost the same extent. Thus, a changing propensity to work part-time explained most of the increase in part-time work in the majority of countries as well as the decline of part-time employment in two countries (Denmark and the USA). For the USA, Williams (1995) found that the decline in the rate of part-time work in the 1980s was essentially due to women moving from part-time to full-time employment, and less frequently from full-time to part-time work (see Williams 1995). Boje (1995) arrives at the same result for the part-time trends in Denmark. Finally, again we see a positive structural effect. The negative structural effect in Denmark is striking. It results from the disproportionate increase of the number of men in the total number of employed persons.

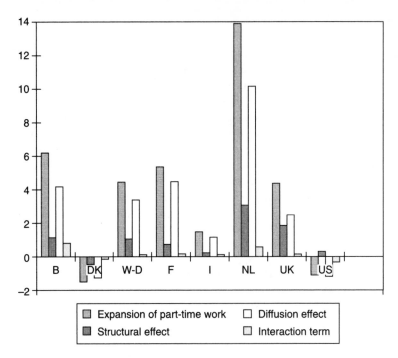

Figure 5.2 Shift in gender-specific characteristics of employment and the dynamics of part-time work (shift-share analysis), 1983–93
Source: OECD (1995a); Eurostat (1985, 1995d)

The above shift-share analyses suggest that part-time employment has developed largely independently of sectoral shifts and changes in gender-specific shares of employment. Thus, even without the increase in jobs in services, and without the increase in women's participation in employment, the trend of part-time employment would have evolved roughly as it did. It is mainly increased rates of part-time work in certain sectors (especially services) and within certain groups of the labour force (especially women) that explain the increased rates of part-time work.

Which factors (employee-related aspects or company-related aspects) are generally promoting the diffusion of part-time work? In Labour Force Surveys the majority of part-time employees state that they choose this form of employment voluntarily (because they do not want full-time work). There may be a permanent or temporary interest in part-time work if full-time work would be incompatible with other activities and responsibilities. This might be family work (for example, child rearing or nursing an older family member), education (for example, university studies or training) or self-employment (for example, for farmers).

Then there are cases in which people opt for part-time work because they cannot find full-time work (see OECD 1995b, pp. 65*ff*.). Involuntary part-time workers as a proportion of employed persons in 1993 occurred most frequently in 1993 in the USA (over 5 per cent), followed by France (4.8 per cent), Denmark (4 per cent) and Belgium (3.7 per cent). In countries where the total part-time rate is still relatively low, for example, in Italy, involuntary part-time work is relatively high: it applies to one-third of all part-timers. Certainly this phenomenon has to be considered in the context of household incomes which are still low in these countries, where to make a living most people must have full-time employment.

During the last decade most of the growth of part-time work is attributable to an increase in voluntary part-time employment. However, subject to certain national conditions (for example, a slack labour market) it can also be caused by growing numbers of involuntary part-time workers (see Walwei and Werner 1996). In most countries (Italy, West Germany, the Netherlands, the UK) the involuntary part-time employment rate underwent only minor changes; in the USA, the total part-time rate and the involuntary part-time employment rate fell almost identically. In three countries, however (Belgium, Denmark and especially France), involuntary part-time employment gained more importance and accounted for a quite significant part of the expansion of part-time work.

With respect to employers' attitudes, comparative international company surveys indicate that part-time work is considered to make the organisation of work more flexible and efficient, enabling labour-use planning to be fine-tuned to suit production requirements (Infratest 1992). Potential direct cost advantages from using part-time work (for example, lower hourly wages or social security payments) are surprisingly rare as an incentive mentioned by companies. The UK is an exception, where lower wage and non-wage costs (statutory and company) are seen as significant advantages. The results for the other countries are nevertheless interesting, because they show that generally putting full-time and part-time employment on an equal footing will not necessarily run counter to the company's interest.

LABOUR MARKET EFFECTS THROUGH THE DYNAMICS OF PART-TIME WORK

Growth in part-time employment can influence both the level of employment and unemployment. However, the question is: To what extent do the dynamics of part-time work actually lead to more employment and less unemployment?

More employment through growth of part-time work?

To assess the possible consequences of part-time work for the labour market, we will first scrutinise the full-time and part-time employment trends in the EU countries between 1983 and 1994. We find both common features and marked differences between countries. We can identify three types of country in Table 5.2. First, there are countries (like France, Italy and the Netherlands) which have experienced a considerable increase in part-time employment during the period under investigation; but the number of full-time jobs have declined. Second, other countries (especially Belgium, Ireland, West Germany and the UK) show at least some increase in full-time jobs in addition to a considerable growth of part-time work. Finally, in a third country type (Denmark, Greece and the USA), employment growth is almost solely supported by the increase in full-time jobs. This comparison shows that an increase in employment does not depend on an expansion of part-time work.

An alternative approach to assess (at least to a certain extent) the effects of more part-time work on employment growth is to decompose employment growth using the equation discussed in the previous section. Table 5.3 shows the results for four countries which are of special interest in this context: two with quite low employment growth between 1973 and 1994 (France and Germany) and two with considerable job creation during that period (the Netherlands and the USA).

With respect to the development of GDP, the European countries show quite similar trends whereas economic growth in the USA has been somewhat higher. Compared to Europe two other developments in the USA indicate even more remarkable differences. First, hourly productivity gains have been significantly lower than in the three European countries. Houseman (1995: 100) argues that the relatively low growth in productivity is closely connected to stagnant real wages in the last two decades. Second, in contrast to the European countries the volume of work has risen in the period under investigation (hours of work per employed multiplied by the total number of employed).[5]

Table 5.2 Employment change according to full-time and part-time employment in selected countries, 1983–94

Countries	Total growth in employment	Growth in full-time employment (as part of total growth in employment)	Growth in part-time employment (as part of total growth in employment)
USA	20.0	17.3	2.7
Belgium	9.7	3.7	6.0
Denmark	5.5	6.9	–1.4
West Germany	8.6	2.3	6.3
Greece	7.9	9.2	–1.3
France	0.0	–5.2	5.2
Ireland	8.0	2.4	5.6
Italy	–2.7	–4.1	1.4
Netherlands	19.9	–2.5	22.4
UK	10.3	3.0	7.3

Sources: Eurostat (1985, 1996); Bureau of Labor Statistics

Table 5.3 Decomposition of GDP growth in selected OECD countries, 1973–94[1]

Components Countries[2]		GDP (ΔY)		Employment (ΔE)		Hours of work per employed person (ΔH)		Productivity per hour (ΔP)
		Indices[2]	ln[3]	Indices[2]	ln[3]	Indices[2]	ln[3]	Indices
France	73–94	154.5	0.43	103.5	0.03	86.3	–0.15	172.9
	73–83	124.9	0.22	103.5	0.03	89.9	–0.11	134.3
	83–94	123.8	0.21	100.0	0.00	96.1	–0.04	128.8
West	73–94	154.1	0.43	105.4	0.05	84.2	–0.17	173.6
Germany	73–83	118.5	0.17	97.0	–0.03	91.6	–0.09	133.3
	83–94	130.1	0.26	108.6	0.08	92.0	–0.08	130.2
Netherlands	73–94	155.2	0.44	124.1	0.22	79.0	–0.24	158.3
	73–83	117.3	0.16	103.5	0.03	88.7	–0.12	128.0
	83–94	132.3	0.28	119.9	0.18	89.2	–0.12	123.7
USA	73–94	165.2	0.50	141.7	0.35	101.1	0.01	115.3
	73–83	119.4	0.18	118.0	0.17	97.8	–0.02	103.4
	83–94	138.3	0.32	120.0	0.18	103.3	0.03	111.5

Sources: OECD *Labour Force Statistics* (different volumes); OECD *National Accounts* (different volumes); *Eurostat (1985)*; Bureau of Labor Statistics
Notes:
1. For the underlying equations see also p. 99
   ($\Delta Y = \Delta E \times \Delta H \times \Delta P$; $\ln(\Delta Y) = \ln(\Delta E) + \ln(\Delta H) + \ln(\Delta P)$).
2. The first year of each period equals 100.
3. The values for ln refer to the indices.

Although developments in employment in the Netherlands are also quite dynamic (especially between 1983 and 1994), the reasons behind these changes are obviously different. There are two components which have driven employment growth (especially in contrast to France and Germany). First, although productivity growth was lower, this did not harm economic growth. Part of the explanation is that a comparatively high share of employees in services may have contributed to a lower increase in productivity. Furthermore, wage moderation (through collective agreements at the sectoral level) has been a key element of Dutch macro economic policy since 1983 (OECD 1996: 48). Second, and even more important, hours of work per employed person fell to the lowest level in the Western world. The considerable growth in part-time employment (which was higher than the growth in total employment) has played an enormous role in this context (see Table 5.2).

To assess the overall employment effects of expanding part-time employment, the potential hourly productivity gains must be taken into account, as must the fact that job-sharing of any kind to a greater or lesser extent involves a higher productivity rate per hour. If the newly created part-time jobs deviate only slightly from full-time jobs then the employment effect for the entire economy will be only minor because of higher productivity. If, on the other hand, the additionally created part-time jobs are much shorter than full-time jobs (as in the Netherlands, for example), creation of a larger number of jobs is to be expected due to the stronger sharing of jobs.

Less unemployment through more part-time employment?

The question of whether job creation through the expansion of part-time employment helps to reduce unemployment has a micro and a macro perspective. As a rule, for employees for whom employment is their main source of income, the major drawbacks are reduced working-time and thus a lower wage compared with full-time employees. One exception is when part-time work is explicitly requested by employees (for example, to reconcile work with other activities and responsibilities). Another is that part-time employment may be assessed more favourably if the alternative is becoming or remaining unemployed. In this case, part-time jobs would have to be considered a 'second-best' solution, forced upon a person for lack of alternatives. However, the advantages of part-time work rather than full-time unemployment are that the individual maintains contact with employment and may gain new job experiences and skills which prevent the devaluation of their human capital. As a rule it should also be easier for them to look for jobs compared to the situation which could possibly arise from long-term unemployment.

Consequently, part-time work should fundamentally be considered as a preferable alternative to unemployment. Of decisive importance in this context is whether part-time employment constitutes a bridge to allow permanent integration into the job market or whether it will trigger an unsteady occupational career. Crucial to the decision about whether to accept an offer of part-time work will be the duration of unemployment (or inactivity) which has already occurred or can be expected. The longer the duration of the current and/or imminent unemployment, the more important contact is with working life. However, it is different when the alternative is between short-term frictional unemployment and part-time employment. Choosing part-time employment too quickly (especially if one were previously employed full-time) could also be interpreted negatively by companies if they perceive part-time workers to be inferior ('stigma').

The assessment of the potential effect of part-time employment on the employment biography thus depends greatly on the circumstances of the particular case. Empirically, it would be important to analyse job mobility patterns over time. Longitudinal data can provide such information. Using the German socio-economic panel, Quack (1993: 217ff.) looked at the extent to which part-time employment can be considered more as a transitional condition or more as a permanent condition, depending on certain demographic characteristics. The study distinguishes four different groups: men, younger single women, single mothers and married women. In the period investigated (1984–8), part-time employment was found to be a transitional stage for men and younger single women, usually followed by full-time employment or continuation of training. The choice of part-time employment following unemployment led to renewed unemployment in only a few cases for these two groups of people. The situation was different for lone and married mothers. Accumulation of marginal and unstable employment occurred particularly for women from households with low per capita income, for those with a relatively low level of skill, and for all lone mothers. People in continuous part-time employment over longer periods, on the other hand, more frequently included women with older children and higher levels of education.

From the macro perspective, there is hardly any connection between national rates of part-time employment and unemployment. In other words, countries with high levels of part-time work are not necessarily those with low unemployment rates. The chief reason for the weak connection is that an increase in employment is always only partly fed by the unemployed. Some of the jobs are taken by a reserve labour force of inactive individuals entering or re-entering employment (see above, p. 101). This is explored in Table 5.4, which indicates the supply-side components which have driven employment growth.

Table 5.4 shows that although there have been significant differences in employment growth in the four countries under survey, all are confronted with a lower rate of employment for the labour force (higher unemployment rate) in 1994 than in 1973. Employment growth in all countries had been mainly fed by the supply of new workers (i.e. changes in the size of the working population). Interestingly, the increase in the working population was not only significantly higher in the USA but also in the Netherlands compared to the situation in France and West Germany. Labour force participation rates remained relatively constant in France and West Germany, increased to some extent in the Netherlands and to a considerable extent in the USA. While the decline in the male labour force participation rate tended to be somewhat less in the USA than in the other countries, the increase in the female labour force participation was much greater (see also Houseman 1995). Finally, the sharp rise in unemployment rates during the 1970s and 1980s in France, West Germany and the Netherlands indicates that employment growth was still too low to compensate for a growing working-age population, an increasing working population and an increasing female labour market participation rate at the same time. But compared to France and West Germany the labour market situation in the Netherlands at least showed some improvements, especially in the latter period (1983–94). This is when the growth in Dutch employment can almost solely be attributed to the 'part-time miracle' (see Table 5.2), when participation rates (especially of women) went up significantly and unemployment rates went down a little (from a high level).

Table 5.4 Decomposition of employment growth in selected OECD countries, 1973–94

Components Countries		Changes in						
		Employment (ΔE)		Working-age population (ΔWP)		Participation rate ($\Delta LFPR$)		Employed as part of labour force ($\Delta(1-UR)$)
		Indices[2]	In[3]	Indices[2]	In[3]	Indices[2]	In[3]	
France	73–94	103.5	0.03	116.6	0.15	98.7	–0.01	89.9
	73–83	103.5	0.03	109.9	0.09	99.9	0.00	94.3
	83–94	100.0	0.00	106.1	0.06	98.8	–0.01	95.4
West Germany	73–94	105.4	0.05	114.1	0.13	99.5	0.00	92.8
	73–83	97.0	–0.03	107.3	0.07	97.2	–0.03	93.1
	83–94	108.6	0.08	106.4	0.06	102.4	0.02	99.7
Netherlands	73–94	124.1	0.22	124.3	0.22	104.8	0.05	95.2
	73–83	103.5	0.03	114.3	0.13	99.5	0.00	90.9
	83–94	119.9	0.18	108.7	0.08	105.3	0.05	104.7
USA	73–94	141.7	0.50	125.2	0.23	115.9	0.15	97.7
	73–83	118.0	0.18	116.0	0.15	107.1	0.07	95.1
	83–94	120.0	0.32	107.9	0.08	108.3	0.08	102.7

Source: OECD *Labour Force Statistics* (different volumes)

Notes:
1 For the underlying equations see also p. 101 ($\Delta E = \Delta WP \times \Delta LFPR \times \Delta (1-UR)$;
   $\lambda n(\Delta E) = \lambda n(\Delta WP) + \lambda n(\Delta LFPR) + \lambda n(\Delta (1-UR))$).
2 The first year of each period equals 100.
3 The values for In refer to the indices.

To sum up, the following mechanism can be expected when the number of part-time jobs in an economy increases. Depending on the availability of workers and the degree of coincidence of their skill profiles with the job requirements, other groups of people are going to take part-time jobs. If, for example, persistent high levels of unemployment have produced a 'sorting process' among the unemployed, these people will be further down the queue than those seeking work again or entering the labour market for the first time. The size of this reserve pool of labour depends on demographic factors and existing participation rates. If, for instance, the female participation rate is still low, a greater reservoir of available workers exists than if the rate is already relatively high – all other conditions being equal. In comparison with the USA, Japan, the UK and the Scandinavian countries, the female participation rates in the other European countries (such as France or West Germany) are usually lower. Thus, in countries with low female participation rates it is likely that an expansion of part-time work will encourage women to enter the labour market and thus do little to reduce recorded levels of unemployment.

CONCLUSIONS

Are part-time jobs really better than no jobs? A simple answer is: it depends. What is certain is that part-time work is growing in most countries and in this sense there is less and less justification for calling it 'non-standard'. However, the shift-share analyses suggest that neither the anticipated change towards a service society, nor the anticipated greater participation of women in the labour force will in itself make part-time employment spread substantially further. The dynamics of part-time employment seem to be determined by behavioural aspects to a much greater extent than structural ones. The 'flexibility in the minds' of the labour market players and the extent to which the interests of the parties in the job market can be fairly balanced will be decisive in the future trends in part-time work. To influence the behaviour of reluctant private companies favourably, moreover, the government as the largest employer could assume a pioneering role in spreading part-time work among its employees.

Although, in principle, a number of more or less disputed approaches actively to further part-time work could be considered (for example, financial incentives for older or younger workers to take up part-time employment) (see O'Reilly 1996), it is more important first to remove existing legal and/or factual discrimination of part-time employment in the law and at the workplace. In addition, to foster the generally recognised principle of 'freedom of choice' for employees, it is important to improve the underlying conditions to reconcile employment and family life (for example, by creating adequate child care facilities or by making part-time child care leave for parents possible). Thus, an important function of the institutional framework for part-time employment would consist in enhancing the conditions for voluntary part-time employ-ment to take place, or at least not impeding it, and in facilitating the transition from part-time to full-time work and back. Greater emphasis on principles such as voluntariness and equal treatment might increase employees' acceptance of part-time work (including men in particular), and in return may also be more acceptable for employers, because better candidates may apply for part-time jobs.

But, as we know, changes in behaviour take time even if the underlying conditions are improved, so that a rapid increase in voluntary part-time employment may appear desirable, but not realistic by any means in countries which still have a low part-time rate. The growth will also be slowed by the fact that when work is to be distributed among more people, qualifications supplied and qualifications demanded rarely coincide (see OECD 1994c: 100). Even if it were economically feasible to divide jobs, the skills of the two – or even more – workers would have to fit the job-share.

There are other reasons why the promotion of part-time work may not be a panacea which substantially reduces unemployment. The expansion of part-time employment, similar to a reduction of full-time weekly hours without higher hourly wages (i.e. to maintain earnings), usually produces productivity gains per worker. If the newly created part-time jobs – as frequently requested by employees or required by operating needs – deviate only slightly from full-time jobs, then, given the productivity effect, employment growth and the effect on relieving unemployment is likely to be small. If, on the other hand, shorter hours part-time jobs are created, more jobs may indeed result, but, as the example of the Netherlands as 'part-time world champion' shows, this mobilises the so-called reserve labour force and only partly reduces recorded unemployment.

NOTES

1 The White Paper of the European Commission on the subject of growth, competitiveness and employment, for example, still assumed the possibility of an average growth rate of 2–3.5 per cent for the gross domestic product of the European Union as a whole through to the end of this millennium (see Europäische Kommission 1993: 52).

2 Employment intensity indicates the percentage by which employment increases (decreases) when economic growth increases (decreases) by 1 per cent. This relationship shows, for example, the extent to which employment is likely to go up during a boom, or how high the growth must be to obtain a certain increase in employment.

3 Table 5.1 confirms this finding. If one compares the threshold levels for GDP growth concerning employment during the two periods 1973–83 and 1983–94 the level is higher for the second period than for the first.

4 Information about part-time employment in labour force surveys is mostly based on the principle of self-assessment, i.e. the interviewees can classify themselves as part-time employees. Due to the many different forms of part-time employment, problems of demarcation and distortion of rates may occur. For instance, full-time jobs lasting less than a year (for example, certain seasonal jobs) are subsumed under 'flexible part-time employment' in the Netherlands (see Bodelier 1994; Walwei 1995). Another (counting) problem concerns the scope of so-called 'marginal' part-time work, i.e. part-time employment for a small number of hours. Both in the Netherlands and in Germany, much ('marginal') part-time employment went unrecorded in 1983 compared to 1993, because these employees did not always classify themselves as gainfully employed. In both countries, corrections to counting methods made during this period explain a significant part (a little more than one-third in each case) of the increase in the number of part-time employees and the part-time employment rate.

5 In Table 5.3 changes in the volume of work can be calculated either by multiplying changes in employment and changes in hours of work per employed person or by adding the corresponding logarithms.

BIBLIOGRAPHY

Bell, L. and Freeman, R. (1995) 'Why Do Americans and Germans Work Different Hours' in F. Buttler, W. Franz, R. Schettkat and D. Soskice (eds) *Institutional Frameworks and Labor Market Performance*, London: New York.

Bodelier, L. (1994) Teilzeitarbeit in den Niederlanden und in Deutschland: Modelle für die Praxis. Einleitung, Arbeitsunterlage für die Fachtagung der Deutschen Gesellschaft für Personalführung (DGFP) am 28.6.1994 in Düsseldorf.

Boje, T. (1995) 'National Report on Denmark' in J. Rubery *et al.* (eds) *Changing Patterns of Work and Working-time in the European Union and the Impact on Gender Divisions.* V/6203/95 – EN, European Commission (DGV), Equal Opportunities Unit.

Delsen, L. (1995) *Atypical Employment: An International Perspective. Causes, Consequences and Policy*, Groningen: Wolters-Noordhoff.

Europäische Kommission (1993) *Wachstum, Wettbewerbsfähigkeit, Beschäftigung*, Brüssels, Luxembourg: Weißbuch.

Eurostat (1985) *European Labour Force Survey*, Results 1983, Luxembourg.

Eurostat (1995a) *Arbeitsorganisation und Arbeitszeit 1983–1992*, Brüssels, Luxembourg.

Eurostat (1995b) Atypische Beschäftigungsformen in der Europäischen Union (1992–1993) Schichtarbeit, Abendarbeit und Nachtarbeit (I), *Statistik Kurzgefasst*, 7/1995.

Eurostat (1995c) Atypische Beschäftigungsformen in der Europäischen Union (1992–1993) Samstags- und Sonntagsarbeit und Arbeit zu Hause (II), *Statistik Kurzgefasst*, 9/1995.

Eurostat (1995d) *European Labour Force Survey*, Results 1993, Luxembourg.

Eurostat (1996) *European Labour Force Survey*, Results 1994, Luxembourg.

Hof, B. (1994) 'Von der Voll- zur Teilzeit. Internationale Erfahrungen und Perspektiven', *iw-trends*, 1.

Hof, B. (1995) 'Gleichgewicht durch andere Verteilung? Arbeitsmarktentwicklung im Systemzusammenhang', *iw-trends*, 3.

Houseman, S. (1995) 'Job Growth and the Quality of Jobs in the US Economy', *Labour* 9: 93–124.

Infratest (1992) *New Forms of Work and Activity. Survey of Experiences at Establishment Level in Eight European Countries*, Munich (mimeo).

Klauder, W. (1990) 'Zur Entwicklung von Produktivität und Beschäftigungsschwelle', *MittAB* 1, S: 86–99.

Kohler, H. and Spitznagel, E. (1995) 'Teilzeitarbeit in der Gesamtwirtschaft und aus der Sicht von Arbeitnehmern und Betrieben in der Bundesrepublik Deutschland', *MittAB* 3: 339–64.

McKinsey (1994) *Teilen und Gewinnen. Das Potential der flexiblen Arbeitszeitverkürzung*, München (mimeo).

Meulders, D., Plasman, O. and Plasman, R. (1994) *Atypical Employment in the EC*, Hants: Dartmouth.

OECD (1994a) *Labour Force Statistics 1972–1992*, Paris.

OECD (1994b) *National Accounts*, Paris.

OECD (1994c) *The OECD Jobs Study, Evidence and Explanations*, Paris.

OECD (1995a) Labour Force Statistics 1973–1993, Paris.

OECD (1995b) *Employment Outlook*, Paris.

OECD (1996) *Economic Surveys*, Netherlands, Paris.

O'Reilly, J. (1996) 'Labour Adjustments through Part-time Work' in G. Schmid, J. O'Reilly and K. Schömann (eds) *International Handbook of Labour Market Policy Evaluation*, Cheltenham: Edward Elgar.

Quack, Sigrid (1993) *Dynamik der Teilzeitarbeit – Implikationen für die soziale Sicherung von Frauen*, Berlin: Sigma.

Walwei, U. (1995) 'Lehre aus dem niederländischen Beschäftigungswunder': in den Köpfen muß sich etwas ändern', *Randstadkorrespondenz* 25, 3: 2–3.

Walwei, U. (1996) 'Mehr Teilzeitbeschäftigung durch flexiblere Arbeitszeitarrangements – Eine Analyse auf der Basis eines InternationalenVergleichs', in D. Sadowski and K. Pull, Vorschläge jenseits der Lohnpolitik. Optionen für mehr Beschäftigung, Frankfurt/New York: Campus.

Walwei, U. and Werner, H. (1995) 'Entwicklung der Teilzeitbeschäftigung im internationalen Vergleich. Ursachen, Arbeitsmarkteffekte und Konsequenzen', *MittAB* 3: 365–82.

Walwei, U. and Werner, H. (1996) 'More Part-time Work as a Cure for Unemployment? Results of an International Comparison', *IAB Labour Market Research Topics* 16.

Williams, D. (1995) 'Women's Part-time Employment: A Gross Flows Analysis', *Monthly Labor Review* 118, 4: 36–44.

6

ARE BENEFITS A DISINCENTIVE TO WORK PART-TIME?

Marco Doudeijns[1]

INTRODUCTION

Although a combination of factors is responsible for the striking growth in part-time employment in recent years, one potentially important factor – changes in the tax and benefit system – has been barely studied to date. A new international database compiled by the OECD on a wide range of benefits and their interactions with the tax system enables us to study this issue in more depth. To date, most part-time jobs have been taken by married or cohabiting women. Thus, the traditional male breadwinner/female carer stereotype that was assumed to be the dominant division of work and family responsibilities is increasingly giving way to dual-earner/dual-carer households (OECD 1994c; Fagan and Rubery 1996).[2] In the latter households part-time work is often sought as a means of combining paid work with care responsibilities. But some people work part-time involuntarily, because they cannot find a full-time job. Employers, on the other hand, can be keen to use part-time work to add flexibility to their workforce, for example, to extend opening hours or to meet peak-hour labour demand (Delsen 1995). There are also financial incentives for employers to use part-time labour to reduce wage costs, such as lower social security contributions or minimum wage exemptions (see Rubery, Chapter 7, this volume). Therefore, two or three part-timers may be cheaper than one full-time employee doing the same amount of work.[3]

The tax and benefit system has an impact on the decision to work part-time for two main reasons. First, there is little financial incentive for someone with an unemployed partner to work part-time. Figure 6.1 illustrates this point using Dutch data.[4] The partner of an employed person can realise increases in net household income over nearly the whole range of earnings from part-time work, whereas the partner of an unemployed person can increase net household income only if their part-time earnings exceed about 70 per cent of the full-time average earnings level. Part-time jobs often do not pay more than the

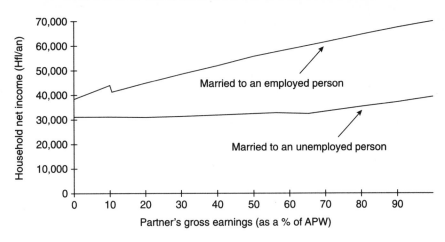

Figure 6.1 Net household incomes when the inactive partner works part-time in the Netherlands
Note: APW = Average Production Worker earnings.

benefit level once income tax, social security contributions and work-related costs are taken into account. The disincentive to take a part-time job increases drastically when the initial unemployment benefit is exhausted and the household has to rely upon assistance-type benefits.

The second influence of the tax and benefit system is that part-time workers can be 'trapped' in their job for three reasons. First, employers are exempted in some countries from paying social security contributions for employees on low wages or in part-time jobs with few hours worked. This creates a strong incentive for employers to offer part-time jobs with only a small number of hours. Second, in some countries benefit entitlements end when the recipient spends more than two or three days in paid employment. Moreover, high clawback rates cause so-called 'poverty traps' that beneficiaries can only exit at high earnings levels. Third, in an attempt to alleviate these problems, some countries have introduced 'in-work benefits' conditional on the number of hours worked. These benefits, however, give rise themselves to poverty traps since they have to be withdrawn at a certain rate once the worker achieves a certain income level.

This aspect of the determinants of part-time work has received little attention in the literature. This chapter aims to help fill this gap. First, potential disincentives arising from the interactions of the tax and benefit systems will be explained and classified. Family level simulation results, based on the *OECD Database on Taxes, Benefits and Incentives* will be used to illustrate, for a number of OECD countries, the extent to which benefit systems alter incentives to take a part-time job. Recent reform proposals will be described and briefly discussed. In the concluding section policy recommendations are outlined.

117

THE FOUR MAIN ELEMENTS IN THE TAX
AND BENEFIT SYSTEM

The ways in which the tax and benefit system traps people in unemployment or poverty through high net replacement rates or high clawback rates are not simply the sum of all separate effects. A micro simulation model is needed to work out the exact effects, which is the route taken later in this chapter. First, however, it is important to outline the four main elements of the tax and benefit system.[5]

Income tax and social security contributions

Disincentives from income and social security taxes occur in three ways. Where a couple's earnings are jointly assessed for tax purposes, taxation of the second earner starts at the last marginal tax rate faced by the higher-earning partner. This means that the second earner in a couple may be taxed at a higher marginal rate than other taxpayers with equivalent earnings. Even when earnings are taxed individually the existence of a dependent partner's allowance may create disincentives for the second earner to enter employment if their partner loses this tax relief as a result. Finally, if social security contributions are only payable above a certain hours or earnings threshold, this can influence the decision to work part-time.

Unemployment benefits

Unemployment Insurance (UI) benefits are paid to unemployed workers who are insured against unemployment and who fulfil certain eligibility conditions. The *benefit unit and the resource unit* of UI are the insured individual: benefit entitlements are not influenced by the other partner's income from work. If the beneficiary him- or herself starts working, however, the benefit is withdrawn. The system of benefit withdrawal may mean that there is little or no financial gain from a part-time wage, thus reducing work incentives.

In some countries, a dependent partner qualifies the UI-beneficiary for a supplement. The subsequent withdrawal of this supplement can form a barrier, discouraging the inactive partner to work part-time. Part-time earnings would have to exceed the dependant's allowance, income and social security taxes plus the value of income tested benefits in order to produce a net financial gain to the household. These supplements and the way in which they are withdrawn create discontinuities in the incentive structure facing each household member.

Assistance and other welfare benefits

Unemployment Assistance (UA) benefits are paid to people who do not qualify for UI benefits or who have exhausted their entitlements, or as first-time benefits where UI-schemes do not exist, as in Australia and New Zealand. Because the resource unit is the household (even if the benefit unit is the individual as in Austria and the Netherlands), receipt of UA affects the incentive structure facing the partner.

The resource unit may in some cases exceed the benefit unit (for example, all household members' resources as well as those of family members of the first or second generation can be important in the assessment). The source of this income, wages or benefits, or from which spouse, is not relevant. Housing benefits are paid to support families with low income and high rents. They can form a substantial part of household income and are income tested. As a consequence, they are an important source of disincentives. Households with incomes below a certain predefined standard of need qualify for Social Assistance (SA) benefits. In many countries, SA serves as an income floor and the standard of need is determined around the minimum subsistence level. Typically, SA benefits have high clawback rates using net household incomes. On the other hand, so-called 'income disregards' in the income testing of welfare benefits have the effect of delaying the income test until the beneficiary's earnings exceed the amount of the disregard. Effectively what this means is a higher payment for people in paid employment; it acts as an incentive to start work. It does not, however, create reductions in high marginal tax rates for people already working.

So-called 'passport benefits' such as free school meals, free dental care, reduced public transport fares, free library services, and so on, can be linked to SA and cease once entitlements to SA no longer exist. The presence of these 'passport benefits' creates a 'notch' where real net income drops significantly. Once the household earnings exceed the standard of need entitlements to SA stop, and so do the benefits associated with it. A similar situation can exist in countries where supplements to SA exist, aiming to cover housing costs.

The lack of child care benefits, and especially the lack of child care opportunities, is a major disincentive to start work. In the countries that do have child care benefits, or benefits implicit in reduced day care-centre fees, a clawback rate can have an impact on the disincentives of people already receiving such a benefit. This is, for example, the case for people to whom working more hours would mean receiving less benefit or paying higher day care-centre fees.

Employment-conditional benefits

The so-called 'in-work benefits' are only available to people who take up paid employment. Alternatively, countries may have employment-conditional provisions in the income tax schedule: allowances for work-related expenses. The difference between these allowances and in-work benefits is that they are a recognition of the cost involved to work and are not designed in an explicit attempt to reduce disincentives to take up paid employment. In-work benefits can make part-time work very attractive compared with full-time work if they are paid conditional on a certain number of hours spent in paid employment and are subsequently withdrawn when earnings increase. Workers could be inclined to reduce their hours worked (or keep them at a part-time level) to maximise their entitlement (see, for example, Duncan and Giles 1996). High clawback rates that come into play with longer hours ensure the net income loss is very small relative to the gain in leisure time.

HOW BIG ARE THE DISINCENTIVES?

The OECD database on taxes and benefits

The OECD Jobs Study (OECD 1994a) identified the tax and benefit system in OECD countries as one of the causes of labour market problems. The research on this subject for the *Jobs Study* and its follow-up has relied heavily on simulation of the benefits received by a hypothetical unemployed person in OECD countries. The *OECD Database on Taxes, Benefits and Incentives* contains data on unemployment and related benefits, housing, family and child care benefits, income and social security taxes and employment-conditional benefits for OECD countries. Net income can be estimated for a wide range of family types in different employment situations and at any point on the earnings distribution (see Martin 1996a). These possibilities have been exploited for the purpose of this chapter, taking for granted the obvious restrictions and limitations of such an approach. (For a full description of this database, see OECD 1997a).

The hypothetical cases considered in this chapter

The purpose of the calculations carried out for this chapter is to illustrate the contribution the different elements of net income make to the immediate financial incentives to work part-time. In order to simplify the presentation, all calculations are based on the case of a married couple with two children under 13 years of age. The contribution of each benefit or tax credit will be similar, though not identical, if other family types are considered. When in full-time employment, the family is assumed to have earnings at the level of the Average Production Worker (APW) (for an explanation of the APW concept, see OECD 1995a). Part-time hourly earnings are at the same hourly wage level as the APW.[6] The unemployment beneficiary is assumed to be 40 years old and to have a 22-year unbroken employment record with earnings in previous employment at the APW level. The other partner is assumed to have never worked and to have no benefit entitlements. Capital income and house ownership are ignored and the family is assumed to rent a house in the private sector with a rent equal to 20 per cent of the APW earnings in that country. It is further assumed that part-time working claimants continue to look for full-time work and continue to qualify for benefit receipt.

Disincentives for partners in work

The first three simulations will seek to answer the following questions:

1   What are the disincentives for an inactive person in a couple to work part-time *given* the employment status of the other partner?
2   How do the part-time employed partner's incentives *change* if the employment status of the other partner changes?

In order to answer these questions, the simulations seek to show how much of the part-time income is retained after payment of income and social security taxes and the withdrawal of income tested benefits. In other words, the analysis in this section aims to illustrate what it is 'worth' to the household if one member takes a part-time job. Formally, this net gain from part-time work is defined as: *100 per cent* * *increase in net household income / gross part-time earnings.*

The results of the first three simulations are shown in Table 6.1: the net gain from working part-time are listed in Panel A for individuals working part-time with an employed partner (simulation one); in Panel B for individuals with an unemployed partner in the first month of unemployment (simulation two); and in Panel C for individuals with an unemployed partner in the sixtieth month of unemployment (simulation three). The family is assumed to receive SA benefits if entitlements exist in Panel C, but SA benefits are not included in the calculations for Panel A and Panel B. Each panel is divided into four columns indicating the number of hours worked in the part-time job.

Simulation one: the normal entry route to part-time work – persons with an employed partner (Table 6.1, Panel A).

In the absence of welfare benefits, disincentives can only be caused by income tax and social security contribution schedules. Consequently, the net gain from part-time work is high in most columns of Panel A in Table 6.1. The exception is Denmark, where means-tested *housing benefits* are still payable if household earnings reach the APW level.

The loss of the *dependent-partner income tax allowance* can play a decisive role for part-time jobs involving few hours. The net gain from part-time work tends to be small for such jobs. This is the case in Denmark and the United States (where the allowance has the form of a dependent-care tax credit). In the Netherlands, where the allowance is withdrawn completely and the partner's income becomes taxable after exactly 4 hours in work, a remarkable picture emerges. Net household income increases more than the part-time earnings if the inactive partner starts to work 4 hours per week due to a 'compensation allowance' paid by the employer to cover social security contributions. Once earnings rise, the partner allowance is lost and part-time earnings become liable to income tax (contributions that must be paid by the employee and social security following a tax reform in 1990). In Switzerland, the dependent allowance comes into play once the partner works 9 hours (at average wages).

Table 6.1 Disincentives for working partners: what percentage of part-time earnings can be retained?

Hours/week	Panel A Partner employed				Panel B Partner unemployed: initial benefits				Panel C Partner unemployed: 60th month benefits			
	4	8	16	20	4	8	16	20	4	8	16	20
Australia	100	100	89	87	63	43	42	36	63	43	42	36
Austria	84	73	78	79	40	48	65	69	0	0	0	0
Canada	69	68	66	66	74	77	75	74	97	91	59	51
Denmark	31	37	42	43	38	39	37	36	−3	−2	−2	−2
Finland	66	56	64	64	66	56	53	56	77	46	30	27
France	65	63	58	57	76	69	62	60	45	41	38	37
Germany	59	58	52	53	23	42	51	57	39	50	48	45
Ireland	89	74	70	69	10	49	72	77	0	0	47	56
Japan	87	89	86	86	87	89	89	89	37	27	19	16
Luxembourg	88	88	88	87	88	88	88	88	88	73	34	26
Netherlands	104	64	65	66	71	59	54	55	0	−1	3	4
New Zealand	65	85	76	76	54	36	27	25	54	36	27	25
Norway	64	64	60	58	67	66	65	65	0	0	28	35
Portugal	89	89	85	84	89	89	89	89	89	89	89	89
Sweden	63	56	63	66	63	56	53	58	0	0	0	0
Switzerland	92	90	88	88	89	89	88	88	0	0	0	0
United Kingdom	49	42	58	60	100	100	93	75	74	37	60	49
United States	38	64	76	78	122	121	114	105	173	146	77	61

Source: OECD Database on Taxes and Benefits
Notes: Earnings are at APW level full-time equivalents.
The working partner does not have any benefit entitlements.

Countries with a *joint taxation* regime (France, Germany, Ireland, Luxembourg, Portugal and Switzerland) do not *per se* stand out because of a low net gain from part-time work. As tax schedules differ between countries, relative differences are more interesting for the question of whether disincentives would be less severe if taxation were individualised. Ideally, calculations for a single person working part-time and not receiving any means tested benefits would serve to illustrate this point. Such calculations are not shown in Table 6.1, but Panel B comes close to this case. UI benefits are individual benefits and as such are not subject to any means testing using the partner's income (with the exceptions of Australia, Austria, Luxembourg and New Zealand). As it turns out, in those countries with a joint taxation regime, the net gain from part-time work is higher in Panel B than in Panel A. This reflects that in Panel B the part-time income is liable to low-bracket income taxes.

Denmark is the only country where, over the whole range, more than 50 per cent of part-time earnings are lost via taxes and income tests. The net gain from part-time work is low, mainly due to the withdrawal of housing benefits. Germany tends to approach a similar situation in many cases.

Simulation two: working part-time with a recently unemployed partner (Table 6.1, Panel B).

We have already noted that those countries with *joint taxation* regimes show a higher net gain from part-time work for people with an unemployed partner (Panel B) compared to those with an employed partner (Panel A). The lower number in the 20 hours column for Germany in Panel A compared with Panel B is due to the reduction of child benefit. In the United Kingdom, *social security contributions* become payable once the partner works more than 8 hours per week. Income taxes become payable once earnings exceed a certain threshold, which is reached when around 13 hours per week are worked. This is also reflected in Table 6.1.

As UI *benefits* are individual benefits, their amounts are not influenced by a working partner's income. The sole exceptions to this rule are Australia and New Zealand, where the net gain from part-time work is noticeably small in the last three columns of Panel B. In Luxembourg, the partner's earnings also give rise to a clawback on the other partner's UI benefit, but only if the earnings exceed 250 per cent of the minimum wage so that part-time workers on average wages are not affected. In Austria, Belgium, Germany and Ireland, the loss of dependants' allowances in the UI benefits, once the partner starts working part-time, results in small net gains from part-time jobs with only a few hours worked. Clawback rates on welfare benefits add to disincentives for part-time work in other countries (for example, *housing benefits* in Australia, Denmark, Germany, Finland, the Netherlands, New Zealand, Sweden and the United Kingdom and *family benefits* in Australia, Ireland and New Zealand). The clawback rates on *housing and council tax benefits* in the United Kingdom start being effective from 16 hours' work per week, which is translated in a low net gain in the 20 hours column.

The United States and Canada have 'in-work benefits' that are phased in over a range of earnings. The effects of this on work incentives are clearly illustrated by the higher net gain from part-time work in Panel B than in Panel A. In the United States, where earned income tax credit (EITC) is not phased out until the partner works more than 16 hours, net income increases faster than gross earnings because the refundable credit exceeds the value of income and social security taxes liable. Family Credit in the United Kingdom, which is paid from the moment the partner works 16 hours, keeps the gain from part-time work at a high level. In Japan, the 'Earned Income Tax Allowance', which increases in value (in this case) once the partner works more than around 16 hours, causes the net gain from part-time work in columns '16' and '20' to be higher in Panel A than in Panel B.

In Panel B well over 50 per cent of part-time earnings flow away in income and social security taxes and income tests in Australia, Denmark and New Zealand for part-time working partners of UI-beneficiaries. In Australia and New Zealand this is due to the fact that the partner's income is taken into account in the income test of the unemployment benefit; in Denmark, it is mainly due to housing benefits. In Germany and Ireland, severe disincentives for part-time jobs with just a few hours worked are mainly due to the loss of partner allowances, but this disincentive is less severe for 'longer' part-time jobs.

Simulation three: working part-time with a long-term unemployed partner (Table 6.1, Panel C).[8]

The effects of the *tax system* on the partner's decision to work part-time are the same as in Panel B, when the other partner receives initial unemployment benefits. A minor difference in countries with *joint tax schedules* can arise from the fact that, if those benefits are taxable, these must be added to taxable income. The disincentive structure in Portugal reflects the tax schedule as in Panel A, because neither UA nor SA benefits are payable.[9]

The income test on *long-term unemployment benefits* is similar to that on initial unemployment benefits in Australia and New Zealand; the disincentive structure for both countries is the same in Panel B and Panel C. In Finland, SA is only payable as a benefit of 'last resort'; 'topping-up' does not frequently happen. For that reason SA is excluded and the disincentive structure is that of a partner of a UA beneficiary.[10] The resource unit of UA *benefits* in other countries is the household. Due to a disregard, the UA income test in Finland and the United Kingdom starts when the partner works just over 3 hours (for an average wage). This causes the sharp drop in net gain from a 4- to an 8-hour job. In Belgium, UI benefits for a family with dependent children are paid indefinitely, which causes the disincentive structure to be as in Panel B. An additional factor in the Belgian incentive structure, however, is the SA income test. If earnings exceed a certain threshold value, the SA payment is reduced. There are four stages on the earnings range at which SA payments are reduced. This causes discontinuities in the incentive structure facing each household member. In Germany, UA benefit is paid indefinitely. It is more generous than SA, so this benefit is not received. UA benefits in Germany are means tested disregarding the spouse's theoretical UA benefit plus 53 per cent of her or his earned income. In spite of this generous disregard, clawback rates on related benefits cause the net gain from part-time work to be below 50 per cent.

The UA income test is dominated in most countries by the *SA income test.* SA benefits are subject to a one-to-one income test using household income in a number of countries. This frustrates any attempt by either partner to increase household income by working part-time as earnings are not enough to exceed the SA payment rate. Austria, Denmark, France, the Netherlands, Sweden and Switzerland are examples where the net gain from part-time work is zero: part-time work does not pay at all in these countries (it may even reduce net household income in the case of Denmark). The same happens in Ireland and Norway for part-time jobs with few hours worked.

Earnings disregards in SA play an important role in reducing disincentives. Canada, France, Japan and the United States disregard 12–22 per cent of earned income. Clawback rates of less than 100 per cent in Canada (75 per cent), France (50 per cent) and Japan (51–77 per cent) moderate disincentives for the members of households on SA benefit even further.

In Canada and the United States, *in-work benefits* cause net gains above 100 per cent; net incomes increase faster than gross part-time earnings. The high value for the United States in the first column of Panel C (173 per cent) is entirely caused by EITC, which turns out to be (net of income taxes) equal to 25 per cent of the gross earned income. Family Credit in the United Kingdom comes into play when 16 hours or more are worked; it prevents a drop in net income when 16 hours or more are worked and when SA payments cease.

DO INCENTIVES TO STAY IN PART-TIME WORK DISAPPEAR IF ONE PARTNER BECOMES UNEMPLOYED?

Table 6.1 illustrates whether or not the incentives for a person to stay in part-time work are modified if their partner moves from employment into unemployment. This is possible by comparing columns with the same hours headings ('4', '8', '16' or '20') across the panels. As the *net gain from part-time work* indicates how much the part-time effort of the partner is 'worth' in terms of extra net income, comparisons can be made using the rule: the lower the number, the lower the (financial) value of part-time work. Hence, suppose the net gain from part-time work in the first column of Panel B is lower than in the first column of Panel A. The part-time working partner, in this case, retains less of his or her earnings when his or her partner is unemployed than when she or he is employed, so incentives to stay in part-time work are reduced. To illustrate this, take the example of Germany. Someone working 4 (8) hours per week with a full-time employed partner may retain 59 per cent (58 per cent) of his or her earnings, but only 23 per cent (42 per cent) if the partner becomes unemployed.

In principle the reasons for the change in disincentives can come from two sources: (1) the value of part-time work for people with an employed partner and (2) the value of a similar part-time job for people with an unemployed partner. For example, compare the loss of the Dependent Care Credit in the United States when a woman who is married to an employed man starts working a few hours in a part-time job with the large financial gain from a similar job for a woman married to an unemployed man. Incentives to work only a few hours per week increase when the partner loses his or her job.

As one would expect, countries with a joint income tax schedule show a slight improvement in incentives for the working partner as the latter is no longer included in high tax brackets. The difference is small, however. The general picture is that incentives to work part-time increase slightly for most countries in the case where the principal earner loses his or her job. The value of part-time work decreases in all 'hours' columns for Australia, while in Austria and Germany incentives to keep the part-time job only decrease for small part-time jobs, but not for 'longer' jobs; the situation in Finland is the reverse. In those countries where 'in-work' benefits exist (Canada, the United States), incentives to maintain 'small' part-time jobs increase if one partner becomes unemployed, but not for 'longer' part-time jobs. In the United Kingdom, Family Credit is paid once the partner works 16 hours per week and ensures the gain from part-time work remains at a high level also when social security payments are due (in this case, once more than 8 hours per week are worked).

Once the unemployed partner has exhausted his or her benefit (Panel C), the incentives to stay in part-time employment are destroyed in most countries. The general picture is that incentives are distorted in more countries when the number of hours worked increases. In Canada, the disregard in the SA income test has the effect of increasing incentives for the partner to work part-time when the partner has exhausted UI entitlements. Similar effects are present in Germany, Finland and the United States. The only country where part-time work is always an attractive option is Portugal, but this reflects the fact that benefits are minimum or absent (see Ruivo et al., Chapter 10, this volume).

Disincentives for unemployed people with benefit entitlements of their own

In Table 6.1 and in the above sections, the focus was on part-time work by the partner of an employed or unemployed person. In this section, the focus is on the transition into part-time work for an unemployed person in receipt of initial unemployment benefits and with an inactive partner. This situation is the focus of most policy debates and it is implicitly about increasing incentives for unemployed men to work part-time.

Table 6.2 shows the indexed net incomes for an unemployed person with a dependent and inactive partner. The indices are constructed such that the unemployment benefit income equals 100. The assumptions are otherwise as for Table 6.1. Table 6.2 is divided in two panels: Panel A lists net incomes excluding child benefits, housing benefits and rent assistance; Panel B shows the same case including child benefits, housing benefits and rent assistance. Each column shows the relative increase or decrease in net income when the unemployment beneficiary starts working the number of hours indicated in the headings. Once the person exhausts his or her initial benefits, a case already included in Table 6.1, it would not make any difference which of the partners would start working. This is due to the fact that the resource unit of assistance benefits is no longer the individual, but the household.

For the withdrawal of UI benefits, most countries apply an 'availability-test'. The benefit is paid only for those days the beneficiary is available for full-time work, based on a five-day working week. The resulting benefit withdrawal translates into little reward for part-time work. In Australia, New Zealand and the United States, different withdrawal methods are used (see p. 123–4), resulting in lower part-time work disincentives. There is an earnings disregard in Canada, which makes part-time work pay in spite of the one-for-one claw-back. The stepwise withdrawal of UI in Ireland in four stages causes a strange pattern in net income when hours worked increase. The reduction in benefit results in a drop in income at each stage. The clawback rates which arise because of housing benefits mean that net incomes show little, if any, gain from a part-time job. The same arguments apply to family benefits in Australia, Ireland and New Zealand. Those are a few cases in Table 6.2 of the complete withdrawal of benefits if only a very small amount is earned. Due to the loss of the UI benefit, there is an absolute drop in net income in Austria once earnings exceed Sch3,500 per month (14 per cent of APW). In Germany, the beneficiary loses his or her entitlements to UI benefit once he or she works more than 18 hours. The same happens in Luxembourg once the UI beneficiary spends more than two days in paid employment per week. Portugal does not allow more than a day in paid employment before UI entitlements are withdrawn.

Panel B clearly shows that over the hours range included, the reward for 'small' part-time jobs is greatest in Australia, New Zealand and the United States. The part-time work disincentives are low in the first two countries because of the moderate income test of UA benefits. The positive effects of the in-work benefit (EITC) are visible in the United States. The income test of SA benefits is the cause of the difficulty in increasing the household income through part-time work in the other countries (apart from Portugal). The lack of an earnings disregard is clear in Austria, Ireland, the Netherlands and the United Kingdom.[11] In the Netherlands, the housing benefit income test causes net incomes to fall if the beneficiary earns less than two-fifths of the APW wage.

Table 6.2 Increases in net income by working part-time in the first month of unemployment benefit receipt for the beneficiary in a one-earner couple

Hours worked/week	Panel A: Without housing benefits				Panel B: With housing benefits			
	4	8	16	20	4	8	16	20
Australia	113	118	128	132	109	112	119	121
Austria	119	133	75	94	100	100	100	100
Canada	113	119	119	119	105	108	113	116
Denmark	103	117	116	121	103	105	111	113
Finland	102	103	106	107	101	101	111	113
France	107	115	129	137	102	104	109	113
Germany	118	127	117	96	109	105	106	90
Ireland	75	78	101	127	100	100	60	73
Japan	114	128	156	168	106	109	113	114
Luxembourg	112	122	141	62	103	103	102	101
Netherlands	104	110	122	128	99	98	104	106
New Zealand	121	128	137	142	110	113	120	123
Norway	105	110	120	125	104	108	115	118
Portugal	114	27	55	68	113	33	58	71
Sweden	102	105	109	111	101	102	105	106
Switzerland	104	108	117	121	102	105	109	111
United Kingdom	125	143	174	189	100	100	108	125
United States	108	116	127	134	117	132	155	157

Source: OECD Database on Taxes and Benefits
Note: Waiting periods are ignored.

HOW DO DISINCENTIVES AFFECT THE LEVEL AND COMPOSITION OF PART-TIME WORK?

Financial incentives do matter; evidence can be found in various sources on both the micro level (Atkinson and Morgensen 1993; Eissa and Liebman 1995; OECD 1996a; Schmid and Reissert 1996) and macro level (Layard and Jackman 1991; OECD 1994b, 1996a; Jehoel-Gijsbers et al. 1995; ILO 1996). The evidence focuses mainly on incentive effects on the supply of full-time work, or more specifically, on the incentives to enter full-time work from 'full-time' unemployment, but extend to part-time work (see, for example, Blundell 1993).

There has been little empirical research on the effects of incentives on part-time labour supply, its level and its composition. Perhaps one of the reasons for this is the complexity of issues at play. The gender-specific nature of part-time work (OECD 1994c; Hakim 1996) plays a role, as well as the question of insurability. If fewer than a certain number of hours are worked or earnings do not exceed a certain amount, the part-time worker is excluded from social insurance schemes (OECD 1997a, 1997b), which can increase net incomes but may lead to poverty in the longer term (see e.g. Blundell 1993). The effects of the tax and benefit system on incentives to work part-time also depend on the starting situation of part-time workers. It is possible to distinguish four different transitions to part-time work: part-time workers can come from a situation of inactivity (for example, dependent spouses or students); from a situation of unemployment (for example, receiving benefits); from another part-time job (for example, increasing the work effort in terms of hours per week); or from a full-time job (for example, transition to part-time work for family reasons or during reduced working hours). Part-time workers receiving a UI benefit form a particular case. Benefit entitlement requires active job search and availability for full-time work if the benefit is based on full-time work. Evidence from Belgium, Norway and the Netherlands indicates a change in behaviour of benefit recipients to ensure continuation of benefits (Jehoel-Gijsbers et al. 1995). In Belgium, part-time working beneficiaries (40 per cent of all beneficiaries) are difficult to persuade to take full-time jobs (i.e. to accept the loss of benefit entitlements) (OECD 1994b: 199). One would expect similar situations in countries where incentives to take a job paying less than the unemployment benefit are totally lacking because beneficiaries can refuse such offers without fear of sanctions (for example, Luxembourg and the Netherlands), as well as in countries where large numbers of beneficiaries are working part-time (for example, in Australia 15 per cent of all beneficiaries are working part-time, but this includes a number of people whose hours of work have been reduced (MISEP 1995)).[12]

A very global idea of the importance of disincentives for unemployment beneficiaries can be obtained by comparing disincentives to work part-time and the incidence of part-time work. The correlation coefficients between the incidence of part-time work (OECD 1996c) and disincentives (Table 6.2, Panels A and B) are positive. [13] This means that in countries where the disincentives to work part-time are high, the incidence of part-time work tends to be low (and vice versa). This might suggest that incentive structures have an actual impact on part-time work decisions; it might also indicate that more and more people have to negotiate poverty traps in countries where the incidence of part-time work is increasing.

The importance of disincentives in the tax and benefit system for couples is illustrated by two observations: women's contribution to household income is low; and women strongly dominate the part-time labour market (OECD 1994c; Hakim 1996). Yet very little research on disincentives from the taxes and benefit system for this group has been done to date.[14] The work done by Gregg and Wadsworth (1996) is therefore very interesting, as it assesses changes in employment at the household level. They demonstrate a simultaneous rise in workless and fully employed households at the expense of households where only one partner is working, using information on the number of two-adult households with one, two or no partner in work. They call this phenomenon *employment polarisation*.

Table 6.3 uses the employment polarisation data for two-adult households (Gregg and Wadsworth 1996, Table 6.2) to explore whether national differences in the extent of polarisation are related to differences in the disincentives structure for part-time work presented in Table 6.1.[15] Thus, Table 6.3 has three columns, referring to Panels A, B and C in Table 6.1.[16] The rows refer to the polarisation data; for example, row one refers to the number of households without any person in paid employment. Each cell contains the correlation coefficient between the data in Table 6.1 and the polarisation data (from Gregg and Wadsworth 1996, Table 6.2). The definitions of employment polarisation reflect the notion that the share of workless households increases at the expense of the number of households with one partner or both in work.

An indication of a possible contribution of disincentives to work part-time to the decline of the number of working households can be obtained from Table 6.3. For example, disincentives to work part-time can lead to the giving up of part-time work in previously two-earner couples. Such a mechanism will contribute to employment polarisation. Strong positive correlations exist between the number of households with no partner in work (first row) and disincentives to work part-time for someone with an unemployed partner.

Table 6.3 Correlations between the disincentives to take a part-time job and the polarisation of employment, the working partner case (see Table 6.1)

	Panel A	Panel B	Panel C
No. of households with no partner in work	0.292	0.661	0.543
No. of households with one partner in work	0.232	0.455	0.545
No. of households with both partners in work	−0.291	−0.602	−0.648

Negative correlations exist between number of households where both partners work (last row) and disincentives to work part-time. Table 6.3 appears to indicate that in countries with low disincentives to work part-time, the number of two-earner households is high. The number of households without any partner in work is higher in countries where disincentives to work part-time are high.

The initial analysis is very general, however, and detailed analysis of the relation between part-time disincentives and the level and composition of part-time work have not been made as yet. Detailed analysis on household level data is needed to draw conclusions, hence a direction for further research.

CONCLUSIONS

This chapter aims to fill the gap in the discussion on work disincentives around the issue of part-time employment. The root of the disincentive problem is the difficult transition from benefit dependency to the labour market. This is reflected in high effective marginal tax rates, which create so-called 'poverty traps', and high net replacement rates, which create so-called 'unemployment traps'. This chapter illustrates how taxes and benefits alter incentives to work part-time. Correlations suggest that incentive structures may have an actual impact on part-time work decisions. In countries where the disincentives to work part-time are high, the incidence of part-time work tends to be low (and vice versa). In countries with low disincentives to work part-time, the number of two-earner households is high. The number of households without any partner in work is higher in countries where disincentives to work part-time are high. Detailed analysis on household level data is needed to draw conclusions, hence a direction for further research.

Recent policy changes have focused on the disincentives for recipients of initial unemployment benefits. Some countries are looking to reduce disincentives to start work,[17] several others to decrease effective marginal tax rates.[18] Initiatives to stimulate part-time work are often seen as a way to 'share' jobs among the employed and unemployed[19] (see Walwei, Chapter 5, this volume).

The concept of these benefits, designed in an era when part-time work was uncommon, certainly needs to be rethought. In addition, this chapter has shown that incentives certainly do not improve once initial benefit entitlements have been exhausted, neither for the one partner, nor for the other, and reforms should take account of unemployment *and* related welfare benefits. Therefore, policies to restore incentives should:

• Facilitate individual choice whether or not to work by concentrating the benefit unit *and* the resource unit around the individual.
  Simulations demonstrate the advantages of individual-based systems such as in Australia. The family-based but partly individualised income tested benefits in New Zealand have similar effects but to a lesser extent.

- Ensure gains from work at all levels of earnings and at all numbers of hours worked per week by setting marginal tax rates on employment income well below 100 per cent.
  The hours rules, ceilings and monetary thresholds in social insurance are only part of the problem. Another part is the high withdrawal rates used in income tests for some welfare benefits. Introducing earnings disregards or reducing clawback rates enhances work incentives as any earned income is not entirely confiscated through the income test. The Canadian example illustrates how much disincentives can be reduced through such measures. One danger of such costly reforms is that the disregards and reduced clawback rates are introduced at the cost of basic payment rates, increasing poverty for recipients unable to work or to look for work.
- Reform the tolerance of UI systems towards part-time income and accept part-time work as an alternative to inactivity or unemployment.
  Low part-time earnings lead to a disproportionate reduction of UI benefits. If getting unemployed men and women back to work through part-time employment is a real policy goal, a system of earnings disregards or employment-conditional benefits is worth considering.

Policy reforms are obviously restricted by their cost. Earnings disregards and moderated clawback rates can be very effective measures but are in fact fiscal transfers to raise income levels for the low paid. Employment-conditional benefits can in principle be taxed back from earnings higher up on the earnings distribution, but they have a number of drawbacks, and their introduction and design depends heavily on a country's earnings distribution. Estimates of budgetary effects calculated on the basis of the present situation have little value, as the effects on employment, wage setting, unemployment and inactivity by introducing such a scheme are unpredictable. Alternatives have been sought via universal benefit systems,[20] but these have one common characteristic: they are too expensive to be realistic. Clearly these issues require further research as such policies are increasingly being used in attempts to reduce unemployment.

NOTES

1 Social Policy Division, Directorate of Education, Employment and Social Affairs, OECD, Paris. Mark Pearson, John Martin and Willem Adema provided helpful suggestions. The author expresses his personal view, which does not commit the OECD Secretariat or any OECD member government.
2 Testimony of this change taking place in the Netherlands is a report developing three scenarios of divisions of work and care in family life (SER 1996a).
3 A recent survey in the United Kingdom has shown that saving on total wage costs is an important reason to employ people part-time (Hewitt 1996).
4 Figure 6.1 is compiled with the use of the OECD *Database on Taxes and Benefits* on the following assumptions: the husband has earnings at the level of the Average

Production Worker (APW) (OECD 1995b) in full-time employment in the chart indicated 'married to employed', while he is unemployed and has exhausted his initial entitlements and receives SA to maintain the family in the chart indicated 'married to unemployed'. In both situations the inactive partner starts working part-time at pro rata APW level earnings, increasing the hours in work (work effort) from zero to 40 hours where he or she has 100 per cent of the APW earnings. The couple have two children aged 11 and 5 attending school and pay rent in the private sector equal to 20 per cent of the APW earnings level, for which housing benefits are received. It reflects the situation in 1995.

5 For a complete description of the tax and benefit system, and an overview of net replacement rates and effective tax rates, see OECD (1997a).

6 As the APW is used for simulations that are not gender specific, no account is taken of the fact that women and part-time workers suffer from hourly wage discrimination (Delsen 1995; Mishell et al. 1996; Gornick and Jacobs 1996; Harkness 1996).

7 The concept employed is in fact the complement of the 'Average Effective Tax Rate', which expresses how much earned income is deducted in the form of income and social security taxes and benefit withdrawal.

8 Dutch statistics illustrate the relevance of this example for women and especially for families of ethnic minorities: one out of every five people without Dutch nationality is dependent on SA in the Netherlands (Potters 1996).

9 In Portugal, there is no SA means test as SA does not exist. Therefore, the gain from part-time work is high, but unemployed people may also be living in poverty.

10 In Austria, take up of SA is small due to the extended maintenance obligations on the family of the beneficiary. Nevertheless, SA has been included there because of the general assumption that resources will have been exhausted after 60 months of unemployment.

11 There is an income disregard in the Netherlands of 70 per cent of gross earnings for jobs not exceeding 5 hours, but the effect of this is destroyed by the housing benefit income test.

12 A quite distinct possibility to work part-time and receive benefits is through a short-time working scheme, in which case a top-up benefit is often possible. Incentives are complicated in this case, and have little to do with the tax and benefit system as described in this chapter.

13 In fact, the correlation coefficients are calculated for relative increases in net income as shown in Table 2. To capture the effect of unemployment benefits, Panel A and Panel B of Table 6.2 are used. For each panel, the average relative increase in income in 4-, 8-, 16- and 20-hour jobs is calculated. The correlation coefficients between these averages and the incidence of part-time work (both sexes) are 0.464 for Panel A and 0.370 for Panel B.

14 There has been research, however, to women's reactions to changes in marginal tax rates (see e.g. Atkinson and Morgensen 1993, and OECD 1995a, not giving unanimous proof).

15 Disincentives are defined as the complement of the values in Table 6.1, which changes the sign, but not the value of the correlation coefficient. Data are taken from Gregg and Wadsworth (1996, Table 2).

16 For each panel, the average disincentive to work 4-, 8-, 16- and 20-hour jobs is calculated.

17 Reforms are generally focused on UI benefits, either to restrict excessive use (Austria, Canada, Denmark) or to tighten eligibility criteria (Belgium, Denmark, France, Luxembourg, Norway and the United Kingdom). Some countries have introduced or increased income disregard in the SA income test (Australia, Canada, the United Kingdom). In Canada, UI entitlements are based on hours worked, with penalties for repeat users and rewards for working while on claim.

18 Some countries have reduced the SA clawback rates (Australia and Canada) or have introduced or extended in-work benefits (Australia, Canada, Ireland, the United Kingdom and the United States) or have reduced income taxes on low incomes (Denmark and the United Kingdom).

19 Numerous countries have installed so-called 'short-time working schemes', whereby the income loss due to reduced hours is compensated by UI payments (Australia, Denmark, Ireland, Luxembourg, the Netherlands, Sweden and the United Kingdom) (MISEP 1995). Other countries (Austria, Belgium, France, Germany, Italy, Portugal and Spain) have schemes with similar purposes but with different funding (Mosely and Kruppe 1996; OECD 1997b).

20 See e.g. Parker (1990, 1996) or Purdy (1996) for discussions of basic income systems; Scharpf (1995) and Havemen (1996) for discussion of wage subsidy systems.

BIBLIOGRAPHY

Atkinson, A. B. and Morgensen, G. M. (eds) (1993) *Welfare and Work Incentives*, Clarendon Press, Oxford.

Blondal, S. and Pearson, M. A. (1995) 'Unemployment and Other Non-employment Benefits', *Oxford Review of Economic Policy* 1: 136–69.

Blundell, R. (1993) in Atkinson and Morgensen (eds) *Welfare and Work Incentives*, Clarendon Press, Oxford.

CLFS (1996) *'Enquete sur les forces de travail*, Resultats 1995', Statistical Office of the European Communities, Luxembourg.

Delsen, L. (1995) *Atypical Employment: An International Perspective. Causes, Consequences and Policy*, Wolters-Noordhoff, Groningen.

Duncan, A. S. and Giles, C. (1996) 'Labour Supply Incentives and Recent Family Credit Reforms', *The Economic Journal* 106 (January): 142–55.

Dutch Central Planning Bureau (1995) Replacement Rates: A Transatlantic View', Working Paper no. 80, The Hague, September.

Eardly, T., Bradshaw, J., Ditch, J., Gough, I. and Whiteford, P. (1996) *SA in the OECD Countries*, HMSO, London.

Eissa, N. and Liebman, J. B. (1995) 'Labour Supply Responses to the Earned Income Tax Credit', NBER Working Paper 5158, National Bureau of Economic Research, Inc, Cambridge, June.

Fagan, C. and Rubery, J. (1996) 'Transitions between Family Formation and Paid Employment', in G. Schmid, J. O'Reilly and K. Schömann (eds) *International Handbook of Labour Market Policy and Evaluation*, Edward Elgar, Cheltenham.

Gornick, C. and Jacobs, J. A. (1996) 'A Cross-national Analysis of the Wages of Part-time Workers: Evidence from the United States, the United Kingdom, Canada and Australia', *Work, Employment and Society* 10, 1, March: 1–27.

Gregg, P. and Wadsworth, J. (1996) 'It Takes Two: Employment Polarisation in the OECD', Discussion Paper no. 304, ESRC, LSE, London, September.

Hakim, C. (1995) 'Five Myths about Women's Employment', *British Journal of Sociology* 46, 3, September: 429–55.

Hakim, C. (1996) 'Labour Mobility and Employment Stability: Rhetoric and Reality on the Sex Differential in Labour-market Behaviour', *European Sociological Review* 12, 1: 1–31.

Harkness, S. (1996) 'The Gender Earnings Gap: Evidence from the UK', *Fiscal Studies* (Institute for Fiscal Studies) 17, 2, May: 1–36.

Haveman, R. (1996) 'Reducing Poverty while Increasing Employment: A Primer on Alternative Strategies, and a Blueprint', *OECD Economic Studies*, OECD, Paris.

Hewitt, P. (1996) 'The Place of Part-time Employment' in P. Meadows (ed.) *Work Out – or Work In, Contributions to the Debate on the Future of Work*, YPS for the Joseph Rowntree Foundation, York.

ILO (1996) 'World Employment 1996/97, National Policies in a Global Context', International Labour Office, Geneva.

Jallade, J. (1984) *Towards a Policy of Part-time Employment*, European Centre for Work and Society, Maastricht.

Jehoel-Gijsbers, G., Scholten, H., Vissers, A. and van den Heuvel, K. (1995) 'Social Zekerheid en Arbeidsparticipatie, inventarisatie van Nederlands empirisch onderzoek', OSA werkdocument W126, Stichting Organisatie voor Strategisch Arbeidsmarkton-derzoek, Den Haag, February.

Maier, F. (1992) 'The Regulation of Part-time Work: A Comparative Study of Six EC Countries', *Report Prepared for the Commision of the EC*, WZB discussion papers, Berlin.

Martin, J. P. (1996a) 'Measures of Replacement Rates for the Purpose of International Comparisons: A Note', *OECD Economic Studies*, OECD, Paris.

Martin, J. P. (1996b) 'Unemployment and Related Welfare Benefits in OECD Countries and their Impacts on the Labour Market', Publikaties van het Belgisch Instituut voor Openbare Financiën, Brussels, vol. 4.

MISEP (1995) *Employment Observatory, Trends*, Issue 22, Commission of the European Communities, DGV, Brussels.

Mishel, L., Bernstein, J. and Schmitt, J. (1996) 'The State of Working America 1996–97', Economic Policy Institute, Washington, December.

Mosley, H. and Kruppe, Th. (1996) 'Employment Stabilisation through Short-time Work' in G. Schmid, J. O'Reilly & K. Schömann (eds) *International Handbook of Labour Market Policy and Evaluation*, Edward Elgar, Cheltenham.

OECD (1994a) *The OECD Jobs Study: Facts, Analysis, Strategies*, Paris.

OECD (1994b) *The OECD Jobs Study: Taxation, Employment and Unemployment: Evidence and Explanation*, Paris.

OECD (1994c) *Women and Structural Change, New Perspectives*, Paris.

OECD (1995a) *The OECD Jobs Study: Taxation, Employment and Unemployment*, Paris.

OECD (1995b) *The Tax/Benefit Position of Production Workers, 1995 Edition*, Paris.

OECD (1995c) *Employment Outlook*, July, Paris.

OECD (1996a) *Making Work Pay: A Thematic Review of Taxes, Benefits, Employment and Unemployment*, Paris.

OECD (1996b) *The OECD Jobs Strategy: Enhancing the Effectiveness of Active Labour Market Policies*, Paris.

OECD (1996c) *Employment Outlook*, Paris.

OECD (1997a) *Benefits and Incentives in OECD Countries*, Paris.

OECD (1997b) 'Working-time Policies' in *Employment Outlook*, Paris.

Parker, H. (1990) 'The Tax and Benefit Systems, and their effects on People with Low Earnings Potential' in A. Bowen and K. Mayhew (eds) *Improving Incentives for the Low-Paid*, Macmillan/NEDO, London.

Parker, H. (1996) 'Taxes, Benefits and Family Life, The Seven Deadly Traps', Research Monograph 50, Institute of Economic Affairs, London.

Potters, L. T. A. M. (1996), 'Partners in de Bijstand', *Social-economische Maandstatistiek*, Centraal Bureau voor de Statistiek, Heerlen, August.

Purdy, D. (1996) 'Jobs, Work and Citizens' Income: Four Strategies and a New Regime', EUI Working Papers 96/1, European University Institute, Florence.

Sargent, Th. C. (1996) 'An Index of UI Disincentives', Economic Studies and Policy Analysis Division, Department of Finance, Ottawa, September.

Scharpf, F. (1995) 'Subventionierte Niedriglohn-Beschäftigung statt bezahlter Arbeitslosigkeit?', *Zeitschrift für Sozialreform*, February, Wiesbaden.

Schingten, R. and Faber, J. (1996) 'Droit du Travail', Grand-Duché de Luxembourg, Ministère du Travail et d'Emploi, Luxembourg.

Schmid, G. and Reissert, B. (1996) 'Unemployment Compensation and Labour Market Transition' in G. Schmid, J. O'Reilly and K. Schömann (eds) *International Handbook of Labour Market Polcy and Evaluation*, Edward Elgar, Cheltenham.

SER (1996a) 'Advies Toekomstscenario's onbetaalde arbeid', Publikatie nr. 6–21 juni 1996, Sociaal-Economische Raad, Den Haag.

SER (1996b) 'Advies stroomlijning gesubsidieerde arbeid', Publikatie nr. 4–16 februari 1996, Sociaal-Economische Raad, Den Haag.

SZW (1995) 'Unemployment Benefits and SA in Seven European Countries, A Comparative Study', Working Document no. 10, September, Ministerie van Social Zaken en Werkgelegenheid, The Hague.

Whitehouse, E. R. (1996) 'Implementing In-work Benefits in Different Labour Markets', *The Economic Journal* 106: 129–41.

7

PART-TIME WORK

A threat to labour standards?

Jill Rubery

INTRODUCTION

Part-time work not only involves fewer hours and a lower weekly remuneration than full-time work, but it can also constitute a different employment form, organised on different principles, and on different terms and conditions to full-time jobs. This chapter explores the nature of part-time work as a form of deviance from the standard full-time employment relationship. This is empirically explored by comparing the differences in remuneration between full- and part-time workers, in order to assess the potential role of part-time work in the restructuring of the wage and employment relationships within advanced economies and whether these differences undermine the form and evolution of the full-time standards.

PART-TIME WORK AND THE STANDARD EMPLOYMENT RELATIONSHIP

Part-time work derives its significance as a form of deviance from the standard employment contract. The establishment of the standard working week was central to the evolution of the modern employment system. Spot contracting, where labour is hired for a specific task and contracts have to be continuously re-negotiated, has been shown in labour market theory to be an inefficient form of labour market organisation for a wide range of employment situations for both employer and employee (Williamson 1975). Yet without collective worker action and resistance, many more employers would have opted to retain the inefficient but low-risk forms of casual employment relationships (Rubery 1978). The passing of responsibility to employers to ensure sufficient work to cover the standard working week was a notable victory for workers and unions, even if it only partially compensated for ceding control of labour power to employers under factory-based wage labour systems

(Marglin 1974). The historical struggles to move away from spot contracting and to establish standard working hours (both minimum and maximum) form the basis of trade union attachment to standard working hours (Bosch et al. 1994).

The standard full-time employment contract also takes on significance as the basis of the standard of living within society. Those in full-time work reasonably expect to earn sufficient for adult subsistence as defined by current historical standards and to be largely independent of state support, except perhaps for subsidies for dependants. Full-time work may pay below subsistence under certain circumstances, for example to young people or to women, but these deviations are legitimised by the assumption that the standard of living for these groups will be guaranteed through the family. Even in times of high unemployment, both policy-makers and the unemployed are still reluctant to entertain wage subsidies as part of a long-term full-time employment package (McLaughlin 1995).

This relationship between full-time work and the standard of living is maintained through state and company benefits linked to full-time continuous employment. Those without such a work history may be excluded from access to benefits and may only be able to derive access through their family relationships to those with standard employment histories.

This system of benefit provision reflects the notion of a male breadwinner form of household organisation (Lewis 1992; Grimshaw and Rubery 1997; Rubery et al. 1997; Pfau-Effinger, Chapter 9, this volume). Many Welfare State systems still only recognise the legitimacy of the male breadwinner's claims for support when partially or fully without employment, while other population groups are expected implicitly to be funded through family relationships. Thus the notion of a full-time continuous male labour market participant underpins the standard employment and benefit relationship.

Part-time work is thus a deviation from the standard in two respects. From the demand side these are jobs which deviate from standard hours as well as a minimum income and employment guarantees. Part-time work can also be used to evade expectations of premia payments for working antisocial hours, and that work would be scheduled on a regular and predictable basis. From the labour-supply perspective, part-time work provides an opportunity to mobilise into the labour force groups who are either excluded from, or exclude themselves from, full-time continuous participation: the young, the retired and those with care responsibilities. These groups may be regarded as not requiring the same income guarantees and minimum subsistence income as the full-time continuous participant. Social norms relating to income security covering periods out of employment such as holidays, sickness and old age may also be breached, and for them an employment relationship closer to spot contracting may be considered appropriate. It is from these two perspectives that we can begin to build up a picture of the dynamics that influence the terms and conditions under which part-time work is organised.

Opportunities to vary conditions between full- and part-timers will depend both on the form of labour market regulation and on the integration of part-time work into standard employment conditions. Variations in these conditions can be expected between countries but also between sectors and organisations dependent upon the strength of regulation and competitive and technical conditions. The incentives to use part-time work include the degree of cost and price pressure, the organisational need for working-time schedules to cover anti-social hours or to provide flexible cover, not necessarily within standard days, and, of course, the characteristics of the workers normally employed, in particular their gender (Horrell and Rubery 1991). These specific organisational and market factors interact with the national systems of regulation to influence the level of part-time working and the terms under which it is offered but there is no simplistic relationship between the relative costs of part-time work and its use compared to full-time work or to other non-standard employment forms (see Smith *et al.*, Chapter 2, this volume).

The situation is further complicated by the fact that segmentation of the employment system applies not only to part-time but also to full-time work. Some full-time jobs are also low paid, providing less than adult subsistence. Moreover the growth of 'deviant' employment forms, like part-time and temporary employment, may undermine the basis for the continuation of the standard employment contract. Thus, over the longer term the gap between full- and part-time work could narrow if the guarantees associated with the standard contract are undermined, particularly in the most competitive and least well-regulated sectors. Indeed, certain groups, such as women, have never been fully integrated in the standard employment conditions, with the result that as many as 40 per cent of full-time female workers in the UK have been estimated as earning below subsistence wages (Siltanen 1994). A small gap between terms and conditions of full- and part-time work may indicate either policies to include part-time work within standard employment conditions or alternatively weakness in the protection afforded to full-timers.

Potentially equally important influences on part-timers' terms and conditions are the characteristics of the job holders themselves which may determine the extent to which they are regarded as having rights to full-time continuous employment or to alternative income support when such employment is lacking. This can lead to variations between part-timers, even within the same labour market. Where part-time workers are recognised to have needs and aspirations similar to full-time continuous participants, the deviation from the standard conditions may be less than where part-timers are regarded as marginal participants. From this perspective variations in part-timers' terms and conditions are likely to reflect gender differences and life cycle patterns of participation. However, where women are expected to be full-time continuous workers, part-time work may be recognised to involve a financial cost, while in countries where the norm for women is still taken to be non-participation, part-time work may be considered a net financial gain. Again the extent to which actual terms and conditions reflect these social norms will depend upon labour market regulations, fiscal policies and the like.

Supply- and demand-side factors can be seen to have independent effects on part-time work, but there is also a 'mutual conditioning' between the two sides (Humphries and Rubery 1984). For example, in some organisations part-timers may not be remunerated for antisocial hours because employers are seeking cheaper ways of extending operating or opening hours; but other employers may do the same more because they consider opportunities to work antisocial hours as a benefit, and not a cost, for those with care responsibilities or in full-time education and not because they face specific cost pressures. Thus, in analysing the empirical evidence on the terms and conditions of part-time work we need to keep this perspective of the mutual conditioning between supply- and demand-side factors in mind.

THE TERMS AND CONDITIONS OF PART-TIME WORK: SOME EMPIRICAL EVIDENCE OF DEMAND- AND SUPPLY-SIDE SEGMENTATION

Labour market regulation and part-time terms and conditions

Despite the absence of harmonised earnings data across countries there have been some recent attempts both to compare part-time pay and full-time pay within and between countries and to identify the impact of labour market regulation on the outcome. Although all the studies utilise different methodologies and datasets the following general points can be drawn.

Part-timers earn lower hourly wages than full-timers

Part-timers earn lower hourly wages than full-timers, even after taking into account occupational and industrial characteristics and/or personal or human capital factors (Simpson 1986; Büchtemann and Quack 1989; Blank 1990; Rosenfeld and Kalleberg 1990; OECD 1994; Paci et al. 1995; Gornick and Jacobs 1996). Significant differences remain between countries, and between studies in the relative size of the differentials, and the extent to which they are 'explained' by differences in full- and part-time employment patterns. A notable difference, for example, is found between the UK and the Netherlands (Fagan et al. 1995; Plantenga et al. 1996; Rubery et al. 1997). On average female part-timers in the UK earn only 75 per cent of female full-timers' pay, while in the Netherlands average pay is similar for women in full- and part-time jobs (in both countries short hours part-time workers are excluded from the data). In the UK much of this difference at the aggregate level arises from the concentration of female part-timers in lower-level jobs. Within individual occupations in the UK there is a smaller full-time/part-time differential than at the aggregate level. The opposite is true in the Netherlands where the equality found at the aggregate level is not reproduced at the individual occupation level where part-timers tend to earn less than their full-time counterparts, although the full-time/part-time gap is still small by UK standards. This equality at the aggregate level can be explained on the one hand by the more comprehensive Dutch collective regulation system in which part-timers' pro rata rights are relatively well established. On the other hand, the equality of part-timers' and full-timers' pay at the aggregate level is due both to the higher share of young and inexperienced workers among full-timers in the Netherlands where almost all older experienced women workers are part-timers, and to the higher share of part-timers in high-level or professional jobs in the Netherlands, compared to the UK (Rubery and Fagan 1993).

Even in the UK, most case studies of organisations find employers paying pro rata pay to part-timers (although additional payments may be lower) (Hunter et al. 1993) and a study of similar jobs in similar organisations found the difference between full- and part-timers' hourly pay to be only 4 per cent (Lissenburgh 1996). Thus, much of the part-time/full-time gap at the aggregate level is associated with differences in types of job held by part-timers (see Smith et al., Chapter 2, this volume).

Part-timers lose out more on benefits than on hourly pay

Differences in labour costs between full- and part-timers in a number of countries are largely related to differences in benefit provisions. In a US study, part-timers were largely excluded from high-cost health and pension schemes while receiving roughly equivalent, or sometimes higher, hourly wage rates (Blank 1990; Mishel and Bernstein 1993). In the UK it has been estimated that to equalise benefits for part-timers with full-timers in the same type of firm (not necessarily in the same type of job) would cost twice as much as to equalise hourly pay with full-timers in the same type of job (Lissenburgh 1996). Even these estimates do not take into account the concentration of part-timers in sectors and organisations where provision of benefits to full-timers also tends to be low. Differences in holiday entitlement are evident both in Britain and in France (Horrell et al. 1989; Dex et al. 1993) with very high numbers of part-timers reporting no or very low holiday entitlement (23 per cent of British part-timers and 28 per cent of French part-timers with less than three weeks or no holiday entitlement). However, other comparative studies of French and British part-timers in banks have found the French to have a more equal access to benefits along with full-timers (O'Reilly 1994: 173–5).

Differences between full- and part-timers' benefit entitlements depend on the system of both labour market regulation and social security provision (Maier 1994). The differences are minimised where labour market regulation requires pro rata benefits for part-timers and where social security provision is either governed by similar regulations for all in the labour market or where access to social protection is based more on citizenship than employment rights. Many European countries now do require part-timers to receive both pro rata pay and benefits (for example, Belgium, Ireland, Luxembourg, the Netherlands) although others still exclude part-timers working below certain hours thresholds from collective agreements and/or state benefits (for example, Germany and Austria). Some countries have inconsistent policies, whereby under labour law pro rata benefits are required, but where social security systems still discriminate against part-timers (see Rubery et al. 1997; Doudeijns, Chapter 6, this volume). In countries where social protection is based on private provision and there are marked variations between organisations and labour force groups in access to private occupational systems or to collectively negotiated fringe benefits, the scope for differentiation between full- and part-timers is high. This reaches particular extremes in the US where access to health care is dependent upon private employer provision and where part-timers do not have pro rata rights with full-timers.

Part-time pay gaps are lowest in centralised and regulated systems

A recent comparative study of part-time/full-time pay differentials in the UK, the US, Australia and Canada found that in all four countries there was a gap between part-time and full-time pay even after accounting for human capital variables, but that the size of the gap varied according to the system of labour market regulation and the degree of wage dispersion (Gornick and Jacobs 1996). Relatively higher pay was found in Australia and Canada compared to the US and UK. The higher pay in Australia was due both to a narrower income distribution and the Australian reward system which provides for a premia of 10–15 per cent for part-timers on casual contracts and for overtime pay for above the usual hours. In Canada there is a wide wage dispersion, even greater than in the US which, other things being equal, tends to reduce part-time pay because of the concentration of part-timers in lower-level jobs. In Canada the relatively high pay for part-timers was explained primarily by higher unionisation among part-timers and the higher pay of these unionised workers. Part-timers in the UK fare somewhat better than part-timers in the US. British part-timers are concentrated lower down the wage hierarchy than American part-timers (possibly because American part-timers are protected by a minimum wage) but the penalty is less in the UK than the US because of less extreme wage inequality between the high and the low paid.

Part-timers are more vulnerable to low pay than full-timers

Data on part-timers in low-paid jobs (i.e. those earning below 66 per cent of full-time median hourly wages) are difficult to obtain. However, a recent EU study which focused on full-timers and low pay also has some data on part-timers in Belgium, the UK, Ireland and the Netherlands (Gregory and Sandoval 1994). In all four cases the share of part-timers among the low paid was considerably higher than the share of full-timers. However, the differences between countries is even more remarkable. At one end of the spectrum the share of low paid rises from 5 per cent to 9 per cent in Belgium when part-timers are considered while at the other end of the spectrum, in the UK the share rises from 17 per cent to no less than 60 per cent. The UK has a high overall share of part-timers in employment and these results might suggest that the opportunity to pay low wages is a major factor encouraging high part-time employment rates. However, the Netherlands, with an even higher share of part-time employment, has a lower overall incidence of low pay, with the share of workers who are low paid rising from 11 per cent to 23 per cent when part-timers are considered. Ireland has the highest share of full-timers in low pay at 19 per cent but in comparison to the UK the share of low-paid part-timers is relatively modest, at one-third instead of two-fifths.

Although part-timers are covered by minimum wage legislation in the US and many European countries the effectiveness of the provision is sometimes questionable. The Netherlands recently extended minimum wage protection to those working less than 14 hours, and the result has been a large increase in the share of the employed population found on the minimum wage rate (Plantenga et al. 1996), indicating the importance of such protection systems for part-timers. Marginal part-time workers on very short hours still lie outside minimum wage protection provided by collective agreement in some countries (for example, Germany and Austria).

Most studies find that part-timers on short hours are more likely to be low paid than part-timers on medium and long hours of work. Büchtemann and Quack (1989) revealed that in Germany there was very little difference in hourly pay between full-timers and part-timers who worked more than 15 hours and were thus within the social security system, but a significant hourly pay gap emerged with part-timers working fewer than 15 hours and outside the social security. In the Netherlands so-called flexible workers, which includes those working variable as well as short hours, earn a great deal less than the average pay for both full-timers and regular part-timers (Plantenga et al. 1996). Low pay in the Netherlands was also concentrated among those part-timers excluded until 1994 from the minimum wage protection; that is, those working for less than 14 hours a week (Plantenga and van Velzen 1993). In the UK, earnings surveys have tended to exclude those earning below income tax thresholds but the inclusion of an earnings question within the Labour Force Survey has enabled some information for the first time to be collected on the full range of part-timers in the labour market. The results suggest that there is indeed a set of low-paid part-time workers not captured by other earnings surveys. Hourly pay for this marginalised group tends to fall below the hourly pay rates for those included within the social security and tax system.

The impact of part-time work on pay cannot necessarily be disentangled from the influence of gender

Disentangling the impact of part-time work on hourly pay rates from that of gender is fraught with difficulties. Controlling for gender may remove much of the apparent impact of part-time work on the pay variable (Horrell *et al.* 1989). Some findings continue to reveal a part-time effect over and above a gender effect: for example, a recent UK study found that part-timers experienced a 14 per cent mark down in pay unexplained by either job or personal characteristics compounding unexplained inequalities between male and female full-timers (Paci *et al.* 1995). Scandinavian and American studies have also found lower wages for part-timers relative to full-timers after controlling for human capital variables and/or industrial and job characteristics (Blank 1990; Rosenfeld and Kalleberg 1990). Blank goes on to undermine her own findings of pay discrimination by adjusting for sample selection bias between full- and part-timers. By modelling the decision to enter employment as well as the decision whether to work full- or part-time, the evidence of lower pay for part-timers in each occupation is reversed into a finding of higher pay. According to Blank, one explanation of this result is as follows:

> there may be unmeasured productivity-related factors that are correlated with the determination of who works part-time that would make these women less productive if they were full-time workers. ... The fact that selection adjustments affect wages implies that the variables entering the selection equation – such as number of young children and total number of people in the household – actually affect the wage determination process for these workers. These workers choose part-time jobs that allow them to work productively and also fulfil their other responsibilities.
>
> (Blank 1990: 153)

These contradictory results perhaps illustrate more clearly the futility of the task of differentiating the impact of part-time work from the more general factors which lead to gender discrimination in pay, including women's assumed household responsibilities. The human capital approach where pay is assumed to reflect individual productivity unless proven otherwise is at odds with a segmentation approach where pay reflects institutional conditions. Under this approach the development of full-time pay in some sectors may be constrained by the existence of a large body of part-time workers providing a ready substitute. Moreover, the prevalence of part-time working helps to maintain the economic subordination of women and reinforces social norms which may affect female full-timers as well as part-timers. For example, the Netherlands offers relatively high pay for part-timers in comparison to female full-timers, but the gender pay ratio for full-timers is low relative to that found, for example, in

Scandinavian countries. Widespread part-time working in the Netherlands may help to reinforce the male breadwinner model of household organisation which in turn reinforces the gender pay gap even among full-timers.

In Scandinavia, wage equality is greater between men and women as well as between full- and part-timers. This equality derives both from the stronger ideological commitment to dual earner households, demonstrated in part by the pay compensation even for part-time parental leave in Sweden, and from the solidaristic wage policy which reduces the overall level of wage dispersion.

The impact of supply-side segmentation on the terms and conditions of part-time work

Evidence from a number of European countries can be drawn upon to illustrate the tendency to link pay to the economic activity status of the job holder. We can differentiate between part-timers as (1) contingent participants, (2) permanent full-time participants in temporary voluntary part-time work, or (3) permanent full-time participants who require compensation for taking part-time work.

Part-time work for contingent participants

Contingent participants are seen as not fully responsible for their own subsistence and cannot expect compensation for short hours below standard or full-time hours. They are most at risk, dependent upon the degree and form of labour market regulation, of receiving below pro rata terms and conditions and access to benefits.

Their contingent status is reinforced as much by the state as by employers: in many countries part-timers have restricted rights to unemployment benefits, pensions and/or sick pay (Rubery *et al.* 1997; Ginn and Arber, Chapter 8, this volume), particularly when they fail to meet earnings or hours thresholds and when combining work with other activities such as education and caring. Thus, the number of hours worked part-time can be an important factor influencing the risk of receiving inferior conditions: the closer part-timers' hours are to those of full-timers, the lower the risk. Longer hours may result in the work being more fully integrated with full-time work because of the nature of the job, or because the part-time worker is closer to being a full-time permanent participant.

Exemption from social protection payments may increase the immediate cash income of part-timers at the loss of forgone benefit entitlements. There may also be very real incentives to avoid social protection payments for contingent part-timers where they are unlikely to result in eligibility for benefits; that is, if unemployed part-timers have to prove availability for full-time work to gain unemployment benefit (for example, in the UK and Germany) or if their independent contributory pension would not exceed the minimum pension to which they would have been entitled without contributions. However, preferences for cash rather than benefits may reflect low income as much as a preference for immediate consumption; part-timers may choose not to join pension schemes not because they have no interest in long-term security but because they have low incomes.

'Fair wages' are traditionally discussed in terms of weekly or monthly income, which can be readily linked to notions of subsistence income, but for part-timers fair wages have to be specified in hourly terms, which are less clearly linked to subsistence. The increasingly complex relationships which emerge between earnings and household living standards as a consequence of both the growth of multi-earner households and of variable and atypical employment contracts may be weakening the strength of social norms such as fair wages, which help protect the real value of pay. Moreover, as contingent part-timers do not usually have access to unemployment benefits there is also no benefit level to provide a floor to wages. Under these conditions it is possible to offer those on part-time work hourly wages which fall well below subsistence norms even defined by unemployment benefits. The emphasis on the contingent nature of the participation of the employees effectively removes the moral burden from employers as well as the state to provide income guarantees at times of no work, including holidays, sickness, downturns in demand and old age. The exclusion of many part-timers from holiday entitlements in deregulated labour markets such as the UK perhaps best illustrates how part-time employment contracts deviate from the social expectations around the full-time open-ended contract. In the UK, most full-timers do receive paid holidays, but around one-third of part-timers have no paid holiday entitlement according to Labour Force Survey estimates (Watson 1993).

Part-time work for continuous participants on a temporary and voluntary basis

This category consists mainly of women who reduce hours over the period of childbirth and child-raising while remaining permanent participants in the labour market and usually in the same job. This group is exemplified by those women who in France take advantage of the right to opt for shorter working hours – *temps choisi* – and who choose by and large to reduce hours to 80 per cent of the standard, taking Wednesdays off to fit in with the free half-day for schoolchildren. This type of voluntary part-time work is most often found in the public sector in France.

It may be more appropriate to call this form of employment reduced full-time working rather than part-time working as there is no tendency to create specific jobs for part-timers and participants can return to full-time work when they wish. Other examples include various job-sharing schemes, or parental leave schemes with the right to reduced hours but without wage compensation (EC Childcare Network 1996; Rubery et al. 1997). In all these cases the right to work part-time is seen as a privilege, thereby removing any burden on the employer or the state to compensate for the gap between full and reduced hours income. It is assumed to be up to the individual and/or the family to make up any shortfall between subsistence needs and actual income. Some parental leave systems may preserve full-time employment rights, but in other cases benefits are reduced and based on part-time hours.

Most people working reduced hours retain the same rights to benefits and working conditions as full-timers. Working reduced hours is unlikely to result in effort-intensification strategies or variable working-time schedules that are associated with specifically designed part-time jobs. Those taking this route may pay penalties over the life cycle in the form of lower promotion opportunities if the decision to opt for reduced hours marks them out as less committed workers, but the immediate short-term costs of changing working-time status may be relatively low.

Those employed in part-time work under these conditions thus occupy an intermediate position between groups considered to be permanent full-time participants and those considered to be contingent participants. The opportunity to reduce hours is usually either guaranteed by the state or derives from the characteristics of the person and the job. Employers are more willing to offer these opportunities to retain employees with relatively high skills. Thus, *temps choisi* is only available to specific types of employee or as a result of equality policies, usually implemented at the level of the state.

Part-time work for full-time continuous participants

Part-timers who are regarded as normally seeking full-time work may be able to claim some degree of compensation for the gap in earnings between full-time and part-time work. Although probably the smallest category in most advanced countries, their numbers may increase as governments adopt policies of extending part-time work to non-traditional sectors of the labour force and as more countries move towards a situation in which women are regarded as permanent and not contingent participants. The degree of compensation will again depend upon labour market status.

Compensation for flexible working

Where women are engaged in flexible working, by and large they receive very limited compensation for lost income. Men are much more likely to be offered schemes which enable them to retain full-time earnings. Two examples illustrate this point. In Spain and Greece men are sometimes asked to work part-time to facilitate the extension of operating hours and receive in return full-time pay for part-time work; in both countries weekend work is allowed if it is organised on a part-time basis (Cavouriaris *et al.* 1994: 61; Moltó 1994: 74).

Self-employment may also be used as an alternative to part-time work to enable men in particular to provide below full-time hours but with the possibility of compensation through working for other employers and by charging a higher hourly rate than direct employees. Where employers seek greater working-time flexibility in female job areas they are more likely to create part-time jobs at the same or lower hourly remuneration as full-timers.

Compensation for work sharing and early retirement

One of the most common forms of part-time work for men which is compensated is short-time working. Where prime-age men are employed, variations in overtime are used to adjust to demand, but when variations are extreme or there are government subsidies available, short-time work with earnings compensation may be used to avoid redundancy. Although these schemes are not explicitly related to gender they are primarily found among male manual workers in heavy industry. There are very few situations in which women would receive compensation for hours not actually worked and in female work areas part-time jobs tend to be used to absorb fluctuations. However, the notion of the male breadwinner has resulted in short-time subsidies remaining a key part of many countries' labour market policies.

Work sharing by full-timers or partial early retirement schemes are other forms of part-time work and also often attract compensation. This may involve partial wage compensation or, even more likely, protection of benefit rights, particularly pension rights at full-time level. Such protection was explicitly advocated by the Delors White Paper on EC employment policy, even though no reference was made to the divisive effect of providing full-time benefits only to those entering part-time work from full-time work (CEC 1994; Rubery 1995). Many women enter part-time work from inactivity and thus would be ineligible for the protection. In France there are subsidies worth up to 30 per cent of gross pay to encourage people to move to partial early retirement (Gauvin et al. 1994: 88) and also policies to encourage people to take up part-time work under redundancy packages. In Belgium, those aged over 50 who work part-time are still eligible for a full-time pension (Meulders et al. 1994: 25, 98). In Germany, those moving from full-time to part-time status retain the right to full-time unemployment benefits if they lose their job (Maier et al. 1994: 82)

Compensation for the unemployed accepting part-time work

Many governments have developed schemes to encourage the unemployed to enter part-time jobs, by providing income subsidies, allowing partial retention of benefits or by providing protected rights to full-time unemployment compensation. Many of these schemes restrict eligibility to those registered as unemployed and/or eligible for benefits (see doudeijns, Chapter 6, this volume). This excludes many of those who normally take up part-time work, as they often enter direct from inactivity and, because of limited prior participation, are not counted as unemployed as far as these benefits are concerned. In the case of Germany there is a scheme specifically designed for those previously in full-time work which allows the unemployed to retain half of their earnings from work up to 18 hours per week, while those working fewer than 18 hours are in fact excluded from the unemployment benefit scheme (Maier et al. 1995; OECD 1996). Ireland has a specific part-time work incentive scheme for those on long-term social assistance (Barry 1995; OECD 1996). Some countries also provide unemployment benefits if there is income loss due to reduced hours of work, for example, the Netherlands (Plantenga and Sloep 1995) and Australia (OECD 1996). Sometimes subsidies are provided to households on the basis of low wage income; these in-work benefits can provide a means of compensation for breadwinners who move into part-time work, but in practice few may opt to take up part-time work as this is not seen as compatible with breadwinner status (McLaughlin 1995).

Compensation for caring work

Where women are treated as full-time permanent participants in the labour market responsible for their own subsistence in the same way as men, the fact that they may need income compensation for periods when they work reduced hours because of care responsibilities may be recognised in the design of parental leave systems. Thus, for example, in Sweden it is possible to take paid parental leave in the form of reduced hours but with partial income compensation.

PART-TIME WORK AND STANDARD EMPLOYMENT CONDITIONS: A DYNAMIC RELATIONSHIP

So far we have been concerned to compare part-time work with full-time work and/or with the standard employment relationship, without considering the impact of part-time work on the terms and conditions for full-timers. As the interrelationships between the terms for part- and full-timers clearly evolve over time, subject to a wide range of influences, it is of course difficult to identify precisely the impact of part-time on full-time conditions and vice versa. Nevertheless, it is important to address these questions so as to avoid the trap of regarding the structuring of employment conditions as static, and the evolution in standard and non-standard employment as independent instead of as interdependent.

The thrust of EU policy has been to extend full-time standard employment conditions to part-timers on a pro rata basis, through the planned directive on part-time workers, which is subject to agreement under the Maastricht social protocol. In many countries pro rata conditions are already enshrined in law or in collective agreements. The Netherlands, for example, has passed a law requiring pro rata conditions unless different conditions can be justified, so part-timers now have rights to accrued holiday entitlements for actual hours and not just contractual hours, wage supplements and additions, training, gratuities, and soon, although rights to overtime pay above contractual, as opposed to standard, hours have not been won. In Luxembourg, part-timers have the right to extra compensation for hours above their own contractual hours (Plasman 1995).

This extension of rights and benefits could be regarded as a further stage in a general process of labour market regulation and organisation whereby weaker labour market groups are brought, often with the aid of the state, within the system of labour market protection. However, while the transfer of rights appears to be in one direction, from full- to part-timers, the indirect impact of part-time work on full-time conditions must also be examined. Historically the incorporation of weaker groups within the collectively regulated system often involved some weakening of the degree of regulation which could be exerted over a smaller, more cohesive group of skilled or privileged workers. It is thus only to be expected that the extension of the related system to cover part-timers may involve some changes in the terms and conditions for full-timers.

The spread of part-time and other atypical forms of employment is a major factor stimulating employer interest in the development of more flexible working-time arrangements for core or full-time workers. Many of the advantages of part-time work lie in the opportunity to intensify work and, relatedly, to target working hours to fit varying schedules and demands. Without the example of part-time work to follow, employers may have been slower to adopt new working-time practices for full-timers involving more variable hours of work, associated, for example, with annualised contracts. Part-time work may also be used to change wage-effort norms within some industries; change to part-timers' hours has been a major way in which public sector organisations have sought to win contracts under compulsory competitive tendering (Cutler and Waine 1994). This increased intensity of work for groups subject to competitive tendering is likely to have a general impact on wage-effort norms within the public sector. The use of part-time work for antisocial hours has also established a new norm, both of operating and opening hours and of expected remuneration for those hours. This new norm impacts on working-time and pay norms for full-timers. Increasingly, organisations are expecting full-timers to accept antisocial working hours and new working-time systems which follow the terms and conditions of part-timers in not offering additional remuneration for antisocial working hours. This pattern can be seen particularly in the case of Sunday opening for shops in the UK. Initially, existing full-time staff were offered double time for Sunday working, but part-timers or new full-time recruits were expected to work at weekends for lower or no premia (Rubery 1994, 1996). Gradually, retail companies are moving over to including Sunday work as part of a normal contract without special remuneration. Moreover, much of the privatisation and indeed decentralisation of pay determination in the public sector in the UK has concentrated on reducing antisocial hours premia for full-timers, a move facilitated by the possibility of using part-time workers for antisocial hours as a cheaper alternative.

The growth of atypical employment, including part-time work, has also been associated with the general trend towards weakening employment protection. Atypical workers often enjoy fewer employment protection rights than full-timers but those enjoyed by full-timers have been reduced through legislative change in a number of countries. These changes have been made in part to reduce the differentiation between standard and non-standard workers, but through levelling down rather than levelling up. At the same time, there has been a move towards decentralisation and increased individualisation in terms and conditions of employment, so that establishing pro rata rights for part-timers to basic terms and conditions provides less protection than where regulations remain a dominant force unifying employment conditions across large labour force groups. Thus differentiation of employment conditions is proceeding alongside the incorporation of part-timers within basic employment protection systems.

CONCLUSION

Part-time work presents a major potential challenge to labour market norms and standards associated with full-time work. Evidence from a variety of countries suggests that this challenge to labour standards can be modified and reduced through the incorporation of part-time work into the system of regulation. While it may not be feasible to prevent the use of part-time work to change some norms and expectations, for example, those relating to antisocial working hours or the continuation of standard 8-hour Monday to Friday working patterns, it is still possible to incorporate part-time work within the general terms and conditions for full-timers and ensure equality of access to hourly pay and to benefits. Employers are still interested in creating and promoting part-time work even when required to meet pro rata conditions, as the advantages of part-time work lie primarily in the opportunities to cut out unnecessary labour hours or to reduce the use of expensive overtime labour. In Scandinavia and to a large extent the Netherlands, part-time work has been incorporated into standard labour market norms and remuneration on a pro rata basis is not challenged (Ellingsaeter 1992).

Commitment to regularise and incorporate part-time work into standard terms and conditions is critical to the protection of both full- and part-time workers. This commitment needs extension to include social protection where this is still linked to full-time participation. Even under pro rata conditions part-time workers will suffer financial penalties which go beyond the shortfall in weekly income; part-timers are less likely to be promoted and thus enjoy less favourable lifetime earnings prospects, and part-time jobs still tend to be created in sectors, organisations and occupations where relative pay even for full-timers is low. Thus, a good deal for part-timers requires not only equality with full-timers in the same job or organisation but also an overall low level of pay dispersion within the economy.

Part-timers need protection in particular from the argument that low pay for part-timers is not a problem, as they are apparently content to supply their labour at low wages. This argument is based on the notion that employers should exploit different supply conditions, paying low wages to part-timers because they lack access to unemployment benefits or are excluded from high-paying full-time jobs, leaving them with little option but to accept low wages. Such an argument suggests that the wage structure should reflect segmentation on the supply-side and not skill and productivity in work. In the long term, of course, according to neo-classical theory these two conditions should converge, but supply-side segmentation has always been a persistent feature of labour markets. As such the role of labour market regulation should be to minimise the impact of supply-side differentiation on labour markets and to go some way to ensure that the notion of equality of pay for the same work is established.

BIBLIOGRAPHY

Barry, U. (1995) *Women and the Employment Rate in Ireland: The Causes and Effects of Variations in Patterns of Female Participation and Employment*. Report for the European Commission, Working Paper, EC Network on the Situation of Women in the Labour Market. Manchester: UMIST.

Blank, R. M. (1990) 'Are Part-time Jobs Bad Jobs?' in G. Burtless (ed.) *A Future of Lousy Jobs? The Changing Structure of US Wages*. Washington, DC: The Brookings Institute.

Bosch, G., Dawkins, P. and Michon, F. (eds) (1994) *Times are Changing?* International Institute for Labour Studies. Geneva: ILO.

Büchtemann, C. and Quack, S. (1989) '"Bridges" or "Trips"? Non-standard employment in the Federal Republic of Germany', in G. Rodgers and J. Rodgers (eds) *Precarious Jobs in Labour Market Regulation: The Growth of Atypical Employment in Western Europe*. Geneva: ILO.

Cavouriaris, M., Karamessini, M. and Symeonidou, H. (1994) *Changing Patterns of Work and Working-time for Men and Women – Towards the Integration or the Segmentation of the Labour Market*. Report for the European Commission, Working Paper, EC Network on the Situation of Women in the Labour Market. Manchester: UMIST.

Commission of the European Communities (CEC) (1993) *Growth, Competitiveness, Employment: The Challenges and Ways Forward into the 21st Century: White Paper*. Luxembourg: Office for Official Publications of the European Communities.

Cutler, A. and Waine, B. (1994) *Managing the Welfare State: The Politics of Public Sector Management*. Oxford: Berg.

Dex, S., Walters, P. and Alden, D. (1993) *French and British Mothers at Work*. London: Macmillan.

Ellingsaeter, A. L. (1992) 'Part-time Work in European Welfare States: Denmark, Germany, Norway and the United Kingdom Compared', Report 92: 10. Oslo: Institute for Social Research.

European Commission Childcare Network (1996) 'Review of Children's Services'. Report prepared for the Equal Opportunities Unit, DGV. Brussels: European Commission.

Fagan, C., Plantenga, J. and Rubery, J. (1995) 'Part-time work and inequality. Lessons from the Netherlands and the UK' in J. Lapeyre and R. Hoffmann (eds) *A Time for Working: A Time for Living*. Documentation of the joint conference of the European Trade Union Confederation (ETUC) and the European Trade Union Institute (ETUI), December.

Gauvin, A., Granie, C. and Silvera, R. (1994) *The Evolution of Employment Forms and working-time among Men and Women – Towards the Integration or the Segmentation of the Labour Market*. Report for the European Commission, Working Paper, EC Network on the Situation of Women in the Labour Market. Manchester: UMIST.

Gornick, J. C. and Jacobs, J. (1996) 'A Cross-national Analysis of Part-time Workers Wages', *Work, Employment and Society* 10, 1, March: 1–27.

Gregory, M. and Sandoval, V. (1994) 'Low Pay and Minimum Wage Protection in Britain and the EC' in R. Barrell (ed.) *The UK Labour Market: Comparative Aspects and Institutional Developments*. Cambridge: Cambridge University Press.

Grimshaw, D. and Rubery, J. (1997) 'Workforce Heterogeneity and Unemployment Benefits: The Need for Policy Reassessment in the European Union', *Journal of European Social Policy* 7, 4: 291–315.

Horrell, S. and Rubery, J. (1991) *Employers' Working-time Policies and Women's Employment*. London: HMSO.

Horrell, S., Rubery, J. and Burchell, B. (1989) 'Unequal Jobs or Unequal Pay?', *Industrial Relations Journal*, Autumn.

Humphries, J. and Rubery, J. (1984) 'The Reconstitution of the Supply Side of the Labour Market: The Relative Autonomy of Social Reproduction', *Cambridge Journal of Economics* 8, 4: 331–46.

Hunter, L., McGregor, A., MacInnes, J. and Sproull, A. (1993) "The 'Flexible Firm": Strategy and Segmentation', *British Journal of Industrial Relations* 31, September: 383–408.

Lewis, J. (1992) 'Gender and the Development of Welfare Regimes', *Journal of European Social Policy* 2: 159–73.

Lissenburgh, S. (1996) *Value for Money: The Costs and Benefits of Giving Part-time Workers Equal Rights*. A report for the TUC, January. London: TUC.

Maier, F. (1994) 'Institutional Regimes of Part-time Working' in G. Schmid (ed.) *Labour Market Institutions in Europe*. New York: M.E. Sharpe.

Maier, F. and Rapp, R. (in collaboration with C. Johnson) (1995) *Women and the Employment Rate in Germany: The Causes and Effects of Variations in Patterns of Female Participation and Employment*. Report for the European Commission, Working Paper, EC Network on the Situation of Women in the Labour Markets. Manchester: UMIST.

Maier, F., Quack, S. and Rapp, Z. (1994) *Changing Patterns of Work and Working-time for Men and Women – Towards the Integration or the Segmentation of the Labour Market*. Report for the European Commission, Working Paper, EC Network on the Situation of Women in the Labour Market. Manchester: UMIST.

McLaughlin, E. (1995) 'Gender and Egalitarianism in the British Welfare State' in J. Humphries and J. Rubery (eds) *The Economics of Equal Opportunities*. Manchester: Equal Opportunities Commission.

Marglin, S. A. (1974) 'What do Bosses do?' in A. Gorz (ed.) (1978) *The Division of Labour: The Labour Process and Class Struggle in Modern Capitalism*. Sussex: Harvester Press.

Meulders, D., Hecq, C. and Ruz Torres, R. (1994) *Changing Patterns of Work and Working-time for Men and Women – Towards the Integration or the Segmentation of the Labour Market*. Report for the European Commission, Working Paper, EC Network on the Situation of Women in the Labour Market. Manchester: UMIST.

Mishel, L. and Bernstein, J. (1993) *The State of Working America 1992–3*. Economic Policy Institute, New York: M.E. Sharpe.

Moltó, M.-L. (1994) *Changing Patterns of Work and Working-time for Men and Women – Towards the Integration or the Segmentation of the Labour Market*. Report for the European Commission, Working Paper, EC Network on the Situation of Women in the Labour Market. Manchester: UMIST.

OECD (1994) *Women and Structural Change: New Perspectives*. Paris: OECD.

OECD (1996) *Employment Outlook*. Paris: OECD.

O'Reilly, J. (1994) *Banking on Flexibility*. Aldershot: Avebury.

Paci, P., Joshi, H. and Makepeace, G. (1995) 'Pay Gaps Facing Men and Women Born in 1958: Differences within the Labour Market' in J. Humphries and J. Rubery (eds) *The Economics of Equal Opportunities*. Manchester: Equal Opportunities Commission.

Plantenga, J. and Sloep, M. (1995) *Women and the Employment Rate in the Netherlands: The Causes and Effects of Variations in Patterns of Female Participation and Employment*. Report for the European Commission, Working Paper, EC Network on the Situation of Women in the Labour Market. Manchester: UMIST.

Plantenga, J. and van Velzen, S. (1993) *Wage Determination and Sex Segregation in Employment: The Case of the Netherlands*. Report for the European Commission, Working Paper, EC Network on the Situation of Women in the Labour Market. Manchester: UMIST.

Plantenga, J., Koch, E. and Sloep, M. (1996) *Trends and Prospects for Women's Employment in the Netherlands in the 1990s*. Report for the European Commission, Working Paper, EC Network on the Situation of Women in the Labour Market. Manchester: UMIST.

Plasman, R. (1995) *Women and the Employment Rate in Luxembourg: The Causes and Effects of Variations in Patterns of Female Participation and Employment*. Report for the European Commission, Working Paper, EC Network on the Situation of Women in the Labour Market. Manchester: UMIST.

Rosenfeld, R. A. and Kalleberg, A. (1990) 'A Cross-national Comparison of the Gender Gap in Earnings', *American Journal of Sociology* 96, 1: 69–106.

Rubery, J. (1978) 'Structured Labour Markets, Worker Organisation and Low Pay', *Cambridge Journal of Economics* 2, 1: 17–37.

Rubery, J. (1994) *Changing Patterns of Work and Working-time – Towards the Integration or Segmentation of the Labour Market in the UK*. Report for the European Commission, Working Paper, EC Network on the Situation of Women in the Labour Market. Manchester: UMIST.

Rubery, J. (1995) 'Synthesis' in *Equal Opportunities for Women and Men: Follow-up to the White Paper on Growth, Competitiveness and Employment*. Report to the European Commission's Employment Task Force (Directorate-General V) V/5538/95-EN, DGV Brussels.

Rubery, J. (1996) *Trends and Prospects for Women's Employment in the 1990s. National Report for the UK*. Report for the European Commission, EC Network on the Situation of Women in the Labour Market. Brussels: European Commission.

Rubery, J. and Fagan, C. (1993) *Occupational Segregation of Women and Men in the European Community*. Luxembourg: Office for Official Publications of the European Communities.

Rubery, J., Smith, M., Fagan, C. and Grimshaw, D. (1997) *Women and European Employment*. London: Routledge.

Siltanen, J. (1994) *Locating Gender*. London: UCL Press.

Simpson, W. (1986) 'Analysis of Part-time Pay in Canada', *Canadian Journal of Economics* XIX, 4: 798–807.

Watson, G. (1993) 'Working-time and Holidays in the EC: How the UK Compares', *Employment Gazette* 101, 9: 395–403.

Williamson, O. (1975) *Markets and Hierarchies*. New York: Free Press.

8

HOW DOES PART-TIME WORK LEAD TO LOW PENSION INCOME?

Jay Ginn and Sara Arber

INTRODUCTION

Employment histories – including periods of part-time, full-time and non-employment – are influenced by both the gender culture surrounding domestic labour and the gendered institutional framework (Pfau-Effinger, Chapter 9, this volume). Thus both agency and social structure contribute to explaining levels of part-time work. This chapter assesses the effect of part-time work on pensions, something women generally do not consider when making employment decisions (Carr 1993), but which is profoundly influenced by two major social institutions: the welfare state and the labour market. Where these institutions privilege the employment pattern associated with middle-class males – full-time continuous employment for most of the working life – those with part-time or interrupted employment are disadvantaged in pension acquisition.

Although part-time employment is becoming more common among men, the timing of part-time employment differs for women and men (see Delsen, Chapter 3, this volume). Men are most likely to work reduced hours at the beginning and end of their working lives, the latter often associated with the shedding of older workers from full-time jobs (Kohli *et al.* 1991; Laczko and Phillipson 1991; Trinder 1992). For many women, however, part-time employment is central to their working lives and hence has more serious effects on pension acquisition. This chapter focuses on how women's part-time rather than full-time employment reduces their pension income; we do not address the issue of part-time work after pensionable age.

We are concerned with pension income to which women have direct access, including pensions derived from husbands' employment records. Widowed and divorced women cannot rely on a husband's financial support throughout life, while married women may not share their husband's income equally (Edwards 1981; Pahl 1989; Vogler 1989; Morris 1996). Discretionary income from another is experienced and used differently from an individual's own income (Sen 1984; Cragg and Dawson 1981; Popay 1989).

The effect of part-time employment on pension income varies among countries and over time, due to differences in the political forces shaping pension systems and the labour market. The balance between public and private pension provision and the redistributional structure of state schemes mediate the effect of part-time employment. It has been suggested that welfare states shaped by labour movements with redistributive, egalitarian aims are more woman-friendly in their provisions (Hill and Tigges 1995). The nature of part-time jobs also varies among and within countries. In the US, Tilly (1992) identifies two types of part-time job – 'retention' and 'secondary' – the latter having more serious implications for long-term earnings and for pension income. Pension outcomes will depend on the extent of segregation of part-time work into low-paid occupations.

We first outline in general terms how part-time employment may affect pension entitlements, then assess the implications for pensions of part-time employment in three EU countries – Britain, Denmark and Germany – with contrasting types of welfare regime. The pension system is outlined for each country, focusing on the interaction of part-time employment with public and private pension schemes. The second section draws on recent research (Ginn and Arber 1996) to demonstrate how part-time employment in Britain reduces pension entitlements, using data on the work histories and pension income of British women and men aged over 60.

Part-time employment and pensions

Earlier chapters show that women's roles as carers for children and others constrain their ability to be employed full-time, although the impact of care responsibilities on hours of employment varies according to state policies towards families and the labour market (Rubery et al. 1995).

Part-time work can lead to lower pension income in two main ways. First, periods of part-time work reduce the lifetime earnings on which pensions generally depend. In Britain, women often leave or change their job when family responsibilities cannot be combined with full-time employment. Taking a part-time job following child-bearing usually entails occupational downgrading, affecting earnings well beyond the period of intensive child-rearing (Martin and Roberts 1984; Joshi 1984, 1989, 1991). Moreover, leaving a job for child-bearing may entail loss of any occupational pension rights acquired (Ginn and Arber 1994a; Glover and Arber 1995). The impact of maternity on employment and pension rights is less negative in Scandinavian countries, where women's rights to return to the same job on reduced hours enable continuity of employment. In mid-life, switching to part-time hours to provide informal care for parents or in-laws can have a disproportionate effect on the amount of pension in final salary schemes.

157

Second, part-time employees are less likely to be eligible to contribute to pension schemes in both state and non-state pension schemes. In the social insurance schemes of five EU states (Austria, Spain, Ireland, Germany and Britain), contributions from those earning below a threshold are not allowed (Luckhaus 1996), while occupational schemes often do not admit part-time employees. An EU Draft Directive of 1982 proposed that part-timers should not be excluded from statutory or occupational pension schemes, although minimum thresholds of hours or earnings were still allowed (Rubery and Tarling 1988). The European Court's judgment (the 1986 Bilka-Kaufhaus case: see Luckhaus and Moffat 1996) ruled that exclusion of part-timers could be in breach of Article 119 of the Treaty of Rome. The German Supreme Court ruling that part-timers should not be excluded from retirement schemes (Hesse 1984) and the European Court's 1994 judgment in two Dutch cases have re-inforced the message to employers. However, the effect of these legal rulings has been slow and limited so that in Britain, for example, less than one-fifth of all part-timers belong to an occupational pension scheme (OPCS 1995).

In practice, most part-timers are unable to acquire an adequate occupational pension because of the combination of low pay and lack of access to schemes. Thus the proportion of the working life in which a person is employed full-time, part-time or not employed profoundly affects their ability to accumulate their own pension entitlements. In addition, the relationship between part-time employment and pension income is mediated by the type of pension provision, whether mainly state or private, the benefit structure of pension schemes and the nature of part-time jobs available. We outline a typology of welfare states below, noting the lack of attention to the gendered nature of welfare.

Gendering welfare regimes

Although industrial societies have developed a wide variety of social security systems, these may be grouped on the basis of entitlement to state support – whether through citizenship, work-merit or need – and whether provision for times of hardship is viewed as mainly the responsibility of the state or the individual and their family (Titmuss 1974; Esping-Andersen 1987; Palme 1990). Titmuss and Esping-Andersen have each distinguished three ideal types of welfare regime which broadly coincide.

Palme (1990) assigns countries to one of four types of pension system. Basic security systems guarantee an adequate income for all in old age; income security systems ensure a certain replacement rate of previous earnings; residual systems provide no guarantee of either of these; and institutional systems provide both a guaranteed minimum and a good replacement rate. The latter are included here with the basic security type. Palme's typology is combined with Esping-Andersen's types of welfare state to provide the models shown in Table 8.1, with Britain, Germany and Denmark as three examples of pension systems (discussed more fully in Ginn and Arber 1992, 1994b).

Table 8.1 Typology of pension systems, with examples

Political philosophy	Type of welfare state		
	Liberal	Conservative/ corporatist	Social democratic /socialist
Welfare policy orientation	*Residual welfare* State plays a minimal role, family and market roles emphasised	*Industrial achievement/ performance* Social needs are met mainly according to work-merit	*Institutional- redistributive* State support based on citizenship, as a universal social right
Type of pension system	*Residual* State provides a minimal safety net for those lacking an occupational pension	*Income security* State ensures a high income replacement rate	*Basic security* State provides a universal benefit
Example	*UK*	*West Germany*	*Denmark*
Key features: (a) State basic pensions	NI basic pension has maximum (£61 pw single, 1996) set below level of means tested benefits; amount depends on years of contributions	None	Major component, social pension paid to all citizens (£101 pw each, 1996). Minor additional quasi-state pension (ATP) depends on years of contributions (not earnings-related)
(b) State earnings- related pensions	Minor additional pension, SERPS, will replace up to 25% of earnings in 1998	Major component of system: social insurance pension replaces up to 40–45% of earnings	None
(c) Private occupational pensions	Major component, benefits mainly male non-manual employees	Commonly integrated with state pension. Mainly benefits higher paid	Mainly benefits salaried staff, but spreading

The residual welfare model of liberal regimes is characterised by minimal state provisions, allowing wide scope for private (non-state) earnings-related pensions. There is no guaranteed pension income for non-earners, who must rely on a breadwinner or on means tested benefits. Based on these criteria and the low-income replacement rate of state schemes, Palme assigned Britain, Ireland and Switzerland to this group.

The income security model of conservative, or corporatist, welfare regimes is founded on earnings-related state social insurance which reflects earnings over the working life. Such societies tend to be family centred and to have no pension income guarantee for non-earners, mainly married women. There is less incentive for the development of private occupational pension schemes than in the residual model. Based on these features and an income replacement rate which exceeds half the average manual earnings, Germany, Belgium, France, Italy, Spain and Portugal were assigned to this model.

In the basic security model of social democratic regimes a basic pension, equivalent to at least one-third of manual earnings, is provided to all residents irrespective of their employment record, funded from general taxation. The Netherlands, Denmark, Sweden, Norway and Finland all met this criterion, but the latter three countries also have an earnings-related state pension with a high replacement rate.

Welfare State theorists have tended to ignore gendered aspects of welfare, such as how part-time and interrupted employment is treated in pension rules, their typologies reflecting the male-dominated class struggle through which state welfare emerged. Public pensions were 'developed by men with men in mind', the outcomes depending on the power of working-class institutions to further the interests of working men (Hill and Tigges 1995: 100). Nevertheless, the type of pension system developed has different implications for women, especially those employed part-time.

Feminist writers have begun to redress the lack of a gender dimension in classifications of welfare states. For example, writers have examined how the model of the family underlying welfare provision influences social security arrangements (Lewis 1992; Allmendinger et al. 1993); whether families or individuals are the basic unit for social security purposes (Langan and Ostner 1991); how far benefits enable women to maintain an autonomous household without financial dependence on a breadwinner (Orloff 1993); whether public pensions serving working-class interests also benefit women (Hill and Tigges 1995); and how far married women are treated as independent individuals in social security (Ginn and Arber 1992, 1994b, 1994c).

We next consider how the pension systems of three welfare states – Denmark, Germany and Britain – treat part-time employment. Part-time employment accounts for 16–24 per cent of all employment in these countries and 34–44 per cent of all women's employment. Part-time hours are longer in Denmark than in Germany or the UK. For example, the proportion of women part-timers in public administration who work over 20 hours per week is 85 per cent, compared with 71 per cent in Germany and 46 per cent in Britain (Ellingsaeter 1992).

Part-time employment and pensions in three welfare states

Denmark

The Danish pension system provides an income in later life which is loosely related to employment participation or hours of work over the life course. There are three main components of the system. The first, a flat rate social pension, is payable to all citizens with forty years' residence at age 67 (see Table 8.1a), although a partial pension may be paid earlier. Funded from general taxation, the pension is independent of employment record. The basic amount is payable to each individual irrespective of marital status (DKr876.5 per week in 1996, equivalent to £101) (Sedgwick Noble Lowndes 1996). Unmarried people receive a 40 per cent supplement (Kvist 1996a).

The second element is a compulsory, funded, defined contribution scheme known as ATP (see Table 8.1a) covering employees aged 16 to 66 working more than 9 hours per week. The scheme, which matures in 2000, provided a maximum pension of DKr276 per week in 1995, equivalent to £32 (Sedgwick Noble Lowndes 1996), or 32 per cent of the basic pension. The pension depends on years employed and contributions paid: it is paid in full if weekly hours employed exceed 27, at two-thirds for 18 to 26 hours and at one-third for 9 to 17 hours (ATP-huset 1994). Two-thirds of the contribution is paid by the employer and the combined contribution for full-time employment (DKr2,683 a year in 1996) represents just over 1 per cent of the average production worker's wage (APWW). From 1993, ATP contributions have been payable by social security benefit recipients, the state contributing two-thirds (ibid.). This helps those with periods out of the labour market to maintain a full ATP contribution record. Periods of part-time employment below 27 hours will reduce the pension but the banding of contributions ensures a more redistributive structure than in an earnings-related pension scheme.

The third element comprises private occupational and individual pension schemes (see Table 8.1c). Until 1993, occupational schemes were confined mainly to salaried employees, less than half the workforce, but coverage has expanded, mainly in the form of defined contribution schemes, with employers paying two-thirds of the contributions (Sedgwick Noble Lowndes 1996). Due to their concentration in the public sector, a higher proportion of women than men belong to an occupational pension scheme, 71 per cent compared with 66 per cent in 1996, although women's part-time and interrupted employment is likely to lead to their pension amounts being lower than men's (Kvist 1996b). The growth of private pensions will magnify inequalities of class as well as gender among pensioners in the future.

In sum, the Danish state pension schemes are inclusive of most part-time employees (and the non-employed). Although private pensions place part-timers at a disadvantage, the generous universal social pension has resulted in a high degree of gender equality of pension income and the lowest pensioner poverty rate in the EU (Walker 1993).

Germany

Both the labour market and pension system differed in the two German states prior to unification, reflecting radically different ideologies. Since it is the institutions of the old Lander which now prevail in unified Germany, it is these we discuss.

In contrast to Denmark, the German pension system assumes women's dependence on a male breadwinner, providing for women mainly as wives or widows and reflecting a strong family orientation (see Pfau-Effinger, Chapter 9, this volume). Women's opportunity to obtain a good pension income through their own employment has been very limited. The pension system thus sets incentives for women to stay at home and support their husbands' careers (Allmendinger et al. 1993).

The main component of the pension system is the state earnings-related pension scheme covering most employees (see Table 8.1b). The contribution rate is 18 per cent, split equally between employer and employee, and the pension replaces up to 45 per cent of earnings (Sedgwick Noble Lowndes 1996). The structure of the scheme's benefits is progressive but provides adequate pensions only for those with a typically male pattern of full-time continuous employment.

Part-time employees are included only if they both work over 15 hours per week and their earnings exceed a specified minimum, which was DM560 a month in 1994 (Marullo 1995), equivalent to £36 a week. This is a lower threshold for social insurance than in Britain, yet it has been estimated that at least 1 million part-time employees in Germany lack full employment protection at any time (Bjurstrom 1992). For women, at least fifteen years of contributions are required for a full pension, of which ten must be in the years between ages 40 and 60 (Sedgwick Noble Lowndes 1996). Even where sufficient contributions have been made, those who work part-time for many years are generally unable to acquire a pension of their own above the level of means tested benefits.

The extension, from 1992, of social insurance credits for child care represents belated recognition that women are workers as well as mothers. A parent taking a career break or switching to part-time work in order to care for a child is credited with contributions at the rate of 75 per cent of national average earnings, for up to three years per child (Ruland 1991). Thus, for credited years, the low wages associated with part-time work do not reduce the pension entitlement.

The private occupational pensions sector benefits mainly well-paid salaried staff (Table 8.1c). Members of these non-contributory schemes can expect a pension replacing 60–70 per cent of final salary for a full career (Sedgwick Noble Lowndes 1996). Pension schemes are selective in coverage, women having less access due to occupational segregation and the exclusion of part-timers (Schmahl 1991).

To summarise, part-timers are often excluded from both state and private schemes. Part-timers who do contribute to the state scheme face dependence on means tested social assistance or on their family, while those admitted to a private scheme receive disproportionately low benefits. The new credits will help women caring for a very young child to work part-time without loss of state pension entitlements.

Britain

By European standards the British basic pension (£61 a week in 1996) is minimal; it is 11 per cent below the level of means tested benefits for a single pensioner (see Table 8.1a). Moreover, the value is indexed to prices and has been falling relative to average male earnings, from 20 per cent of male earnings in 1981 to 16 per cent in 1990 with a projected fall to 14 per cent by the year 2000 (Johnson and Falkingham 1992).

The pension is payable in full to those with the required years of National Insurance (NI) contributions (39 years for women and 44 for men), at age 60 for women and 65 for men; but from 2020 women's pension age will be 65, the increase being phased in from 2010. Married women may receive either a pension based on their own contributions or a dependant's pension of 60 per cent of their husband's pension, whichever is greater. Widows and divorced women may use their ex-husband's contribution record during the marriage to help them qualify for a basic pension. Only a minority of pensioner women, 28 per cent, receive any basic pension from their own employment (Retirement Income Inquiry 1996), due mainly to past state pension rules which acted as disincentives to married women contributing (Groves 1991). Although these rules no longer apply, long periods of part-time employment may still exclude women from earning a basic pension; where annual earnings are below the Lower Earnings Limit (LEL) (£3,172 a year in 1996–7), NI contributions are not payable. Because of the relatively short hours worked by women part-timers and the lack of any minimum wage in Britain, this threshold excludes up to 2.5 million women from NI each year (Equal Opportunities Commission 1996), including nearly half of women working part-time (Hutton *et al.* 1995).

The adverse impact of part-time employment on the basic pension will in future be mitigated by Home Responsibilities Protection (HRP), operative since 1978, whereby the required contribution years are reduced by the number of years (up to twenty) in which a person is caring for dependent children or a sick or disabled relative. By 2020 most women will retire with some entitlement to basic pension but up to half of them will have a reduced pension (Hansard 1994) due to years where earnings were below the LEL but were not covered by HRP.

It is instructive to compare the value of the British basic pension and Danish social pension relative to the average gross production worker's wage (APWW) (Table 8.2). In Britain, husbands with a full contribution record receive 20 per cent of the APWW, but most wives receive the married women's allowance which is equivalent to only 12 per cent at the maximum. In Denmark, the basic amount received by both husbands and wives in 1996 was 19 per cent of the APWW (calculated from Sedgwick Noble Lowndes 1996 and Kvist 1996b). Thus, while the British state pension leaves married women financially dependent on their husbands, the individualised state pension in Denmark promotes their independence. Comparing non-married pensioners,

Table 8.2 State pension relative to average gross wages, by gender and marital status, Britain and Denmark, 1996

Marital status	Basic pension, Britain		Social pension, Denmark	
	£/week	% of APWW*	£/week**	% of APWW*
Married/cohabiting:				
Husband	61	20	101	19
Wife	37	12	101	19
Couple's pension	98	32	202	37
Unmarried:				
Man	61	20	101 + 40 = 141	26
Woman	61	20	101 + 40 = 141	26

Sources: Sedgwick Noble Lowndes (1996: 29); ONS (1996); Kvist (1996a)
Notes:
1   The amounts of pension shown exclude means tested supplements.
2   In 1996, the average production worker's wage (APWW) for Britain was £303pw (mean gross weekly earnings of full-time workers in manufacturing; for Denmark the APWW was £539pw (DKr4,692) (mean gross wage of production workers in the private sector).
3   For men and single women in Britain, a full contribution record of 44 and 39 years respectively is assumed. For widows and divorced women, it is assumed their deceased/ex-husband had a full contribution record. In practice, many people have fewer years and a reduced pension.
* APWW – Average Production Worker's Wage
** Calculated using the 1996 official exchange rate: £1 = DKr8.70

these received a maximum basic pension equal to 20 per cent of the APWW in Britain but a guaranteed 26 per cent of the APWW in Denmark. Relative to the APWW, the basic pension in Denmark was 1.6 times higher for married women and 1.3 times higher for non-married women compared with their counterparts in Britain, helping Denmark to avoid the feminisation of older people's poverty seen in most European societies (Walker 1993). The advantage of Danish pensioners relative to British is even greater if net wage replacement rates are compared, because Danish tax rates are considerably higher than in Britain.

The British second-tier state pension, the State Earnings Related Pension (SERPS), is based on average pensionable earnings over the working life (44 years for women and 49 for men) and is therefore reduced by periods of part-time employment and non-employment (see Table 8.1b). The level of SERPS, even for those employed continuously and full-time, is low by European standards, replacing a maximum 25 per cent of average earnings in 1998.

From 1998, Home Responsibilities Protection (HRP) may be extended to SERPS, allowing up to twenty-four years to be disregarded in the calculation of average earnings. HRP may apply to years when a person is caring for children or elderly parents, if they are not employed or earn less than the Lower Earnings Limit (LEL). However, years of part-time work where earnings exceed the LEL will count and may substantially reduce the pension payable. Thus a woman employed part-time while caring could receive, other things being equal, a lower SERPS pension than one who stays at home while caring.

Raising the state pension age for women to 65 will reduce their SERPS pension. Although the basic pension will be protected during the extra five years for women who are not employed, these years will be counted in the calculation of average earnings and will therefore reduce the amount of SERPS pension for women who are not employed or who work part-time (Hutton *et al.* 1995). Only the minority of women employed full-time from ages 60 to 65 (less than 6 per cent in 1995) will be able to avoid this loss.

Private pensions, including occupational and personal pension schemes, are a larger component of the pension system in Britain than in the rest of the EU and are mainly responsible for class and gender inequality of income in later life (Ginn and Arber 1991; Arber and Ginn 1991, 1994). Such pension schemes are usually 'contracted out' of SERPS, replacing its provisions with equivalent or better benefits (see Table 8.1c). Occupational pension schemes, to which employers and employees contribute, cover only half of employees, mainly full-timers working for larger employers.

Part-time employees have low coverage in occupational pension schemes. In 1994, over two-thirds of full-time employees belonged to a scheme but only 19 per cent of part-timers (working fewer than 30 hours per week) did so (OPCS 1995). Research shows that the reasons for part-timers' low membership differ according to sector of employment. In the public sector, part-timers' non-membership was mainly because the scheme's rules excluded them, but in the private sector many employers of part-timers did not operate a scheme. Even when family circumstances and labour market factors such as earnings, length of job tenure and occupational class were controlled, full-timers had five times greater odds than part-timers of belonging to a scheme (Ginn and Arber 1993).

Recent EU moves to discourage indirect discrimination against women have brought a modest improvement in the occupational pension coverage of part-timers in Britain. Nevertheless, even among the larger schemes, 30 per cent of schemes in the private sector and 8 per cent in the public sector still exclude some part-timers; the hours limit for eligibility varies among schemes (NAPF 1996).

Where part-timers do join an occupational pension scheme, their pension benefits will be much reduced, relative to full-time employees. Because the amount of the British basic state pension is well below the threshold at which means tested benefits are payable, a small occupational pension may bring no financial advantage. It may even leave the recipient financially worse off than if she had no private pension at all, if it disqualifies her from receiving means tested benefits, especially income support and housing benefit – the 'occupational pensions trap' (Walker *et al.* 1989).

Personal pension schemes in Britain are theoretically open to any employed person, irrespective of hours worked. By 1993 5 million people had joined an Appropriate Personal Pension scheme (APP), approved by the government as an alternative to SERPS (Department of Social Security 1994: 9). Personal pensions provide less generous benefits than occupational pensions, mainly because employers usually contribute little (Davies and Ward 1992). Part-time employees and others who are low paid receive a particularly poor return on contributions, due to the high sales and administrative costs (Ward 1996: 43–4). Those earning less than £10,000 a year do not benefit from joining an APP, compared with remaining in SERPS, although 70 per cent of women with an APP were earning less than this amount in 1992–3 (Waine 1995). Many of these women will have been working part-time and will receive a very poor pension even after many years in an APP. A small personal pension, like small occupational pensions, is likely to bring no financial gain.

In sum, part-time employees fare badly in the British pension system, mainly because of the very low level of the basic state pension, which provides an inadequate platform on which to build additional income. Although carers will be entitled to some disregarded years in the state earnings-related pension, combining caring with part-time employment may reduce the pension. Many part-timers still lack access to occupational schemes and are left to rely on personal pensions providing a poor return on investment. Even where part-timers are able to contribute to an occupational pension, their low earnings often result in a pension too small to bring any financial gain. Part-timers face a highly complex and changing pension system which makes planning almost impossible.

We have considered the pension systems of three countries exemplifying the social democratic, the conservative/corporatist and the liberal welfare policies. It is important to distinguish between welfare policy orientations (or intentions) and the actual outcomes (which may be unintended) for different population groups. Denmark's tradition of social solidarity, reflecting the historical strength of the male-dominated labour movement, has resulted in a pension system which is inclusive of part-timers, who are mainly women. This supports the socialist feminist view that 'working-class institutions promote classwide interests that benefit women as well as men' (Hill and Tigges 1995: 99). Germany and Britain, in spite of ostensibly different welfare policies, the one to maintain occupational stratification, the other to minimise the role of the state in favour of the market, both have pension systems which marginalise part-time employment, leaving part-timers vulnerable to personal poverty in later life. The predominant role of the private sector in Britain, combined with the low level of state pensions, makes the impact of part-time work on individual pension income particularly severe.

Part-time employment is not, of course, a permanent situation; people move between periods of full-time employment, economic inactivity and part-time employment. Pension income is likely to depend on the relative proportions and sequencing of these periods over the working life. In the next section, we examine the cumulative effect of part-time employment on private pension acquisition in Britain, using research described more fully in Ginn and Arber

(1996). The analysis is mainly of older women's employment histories, since few older men had periods of part-time work during their employment history. We focus on private pensions since it is the possession of a good occupational or personal pension which differentiates those with a good standard of living in later life from those with incomes near poverty level.

Women's employment histories and pension income in Britain

The research used data from the OPCS *Retirement and Retirement Plans Survey* of 1988 (Bone *et al.* 1992). This government survey interviewed a nationally representative sample of 3,542 British men and women aged 55 to 69 living in private households. Respondents were asked for a full employment history including the month and year of starting and ending jobs, as well as information on current income, including occupational and personal pensions. Cohabiting couples were grouped with married. 'Part-time employment' refers here to employment for 30 hours or less. Since the employment histories of those aged between 55 and 60 were not necessarily complete, detailed analysis of the histories includes only employment up to age 55.

Women's average time employed since their first job was 27 years (57 per cent of the time), of which 8 years were part-time. This compares with men's 43 years employed (97 per cent of the time), with 0.4 years part-time. From age 20–55, women's mean years employed was less than 20, compared with men's 34 years.

Since pension acquisition depends on length of employment and timing of return as well as hours worked, time spent by women in employment at different stages of the life course was summarised in a fivefold typology (see Table 8.3). Each employment history type was further subdivided according to whether employment had been mainly full- or part-time. For those with continuous employment, the key division was between those with at least 90 per cent full-time employment and those with less.

While the overwhelming majority of men – 90 per cent – had a long period of continuous full-time employment, only 12 per cent of older women did so (Type 1a). Eight per cent of women had worked continuously but with at least 10 per cent of their employment part-time. One-third of women, the largest group, were stable returners, with only three years or less out of employment between ages 40 and 55. Seventeen per cent returned to employment but for less than twelve years between 40 and 55, while 15 per cent returned only briefly. Among returners, the majority had worked full-time for over half of their working life. The domestic career, in which employment was mostly before age 30, accounted for 17 per cent of women.

Figure 8.1 shows that among those over state pension age nearly 70 per cent of men but 25 per cent of women received an occupational or personal private pension. For women, the likelihood of pension receipt varied with employment pattern and whether or not employment was mainly full-time. Women whose

167

Table 8.3 Employment history types: percentage of women and men aged 55–69 with each type

Employment history type		Women	Men
1 Continuous:			
	(a) at least 90% FT	12	90
	(b) at least 10% PT	8	3
2 Stable returner:			
	(a) mainly FT	19	2
	(b) mainly PT	14	0
3 Intermediate returner:			
	(a) mainly FT	11	4
	(b) mainly PT	6	0
4 Brief returner:			
	(a) mainly FT	11	0
	(b) mainly PT	4	0
5 Domestic:			
	(a) mainly FT	14	1
	(b) mainly PT	3	0
Col %		100	100
N =		1,859	1,684

Source: OPCS *Retirement and Retirement Plans Survey*, 1988 (authors' analysis)
Note: 'Mainly' is defined as at least half of total employed time since the first job.
Employment history types
1 Continuous – employed for at least 30 years from age 20–55.
2 Stable returners – employed for at least 12 years from age 40–55 but less than 30 years from age 20–55.
3 Intermediate returners – employed for at least 10 years from age 30–55 but less than 12 years from age 40–55.
4 Brief returners – employed for at least one month but less than 10 years from age 30–55.
5 Domestic career – employed for less than one month from age 30–55.

employment was mainly part-time were less likely to have a private pension, within the four main patterns. For example, among stable returners nearly half of those employed mainly full-time received some non-state pension (Type 2a), compared with only 14 per cent where employment was mainly part-time (Type 2b). Among women with continuous employment, the effect on the chance of pension receipt of part-time work for less than 10 per cent of their working career (i.e less than four years) (Type 1b) is striking; only 25 per cent received a private pension compared with 62 per cent of women with at least 90 per cent full-time employment.

Among those with a private pension, the median amount for all women aged 60–69 was £18 per week, compared with £32 for men aged 65–69. For women employed continuously and mainly full-time (Type 1a), the median was £34 per week but was only £19 where the proportion of full-time employed years was less than 90 per cent (Type 1b). For stable and intermediate returners (Types 2 and 3), the median amount was £15 per week where employment had been mainly full-time but less than £10 for part-timers.

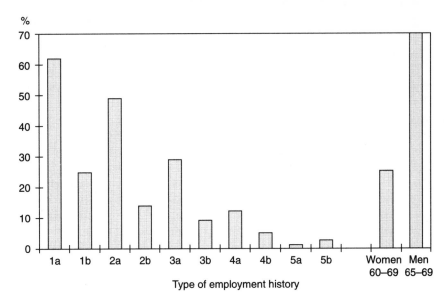

Figure 8.1 Percentage with independent private pension by type of employment
history: women aged 60–69
For key to employment history types, see table 8.3, p. 168

To summarise, maintaining continuous and full-time employment maximised older women's likelihood of obtaining a private pension and the amount. Both taking a career break and having any periods of part-time employment substantially worsened women's pension position.

Multivariate analysis, in which occupational class, educational level and marital status were included in the model, showed that the chance of entitlement to a private pension among women and men aged over 60 increased according to the years of full-time employment. The number of years of *part-time* employment had no effect on entitlement, nor did the total number of years employed (Ginn and Arber 1996).

The analysis of British women's private pension acquisition has shown that it is the years of full-time employment which are crucial: part-time years make little contribution to receipt or amount. The pensions trap (Walker *et al.* 1989), which can make a small pension financially worthless, will arise more frequently in the future in Britain as the flat rate basic pension loses its value and falls further below the level of means tested benefits. This will exacerbate the consequences of part-time work for individual income in later life.

CONCLUSIONS

Women's employment is increasing in most countries and later cohorts of women, born after 1950, will have spent more years in employment than current pensioners. However, because most of the increase has been in part-time employment (Hakim 1993), it will not necessarily remove women's disadvantage in individual income in later life: this will depend on the pension system.

This chapter has shown how pension schemes penalise periods of part-time employment and that in private pension schemes the effect is particularly severe. The structure of state pension schemes, the balance between state and private pensions and the nature, timing and duration of part-time jobs all influence the extent to which part-time work leads to low pension income.

In Britain and Germany, where earnings-related pensions predominate (operated by the private sector in Britain and by the state in Germany), it is only by adopting the traditionally male career pattern of full-time continuous employment, which generally means forgoing parenthood, that most women can ensure a good private pension income in later life. In Britain, the 'independence model' of pension provision, in which there is no need to depend on a husband for financial support, is only viable for a minority of women, whereas Danish state pension schemes ensure an adequate independent income for those with periods of part-time employment.

Cuts in state pensions will particularly disadvantage part-timers, since private pensions cannot fill the gap. Although reform of occupational pensions to include part-timers is welcome, it will do nothing for part-timers in small organisations lacking a pension scheme. Even mandatory private pensions would leave the low paid, mainly part-timers, with trivial pensions, caught in the pensions trap.

Recent pension reforms by European governments have tended to link pensions more closely to lifetime earnings (Palme and Stahlberg 1993), increasing the pension disadvantage of part-time work. Such reforms have met resistance from the organised working class, except in Britain, where cuts in state pensions have been achieved against a background of relentless attacks on trade union power. Insofar as women rely on state pensions more than men, this lends support to Hill and Tigges's (1995) thesis linking working-class strength with women's interests.

It is a paradox that part-time work is growing and working-time flexibility being promoted at a time when pension policies are magnifying the penalties of part-time work. In terms of the gender arrangement (see Pfau-Effinger, Chapter 9, this volume), cultural change is evident, with growing support for a more equal gender division of domestic labour, for women's financial independence and for women's equality in employment. Yet the institutional conditions, particularly pension arrangements, are becoming more hostile to the spread of part-time employment which more equal gender roles requires. If the potential benefits of part-time work are to be realised, it is essential that these adverse effects are tackled. In particular, state pensions need to be aligned to working patterns which include periods of part-time work. For example, a citizen's pension funded from general taxation (similar to the Danish social pension) would greatly benefit those with periods of part-time employment or unemployment.

Reforming pension systems to ensure full inclusion of part-timers would not only reduce poverty and social exclusion in later life; it would also fit better with a post-modern flexible working life and would reflect public recognition of the social value of caring work which usually underlies part-time employment.

ACKNOWLEDGEMENTS

For access to *Retirement and Retirement Plans Survey* data we are indebted to the ESRC Data Archive, University of Essex. We are grateful to the Office of Population Censuses and Surveys for permission to use the data. The chapter is based on a research project funded by the Economic and Social Research Council (Grant No. R000233240).

BIBLIOGRAPHY

Allmendinger, J., Bruckner, H. and Bruckner, E. (1993) 'The production of gender disparities over the life course and their effects in old age – results from the West German Life History Study', in A. Atkinson and M. Rein (eds) *Age, Work and Social Security*, Basingstoke: Macmillan.

Arber, S. and Ginn, J. (1991) *Gender and Later Life: A Sociological Analysis of Resources and Constraints*, London: Sage.

—— (1994) 'Women and aging', *Reviews in Clinical Gerontology* 4(4): 93–102.

ATP-huset (1994) *The Wage Earner's Guide to ATP*, Hilleroed: ATP-huset.

Bjurstrom, H. (1992) *Deltidsansattes rettigheter. En komparativ studie av Danmark, Norge, Storbritannia og Tyskland*, Oslo: Institute for Social Research.

Bone, M., Gregory, J., Gill, B. and Lader, D. (1992) *Retirement and Retirement Plans Survey*, London: HMSO.

Carr, M. (1993) 'Women, pensions and the state', *Benefits* 8: 9–13.

Cragg, A. and Dawson, T. (1981) *Qualitative Research among Homeworkers*, Research Paper no. 21, London: Department of Employment.

Davies, B. and Ward, S. (1992) *Women and Personal Pensions*, Manchester: Equal Opportunities Commission.

Department of Social Security (1994) *Personal Pension Statistics, 1992/3*, revised edition, London: Government Statistical Service.

Edwards, M. (1981) *Financial Arrangements within Families*, Canberra: National Women's Advisory Council.

Ellingsaeter, A. (1992) *Part-time Work in European Welfare States*, Oslo: Institute for Social Research.

Equal Opportunities Commission (1996) *Part-time and Atypical Work*, Manchester: EOC.

Esping-Andersen, G. (1987) *State and Market in the Formation of Social Security Regimes. A Political Economy Approach*, Working Paper 87/281, Florence: European University Institute.

Ginn, J. and Arber, S. (1991) 'Gender, class and income inequalities in later life', *British Journal of Sociology* 42(3): 369–96.

—— (1992) 'Towards women's independence: pension systems in three contrasting European welfare states', *Journal of European Social Policy* 4(2): 255–77.

—— (1993) 'Pension penalties: the gendered division of occupational welfare', *Work, Employment and Society* 7(1): 47–70.

—— (1994a) 'Heading for hardship: how the British pension system has failed women' in S. Baldwin and J. Falkingham (eds) *Social Security and Social Change: New Challenges to the Beveridge Model*, Hemel Hempstead: Harvester Wheatsheaf.

171

—— (1994b) 'Gender and pensions in Europe: Current trends in women's pension acquisition' in P. Brown and R. Crompton (eds) *A New Europe: Economic Restructuring and Social Exclusion*, London: UCL Press.

—— (1994c) 'Women's independent and derived pensions compared in Britain and Denmark' in H. Peemans-Poullet and J. Carton de Tournai (eds) *L'Individualisation des Droits dans le Secteur des Pensions des Travailleurs Salaries*, Brussels: Université des Femmes.

—— (1996) 'Patterns of employment, pensions and gender: the effect of work history on older women's non-state pensions', *Work Employment and Society* 10(3): 469–90.

Glover, J. and Arber, S. (1995) 'Polarisation in mothers' employment: occupational class, age of youngest child, employment rights and work hours', *Gender, Work and Organisation* 2(4): 165–79.

Groves, D. (1991) 'Women and financial provision for old age' in M. McLean and D. Groves (eds) *Women's Issues in Social Policy*, London: Routledge.

Hakim, C. (1993) 'The myth of rising female employment', *Work Employment and Society* 7: 97–120.

Hansard (1994) *House of Commons*, 21 June, col. 146.

Hesse, B. (1984) 'Women at work in the Federal Republic of Germany' in M. Davidson and C. Cooper (eds) *Working Women: An International Survey*, Chichester: John Wiley & Sons.

Hill, D. and Tigges, L. (1995) 'Gendering welfare state theory. A cross national study of women's public pension quality', *Gender and Society* 9(1): 99–119.

Hutton, S., Kennedy, S. and Whiteford, P. (1995) *Equalisation of State Pension Ages: The Gender Impact*, Manchester: Equal Opportunities Commission.

Johnson, P. and Falkingham, J. (1992) *Ageing and Economic Welfare*, London: Sage.

Joshi, H. (1984) *Women's Participation in Paid Work: Further Analysis of the Women and Employment Survey*, Research Paper no. 45, Department of Employment, London: HMSO.

—— (1989) 'The changing form of women's economic dependency' in H. Joshi (ed.) *The Changing Population of Britain*, Oxford: Basil Blackwell.

—— (1991) 'Sex and motherhood as handicaps in the labour market' in M. McLean and D. Groves (eds) *Women's Issues in Social Policy*, London: Routledge.

Kohli, M., Rein, M., Guillemard, A.-M. and van Gunsteren, H. (eds) (1991) *Time for Retirement. Comparative Studies of Early Exit from the Labour Force*, Cambridge: Cambridge University Press.

Kvist, J. (1996a) 'Retrenchment or restructuring? The emergence of a multi-tiered welfare state in Denmark', Paper presented to the Comparative Social Policy Group Seminar 'Social Insurance in Europe – an Outdated Social Policy Design?', Sheffield Hallam University, 15 July.

—— (1996b) Personal communication.

Laczko, F. and Phillipson, C. (1991) *Changing Work and Retirement*, Milton Keynes: Open University Press.

Langan, M. and Ostner, I. (1991) 'Gender and welfare' in G. Room (ed.) *Towards a European Welfare State?*, Bristol: School for Advanced Urban Studies.

Lewis, J. (1992) 'Gender and the development of welfare regimes', *Journal of European Social Policy* 2(3): 159–73.

Luckhaus, L. (1996) 'Privatisation and pensions: some pitfalls for women?' Paper presented to the International Conference 'Beyond Equal Treatment: Social Security in a Changing Europe', Dublin, 10–12 October.

Luckhaus, L. and Moffat, G. (1996) *Serving the Market and People's Needs? The Impact of European Law on Pensions in the UK*, York: Joseph Rowntree Foundation.

Martin, J. and Roberts, C. (1984) *Women and Employment. A Lifetime Perspective*, London: HMSO.

Marullo, S. (ed.) (1995) *Comparison of Regulations on Part-time and Temporary Employment in Europe*, London: Employment Department.

Morris, L. (1996) 'Researching living standards: some problems and some findings', *Journal of Social Policy* 25(4): 459–83.

National Association of Pension Funds (NAPF) (1996) *NAPF Annual Survey, 1995*, London: NAPF.

OECD (1996) *Employment Outlook*, Table E, Paris: OECD.

ONS (1996) *Labour Market Trends*, November, London: HMSO.

OPCS (1995) *General Household Survey 1994*, London: HMSO.

Orloff, A. (1993) 'Gender and the social rights of citizenship: the comparative analysis of gender relations and welfare states', *American Sociological Review* 58(3): 303–28.

Pahl, J. (1989) *Money and Marriage*, London: Macmillan Education.

Palme, J. (1990) *Pension Rights in Welfare Capitalism: The Development of Old Age Pensions in 18 OECD Countries, 1930–85*, Stockholm: Swedish Institute for Social Research.

Palme, J. and Stahlberg, A.-C. (1993) 'European pensions reform. A view from Scandinavia: reforms in Sweden', *Journal of European Social Policy* 3(1): 53–6.

Popay, J. (1989) 'Poverty and plenty: women's attitudes towards and experience of money across social classes' in *Women and Poverty: Exploring the Research and Policy Agenda*, London: Institute of Education/University of Warwick.

Retirement Income Inquiry (1996) *Pensions: 2000 and Beyond*, London: RII.

Rubery, J. and Tarling, R. (1988) 'Women's employment in declining Britain' in J. Rubery (ed.) *Women and Recession*, London: Routledge & Kegan Paul.

Rubery, J., Fagan, C. and Smith, M. (1995) *The Changing Pattern of Work and working-time in the European Union and the Impact on Gender Relations*, V/6203/95–EN, Brussels: European Commission (DGV-Equal Opportunities Unit).

Ruland, F. (1991) *Survivors' Benefits of the Pension Scheme in Germany: Current Issues and Future Perspectives*, Geneva: International Social Security Association.

Schmahl, W. (1991) 'On the future development of retirement in Europe, especially of supplementary pension schemes. An introductory overview' in W. Schmahl (ed.) *The Future of Basic and Supplementary Pension Schemes in the European Community – 1992 and Beyond*, Baden-Baden: Nomos Verlagsgesellschaft.

Sedgwick Noble Lowndes (1996) *The Guide to Employee Benefits and Labour Law in Europe 1996/7*, Croydon: Sedgwick Noble Lowndes.

Sen, A. (1984) 'Rights and capabilities' in *Resources, Values and Development*, Oxford: Basil Blackwell.

Tilly, C. (1992) 'Two faces of part-time work: good and bad part-time jobs in US service industries' in B. Warme, K. Lundy and L. Lundy (eds) *Working Part-time: Risks and Opportunities*, New York: Praeger.

Titmuss, R. (1974) *Social Policy*, London: Allen & Unwin.

Trinder, C. (1992) *Present and Future Patterns of Retirement*, London: Public Finance Foundation.

Vogler, C. (1989) *Labour Market Change and Patterns of Financial Allocation within Households*, Working Paper no. 12, Economic and Social Research Council.

Waine, B. (1995) 'A disaster foretold? The case of the personal pension', *Social Policy and Administration* 29(4): 317–34.

Walker, A. (1993) 'Achieving (or not achieving) economic security in old age: the EC's pension systems compared', *Benefits* 8: 6.

Walker, R. Hardman, G. and Hutton, S. (1989) 'The occupational pension trap: towards a preliminary specification', *Journal of Social Policy* 18(4): 575–93.

Ward, P. (1996) *The Great British Pensions Robbery*, Preston: Waterfall Books.

Part II

INTERNATIONAL
PERSPECTIVES

9

CULTURE OR STRUCTURE AS EXPLANATIONS FOR DIFFERENCES IN PART-TIME WORK IN GERMANY, FINLAND AND THE NETHERLANDS?

Birgit Pfau-Effinger

INTRODUCTION

Despite the universal increase in female employment, particularly among married women with children, what accounts for the differentiated growth of part-time work across countries? Explanations usually focus on the differential effect of welfare state policies to facilitate full-time female employment, or on the strategies of employers to divide and segment the labour market, by offering secondary sector marginalised part-time jobs to women. However, these arguments are often based on the assumption that women want full-time work; part-time work is a second best solution which mothers only choose in the context of institutional constraints. There is no doubt that the institutional framework created by the labour market and the state is of substantial importance for the employment behaviour of women. Nevertheless, explanations which stress these institutional factors can become too one-sided. This results in a neglect of the way that women's social practices also reflect deep-rooted differences in cultural ideals, norms and values concerning childhood and the gendered division of labour within the family. The dimension of 'culture' is important in explanations of cross-national differences but it has usually been excluded or only marginally integrated in theoretical explanations. Instead, culture is often treated as the residual explanatory variable (Duncan 1993; Pfau-Effinger 1993; O'Reilly 1996).[1]

The aim of this chapter is to present an explanatory theoretical approach for cross-national differences in the share of women working part-time which is illustrated using the cases of West Germany, Finland and the Netherlands. This 'gender arrangement' approach conceptualises the complex interrelationship between culture, structure and action and allows us to analyse the different societal processes which influence women's decisions to seek gainful employment.[2]

THE THEORETICAL FRAMEWORK FOR CROSS-NATIONAL ANALYSIS OF PART-TIME EMPLOYMENT: GENDER ARRANGEMENT

The theoretical approach used here is based on three basic concepts: gender culture, the gender order and gender arrangements. A central concern of this approach is to differentiate between culture and the institutions that structure society. The concept of *gender culture* refers to common assumptions about the desirable, 'normal' form of gender relations and the division of labour between women and men. These are institutionalised as norms and can remain relatively constant for some time (Kaufmann 1989). Even so, the dominant gender culture is not necessarily shared equally by all social groups in a given society. Its normative validity may vary according to regions (Häussermann and Sackmann 1993; Duncan 1995), according to ethnicity (Dale and Holdsworth, Chapter 4, this volume; Duncan and Edwards 1995) and according to social strata. The analyses of these differences can be important for they may be the starting point for further change in the overall gender arrangement (see Figure 9.1).

The *gender order* refers to the structure of gender relationships and the relations between different societal institutions. Connell (1987) differentiates between three interrelated but relatively autonomous gender structures: the division of labour, power and 'cathexis', that is, emotional and sexual relationships. Societal institutions are important in relation to the gendered division of labour: the labour market, the family, the state, and the education system. Power relations need to be understood in terms of the strategies adopted by collective actors such as trade unions and the feminist movement (O'Reilly 1995; Mósesdóttir 1996).[3]

Finally, the *gender arrangement* refers to the generally binding forms resulting from negotiations between actors relating to the gender culture and institutions within the gender order. This idea is central to the work of Hirdman (1988 and 1990) who examines the relationship between the 'gender system' and the 'gender contract'. Unfortunately, her analysis neglects the way culture and social order are interrelated (see also Pfau-Effinger 1994a and 1994b; Duncan 1995). The concept of a gender arrangement elaborated here is an attempt to bridge this gap theoretically. It is important that this concept should be seen in relation to the actors who, with different resources, negotiate the arrangement between norms and structures. Contrary to concepts which focus on the effects of patriarchal structures, this approach also treats women as self-determining actors.

Although a significant degree of stability is found in the gender arrangement, which can be explained by the 'long duration' of institutions (Braudel 1972), a dynamic approach is required. In phases of rapid societal modernisation or transformation, the speed of change in the gender culture and the gender order can differ, which may be at variance, or correspond to broader

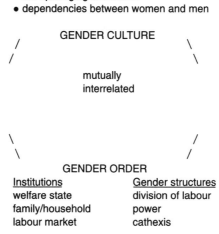

Cultural constructions with reference to:

- spheres of work of women/men
- societal valuation of these spheres
- childhood and main sphere for
  the upbringing of children
- dependencies between women and men

GENDER CULTURE

COLLECTIVE
SOCIAL
ACTORS/
INDIVIDUALS

mutually
interrelated

GENDER ORDER

Institutions	Gender structures
welfare state	division of labour
family/household	power
labour market	cathexis

Figure 9.1 The mutual interrelationship of gender culture, gender order and social action in the gender arrangement

social changes occurring simultaneously. This may increase pertinent tensions and contradictions in the existing 'power-balance' between men and women (Elias 1986, 1987), potentially leading to a process of re-negotiation of the gender arrangement by individuals and/or collective actors.

Factors which make the process of change stronger and more dynamic include: the extent to which the traditional gender culture was entrenched before a period of change; the extent to which the process of cultural modernisation starts in relation to surrounding societies; and finally the scope actors have to find consensus on a new gender arrangement in relation to existing cultural principles of social integration and political practices. In sum, this approach allows us more adequately to explain cross-national structural differences in the share of women working part-time by taking account for the gender arrangement and gender culture in a given society.

Classification of gender arrangements

Societies can be classified and differentiated in relation to the existing gender arrangement. The gender culture can act as a foundation establishing the specific characteristics of a particular gender arrangement using the following four dimensions. First, the conceptualisation of the social spheres by which women and men should be integrated into society and the way the interrelationship of these spheres is constructed (symmetry versus complementarity). Second, by the social value accorded to each of these spheres (equality versus hierarchy). Third, by the way dependencies between women and men are constructed (autonomy versus one-sided or mutual dependency). And, finally, by the cultural construction of responsibility for caring relations between generations. By this I mean the construction of childhood, motherhood and fatherhood in relation to the division of caring responsibilities between the family, state, market or intermediary sector.

Modernisation theories, such as those developed by Parsons as well as those found in substantial parts of feminist discourse, have often assumed industrial societies to have a single model of gender relations, that is, the male bread-winner model. However, I would argue that it is possible to distinguish between at least four gender culture models in Western Europe, with the possibility of numerous sub-variants. Each category constitutes an 'ideal type' in the Weberian sense and can be characterised as follows (Pfau-Effinger 1996).

The family economic gender model

This model is where both sexes contribute substantially to the survival of the family economy by working in their own family business, for example, in agri-culture or trade. Children are treated as members of the family economic unit, that is, as workers, as soon as they are physically able to contribute. There may exist a strong sexual division of labour within the family economy, which in fact varies according to the context of time and space (Honegger and Heintz 1981). Within the family economy there is a mutual dependence: the work of women is seen as being important as that of men for the survival of the family. Therefore, the position of women can, in principle, be as highly valued as that of men. In history the degree to which a gender hierarchy was constructed within this model varied with respect to time and space.

The male breadwinner/female carer model

This model conforms to the idea of the basic differentiation of public and private social spheres. Male breadwinners provide income for their family through waged employment in the public sphere, whereas women are primarily responsible for unpaid caring tasks for their families in the private household. In this model, childhood is constructed to require the special care of a full-time mother.

The dual breadwinner/state carer model

This model conforms to the idea of the 'completed labour market society' (Beck 1986) with full-time integration of both sexes into the employment system. Women and men are seen as individuals, who both earn income for their own

180

living and that of their children. Like the male breadwinner/female carer model, childhood is constructed as a phase in the life cycle requiring much care and support, but this responsibility is more competently performed by the welfare state than by the family.

The dual breadwinner/dual carer model

This model reflects the notion of a symmetrical and equitable integration of both sexes into society. In contrast to the preceding models, child-rearing is to a large extent a family responsibility. The household consists of an equal distribution of domestic and waged labour for women and men. This is only possible because the labour market is organised in such a manner that structurally allows for parents to fulfil their 'dual responsibility'. Such a model requires that domestic labour be financed on the basis of a family wage or on the basis of a state transfer system.

Different gender culture models may dominate in any particular gender arrangement and they also have the potential to change existing patterns.[4] It is important to treat this classification as dynamic rather than static. This classification and the theory of a 'gender arrangement' can help to account for the differences observed in the role of part-time work in West Germany, Finland and the Netherlands.

PART-TIME WORK AND THE MODERNISATION OF THE GENDER ARRANGEMENT IN CROSS-NATIONAL COMPARISON

Most Western European societies have experienced a 'leap in modernisation' (Beck 1986) and a significant increase in female labour force participation, albeit using different combinations of full- and part-time work. Using the 'gender arrangement' approach to provide a dynamic analysis of the differences in the socio-historical development, I will seek to explain why part-time work has been so important in the Netherlands and to a lesser extent in West Germany; in contrast, why it has been so insignificant in Finland in integrating women into paid employment.[5]

At the end of the 1950s, just over a quarter of working-age women were in paid employment in the Netherlands, compared to nearly 50 per cent in West Germany and 66 per cent in Finland (Table 9.1). In the following thirty years female participation increased substantially, especially in the Netherlands, so that by 1990 slightly more than half of the working-age women in the Netherlands and West Germany were active compared to a much higher rate of 74 per cent in Finland. The role of part-time work in this process varies considerably between the countries. Although part-time rates were higher in the Netherlands than elsewhere, these received a dramatic boost during the

Table 9.1 Change of employment patterns of women

	Netherlands (1)	West Germany	Finland
Labour force participation rates of women (percentages)(2)(a)			
1960	26	49	66
1973	29	50	64
1983	40	50	73
1990	53	56	74
Labour force participation rates of married women (percentages)(b)			
1960	6	33	66
1970	15	36	64
1980	29	41	70
1990	41	47	77
Part-time rates of women (percentages)(3)(c)			
1979	44	24	11
1990	62	31	10

Sources: (a) OECD 1992: 46 and OECD 1995: 215; revised statistics for Finland see Allen 1991: 56 (b) Pott-Buter 1993: 200; Allen 1991: 55 (c) OECD 1995: 210; there are no data available for former years.

Notes: (1) Until 1987, the share of employees in part-time work; as a result the labour force participation rate has been higher in reality than the statistics show, because some groups of part-time workers have been excluded from statistics (Pott-Buter 1993: 29; OECD 1995: 211). (2) Proportion of all employed and unemployed women to the female population 15–64 years of age. (3) Share of part-time working women to all employed women. Definition of 'part-time': Finland 1–29 hours (Nätti 1991), West Germany 1–34 hours, the Netherlands 1–30 hours (OECD 1995: 211).

1980s so that by 1990 62 per cent of women were working part-time compared to only 31 per cent in Germany and only 10 per cent in Finland.

This three-country comparison clearly indicates how increased labour force participation in the Netherlands and West Germany is more closely associated with the rise in part-time work than is the case in Finland. These differences can be largely explained, first, in relation to the gender culture which formed the historical basis for the changes in the gender arrangement in each society at the beginning of the period of analysis; and, second, in terms of the different state policies, firms' behaviour and the action of collective actors.

Modernisation of the gender culture and orientation of women to part-time work

In the 1950s and 1960s, the gender arrangements in the Netherlands and in West Germany primarily reflected the male breadwinner/female carer family model. After the Second World War, this expressed itself in the predominance and institutional backing of the housewife marriage. This principle was particularly central to the gender arrangement in the Netherlands where it was not socially acceptable for wives to take up paid work (Ishwaran 1959), although this did not apply to the same degree for West Germany (Sommerkorn 1988).

These differences can, in part, be explained in relation to the foundations of the housewife marriage model, and the function of the family ideal in society in general. In West Germany, the idea of the 'home caring society' was not as deeply anchored in cultural traditions as in the Netherlands. In West Germany, housewife marriage was the dominant cultural ideal from the turn of the twentieth century, whereas in the Netherlands, the dominance of this notion in the gender arrangement can be traced back to the seventeenth century (Schama 1988). Moreover, the gender culture of the Netherlands was traditionally much more centred on children, and on the ideal of having many children who would be cared for in the home (Pott-Buter 1993; Knijn 1994a). Differences in the institutional foundation of religion were also important. The Netherlands was a multi-confessional society, split into many different religious associations, which were hostile even to each other. Society was 'pillarised' in that it was deeply segregated culturally, politically and socially (Felling *et al.* 1987) . There was, nevertheless, a strong cultural homogeneity with reference to the ideal of the housewife marriage and the importance of having children. According to Ishwaran (1959), the author of a comprehensive sociological study on the Dutch family in the fifties, the family ideal played a very important role in the integration of society, for it was a central common idea that went beyond cultural fragmentation. In West Germany the family ideal did not have to play a similar function to the same extent. The gender arrangement in Finland, in contrast, was based on the agrarian family economic model up to the 1950s. There was a gender-specific, but egalitarian division of labour within an agrarian family. Both gender domains were ascribed comparable social worth and gender relations within marriage had a partner-like nature (Voipio-Juvas and Ruohtula 1949; Julkunen 1991).

Rapid modernisation has taken place in all three societies since the Second World War. Secularisation, democratisation and the expansion of professional education were all part of this development which broadened the life course options for some individuals. These processes led to an intensification of the contradiction in the Netherlands and West Germany between the notion of equality in bourgeois ideology and the construction of inequality in the male breadwinner/female carer model. Women reacted to this by increasingly questioning the housewife arrangement at the level of everyday life and by founding a feminist movement which fought for gender equality at the political and cultural level. This change can also be seen in the fact that it has become more acceptable for married women to work through the expansion of job opportunities in the service sector, declining birth rates[6] and rising rates of divorce and single parenthood. Women developed a new identity as mothers and workers who combine both spheres of life (Geissler and Oechsle 1994). Beck-Gernsheim (1983) describes this as a process of 'late, adapting individualisation'.

In the Netherlands the process of change was much stronger than in West Germany. One of the most significant bases for this 'cultural revolution' (Peters *et al.* 1993) was the process of secularisation which eroded the previous 'pillarisation'. Within four decades a substantial break with the centuries-old tradition of housewife marriage took place. Mothers were no longer seen as the only people competent to care for their children, and it became increasingly accepted that they share this task with others, both inside and outside the home (Heiligers 1992:5ff.). Similar but less dramatic changes occurred in West Germany. This can be seen, for example, in the acceptance of maternal employment: 46 per cent of the population in the Netherlands compared to 24 per cent in West Germany think that mothers of pre-school children should be employed. A similar pattern is also seen with those positively supporting employed mothers of schoolchildren: in the Netherlands 86 per cent compared to 51 per cent in West Germany (Höllinger 1991: 769). On the basis of data from the International Social Survey Programme, Höllinger (1991) concludes that the Netherlands is one of the few countries in which a more 'modern' type of attitude towards employment of mothers prevails, whereas West Germany belongs to the more 'traditional' societies in this respect.

The reason cultural change was more rapid in the Netherlands than in West Germany was because, first, the family played a much greater role in cultural integration than in West Germany and was therefore more entrenched, before this role was undermined in the secularisation process. Second, the Netherlands was a latecomer with respect to cultural modernisation. While the economy and education system modernised, this remained set within a rather conservative gender culture; West Germany, in contrast, had always had a more diverse culture and change started earlier. Third, it was easier for the main actors in the Netherlands to find a new social consensus than in West Germany. Dutch society had been horizontally rather than vertically divided; when secularisation eroded pillarisation it was easier to build a new consensus on the principles of solidarity and equality, while stronger hierarchical divisions in Germany were reproduced in a redefinition of gender relations (Plantenga 1993).[7]

Traditional attitudes in favour of a purely housewife role are stronger in West Germany than in the Netherlands: 26 per cent of West German women compared to 14 per cent of Dutch women said they would prefer to stay out of employment (IPOS 1992; van den Putte and Pelzer 1993: 490). In contrast, more Dutch women prefer part-time work to being a housewife. They also appear to be more satisfied with part-time employment: only 12 per cent said they would prefer to take up a full-time job compared to 35 per cent of West German women. In the Netherlands, this seems to indicate a general cultural trend away from the 8-hour standard working day. This is supported by the results of an investigation on employment preferences of men. More than two-thirds of men (69 per cent) would prefer a part-time job to full-time employment, if they could choose. In West Germany on the other hand, only a quarter of men (28 per cent) would prefer part-time work (sources of data are based on IPOS 1992 for Germany and van den Putte and Pelzer 1993: 490 for the Netherlands).

In both countries, however, the traditional ideal of privatised childhood still dominates (Knijn and Verheijen 1988; Pfau-Effinger and Geissler 1992). According to a recent survey, 47 per cent of women and 46 per cent of men in West Germany thought that all-day pre-school programmes would be detrimental to their children's development (IPOS 1992: 68). If they could choose between school instruction on a half-day and full-day basis, only 19 per cent of women and men would choose all-day school (IPOS 1992: 72). This causes a 'moral dilemma' for mothers, according to Gerson (1995), between the aim of individual self-fulfilment and care for their children. Although there is an increased demand for part-time work as a way of managing maternal employment, this reflects how women's demand for paid employment is set against institutional constraints such as unfavourable school timetables in Germany. Part-time work is a substantial factor influencing the modernisation of notions of women's roles in society (Pfau-Effinger and Geissler 1992) and it has a central position in the new gender arrangement in both countries.

Cultural change in the Finnish gender arrangement took a distinctly different avenue. In the 1950s and 1960s there were strong signs of modernisation evident in the societal transformation to an industrial society and then directly to a service society (Alestalo and Kuhnle 1991). The basic symmetry between the gender-specific division of labour and the more egalitarian relations between spouses was maintained within their modernised forms. What changed was the cultural ideal of childhood: children were seen increasingly as individuals who need a lot of care. Child care in this arrangement is primarily a task of the welfare state (Julkunen 1991). Since the labour market crisis at the beginning of the 1990s, neither part-time work for mothers nor a retreat to the household has been seen as a societal solution. Women seem to be exclusively oriented towards full-time work. One important reason for this difference compared to other countries seems to be that Finnish mothers do not face the same 'moral dilemma' as mothers in the Netherlands or West Germany. Finnish mothers are not torn between 'self' interests and 'care' interests, between the demand or expectation to be in two different places at the same time – in the office and at home. This is because 'childhood' is largely constructed as 'public'. This attitude is supported by the provision of a personally and financially well-equipped system of public child care on a highly professional basis.

Thus we find two different paths towards a more egalitarian gender culture model. In this respect, the Netherlands and Finland are further advanced than West Germany, though the modernisation paths in both countries differ substantially and part-time work plays a very different role. The Dutch path began with a dominant male breadwinner/female carer model and is now progressing towards a dual breadwinner/family carer model, which is not the case in West Germany where the male breadwinner model was simply modernised. The Finnish path in contrast went from a family economic model towards an individualistic-egalitarian model. In Finland, as well as in the Netherlands, the attitudes and the behaviour of men contributed to the extension of a more egalitarian gender culture. This can be seen in the higher level of participation of men in family work. As empirical research has shown, men in Finland and the Netherlands contribute more to caring and household labour than men in West Germany, where the domestic division of labour is still very traditional (Nikander 1992; Künzler 1995).[8]

Constraints and opportunities at the level of the gender order

The constraints and opportunities for women to realise their aspirations are different in the gender orders of all three countries. There is a relatively high level of correspondence between the demand for full-time employment and the percentage of those working full-time in the Netherlands and West Germany: 12 per cent want full-time work compared to 16 per cent of women who are working full-time in the Netherlands; the respective figures for West Germany are that 35 per cent want to work full-time and 35 per cent work full-time. However, because of institutional lags in development, the share of women who want to work part-time is much higher than the number of women working part-time: in the Netherlands 74 per cent of women want part-time work compared to 25 per cent who are working part-time; in West Germany the corresponding figures were 35 per cent and 15 per cent. Particularly among the non-employed and unemployed there is a high proportion of women who would prefer part-time employment to staying at home. (Sources of data for 1988–90 are drawn from van den Putte and Pelzer (1993: 490) and Schupp (1991: 220). Data for 1990 are based on OECD (1995: 215) and OECD (1991: 41).)

In the Netherlands, paradoxically, this is a 'double mismatch': on one hand, there is a rather high surplus of women who say they would prefer a part-time job compared with those women who are working part-time. On the other hand, there is also a large number of women who are involuntarily working part-time: nearly a quarter of part-time working women would prefer full-time employment.[9] In most cases involuntary part-timers seem to be mothers who were unable to move from part- to full-time employment once their grown-up children had left home (Plantenga and van Velzen 1994).

In Finland, by contrast, there is a close correspondence between the preference for, and level of, part-time employment. The proportion of full-time working women who said that they would prefer a part-time job of between 1 and 29 hours in 1993 was only 4.4 per cent, although the overall share of women working part-time is rather low. Among the non- and unemployed there is very little demand for part-time work (Nätti 1995). In contrast, the rate of involuntary part-time work is relatively high: according to Nätti (1995: 17) 49 per cent said they did not want a part-time job (see Annual Labour Force Survey 1993).

Discrepancies between employment orientations and real employment are a result of time lags and discrepancies between gender culture and gender order. It should be noted, however, that in times of transformation there may exist ambivalence within the orientations of individuals with consequences for their social practice, which are possibly not visible in representative investigations on the basis of questionnaires (see also Dex 1988).[10]

Changes in the gender policies of the welfare state

The West German welfare state was reconstructed after the Second World War on conservative-corporatist principles. Social provision was organised to reflect and reproduce existing status hierarchies (Leibfried and Tennstedt 1985; Kaufmann 1989, Esping-Andersen 1990). This system was based on, and its policies continue to support, the male breadwinner family model. The main reference point of the standard (male) employment relationship became the basis of the social insurance system, which resulted in disadvantages that women had to accept in the employment system (Pfau-Effinger 1990, 1993; Plantenga 1992b; Rubery, Chapter 7, this volume). Neither the possibility for mothers to stay home and care for their children independent of a family breadwinner nor the integration of mothers into the labour market has been actively promoted in West Germany (Pfau-Effinger and Geissler 1992; Quack 1993). Part-timers, especially those working less than 20 hours a week or earning less than DM610 (1997) a month do not contribute to the social security system. Restricted child care provision sought to meet educational goals rather than female emancipation (Kaufmann 1989), reinforcing the cultural ideal of private caring being coupled to marriage. Part-time work for mothers is only possible for women living with a male breadwinner. Among single mothers, in contrast, there is a relatively high rate of 'involuntary' full-time employment since they usually cannot afford to work part-time or take a family break because they lack a male breadwinner. Market solutions provided by private childminders are really only an alternative for middle-class women.[11] In terms of the social actors in the German system the trade unions have for a long time oriented their policies towards the security of the standard employment relationships of their male clients (Wiesenthal 1987). The feminist movement supported full-time integration of all women into waged work, but the expansion of part-time jobs was never a political goal (Pfau-Effinger and Geissler 1992).

In contrast, the welfare states in the Netherlands and Finland were in substantial parts organised as 'social democrat' welfare regimes (Esping-Andersen 1990). Cultural values and regulation were based on solidarity and the principle that all citizens should have equal access to welfare benefits and services. However, both welfare states represented a very different combination of welfare regime and gender culture. In Finland, there was a combination of a social democratic welfare regime with a gender policy which promoted an egalitarian-individualistic family model, while in the Netherlands, a welfare regime based on social democrat principles of social redistribution was combined with a rather traditional gender policy in favour of the housewife–male breadwinner family model until the beginning of the 1980s. Further, the policies of the Dutch welfare state were based on a concept of social citizenship with universal rights in contrast to the Finnish system of social rights based on more employment. The Dutch welfare system is considered to be one of the most generous of all Western industrial countries (Heiligers 1992; Bussemaker 1994: 9).

In the Netherlands, from the 1970s until the mid-1980s, state policies chiefly promoted housewife marriage. There was no expansion of the practically non-existent public child care system until the beginning of the 1980s (see Bussemaker 1994). Nevertheless, unlike West Germany single mothers were included into the general cultural ideal of the caring housewife. Since 1965 generous social benefits for single mothers allowed them to stay at home until their children had grown up. During the 1980s, however, the gender policies of the welfare state were substantially transformed. Two equality promotion programmes sought to further the possibility for women to have an independent existence beyond a purely caring and housework orientation. At the highest political level, a commission for the promotion of gender equality was founded (Emancipatieraad), in which representatives of the feminist movement worked together with government, unions and employers' representatives (Bussemaker 1994).[12]

The promotion and protection of part-time work for women and men was part and parcel of a positive equality policy and in response to demands from the feminist movement (Plantenga 1992a: 84). Dutch mainstream feminists were relatively homogeneous in their political aims. They struggled for a fundamental restructuring of paid and unpaid work according to which men and women could distribute their working time equally between caring and waged work (Plantenga and van Velzen 1994). Further, the unions, in co-operation with representatives of the state and the women's movement, participated in developing a strong policy for the promotion of part-time work, which has led to a relatively high standard of working conditions and social security of part-time jobs. In sum, welfare policies in the Netherlands, unlike West Germany, have promoted the development of a more egalitarian dual breadwinner/dual carer model based on part-time work opportunities for mothers and fathers. It would appear that welfare state policy, shaped by social democratic ideas, offers better opportunities for a modernisation of the male breadwinner model which favourably affects women's social status than policy which has been shaped by a corporatist-conservative welfare state regime. Nevertheless, the persistence of policies which make financial transfers dependent on a male breadwinner marriage, as in Germany, reinforces the wife's dependency on her husband.

In contrast to the Netherlands and West Germany, the Finnish welfare state was shaped by a social democrat welfare regime tailored to a dual breadwinner/dual carer gender arrangement. Since the beginning of the 1970s, married women and men have been treated as individuals for social insurance and tax. A comprehensive public child care system was developed which allows both parents to work full-time. The state also promoted waged work of women in its role as employer, by largely extending the number of service jobs in welfare administration, so that it was possible for women to remain continuously in full-time employment (Korppi-Tommola 1991). Because of this individualisation in terms of social security and income, and because of the full integration of all adults into the employment system, single mothers are not discriminated against in terms of income and social security. The 'women friendly' policies of the welfare state were substantially influenced by women themselves, who largely formed the staff in the public welfare service sector (Simonen 1990). The social mobilisation of women within comprehensive women's federations already had a long tradition in Finland and these associations had to a great degree contributed to the building of the welfare state.

LABOUR MARKET DEVELOPMENTS AND PART-TIME WORK

During the 1950s in West Germany a considerable proportion of married women was integrated into the labour force, the majority of them working as blue-collar workers in the manufacturing sector. A certain proportion of women stayed in employment after marriage or returned to work after active motherhood (Willms-Herget 1985; Pfau-Effinger 1990; Lauterbach 1991). In the Netherlands during the same period, women were more likely to have a two-phase biography: working prior to marriage and withdrawing from the labour market afterwards (Plantenga 1992b) (as can be seen from activity rates cited in Table 9.1). The main explanation for this difference is that the idea of the 'home caring' and child-centred society was more deeply anchored in the culture of the Netherlands than in West Germany. Moreover, German society was also less prosperous than the Netherlands: the distribution of wealth did not allow most working-class German women to be full-time housewives, despite the popular ideal of a housewife marriage since the turn of the century (Rosenbaum 1982; Willms-Herget 1985; Plantenga 1992a).

Labour shortages in the early 1960s in West Germany and the Netherlands prompted many companies to offer part-time work as a means to attract married women back to work. However, these private sector initiatives did not result in a significant increase in the number of women in work (Pott-Buter 1993), because cultural ideals about the structure of the family were changing at a slower rate than practices within firms (Willms-Herget 1985; Plantenga 1992a). During the recession years of the 1970s female labour market participation continued to grown in West Germany and the Netherlands, independently of economic cycles, although levels of female unemployment grew faster than levels of female employment (Pfau-Effinger 1990). Hidden female unemployment increased, partly because of a deficit in the supply of part-time jobs for women: many mothers who wanted a part-time job preferred to stay at home instead of accepting a full-time job (Brinkmann and Kohler 1989). High female unemployment was also a result of a time lag between the increase in the share of women who wanted to work part-time and the somewhat limited development of part-time jobs.

In West Germany the labour market remained relatively closed with respect to job opportunities for women, although a moderate and rather slow growth of the service sector has led to an increase in part-time jobs for women.[13] Restructuring was more rapid in the Netherlands where the proportion of women's jobs doubled in less than two decades, and female-dominated jobs were constructed mainly on a part-time basis. However, as the chapters by Smith *et al.* (Chapter 2), Delsen (Chapter 3) and Walwei (Chapter 5) in this volume show, there is not a uni-causal relationship between the development of service jobs and the rise of the female labour force participation, although the more extensive provision of public and private services created both job opportunities and the possibility for women to go out to work (see Häußermann and Siebel 1991). The more positive attitude to part-time work in the Netherlands seems to have stimulated the use of part-timers in firms more than in West Germany, even though part-time work is more protected in the Netherlands than in West Germany (Plantenga 1992a). The prospects for part-time work have become less certain since the impact of German unification which resulted in two contrasting gender culture models being brought together: in the East a tradition of a dual breadwinner/state carer model based on full-time working mothers with a 'modernised' male breadwinner model supplemented by mothers working part-time in the West (Geissler 1991). It seems as if these cultural differences will persist despite unification under a common male breadwinner model in the welfare state and the labour market (Quack and Maier 1994; O'Reilly 1995).

In the past thirty years the Finnish labour market has also experienced a dramatic restructuring. Until the 1960s nearly all women (96 per cent) were working, usually in their own agricultural family business (Allen *et al.* 1990). Within a couple of decades a modern service economy was created which guaranteed full employment for women. The proportion of service jobs has doubled in Finland from 33 per cent in 1960 to 61 per cent in 1990 (Finnish Ministry of Labour 1993: 17, 25). Unlike West Germany or the Netherlands, the guarantee of full-time employment for women was only possible because of the central role played by the welfare state in the dramatic increase of service jobs for women, particularly in public caring institutions. Today, 43 per cent of Finnish women are employed in the public sector, more than half of them in social services (Nordic Council of Ministers 1994: 87). During this process of change, women retained their former pattern of full-time work on a par with that of men (Nikander 1992: 109).[14]

Although horizontal gendered segregation is very marked in the Finnish labour market, this does not correspond to a high degree of vertical segregation as in West Germany and the Netherlands. In the process of expansion of the welfare state, women have increasingly occupied high positions in the public sector. The share of women in top positions of public services today is 41 per cent (Kolehmeinen 1992: 13). The wage gap between men and women is very small in Finland where the average monthly net income of women is 94 per cent of that of men (Nordic Council of Ministers 1994: 92). One explanation for this is that the level of average and professional education for women is higher than for men (Anttonen 1990; Nikander 1992). Furthermore, 'female' occupations like those in the social services are valued more highly in Finnish society than in other countries. This is to a large extent due to a fundamental principle of the Scandinavian welfare state holding that social services should be offered by the state on a relatively highly qualified level (Esping-Andersen 1990; Alestalo and Kuhnle 1991). Furthermore, the redistributive effect of the policies of the welfare state with respect to gender may play a role here. One important insight to take away from this comparison is that strong gender segregation of occupations does not automatically correspond with strong vertical segregation (Kolehmeinen 1992). The gendered segregation of the labour market in Finland also resulted in many more men than women losing their jobs in the heavy economic crisis since the beginning of the 1990s: in general, the decrease in the number of jobs in the private industrial sector was much higher than in the public sector (Koistinen and Suikkanen 1992).

Neither the private sector nor the state in Finland actively sought to expand the use of part-time work radically. Sporadic attempts of firms in retail trade in this direction during the 1970s and the 1980s failed because there were practically no workers willing to accept these jobs (Allen et al. 1990; Nätti 1995). This is partly due to the strong work ethic in Finland where full-time employment is the cultural norm; while working part-time or taking lengthy parental leave is associated with a high risk of social stigmatisation.

Although at the beginning of the 1990s more firms, particularly in the service sector, expressed an interest in expanding their use of part-time work (Erikson and Fellman 1991), in practice the proportion of part-time jobs increased only marginally (Nätti 1995: 10). The demand for part-time jobs among women is very low in Finland: the proportion of full-time employed women who would have preferred to work fewer than 30 hours per week increased from 6 to 9 per cent during the 1980s but fell to 4 per cent in 1993 (Nätti 1995: 20).

CONCLUSIONS

In this chapter I have argued that cross-national differences in the use of part-time work cannot only be explained by structuralist accounts of post-Fordist flexible employment strategies of firms or the institutional frameworks established by welfare states. Comparing part-time working in the Netherlands, West Germany and Finland shows the significant effects of the interplay of gender culture, gender order and the behaviour of women within the framework of a gender arrangement. Cross-national differences in the development of the share of women working part-time can be primarily explained by differences in the gender culture and particularly of the cultural ideals about the work of mothers and the appropriate sphere for bringing up children.

State policies and firm strategies in relation to the behaviour of collective actors affect the degree and speed of change. As we have seen in the post-war period, the basic characteristics of the gender culture already differed significantly between the countries examined here, exemplified by the rates of female activity.

In the following decades, in all three countries, processes of re-negotiation of the gender arrangement between societal actors and a change in cultural ideals took place which was primarily initiated by women and in which men participated to a different degree. The new ideals are, more than before, based on the cultural construction of the 'employed mother'. Differences in the degree and forms in which women were integrated into the labour market can be primarily explained by the fact that cultural change was based on different cultural traditions, proceeding under different dynamics of change which resulted in divergent paths. In those countries where the tradition of the male breadwinner/female carer family prevailed, the idea of privatised childhood survived in part. As a consequence, part-time work was a substantial element of the modernisation of the male breadwinner family model. Though in parts precarious, part-time work turned out to be a new form of employment for women in the biographical phases of active motherhood. This is even more true for the Netherlands than for West Germany. These differences can be explained by the fact that the tradition of the 'home caring society' and the housewife marriage was more deep-rooted in the Netherlands. Institutional regulation has in part reinforced the orientation of women towards part-time work in these countries. In contrast, in Finland, where the male breadwinner/female carer model was never dominant, the tradition of women's full-time participation in the production sphere was maintained during the modernisation process and change in the gender arrangement.

Differentiating at the conceptual level between the gender culture and the gender order of a particular society is fruitful in identifying existing contradictions, asynchronies and discrepancies between the different levels, and their consequences for the development of part-time work. The policies of the welfare state, the conditions of the labour market and the gendered division of labour within family, as well as policies and alliances of collective actors, are important factors to explain how fast social practice has adapted to the increase in the orientation of women towards part-time work in the Netherlands and West Germany. In the Netherlands we have seen how a social democrat welfare state and a fairly unified feminist movement, integrated into the decision-making process of the welfare state, promoted new patterns of employment orientation in favour of part-time work in the phases of active motherhood. In West Germany a more corporatist-conservative welfare regime and a divided protest feminist movement has not integrated itself into welfare state institutions, with the consequences that part-time work is less well developed and less well protected.

When we find that women (and men) in different countries have rather different interests in part-time work, what could be the consequence for policy recommendations at the European level? Part-time work should be one among several options for parents to combine family and employment in times of active parenthood. A central precondition for a real choice would be a comprehensive public child care provision and a full coverage of part-time work with respect to social benefits. Moreover, private caring work of parents should be respected as a central contribution to society, and a legal right for parental leave with an allowance which is based on an income substitute should be introduced. This would allow a real choice between staying at home or working intermittently part-time. Moreover, to avoid discrimination of part-time workers within the employment system, the strong connection of working-time and career which exists in most Western European countries should be decoupled. It is even outdated today when societies can no longer guarantee full employment of all those who want a job.[15]

ACKNOWLEDGEMENTS

Thanks to Simon Duncan, Pertti Koistinen and Faith Dasko for useful comments on an earlier version of this chapter, to Faith Dasko for her translation of parts of this chapter and to Jackie O'Reilly and Colette Fagan for their very useful suggestions in clarifying the arguments.

NOTES

1 O'Reilly (1996) discusses the way theoretical approaches to cross-national employment research integrate 'culture' as a dimension. She argues that a combination of 'ideational' and institutional approaches is fruitful for cross-national comparisons. See also the introductory chapter to this book by Fagan and O'Reilly where they argue for giving gender a more central focus.

2 International structures of social inequality comprise another important dimension of gender differences; see Lenz (1996).

3 In this chapter I am not able to discuss cathexis.

4 An extension of the analysis outside of Western Europe would expose other types of gender culture models. For example, Weber (1996) found that the modern Japanese family represents a mixture of a traditional Japanese model, based on the Samurai family and Confucian gender morals, together with an adopted Western male breadwinner/female carer model.

5 Unfortunately, given the limits of this chapter it is not possible to discuss in any detail the differences relating to social stratification, regions and ethnic groups within these countries.

6 The birth rate in the Netherlands decreased from an average of 3.1 per woman in the child-bearing age group in 1969 to 1.6 in 1990 (Centraal bureau voor de Statistiek 1992).

7 This may also explain why in the former DDR a rather hierarchical social construction of gender relations had partly survived besides the full integration of women into waged work, as feminist studies after unification have found (Quack and Maier 1994).

8 It seems to be paradoxical that Dutch husbands are so progressive with respect to their participation in caring and housework even though the housewife model was so deeply rooted in the Dutch culture. There are some indicators, however, that the 'father' was already traditionally constructed here not only as breadwinner but also in parts as 'carer' (see Ishwaran 1959; Schama 1988).

9 According to the OECD (1990: 181; and my own calculations) the proportion of all employed women working 'voluntarily' part-time. This is still much higher than the rate of women working part-time in other Western European countries (see other chapters in this volume on Australia, New Zealand and Japan).

10 Dex talks about 'lagged adaptation' at the level of individuals which means that it needs a certain space of time until women adjust their aspirations to their contemporary experiences and practices.

11 The growing use in Germany of the cheap labour of highly qualified migrants from Eastern European countries creates new problems of inequality among women (Friese 1996; Rerrich 1996).

12 Trudi Knijn (1994b) argues that while this process was to support women it also meant a loss of security previously provided by the welfare state (see also Heiligers 1992).

13 In 1990 69 per cent of all employees in the Netherlands were working in the service sector, compared to 57 per cent in West Germany (OECD 1995: 209).

14 Most women stay outside employment for about one year after childbirth, though the parental leave legislation would allow them to stay outside the labour force until the child is 3 with a considerable income substitute.

15 Some big Swedish firms could be examples here which institutionalised 'Schemes for the promotion of parents' according to which parents can make a career independent of their working time.

BIBLIOGRAPHY

Alestalo, M. and Kuhnle, S. (1991) 'The Scandinavian Route: Economic, Social, and Political Developments in Denmark, Finland, Norway and Sweden' in R. Ericson, E. J. Hansen, S. Ringen and H. Uusitalo (eds) The Scandinavian Model. Welfare States and Welfare Research, Armonk, London: M.E. Sharpe.

Allen, T. (1991) Kotilaloustuotanto ja naisten palkkatyö – Muuttvuko näkymätön näkyväksi markkinoilla? TTT Katsaus 4: 50–62.

Allen, T., Laaksonen, S., Keinänen, P. and Ilmakunnas, S. (1990) Wage from Work and Gender. A Study on Differentials in Finland in 1985, Statistics Finland, Studies 190 (in English 1992), Helsinki: Statistics Finland.

Anttonen, A. (1990) 'The Feminization of the Scandinavian Welfare State' in L. Simonen (ed.) Finnish Debates on Women's Studies, Tampereen Yliopist, Yhteiskuntatieteiden tutkimusleitos, Naistutkimusyksikkö, Työraportteja 2.

Beck, U. (1986) Risikogesellschaft. Auf dem Weg in eine andere Moderne, Frankfurt: Suhrkamp.

Beck-Gernsheim, E. (1983) 'Vom "Dasein für andere" zum Anspruch auf ein Stück "eigenes Leben" – Individualisierungsprozesse im weiblichen Lebenszusammenhang', Soziale Welt 34: 307–39.

Braudel, F. (1972) 'Geschichte und Sozialwissenschaften – Die "Longue Duree"' in H.-U. Wehler (ed.) Geschichte und Soziologie, Köln: Kiepenheuer & Witsch.

Brinkmann, C. and Kohler, H. (1989) 'Teilzeitarbeit und Arbeitsvolumen', Mitteilungen aus der Arbeitsmarkt- und Berufsforschung 3: 472–82.

Büchtemann, C. F. and Schupp, J. (1986) Zur Sozio-Ökonomie der Teilzeitbeschäftigung in der Bundesrepublik Deutschland, discussion papers of the Wissenschaftszentrums Berlin für Sozialforschung, IIM/LMP 86–15, Berlin: WZB.

Bussemaker, J. (1994) 'Gender Regimes and Welfare State Regimes: Gender Relations and Social Politics in the Netherlands', paper presented at the conference 'Crossing

Borders. International Dialogues on Gender, Social Politics and Citizenship', Stockholm, 27–9 May.

Centraal bureau voor de Statistiek (CBS) (1992) *Negentig jaren statistiek in tijdreeksen*, Den Haag: CBS.

Connell, R. (1987) *Gender and Power. Society, The Person and Sexual Politics*, Cambridge, Oxford: Polity Press.

Dex, S. (1988) *Women's Attitudes towards Work*, London: Macmillan.

Duncan, S. (1993) 'Spatial Divisions of Patriarchy?' in S. Duncan (ed.) *Spatial Divisions of Patriarchy in Western Europe*, Special Issue of 'Environment and Planning' A, 26.

—— (1995) 'Theorizing European Gender Systems', *Journal of European Social Policy* 4: 263–84.

Duncan, S. and Edwards, R. (1995) 'Lone Mothers and Paid Work: Neighbourhoods, Local Labour Markets and Welfare State Regimes', *Social Politics* 2: 149–73.

Elias, N. (1986) 'Wandlungen der Machtbalance zwischen den Geschlechtern. Eine prozeßsoziologische Untersuchung am Beispiel des antiken Römerstaats', *Kölner Zeitschrift für Soziologie und Sozialpsychologie* 38: 425–49.

—— (1987) *Der Prozeß der Zivilisation*, 2 vols, Frankfurt: Suhrkamp.

Eriksson, T. and Fellman, S. (1991) *Työajat yritysten näkökulmasta*, ETLA B 72, Helsinki.

Esping-Andersen, G. (1990) *Three Worlds of Welfare Capitalism*, Cambridge, Oxford: Polity Press.

Felling, A., Peters, J. and Schreuder, O. (1987) *Religion im Vergleich: Bundesrepublik Deutschland und Niederlande*, Frankfurt, Bern, New York, Paris: Peter Lang.

Finnish Ministry of Labour (1993) *Finnish Labour Review* 1, Helsinki: Ministry of Labour.

Friese, M. (1996) 'Soziale Ungleichheit-Bildung-Geschlecht-Ethnizität. Modernisierungsfallen und ihre Überwindung' in P. Ahlheit *et al.* (eds) *Von der Arbeitsgesellschaft zur Bildungsgesellschaft. Perspektiven von Arbeit und Bildung im Prozeß europäischen Wandels*, Bremen: University of Bremen.

Geissler, B. (1991) 'Arbeitsmarkt oder Familie: Alte und neue gesellschaftliche Integrationsformen von Frauen', *Zeitschrift für Sozialreform* 11/12: 663–76.

Geissler, B. and Oechsle, M. (1994) 'Lebensplanung als Konstruktion: Biographische Dilemmata und Lebenslauf-Entwürfe junger Frauen' in U. Beck and E. Beck-Gernsheim (eds) *Riskante Freiheiten*, Frankfurt: Suhrkamp.

Gerson, K. (1995) 'Gender and Modernization: Women, Men, and Moral Dilemmas in an Age of Gender and Family Change', unpublished manuscript.

Häußermann, H. and Siebel, W. (1991): 'Soziologie des Wohnens', in H. Häußermann, D. Ipsen, T. Krämer-Badoni, D. Läpple, M. Rodenstein and W. Siebel (eds) *Stadt und Raum. Soziologische Analysen*, Pfaffenweiler: Centaurus.

Häußermann, H. and Sackmann, R. (1993) 'Regional Differences of Female Labour Force Participation in West-Germany' in P. Koistinen and I. Ostner (eds) *Women and Markets*, Tampere: Yliopisto.

Heiligers, P. (1992) 'Gender and Changing Perspectives of Labour and Care', paper presented at the First European Conference of Sociology, August.

Hirdman, Y. (1988) 'Genussystemet – reflexioner kring kvinnors sociala underordning', *Kvinnovetenskapligtidskrift* 3: 49–63.

Hirdman, Y.(1990) 'Genussystemet' in Statens Offentliga Utredningar: 44, *Demokrati och makt i Sverige*, Stockholm: SOU.

Höllinger, F. (1991) 'Frauenerwerbstätigkeit und Wandel der Geschlechtsrollen im internationalen Vergleich', *Kölner Zeitschrift für Soziologie und Sozialpsychologie* 43: 753–71.

Honegger, C. and Heintz, B. (eds) (1981) *Listen der Ohnmacht. Zur Sozialgeschichte weiblicher Widerstandsformen*, Frankfurt: Europäische Verlagsanstalt.

Institut für praxisorientierte Sozialforschung (IPOS) (1992) *Gleichberechtigung von Frauen und Männern – Wirklichkeit und Einstellungen in der Bevölkerung*, Schriftenreihe des Bundesministers für Frauen und Jugend, Stuttgart, Berlin, Köln: Kohlhammer.

Ishwaran, K. (1959) *Family Life in the Netherlands*, The Hague: Utgeverij van Keulen n.V.

Julkunen, R. (1991) 'Women in the Welfare State' in M. Manninen and P. Setälä (eds) *The Lady with the Bow*, Helsinki: Otava.

Kaufmann, F. X. (1989) *Zukunft der Familie. Stabilität, Stabilitätsrisiken und Wandel familialer Lebensformen sowie ihre gesellschaftlichen und politischen Bedingungen*, Gutachten zu Händen des Bundeskanzleramtes, Bonn: Bundeskanzleramt.

Knijn, T. (1994a) 'Social Dilemmas in Images of Motherhood in the Netherlands', *European Journal of Women's Studies* 1, 2: 183–206.

—— (1994b) 'Fish without Bikes: Revision of the Dutch Welfare State and its Consequences for the (In)dependence of Single Mothers', *Social Politics* 1: 83–105.

Knijn, T. and Verheijen, C. (1988) *Tussen Plicht en Oontplooiing: Het Welbevinden van Moeders met Jonge Kinderen in Een Veranderende Cultuur*, Nijmegen: ITS.

Koistinen, P. and Suikkanen, A. (1992) 'How to Manage the Decline: Are Finnish Employers and State Actors Following a New Strategy in the Current Economic Decline?' in P. Koistinen and A. Suikkanen (eds) *Finnish Labour Market Policy in Trial – Evaluation on the 1980s*, Työelämän tutkimuskeskus Työraportteja 27.

Kolehmeinen, S. (1992) 'Occupational Gender Segregation in the Finnish Labour Market – Change in Employment or in Segregation?' Paper presented at the First European Conference on Sociology at Vienna, August.

Korppi-Tommola, A. (1991) 'Education – The Road to Work and Equality' in M. Manninen and P. Setälä (eds) *The Lady with the Bow*, Helsinki: Otava.

Künzler, J. (1995) 'Geschlechtsspezifische Arbeitsteilung: Die Beteiligung von Männern im Haushalt im internationalen Vergleich', *Zeitschrift für Frauenforschung* 13: 115–32.

Lauterbach, Wolfgang (1991) 'Erwerbsmuster von Frauen. Entwicklungen und Veränderungen seit Beginn dieses Jahrhunderts. S. 23–56' in K. U. Mayer, J. Allmendinger and J. Huinink (eds) *Vom Regen in die Traufe: Frauen zwischen Beruf und Familie*, Frankfurt/New York: Campus Verlag.

Leibfried, S. and Tennstedt, F. (1985) 'Einleitung' in S. Leibfried and F. Tennstedt (eds) *Politik der Armut und Spaltung des Sozialstaats*, Frankfurt: Suhrkamp.

Lenz, I. (1996) 'Geschlecht, Herrschaft und internationale Ungleichheit' in R. Becker-Schmidt and G.-A. Knapp (eds) *Das Geschlechterverhältnis als Gegenstand der Sozialwissenschaften*, Frankfurt, New York: Campus Verlag.

Mósesdóttir, L. (1995) 'The State and the Egalitarian, Ecclesiastical and Liberal Regimes of Gender Relations', *British Journal of Sociology*, December: 623–42.

Nätti, J. (1991) *Part-time work in the Nordic Countries*, Jyväsklä: University of Jyväsklä.

Nätti, J. (1995) 'Working time policy and work sharing in Finland', paper presented at the International Workshop on 'Work-sharing in Order to Protect and Expand Employment', Brussels, 7–9 December.

Nave-Herz, R. and Krüger, D. (1992) *Ein-Eltern-Familien. Eine empirische Studie zur Lebenssituation und Lebensplanung alleinerziehender Mütter und Väter*, Bielefeld: Kleine.

Nikander, T. (1992) *The Woman's Life Course and the Family Formation*, Helsinki: Statistics Finland.

Nordic Council of Ministers (1994) *Women and Men in the Nordic Countries. Facts and Figures 1994*, Copenhagen: Nordic Council of Ministers.

OECD (1990, 1991, 1992, 1995) *Employment Outlook*, Paris: OECD.

O'Reilly, J. (1994) 'Theoretical and Methodological Approaches to Cross-national Employment Research', paper presented at the Sixteenth World Conference of the International Working Party on Labour Market Theory, Strasbourg, 15–19 July.

—— (1995) 'Teilzeitarbeit ind Ost- und Westdeutschland: Ansätze zu einem geschlechterspezifischen gesellschaftlichen Modell', unpublished paper, Berlin: Wissenschaftszentrum Berlin.

—— (1996) 'Theoretical Considerations in Cross-national Employment Research', Sociological Research Online, 1, 1: http:\\www.soc.surrey.ac.uk.

Peters, J., Felling, A. and Scheepers, P. (1993) 'Individualisierung und Säkularisierung in den Niederlanden in den achtziger Jahren' in B. Schäfers (ed.) Lebensverhältnisse und soziale Konflikte im neuen Europa, Verhandlungen des 26. Deutschen Soziologentages in Düsseldorf 1992, Frankfurt, New York: Campus Verlag.

Pfau-Effinger, B. (1990) Erwerbsverlauf und Risiko. Arbeitsmarktrisiken im Generationenvergleich, Weinheim/Basel: Deutscher Studien-Verlag.

—— (1993) 'Modernisation, Culture and Part-time Work', Work, Employment and Society (Journal of the British Sociological Association) 3: 383–410.

—— (1994a) 'Erwerbspartnerin oder berufstätige Ehefrau?' Soziale Welt 3: 322–73.

—— (1994b) 'Women's Work and New Forms of Employment in Germany' in I. Ostner and P. Koistinen (eds) Women and Markets, Tampere: Yliopisto.

—— (1996) 'Analyse internationaler Differenzen in der Erwerbsbeteiligung von Frauen – theoretischer Rahmen und empirische Ergebnisse', Kölner Zeitschrift für Soziologie und Sozialpsychologie 3: 462–92.

Pfau-Effinger, B. and Geissler, B. (1992) 'Institutioneller und soziokultureller Kontext der Entscheidung verheirateter Frauen für Teilzeitarbeit – Ein Beitrag zur Soziologie des Erwerbsverhaltens', Mitteilungen aus der Arbeitsmarkt- und Berufsforschung 3: 358–70.

Plantenga, J. (1992a) 'Women and Work in the Netherlands. Some Notes about Female Labour Force Participation and the Nature of the Welfare State' in G. Buttler, H.-J. Hoffmann-Nowotny and G. Schmitt-Rink (eds) Acta Demographica, Heidelberg: Physika.

—— (1992b) 'Differences and Similarities: The Position of Women on the Dutch Labour Market from a European Perspective', Bevolking en Gezin 1: 101–20.

—— (1993): Een afwijkend patroon. Honderd jaar vrouwenarbbeid in Nederland en (West–)Duitsland, Dissertation, Rijksuniversiteit Groningen.

Plantenga, J. and van Velzen, S. (1994) Changing Patterns of Work and Working-time for Men and Women. Towards the Integration or the Segmentation of the Labour Market, External report commissioned by and presented to the European commission, Utrecht: Economic Institute/CIAV.

Pott-Buter, H. (1993) Facts and Fairy Tales about Female Labor. Family and Fertility. A Seven-country Comparison 1850–1950, Amsterdam: Amsterdam University Press.

Quack, S. (1993) Dynamik der Teilzeitarbeit. Implikationen für die soziale Sicherung von Frauen, Berlin: Edition Sigma.

Quack, S. and Maier, F. (1994) 'From State Socialism to Market Economy – Women's Employment in East Germany', Environment and Planning A 26, 8: 1257–6.

Rerrich, M. S. (1988) Balanceakt Familie. Zwischen alten Leitbildern und neuen Lebensformen, Freiburg i.Br.L Lambertus.

—— (1996). 'Modernizing the Patriarchal Family in West Germany', European Journal of Women's Studies 3, 1: 27–38.

Rosenbaum, H. (1982) Soziologie der Familie. Untersuchungen zum Zusammenhang von Familienverhältnissen, Sozialstruktur und sozialem Wandel in der deutschen Gesellschaft des 19. Jahrhunderts, Frankfurt: Suhrkamp.

Schama, S. (1988) The Embarrassment of Riches. An Interpretation of Dutch Culture in the Golden Age, Berkeley, London: University of Berkeley Press.

Schupp, J. (1991) 'Teilzeitarbeit als Möglichkeit der beruflichen (Re-)Integration' in K.-U. Mayer, J. Allmendinger and J. Huinink (eds) Vom Regen in die Traufe: Frauen zwischen Beruf und Familie, Frankfurt, New York: Campus Verlag.

Simonen, L. (1990) *Contradictions of the Welfare State: Women and Caring*, Acta Universitatis Tamperensis ser A, Bd. 295, Tampere: University of Tampere.

Sommerkorn, I. (1988) 'Die erwerbstätige Mutter in der Bundesrepublik: Einstellungs- und Problemveränderungen' in I. Nave-Herz (ed.) *Wandel und Kontinuität der Familie in der Bundesrepublik Deutschland*: Frankfurt am Main: Campus Verlag.

van den Putte, B. and Pelzer, A. (1993) 'Wensen, motieven en belemmeringen ten aanzien van de arbeidsduur', *Sociaal Maandblad Arbeid* 47: 487–95.

Voipio-Juvas, A. and Ruohtula, K. (1949) *The Finnish Woman*, Helsinki: Werner Söderström Osakeyhtiö.

Weber, C. (1996) 'Geschlechterordnung, Arbeitsmarktintegration und Familienform: Japan im Vergleich' in I. Lenz, and M. Mae (eds) *Getrennte Welten, gemeinsame Moderne? Geschlechterverhältnisse in Japan*, Opladen: Leske & Budrich.

Weber, M. (1963) *Gesammelte Aufsätze zur Religionssoziologie*, Bd. I, Tübingen.

Wiesenthal, H. (1987) *Strategie und Illusion – Rationalitätsgrenzen kollektiver Akteure am Beispiel der Arbeitszeitpolitik 1980–1985*, Frankfurt/New York: Campus Verlag.

Willms-Herget, A. (1985) *Frauenarbeit. Zur Integration der Frauen in den Arbeitsmarkt*, Frankfurt, New York: Campus Verlag.

10

WHY IS PART-TIME WORK SO LOW IN PORTUGAL AND SPAIN?

*Margarida Ruivo, Maria do Pilar González
and José M. Varejão*

INTRODUCTION

The use of part-time work has evolved in distinctively different ways in Northern and Southern European countries. In Northern Europe, higher rates of female labour force participation are often associated with a high level of part-time work, whereas in Southern Europe both female participation rates and the share of part-time work are lower (see Smith *et al.*, Chapter 2, and Pfau-Effinger, Chapter 9, this volume). Nevertheless, despite this association, there are also outlying cases where women have very high levels of labour market participation but where part-time work is not very significant, as in Portugal and Finland.

In this chapter, we focus on the Southern European experience and compare the cases of Portugal and Spain (Pfau-Effinger examined the Finnish case in the Northern European context in the previous chapter). Although Portugal and Spain share similar social, cultural and political backgrounds, they differ in many important ways, particularly in terms of their labour market performance. For example, the unemployment rate in 1995 in Portugal was 7.3 per cent, compared to 22.9 per cent in Spain. There are also important differences in female participation rates, which are much higher in Portugal (61.4 per cent of the female population aged 15–64 were economically active in Portugal, compared to 45.6 per cent in Spain in 1995) (European Commission 1996: 152 and 159). Nevertheless, the overall part-time rate is very low in both countries, having risen from around 6 per cent in 1987 to 7.5 per cent in 1995.

In this chapter, we set out to examine why Portugal and Spain have such low levels of part-time work despite different levels of female participation. In the first section we identify the characteristics of part-time employment in the two countries. In the second section we consider the influence of labour market regulation on the demand for labour and discuss the issue in the broader context of the debate on labour market flexibility. In the third section we focus on the supply side of the labour market and discuss women's decisions on whether or not to participate. Such decisions are seen here as essentially twofold: if a woman decides to enter the labour market, she also has to decide whether to do so on a part-time or full-time basis. This framework seems to be the most appropriate one for discussion of the Portuguese and Spanish cases, since the choice here seems to be between non-participation (in Spain) and full-time participation (in Portugal), with part-time work not apparently an option in either country. We conclude by considering the prospects for part-time employment in these two countries, bearing in mind that one of the objectives of this book is to discuss whether differences in part-time work across countries are likely to persist or to converge, and whether the expected changes will tend to encourage marginalised or more integrated forms of part-time work (see Fagan and O'Reilly, Chapter 1, this volume).

CHARACTERISTICS OF PART-TIME EMPLOYMENT IN PORTUGAL AND SPAIN

First, women dominate part-time employment in both countries (67.1 per cent in Portugal and 74.9 per cent in Spain), as they do in the rest of Europe (81.8 per cent in E12). However, the part-time employment rates for women in Portugal (12.1 per cent) and in Spain (15.3 per cent) are much lower than in the EU as a whole (30.3 per cent). Male part-time rates are very low in all cases, although they are slightly lower than average in Spain (2.6 per cent); in Portugal (4.7 per cent) they are approximately the same as in the EU as a whole (4.8 per cent). However, the fact that in Portugal men account for about 33 per cent of all part-timers should be emphasised, as this is a higher share than anywhere else in Europe.

Second, in both Spain and the E12, part-time employment, like employment as a whole, is dominated by individuals in the 25–49 age group. However, this is not the case as far as Portuguese men are concerned. Here, higher age groups are predominant (60 per cent of all male part-timers are over 50, and 29 per cent over 65). Although this age effect is not as marked in the case of female part-timers, older women still account for 42 per cent of total female part-time employment (compared with about 20 per cent in Spain and 22 per cent in the E12). It is also worth mentioning that in Spain, the younger age groups account for a higher share of total part-time employment (31.4 per cent for men and 18.8 per cent for women) than either in the E12 (29.7 per cent and 10.5 per cent) or in Portugal (17.1 per cent and 10.1 per cent). Comparison of the part-time rate across age groups in Portugal, Spain and the E12 produces similar results – in Portugal, part-time employment is more widespread in the higher age groups (particularly among men), whereas in Spain, where the age profile of part-time employment is closer to the European average, part-time work is slightly more common among young people (see Table 10.1).

Table 10.1 Part-time employment, breakdown by gender and age group (%), 1994

	Portugal	Spain	E12
Men			
15–24 years	17.1	31.4	29.7
25–44 years	23.1	46.1	40.2
45–64 years	29.9	16.7	19.6
65 years and over	29.1	6.4	10.4
Women			
15–24 years	10.1	18.8	10.5
25–44 years	47.9	60.5	66.2
45–64 years	29.4	18.8	21.4
65 years and over	13.0	1.8	1.9

Source: Eurostat (1994)

Third, in all countries, the majority of part-timers is employed in the service sector. However, there are marked differences between countries. In Portugal, the share of part-timers in services is 50 per cent, compared with 81 per cent in Spain and 83 per cent in the E12. The agricultural sector accounts for 34 per cent of all part-time employment in Portugal. This is a characteristic of part-time employment that is specific to Portugal; in Spain it is approximately 9 per cent and among the E12 it is 5 per cent. Unlike in many other European countries, the part-time employment rate in Portugal is highest in agriculture, whereas in Spain, as in the majority of other European countries, it is highest in the service sector. The distribution of part-time employment across sectors in Portugal is common to both men and women. However, the share of agriculture is even higher for male part-timers (44 per cent), while the service sector does not provide the majority of male part-time jobs.

Fourth, whereas in Spain and the E12 as a whole more than two-thirds of all part-timers are employees, in Portugal, more than half of all part-timers are employers or self-employed workers. This high share of employers and self-employed workers among part-timers in Portugal is particularly marked among men, although it is also discernible among women. In Spain, as in Portugal, family workers are also over-represented among part-timers (particularly among men).

Fifth, the hours usually worked by part-timers are higher than the European average in Portugal (21.6 hours per week compared with 19.6) but lower in Spain (18 hours per week). In this respect as well, part-time work in Portugal is somewhat different from the rest of Europe, with a much higher share of all part-timers working long hours: 17.4 per cent of all part-timers in Portugal usually work 31 hours per week or more, compared with only 1.2 per cent in Spain and a European average of 9.8 per cent.

Finally, part-time work in the EC is mostly a voluntary form of work, particularly for women (59 per cent of all part-timers and 65 per cent of women working part-time do so because they do not want a full-time job). However, in Portugal and Spain only a minority of part-timers (10 per cent in Portugal and 3 per cent in Spain) are content with their situation. In these countries, the main reason for acceptance of a part-time job is the failure to find full-time work; this applies to 19 per cent of all part-timers in both countries. However, these figures are not particularly informative, since the majority of individuals surveyed give 'other reasons' for working part-time rather than citing any of the more precise alternatives such as schooling/training, illness/handicap, failure to find a full-time job, no desire for a full-time job and so on. This suggests that the response options have little meaning in these countries.

In sum, there are two fundamental similarities between part-time work in Europe as a whole and in Portugal and Spain in particular. In all countries, it is a largely female phenomenon and is highly concentrated in the service sector (see Table 10.2). A major difference is that, in both Portugal and Spain, part-time work seems to be mainly involuntary, since only a small minority of part-timers claims to be working part-time because they do not want a full-time job. For the most part, however, part-time work in Spain conforms more closely to the European pattern than it does in Portugal. Although there is no evidence to confirm this, the fact that male part-time work in Portugal is more widespread among older workers, employers or the self-employed and those working in agriculture suggests that here it is to some extent an archaic form of work that allows older (male) workers to go on working after retirement and thereby contribute to their own subsistence.

Table 10.2 Part-time work characteristics (%), 1994

	Portugal	Spain	E12
Breakdown by professional status			
Employers and independent workers	53	18	10
Employees	39	71	86
Family workers	8	11	4
Breakdown by sector of activity			
Agriculture	34	9	5
Industry	16	10	12
Services	50	81	83
Breakdown by reason to work part-time			
Schooling/Training	7	6	9
Illness/Handicap	18	2	2
Couldn't find a full-time job	19	19	18
Doesn't want a full-time job	10	3	59
Other reasons	46	69	12
No answer	–	2	1

Source: Eurostat (1994)

THE DEMAND FOR PART-TIME WORK AND
LABOUR MARKET REGULATION

Traditionally, employers hire part-time workers in order to increase staffing levels during peak business hours or to solve specific scheduling problems. This is why part-time work is used more intensively in areas such as the retail trade, hotels and catering and personal services, where employers have to deal more frequently with regular and periodic peaks of demand and/or where opening hours are too long for the demand for labour to be met solely by full-timers working a single shift.

In the late 1970s, following the first oil crisis, employers began to find other reasons for hiring part-timers. The need to cope with an increasingly uncertain and competitive environment made employers more aware of the advantages, to them, of so-called atypical forms of work, which were seen as more flexible and less expensive. Part-time work was immediately recognised as one such form of work, together with others such as temporary and agency work and those involving antisocial hours, variable schedules or split shifts. In recognition of these two sets of reasons, some authors refer to 'traditional reasons' and 'new reasons' for hiring part-time workers (see, for instance, Bentolila and Dolado, 1994; a comprehensive list of reasons for using part-time work is presented in Chapter 2 by Smith et al. in this volume).

These two sets of reasons undoubtedly overlap, since industries that have traditionally used part-time work are now confronted with a 'new competition', which has made employers even more eager to adopt more flexible forms of employment (see Rubery, 1991). Nevertheless, the distinction is quite useful in analysing why part-time work is so rare in Portugal and Spain. If traditional reasons prevail, part-time work should, logically, remain concentrated in the same areas of activity and the extent to which it is used should depend on the growth in such activities. If, on the contrary, new reasons are dominant, we should expect part-time work to be more evenly spread across a wider range of industries (though not manufacturing, for reasons that Delsen discusses in Chapter 3, this volume) and to be more sensitive to the economic cycle than full-time work. Unless there are national specificities at work, we should also expect that in countries where part-time work is more common, after controlling for the size of the industries using it for traditional reasons, new reasons predominate (this is consistent with the fact that in the last twenty years part-time work has increased the most in the majority of countries where it is now more widespread).

Although there are no data available on the reasons why firms in Portugal and Spain use part-time work, the relatively little use employers in these two countries make of it may perhaps be explained both by the relative unimportance of new reasons and the late development of the service sector, particularly in Portugal. The fact that, within the service sector, part-time work is concentrated in areas such as the retail trade, hotels and catering and personal services, and that agriculture is also an important user of part-timers, provides some initial support for this argument. It is further reinforced by an examination of firms' flexibility needs and of the degree of flexibility that part-time work in these two countries actually provides in comparison with other atypical forms of employment, particularly fixed-term contracts.

Labour market legislation in both Portugal and Spain has long been recognised as very stringent. Grubb and Wells (1993), in a comparative study of labour market regulation in eleven EC countries, find that it is in the Southern European countries, and particularly in Portugal and Spain, that firms' strategies are most constrained by a lack of labour flexibility. In all the areas considered, from dismissals to working-time organisation and temporary work, the Portuguese and Spanish labour markets rank as the most rigid. Only in the use of fixed-term contracts and the organisation of standard working time are they considered to enjoy an intermediate degree of flexibility. This is confirmed by persistent calls by Portuguese and Spanish employers for changes to labour legislation.

In both countries, the regulation of dismissals was a matter for major concern, because, until as recently as the late 1980s, employers enjoyed only very restricted room for manoeuvre in this respect. Unlike most other European countries, these restrictions applied both to administrative requirements (for instance, mandatory procedures, advance notice) and to redundancy pay. Furthermore, the fact that bringing a dismissal action to court is a very slow process not only increases firing costs but also makes firms willing to accept more expensive ways of terminating employment contracts, even when they have a case for lawful dismissal (Sebastián, 1995). Some studies have also suggested that high firing costs were responsible for a lower rate of job creation (García-Perea and Gómez, 1996; Pinto et al., 1996) and had a negative impact both on employers' ability to cut their workforce to desirable levels and on firms' chances of surviving (Teixeira, 1995).

Another major consequence of legal restrictions on the dismissal of permanent employees was an increase in the use of fixed-term contracts. Since employers' main concern was to improve external flexibility, the preference for temporary contracts and other atypical forms of employment seems perfectly logical, particularly since the legislation on fixed-term contracts deliberately provides greater flexibility. It is worth noting that legislation on fixed-term contracts was introduced in Portugal explicitly in order to allow employers to avoid some of the firing costs associated with legislation on dismissal protection applying to permanent workers. As a result, when the use of such contracts was at its peak, temporary employment accounted for 19 per cent of all wage employment in Portugal and 31 per cent in Spain.

As far as part-time work itself was concerned, neither in Portugal nor in Spain was it any more or less flexible than other forms of work. In fact, part-time work, which has been legally regulated since 1971 in Portugal and since 1984 in Spain, is subject to the same rules (pro rata) as full-time work. In statutory terms, therefore, part-timers enjoy the same degree of job security as full-timers, and for both categories the degree of job security depends on the nature of their contracts (whether they are permanent or temporary). The available data (OECD, 1993) shows that almost two-thirds of part-timers in Portugal are on permanent contracts, whereas in Spain 57 per cent have temporary contracts. The pro rata clause further ensures that the use of part-time work has no substantial cost advantages. On the contrary, evidence from Portugal suggests that, after controlling for individual characteristics, young part-timers are paid a higher hourly wage than full-timers (Oliveira et al., 1994).

In the late 1980s, however, less optimistic employment prospects, together with the impact of globalisation on firms' competitiveness, paved the way for changes to labour market legislation. The new legislation was introduced in 1989/91 in Portugal and in 1994 in Spain. The aim of the changes was similar in both countries, namely to improve firms' ability to react to a changing economic environment by increasing labour market flexibility. Despite this common aim, the nature of the changes in each country was somewhat different.

In Portugal, the changes were the result of the realisation that the restrictions imposed on employers in respect of dismissals were the direct cause of the excessive increase in the use of fixed-term contracts. The new rules made it easier to dismiss employees (by shortening the decision process and widening the scope for individual dismissal) while at the same time restricting the use of fixed-term contracts. The legislation governing part-time work was left unchanged. Part-time work is still defined as a form of work involving shorter hours than the standard working time in the industry in question. Part-time workers are still granted the same rights as full-timers, although on a pro rata basis in accordance with the number of hours worked relative to standard daily or weekly working time. Collective agreements can contain provisions on part-time work, although most agreements concluded since 1989 have not done so. It is only recently that some agreements have begun to include clauses on the recruitment of part-timers and the organisation of their work schedules. However, these agreements have been concluded in industries facing major changes in their markets that also make more intensive use of part-timers for traditional reasons (for example, the retail trade). For the most part, part-time work in Portugal remains a form of employment that employers have to accept when employees request it. Interestingly, following these regulatory changes, there was a decline in the share of fixed-term contracts in total wage employment, from 18.7 per cent in 1989 to 9.3 per cent in 1994; however, part-time work continued to grow only slowly.

The changes in Spain were also intended to make the dismissal process easier. Dismissals for economic reasons became possible, although firing costs were not substantially reduced. Despite the new regulations, there is no evidence that either the volume or the nature of dismissals has changed (see García-Perea and Gómez, 1996). In contrast to what happened in Portugal, the legislation governing fixed-term contracts did not change significantly, although some recently concluded collective agreements do contain clauses intended to encourage the creation of permanent jobs (in exchange for a relaxation of the regulations governing dismissals for economic reasons or reductions in wage rates for new recruits). The legislation on part-time work underwent considerable change, however. On the one hand, several of the restrictions on part-time work were lifted, in particular those requiring the establishment of maximum daily and weekly working hours and an absolute upper limit of two-thirds of standard full-time hours. On the other hand, social security contributions were reduced for workers working fewer than 12 hours per week or 48 hours per month. As a result, there was a sharp increase of 18.3 per cent in the use of part-time work between 1994 and 1995.

The response of both labour markets to these reforms of the legal framework seems to confirm the important influence of labour regulation on the incidence of new employment forms. The use of fixed-term contracts declined sharply in Portugal after the legislation became more stringent, whereas the evolution of part-time work, regulation of which remained unchanged, continued to follow its previous trend. In Spain, fixed-term contracts were largely unaffected by the reform and account for approximately 33 per cent of total employment, whereas the use of part-time work increased significantly once the legislation became more flexible. Changes in the regulations governing dismissals did not produce such clear-cut results; however, the changes introduced were not very significant, particularly in Spain (Addison and Teixeira, 1995; Jimeno, 1996).

Reconciling paid work and family responsibilities: is there a role for part-time work?

Variations in part-time rates from country to country are also affected by individual decisions on labour market participation, which are influenced in turn by cultural, economic and legal considerations. Part-time work is frequently regarded as a form of employment intended to encourage the entry into the labour market of specific categories of workers whose labour market behaviour diverges from the adult male norm (i.e. women and younger and older workers). Given the fact that part-time work in all European countries is a predominantly female phenomenon, we shall confine ourselves here to the discussion of the particular characteristics of the female labour supply. Two questions will be addressed: Why is part-time work so much more unattractive to Portuguese and Spanish women than to their counterparts in Northern European countries? And why does female labour market behaviour tend towards non-participation in Spain and full-time work in Portugal, with the part-time option being ignored in both countries?

Before they began to enter the labour market, non-participation among women reflected both their central role in the family and the prevailing forms of family organisation. Thus the increase in female participation rates that has characterised Western European societies in recent decades is associated with changes in family organisation, and in particular in the ways in which each member of the household seeks (or fails) to reconcile family responsibilities and paid work.

One of the most striking and widespread consequences of attempts to reconcile family responsibilities and paid work is the change in fertility patterns that can be observed in European countries. When women enter the labour market (as a result of social or cultural change and/or low household income), the number of children born to each household tends to decline. This change in fertility pattern is quite noticeable in both Portugal and Spain. After a long period of stability from 1960 to 1975, the fertility rate dropped sharply, to levels below the E12 average (see Almeida et al., 1995). This has led to changes in household structures and the labour market status of each of its adult members. In Spain, in families where the household's core is a couple with children, men are typically employed and women are inactive (see Cébrian and Moreno, 1995). In Portugal, the decline in the birth rate seems to have been accompanied by an increase in the number of households in which both partners are economically active.

In general, there are several different ways of reconciling paid work and family life, with one or the other (or a particular mix of the various possibilities) prevailing in each country (see Pfau-Effinger, Chapter 9, this volume). If this reconciliation process is to be successful, a certain degree of material and legal support from social institutions is required, particularly in terms of the provision of care facilities for dependent individuals, especially child care services, flexible working time arrangements, and maternity leave arrangements.

The level of such support is somewhat weak in both countries. Despite the difficulties of accurately estimating the existing level of child care provision, the available evidence suggests that, in both countries, it is far from sufficient. Reliance on family help (particularly on grandmothers) is a well-established practice, which seems to be further encouraged by the lack of public provision (see Silva, 1983; Commission for Equality and Women's Rights, 1994; Lopes, 1994; Portugal, 1995; Tobio, 1995).

Standard weekly hours for full-timers are high in both countries (40 hours in Spain, 42 in Portugal), and changes are not on the agenda for public debate, despite the fact that the issue did gain a little in prominence in Portugal in 1996, following the introduction of new working-time legislation that established a weekly maximum of 40 hours. However, despite the fact that negotiations on working-time reorganisation and new forms of work have been possible since 1991, very little use has been made of the new opportunities (see Varejão and Ruivo, 1996). In consequence, full-time work and long working hours remain the norm in both Portugal and Spain, making it more difficult for individuals to reconcile family and working lives. It is sometimes suggested that women may solve this problem simply by being absent from work; levels of absenteeism seem to be high in both countries (see Tobio, 1995; Varejão and Ruivo, 1996).

Legislation on maternal protection is similar in both countries. The provisions include paid maternity leave, a working time reduction for breast-feeding women, long-term unpaid parental leave and the right to return to the same job after maternity or other leave (Ditch *et al.*, 1994). In both countries, the aim of the legislation is to guarantee workers' income and/or job when they are forced to be absent from work in order to care for very young children.

If working mothers enjoy rights, but no more than elsewhere, if the provision of child care facilities is inadequate and if working hours for full-timers are too long, it might reasonably be expected that women seeking to enter the labour market would prefer to do so on a part-time basis, or at least to consider the possibility of working part-time. Because of these factors, it might be expected that the preference for part-time work would be greater in Portugal and Spain than in other European countries, where the alternatives are more highly developed. Yet, as we have already seen, this is not the case, which leads us to ask why.

The cumulative burden of paid work and family responsibilities is still the major issue affecting women's labour market behaviour. Yet none of the available evidence suggests that women would prefer to work part-time rather than full-time, or to remain outside the labour market altogether (see Table 10.2). Although one could argue that this is so because the supply of part-time jobs is scarce, the possibility that such preferences are determined largely by household income considerations should not be ignored. According to Eurostat data on net monthly family income, Portuguese families have the lowest income levels in the European Union (about 35 per cent of the average value in the EU as a whole). Even compared with other countries with low levels of family income (after Portugal, the countries with the lowest family incomes are Greece and Spain), Portuguese families have a particularly low income (less than 50 per cent that of Spanish families). Thus, in Portugal in particular, it is likely that women's preferences for full-time jobs are attributable largely to the need to boost family income in order to acquire the means to raise the level of household consumption. Given the low wage levels in Portugal, this could not be achieved either in single breadwinner families (which explains why female participation rates are high) or in those where women work part-time.

The low level of demand for part-time jobs among Portuguese and Spanish women is, nevertheless, only one of the characteristics of female labour market behaviour in the two countries. There are differences in this respect between the two countries, with Portuguese women having higher participation rates than their Spanish counterparts. First, the difference in female participation rates between the two countries reflects the fact that women in Spain and Portugal began to enter the labour market at different times. In Portugal, the growth in the female participation rate began in the 1970s, a decade before it started to rise in Spain, and the upward trend has persisted ever since (González *et al.*, 1991; González, 1992). Historical and cultural differences between the two countries are obviously relevant in accounting for this difference. During the 1960s and 1970s, women played a greater part in agriculture in Portugal than in Spain. This was largely because of a greater shortage of male labour in Portugal due both to emigration and military recruitment, and in Spain to the fact that peasant agriculture had been dismantled earlier than in Portugal. Moreover, the political changes that occurred in both countries in the 1970s seem to have produced more profound cultural changes in Portugal than in Spain (see González, 1992).

Recent developments also show that the female participation rate in Spain, unlike that in Portugal, is highly sensitive to the labour market situation (Garrido, 1993; Castillo and Toharia, 1993; Lázaro and Sánchez, 1993; Moltó, 1993), although it has recently been losing some of its pro-cyclical nature (see Bover and Arellano, 1994). As both economies have differed markedly over recent decades in their ability to create jobs (employment grew throughout the 1970–90 period in Portugal, with a remarkable number of new jobs being created every year, whereas in Spain there was a net loss of jobs between 1975 and 1985), the number of jobs being created every year seems to be a more important factor in understanding the evolution of female participation rates than the unemployment record. The fact that a large number of jobs was created every year in Portugal but not in Spain is consistent with the persistence of high female participation rates in Portugal and their slow (and pro-cyclical) growth in Spain.

CONCLUSIONS

Both demand- and supply-side factors explain why part-time employment rates are so low in Portugal and in Spain. Employers in these two countries do not benefit from any special advantages that part-time work could offer, other than its ability to meet specific scheduling problems. In neither country does labour legislation make part-time work particularly advantageous; in terms of both costs and flexibility, it compares unfavourably with other atypical forms of employment (particularly temporary employment and self-employment). Thus one of the reasons why the part-time rate is so low in Spain and Portugal is that it remains unattractive to employers because it fails to meet their flexibility needs. Or, to put it in another way, new reasons, which account for at least part of the growth of part-time work in many European countries, do not apply here. Thus the only valid reasons for hiring part-timers in Portugal and, until recently, in Spain are the traditional ones outlined above or a desire on the part of employees to work part-time.

The distribution of part-time employment across sectors would suggest that 'traditional reasons' are important for any understanding of the patterns of part-time work in Spain and Portugal. Thus one of the reasons why part-time rates remain low is because activities that traditionally use this form of employment are less highly developed, particularly in Portugal, than in the rest of Europe.

Finally, there is no tradition of voluntary (i.e. freely entered into) part-time work that could help to foster the growth of this particular employment form. There are historical, cultural and economic reasons why this is so.

Labour shortages in the 1960s, an abrupt change in social and cultural practices in the 1970s and low average wage levels are all reasons why current patterns of female labour market behaviour in Portugal favour full-time work. In Spain, the main phase of women's entry into the labour market took place at a later date and against a background of high unemployment. This created a situation where women were either discouraged workers or adopted a pattern of continuous full-time employment similar to the dominant male model (see Rubery, Chapter 7, this volume); in such a context the decision to become active is more likely to reflect a generational lifestyle option.

However, certain recent developments may challenge this diagnosis, thereby changing the prospects for part-time work in Spain and Portugal and at the same time raising important policy issues. The share of part-time work to which the 'traditional reasons' explanation applies is likely to grow as the service sector expands (this is particularly true of Portugal, which lags considerably behind most other European countries in this respect).

As far as the flexibility aspect of part-time work is concerned, the prospects in Portugal and Spain seem to differ. Assuming that the regulation of part-time work remains unchanged in Portugal (although the possibility of abandoning the strict pro rata system has been recently considered), there is no reason to suppose that the part-time rates will increase any further. In Spain, things may be different, since the recent changes to the legal framework give employers an incentive to recruit part-timers. As a result, part-time employment can be expected to grow at a faster pace than in the past, just as it did in 1995, immediately after the changes came into force. Prospects for part-time work in the two countries may also differ somewhat from the point of view of the labour supply.

Since it is unlikely that average wage levels in Portugal will rise rapidly, the supply of adult men and women voluntarily opting for part-time work is unlikely to increase significantly for family budget reasons. The supply of involuntary part-time labour will follow a trend close to that of unemployment. Individuals at either end of the age spectrum may, however, become major suppliers of part-time work as a result both of increased life expectancy (coupled with very low retirement pensions) and the increase in the length of time young people are staying in the education system (coupled with the expected increase in tuition fees in public universities, which are currently minimal).

The situation in Spain is different, for two main reasons. First, the low levels of female labour force participation mean there is still scope for more women to enter the labour market (at least, more so than in Portugal and other countries with higher female participation rates). In this situation, part-time work would be seen as a source of additional income rather than a cause of income reduction. Furthermore, the restrictions on family budgets are not as constrained as in Portugal, since Spanish wage levels are higher. However, given the high levels of unemployment in Spain and the disproportionately high incidence among young people and women, most of the increase in the supply of part-time work in Spain is likely to be involuntary.

To turn now to one of the issues raised by Fagan and O'Reilly in Chapter 1, it is fairly safe to say that levels of part-time work are likely to grow in both Portugal and Spain, although at different rates and for different reasons (faster and with greater importance attached to flexibility in Spain than in Portugal). Thus Spain should converge more rapidly than Portugal towards European levels. This faster rate of convergence in Spain will come at the cost of more marginalised forms of part-time work (more precarious and less protected), whereas in Portugal it will remain a less widespread but more secure form of work.

Thus there seems to be a trade-off between the part-time employment rate and the quality of part-time jobs (integrated versus marginalised jobs). This raises two interesting policy issues. The first concerns the role played by government intervention in shaping the characteristics of part-time work. The example of these two countries shows that stricter regulation of part-time work certainly limits its growth but also ensures that part-time jobs will not differ substantially from full-time jobs as far as pay, precariousness and protection are concerned. Although this may make it more difficult for those workers who attach varying degrees of importance to these aspects (for example, those with an interrupted participation record) to find a part-time job, it also makes it harder for part-timers to be relegated to a secondary labour market. Thus government intervention can prevent part-time work from becoming just another source of labour market segmentation, although at the cost of a lower level of part-time employment.

The second policy issue (in fact, a consequence of the first) concerns the perception of low part-time rates. Should they be regarded as an indication of backwardness, and should convergence with countries with higher part-time rates be seen as a desirable goal? If there is indeed a trade-off between the quantity and quality of part-time work, it may well be that some of the countries with higher shares of part-time work should converge towards those in which part-time rates are lower but job quality is higher.

ACKNOWLEDGEMENTS

The authors are grateful to Professors Alberto Meixide and Albert Recio for their suggestions and help with the collection of data and bibliography on the Spanish case. The usual disclaimers apply.

BIBLIOGRAPHY

Addison, John T. and Teixeira, Paulino (1995) 'Dismissals Protection and Employment: Does the Lazear Model Work for Portugal', University of South Carolina, mimeo.

Almeida, Ana Nunes and Wall, Karin (1995) 'A Família', in *Portugal Hoje*, Instituto Nacional de Administração: 33–53.

Bentolila, Samuel and Dolado, Juan J. (1994) 'Labour Flexibility and Wages: Lessons from Spain', Centro de Estudios Monetarios y Financieros: Documento de Trabajo no. 9406.

Bover, Olympia and Arellano, Manuel (1994) 'Participación Laboral Feminina en España Durante los Ochenta', Banco de España, *Boletin Economico*: 63–67.

Blanchard, Olivier and Jimeno, Juan F. (1995) 'Structural Slumps and Persistent Unemployment. Structural Unemployment: Spain versus Portugal', *American Economic Review*, May: 212–18.

Castillo, Sonsolles and Toharia, Luis (1993) 'Mercado de Trabajo y Desigualdad', proceedings of the First Simposio sobre Igualdad y Distribución de la Renta y la Riqueza, Madrid: Fundación Argentaria.

Castro, Alberto, González, Maria Pilar and Osório, António (1996) 'The Portuguese and the Spanish Labour Markets: So Close and Yet So Different', paper presented at the Eighteenth Annual Conference of the International Working Party on Labour Market Segmentation, Tampere.

Cébrian, Immaculada and Moreno, Gloria (1995) 'The Incidence of Household Characteristics on Labour Decisions: The Case of Spain', *Labour* 9: 207–31.

Commission for Equality and Women's Rights (1994) *Portugal. Status of Women. 1994*, Lisbon: CIDM and MESS.

Ditch, John, Barnes, Helen, Bradshaw, Jonathan, Commaille, Jacques and Eardley, Tony (1994) *A Synthesis of National Family Policies 1994*, European Observatory on National Policies, Social Policy Research Unit, University of York.

Eurostat (1994) *Labour Force Survey*, Paris: Eurostat.

Garcia-Perea, Pilar and Gómez, Ramon (1996) 'Evolución Reciente de la Contratación Laboral', Banco de España, *Boletin Economico*, May: 29–37.

Garrido, Luís J. (1993) *Las Dos Biografías de la Mujer en España*, Madrid: Instituto de la Mujer, Ministerio de Asuntos Sociales.

González, Maria Pilar (1992) *Etude de Longue Periode du Rapport Salarial au Portugal*, Thèse pour le doctorat en Sciences Economiques, Paris: Université Paris I.

González, Maria Pilar, Ruivo, Margarida and Varejão, José M. (1991) 'Les Femmes Portugaises – des Comportements d' Activité Atypiques dans le Cadre de l' Europe du Sud', paper presented at the Third Annual Conference of the European Association of Labour Economists, Madrid.

Grubb, David and Wells, William (1993) 'La Réglementation de L'Emploi et les Formes de Travail dans les Pays de la CEE', *Revue Économique de l'OCDE* 21: 7–62.

Jimeno, Juan F. (1996) 'Los Efectos Visibles de la Reforma Laboral de 1994', FEDEA y Universidad de Alcalá de Henares, Documento de Trabajo: 96–109.

Lázaro, Nieves and Sánchez, Rosario (1993) 'Las Mujeres y el Mercado de Trabajo en España: de la Transición a la Democracia' in Jill Rubery (ed.) *Las Mujeres y la Recesión*, Madrid: Ministerio de Trabajo y Seguridad Social.

Lopes, Margarida Chagas (co-ordinator) (1994) *A Evolução das Modalidades de Trabalho dos Homens e das Mulheres: para uma Integração ou uma Segmentação do Mercado de Trabalho?*, Rede de Peritos sobre a Situação das Mulheres no Mercado de Trabalho, Lisbon.

Moltó, María Luísa (1993) 'Las Mujeres en el Proceso de Modernizacion de la Economia Española', in Jill Rubery (ed.) *Las Mujeres y la Recesión*, Madrid: Ministerio de Trabajo y Seguridad Social.

OECD (1993) *Perspectives de l'Emploi*, Paris: OECD.

Oliveira, M. Mendes, Portugal, Pedro and Santos, Maria Clementina (1994) 'Wage Growth and Turnover in the Portuguese Youth Labour Market', paper presented to the Sixth Annual Conference of the European Association of Labour Economists, Warsaw.

Pinto, Mário, Martins, Pedro Furtado and Carvalho, António Nunes (1996) *Glossário de Direito do Trabalho e Relações Industriais*, Lisbon: Universidade Católica Editora.

Portugal, Sílvia (1995) 'As Mãos que Embalam o Berço. Um Estudo sobre Redes Informais de Apoio à Maternidade', *Revista Crítica de Ciências Sociais* 42, May: 155–75.

Rubery, Jill (1991) 'The New Competition and Working Time', paper presented at the Fourth Conference of the International Seminar on Working Time, Gelsenkirchen, December.

Sebastián, Carlos (1995) 'El Desequilibrio en el Mercado de Trabajo', *Papeles de Economia Española* 62: 344–60.

Silva, Manuela (1983) *O Emprego das Mulheres em Portugal. A 'Mão Invisível' na Discriminação Sexual no Emprego*, Porto Ed. Afrontamento.

Teixeira, Paulino (1995) 'Lei dos Despedimentos: O Percurso de Uma Lei': paper presented to the 4º Encontro Nacional de Economia Industrial, Lisboa.

Tobio, Constanza (1995) 'La relation Famille-Emploi en Espagne', in Linda Hantrais and Marie-Thérèse Letablier (eds) *La Relation Famille-Emploi. Une Comparaison des Modes d'Ajustement en Europe*, Centre d'Etudes de l'Emploi, Dossier 6: 157–66.

Varejão, José Manuel and Ruivo, Margarida (1996) 'As Condicionantes da Organização do Tempo de Trabalho. Estudo de um Caso', *Cadernos de Ciências Sociais* 17: 77–90.

11

HOW DOES THE 'SOCIETAL EFFECT' SHAPE THE USE OF PART-TIME WORK IN FRANCE, THE UK AND SWEDEN?

Anne-Marie Daune-Richard

Like all industrialised countries, France, the UK and Sweden have experienced a sharp rise in female employment in recent years. Sectoral and occupational segregation between men and women in the labour market is similar in all three countries. Beyond these broad similarities, however, analysis of the various patterns of female labour market participation reveals major differences, which are rooted in historical and social constructions specific to each country. In this chapter I set out to examine the varying significance of part-time work in integrating women into paid employment in these countries with a framework informed by the founders of the 'societal effect' (Maurice *et al.* 1982).

This original approach was largely concerned with differences in the social construction of managerial hierarchies in France and Germany and did not set out to examine the differences between men and women. This approach has been criticised for overemphasising the differences between societies and internal coherence within national systems (Rubery 1988), which can lead to an ahistoric or 'static' view of societies (Lutz 1989). Nevertheless, it can still provide a useful tool to examine women's employment from a cross-national perspective because gender relations have tended to be viewed through the fixed lenses of the biological/naturalistic approach for too long (Daune-Richard 1988). A 'societal effect' framework enables us to go beyond a universalist account of social trends in different societies, which ignores country and actor specificities within particular institutional arrangements. In addition, it also goes beyond a culturalist approach which reduces differences to an ill-defined set of residual cultural values and characteristics. Therefore, an institutionally informed, relativist approach can still shed a great deal of light on the soci-ology of women's work. In adopting such an approach, our aim is to reveal not only the differences but also the similarities that exist between countries. Above all, we aim to highlight the different meanings that the same phenomenon, in this case part-time work, can have in respect of women's participation in the labour market and, more generally, in gender relations between men and women. Finally, in seeking out these differences, I will attempt to locate the origin and meaning of recent developments that may help to clarify the shifts in, and general dynamics of, the 'societal effect', as well as the internal tensions that may emerge from it.

I shall take as my starting point the notion that the differences between male and female patterns of labour market participation are rooted in the modes of articulation between the production of goods and services and the repro-duction of individuals (see *Le sexe du travail* 1984). Macro-level analysis will focus, therefore, on two areas: on the one hand, the correlation between various modes of labour market organisation in terms of the divisions they create between different categories of labour and, on the other, the various ways in which the labour supply is constructed by state employment, social, family and fiscal policies, seen against the background of the division of domestic work and child-raising within the family. I will start by examining the social construc-tion of the female labour supply, before going on to locate the meaning of part-time work in the three countries relative to the various historical forms of women's entry into wage work.

THE SOCIAL CONSTRUCTION OF THE FEMALE LABOUR SUPPLY

The evolution of participation rates in all three countries has been broadly similar since the 1960s, although the degree of change varies. There has been a considerable decline in male participation rates and, in Sweden, a very signif-icant rise in the female rate (+15 per cent) which is echoed to a lesser extent in the UK (+13 per cent) and France (+10 per cent) (Table 11.1). Overall, the share of women in the economically active population is continuing to rise in all three countries, particularly in Sweden, where they have nearly achieved parity with men and now account for 48 per cent of the labour force, compared with 42 per cent in France and 43 per cent in the UK (*OECD Labour Force Statistics* 1995). In 1995, the share of women in total employ-ment was similar in France and the UK: in the 25–49 age group, 68.4 per cent and 69.9 per cent respectively were in employment, compared to nearly 83 per cent in Sweden. In the first two countries, moreover, men in the same age group were considerably more likely to be in employment than women (+15 per cent to 20 per cent), which is not the case in Sweden (+3 per cent) (Eurostat 1995).

Institutional aspects, such as pay policies, fiscal policies, working-time arrangements and the provision of child care in the different countries, shape the forms of female labour market participation, particularly among women with children.

Table 11.1 Activity rates (% working population 15–64 years old), 1970–93

	1970			1980			1989			1993		
	FR	UK	SW	FR	UK	SW	FR	UK	SW	FR	UK	SW
Employment rates												
Men	86.0	96.1	90.6	83.4	91.5	89.8	76.8	86.3	88.7	74.5	84.0	79.3
Women	49.8	53.5	60.6	55.6	61.7	75.8	57.6	66.0	83.2	59.0	65.3	75.7
Both	68.3	74.6	75.8	69.5	76.6	82.9	67.1	76.2	86.0	66.7	74.7	77.5

Source: OECD (1990, 1995)

In all three countries, the wage gap between men and women has narrowed considerably, so that women in employment can expect to earn more than they used to. However, this is particularly true of Sweden, where the 'wage solidarity' policy, part of the general drive to reduce inequalities, is one of the principles underpinning the 'Swedish model' that has led to a general narrowing of the wage gap, particularly between men and women, to the point where average female pay is now about 80 per cent of that of men (Anxo and Johansson 1995). However, since the mid-1980s, the wage gap has tended to widen again as a result of decentralised pay bargaining. In France, a sustained policy of increasing low wages, combined with rising skill levels among women, has reduced the pay gap between men and women to the point where average female pay was 79 per cent of that of men in 1992 (INSEE 1995). However, this trend has tended to stagnate since 1981 (CERC 1989). In the UK, pay discrimination remains very strong: women's hourly earnings have reached 80 per cent of those of men among manual workers and 58 per cent among non-manual workers (*Bulletin sur l'emploi des femmes* 1994). However, these figures refer only to full-timers, and the gap widens further when female part-timers are taken into account: preliminary results from the Family and Working Life Survey show that, when the average salary of all workers, both full-timers and part-timers, is calculated, women's pay is only 55.5 per cent that of men (King and Murray 1996: 118; see also Rubery, Chapter 7, this volume).

The Swedish taxation system is neutral as far as the household is concerned. The changeover in 1970 from joint to individual taxation meant that married women in employment were no longer penalised and had a considerable incentive to enter the labour market.[1] France still has joint taxation of married couples, but the effect of fiscal policies is difficult to measure since it interacts with that of transfer payments (Bourguignon 1985). Individual taxation was introduced in the UK in 1990, although there is still a special allowance for married men living with a non-working wife.

Policies to reduce working hours and to implement flexible working time in Sweden have led not only to a general reduction in hours worked (although the trend has tended to rise again in the past few years) but also to an enormous increase in permitted absence, particularly but not only among mothers: they get fifteen months' paid parental leave at 75 per cent of their previous salary for the first twelve months[2] and sixty days per year and per child of paid leave if their children fall ill. This leave entitlement, introduced in the 1970s and available to men and women alike, has considerably reduced discontinuity in women's employment.

In France, the opportunities to take leave for family reasons are much more restricted, and the conditions much tighter, than in Sweden. Since 1994, there has been a legal entitlement to three days' leave per year per sick child under the age of 16.[3] Most of the gains made in this field are the result of collective bargaining.[4] Parental leave has existed since 1977, but is unpaid; there is, however, a child-raiser's allowance[5] (Allocation Parentale d'Education (APE)), available to parents who leave their job or reduce their working time (the APE is then reduced pro rata) following the birth of a second or subsequent child;[6] the allowance is payable until the child's third birthday. Given these conditions, take-up rates for the child-raiser's allowance have been low among French women, and even lower among men (*Premières informations* 1992): to date, it has been the exception rather than the rule, and those taking advantage of it have been mainly women who have just had their third child (Barbier 1995). General measures on the organisation of working time in France have tended to be based on principles that are, *de facto*, discriminatory: those affecting men often involve wage compensation (for example, reduced weekend working time without any reduction in pay for men or phased early retirement), while those affecting women tend to involve the introduction of jobs with shorter hours and lower pay (Boisard *et al.* 1986; Bloch-London *et al.* 1996).

Family policy in the UK is based on a notion of women defined by their roles as mothers and wives. Parental leave does not exist – it is merely an extension of maternity leave and is not, therefore, available to fathers. Moreover, the regulations governing access to maternity leave were until recently very restrictive: in 1988, only 60 per cent of working women were entitled to it. Even though a European directive has now extended maternity leave (fourteen weeks, together with a lump-sum payment) to all women irrespective of their previous work situation, the conditions governing access remain restrictive. It applies only to employees, and thus excludes the self-employed, registered unemployed and economically inactive; moreover, women working less than 16 hours a week have to have worked with the same employer for two years, or five years in the case of those working fewer than 8 hours per week. In any event, entitlement to maternity leave is not enshrined in law but arises solely out of agreements between employers and employees (OECD 1995: 211). Parents receive child benefit, but there are no other family allowances or tax credits to ease the burden of child care, unlike in Sweden and France (OECD 1990: 162).

As far as the care of young children is concerned, the provision of public child care facilities in Sweden, which was very underdeveloped at the beginning of the 1970s, has increased considerably: in 1972, 10 per cent of children aged between 4 months and 6 years had a place; the figure today is 50 per cent. In total, 58 per cent of Swedish pre-school children are cared for outside their home. However, these forms of care are expensive until children go to school at the age of 7, or from 1997 at the age of 6 (Pauti 1992; Daune-Richard and Mahon 1997).

In France, child care is made particularly easy for families since there are free nursery schools available to all children from the age of 3 and sometimes even earlier (at present, 94 per cent of children aged 3 go to school), with compulsory primary school starting at the age of 6. In addition, school does not finish until 4.30 p.m. and most schools, at least in urban areas, have a canteen and after-school supervision or homework rooms where children can stay until 6 p.m. On the other hand, up to the age of 3, 52 per cent of French children are looked after by their mothers and only 40 per cent are cared for outside the home (by childminders, in crèches, play groups or nursery school) (Desplanques 1993).

In the UK, the public provision of child care for very young children is poor. Only about 12 per cent of children under 2 years old are cared for outside their homes: 2 per cent in state-run facilities and 5–10 per cent, for a few hours a day, in private play groups. It is estimated that these play groups, around 25 per cent of which receive public funding, provide part-time care for between 40 and 45 per cent of children aged between 3 and 4. Around 44 per cent of this age group have a place in state nursery schools, although about half of them only attend for a few hours a day. Primary school starts at the age of 5: children attend school from 9 a.m. to 3 p.m. and are supervised during their lunch break, although there are virtually no facilities for after-school supervision (Moss 1991). According to a recent survey of working mothers with at least one child under age 5, 48 per cent use one (or more) forms of informal care, while 47 per cent pay for child care or use a combination of informal and paid forms of care (Finlayson *et al.* 1996: 297).

In sum, even though all three countries considered here have seen a considerable increase in female employment, the economic and institutional context has a qualitatively different impact on the form this employment takes.

Until the late 1980s, Sweden was making use of female labour against a background of full employment and even, on occasion, of labour shortages; however, the situation has changed dramatically since the beginning of the 1990s. This economic context is a product of the 'Swedish model' which, since the 1930s, has sought to place the reduction of inequalities and the redistribution of wealth at the heart of social development. Women have benefited in several ways from general measures resulting from these principles. In this context, the development of part-time work has been a flexible and adaptable form of employment for married women in a country that has opted for full employment. Indeed, it was with the expansion of female labour market participation in the 1960s that female part-time work began to increase (Thirriot 1990: 146); it has been on the decrease since the beginning of the 1980s (Table 11.2) while part-timers now work longer hours, in contrast with what is happening in the UK.

Table 11.2 Growth and composition of the part-time workforce (as % of total male or female workforce), 1979–94

| | Part-time work as a % of | | | | | | | | | | | | Proportion of women in part-time work | | | |
| | Total workforce | | | | Male workforce | | | | Female workforce | | | | | | | |
	1979	1983	1990	1994	1979	1983	1990	1994	1979	1983	1990	1994	1979	1983	1990	1994
FR	8.2	9.7	12.0	14.9	2.4	2.6	3.5	4.6	16.9	20.0	23.8	27.8	82.2	84.4	83.1	82.7
SW	23.6	24.8	23.0	24.9	5.4	6.3	7.3	9.7	46.0	45.9	40.5	41.0	87.5	86.6	83.7	80.1
UK[1]	16.4	19.4	21.8	23.8	1.9	3.3	5.0	7.1	39.0	42.4	43.8	44.3	92.8	89.8	87.0	83.6

Source: OECD (1990: 48 and 1995: 224)
Note:
1 1990 data are for 1989.

In France, the increase in female employment took place against a background of a relative shortage of labour until the beginning of the seventies and of a shortage of jobs from 1975 onwards. The female labour supply, which has been maintained despite the jobs crisis, has contributed enormously to the increase in the size of the working population, whereas male employment has declined very considerably. Female part-time work is not a tradition in France where, until recently, the norm of full-time male employment dominated the labour market (see Rubery, Chapter 7, this volume). It was only with the jobs crisis of the late 1970s that part-time work began to spread in France, although it is much less widespread than in Sweden and the UK. In this respect, it is closely linked to the reduction and flexibilisation of employment.

In the UK, it would seem that the institutional framework tends to encourage women with children living with a partner to work part-time rather than dissuading them from working altogether. Indeed, in addition to the absence of public support for child care, whether material or financial, there are social and fiscal policies that offer considerable incentives to married women to work part-time. Below a certain number of hours worked (16 hours a week until 1994, 8 hours since then) or below a certain income level, part-timers and their employers do not have to pay any social security contributions; however, workers in this category are not entitled to any social protection. Income from such jobs is not taxed. According to the New Earnings Survey of 1995, around one-third of British female part-time workers fall below this threshold (Osborne 1996: 235). This type of short hours working, considered as a second income, is largely the province of workers whose social protection is derived from other sources, particularly married women, and especially so since these families also benefit from the special married women's allowance. Thus in 1995, 25 per cent of British women with a part-time job usually worked fewer than 10 hours a week, compared with 11 per cent of French and Swedish women (Eurostat 1995: Table 78).

THE HISTORIC SIGNIFICANCE OF PART-TIME WORK FOR WOMEN'S ENTRY INTO WAGE WORK

The observable differences of institutional arrangements affect the forms of female labour market participation, which arise out of specific historical constructions, of particular 'societal configurations'. These are as much a reflection of differing definitions of the relationships between the public and private spheres as of the relationship between men and women, or of the place of the individual, male or female, in each society (see also Pfau-Effinger, Chapter 9, this volume).

In the UK, industrialisation occurred earlier and marked a more radical break with the past than in Sweden and France; it was based almost wholly on the development of large-scale manufacturing industry, and was accompanied by a rapid decline in the size of the agricultural labour force. These changing patterns of work were paralleled by the emergence, at a much earlier stage than in France or Sweden, of the single breadwinner model of the family (Tilly and Scott 1978). The so-called 'marriage bar', which was defended by both unions and employers, illustrates this development. Introduced in the second half of the nineteenth century, the rule meant that women had to give up their jobs once married. It helped to exclude married women from the labour market until the Second World War: it was gradually phased out between the 1940s and the end of the 1970s.[7] Thus, in 1901 and 1931, the employment rate among married women was 10 per cent in the UK, whereas in France it was 50 per cent and 44 per cent respectively (Hantrais 1990: 109).

Women's participation in the labour market increased significantly but gradually after the Second World War, albeit in ways that ensured they maintained their family responsibilities. They tended to enter and leave the labour market as children were born or family needs changed, and mothers of school-age children tended to work part-time. Thus, until recently, participation rates among British women declined considerably during the child-bearing years; those who went back to work did so on a part-time basis and tended to remain in part-time employment even after their children had grown up (Martin and Roberts 1984). This model of 'intermittent' and part-time employment was very common among women with children in all occupational categories in the 1980s, even if it was less widespread in intermediate and higher occupations (Dex et al. 1993).

However, this model is changing dramatically. Participation rates among women with children have increased considerably in the past few years, particularly among those with young children: in 1995, 55 per cent of women with at least one child under 5 were economically active, compared with 45 per cent in 1985 (Sly 1996: 91). Overall, although participation rates for women with children are still significantly more affected by the presence of young children in the UK than in France (in 1990, 53 per cent of British mothers of children aged below 7 were economically active, compared with 65 per cent of their French counterparts), this is no longer true of mothers with children of school age (72 per cent of French women with children aged between 7 and 14 are economically active, compared with 76 per cent of British women; see Bulletin sur l'emploi des femmes1992).

However, this increasing labour market participation among women with children largely continues to take the form of part-time work. Not only is this form of employment accountable for an increasing share of total female employment (39 per cent in 1979, 44 per cent in 1994: see Table 11.2) but, in 1991, it represented no less than 65 per cent of all employment for women with children, compared with 28 per cent for French women with children (CEE 1993: 160).

In the UK, part-time work seems to characterise the most disadvantaged category of workers: an overwhelmingly female phenomenon, it reduces competition between men and women for the lowest-paid, least interesting jobs

(Rubery and Tarling 1988). By focusing their claims on improving the protection afforded to part-time workers, the trade unions have, paradoxically, helped to reinforce the distinction which separates them from full-time workers and makes them a distinctive category (O'Reilly 1994). It would seem that, as married women gradually entered the labour market, they were relegated structurally to this employment form, whose main attraction to employers has been shown to be its flexibility (Beechey and Perkins 1987). The 'liberation' of married women's labour, which is a recent but now very widespread phenomenon, has taken place in a context in which child care is still regarded as a private matter to be dealt with within the family, by involving the father, grandparents and other members of the extended family and by mothers working part-time, often on atypical hours, in the evening or at night (Brannen 1995). Since they are less likely than their French and Swedish counterparts to go into further or higher education (Table 11.3), there are social pressures on them, as soon as they have family responsibilities, to take unfavourable part-time jobs. This is probably one of the reasons for the greater employability of British women compared with both British men and French women: despite the differences in the measurement of unemployment in the two countries (Barrère-Maurisson et al. 1989), British women are more likely than men to be employed in these undesirable jobs and less likely to register as unemployed between two precarious contracts. In other words, the notion of the 'woman who stays at home' carries greater weight in social perceptions of women's role in the UK.

In France, industrialisation was a more gradual process and a less immediately urban phenomenon than in the UK. It did not lead to a sudden and drastic decline in the size of the agricultural workforce,[8] and the industrial and agricultural worlds remained entwined for a long time. Family forms of production (agriculture, small shops and craft or artisanal activities) persisted for a long time as the main source of work for women, while the industrial wage-earning class emerged particularly in small and medium-sized factories

Table 11.3 Percentage enrolled in full-time education

	Secondary education[1]				Higher education[2]			
	Men		Women		Men		Women	
	1980	1990	1980	1990	1980	1990	1980	1990
France	81.0	92.0	90.0	98.0	26.6	36.6	23.3	42.8
UK	82.0	82.0	85.0	85.0	23.7	29.5	14.3	28.1
Sweden	82.0	88.0	93.0	92.0	–	28.4	–	34.8

Source: UNESCO (1993)
Notes:
1 As a percentage of the population who should officially be at secondary school.
2 Total numbers of students in higher education as percentage of the age group.

and homeworking (Bouillaguet-Bernard and Germe 1981). Women did not enter the wage-earning class until later. In contrast to the UK, there is a long tradition of economic activity among French women, even married ones, but for a long time this was confined to family production units, where they enjoyed neither status nor remuneration.[9] Since the 1960s, women's educational attainment has soared dramatically, leading in turn to a high level of demand for advanced skills in the labour market (Table 11.3). The public provision of care for children aged 3 years and over is both extensive and free, which is unusual in an industrialised country. However, while French men perform a greater share of domestic tasks than their British counterparts, French women still devote a very substantial amount of time to such tasks, on top of very heavy work schedules outside the home. Thus the heavy workload resulting from women's involvement in the labour market and their domestic responsibilities is shared more equally with men and public institutions than in the UK, but generates long working hours (in 1986: a total of 68 hours per week (domestic work plus paid work) for female full-timers and 62 hours for female part-timers) (Roy 1990).

When women entered the labour market in large numbers in France in the 1970s, they followed the male model of full-time work; this was made easier by considerable state support in the spheres of education and child care.[10] At the same time, part-time work was not attractive to employers since their social security contributions were based on the number of employees and not on the number of worked hours;[11] moreover, it was opposed by the unions, who saw it as a threat to the cohesion of standard employment. However, because their working day was so long, a lot of women were forced to give up their jobs once they had family responsibilities, and particularly if they had a large number of children. The state encouraged this by providing financial support through the family allowance system to help mothers of large families to bring up their own children. However, the number of large families has declined dramatically, and at the same time there has been a considerable reduction in the number and duration of career interruptions due to childbirth. Nevertheless, discontinuity of employment, although much diminished, remains strongly correlated with size of family and skill level (expected earnings and working conditions).

Thus there is little tradition of women working part-time in France:[12] it was against the background of the employment crisis and the shortage of full-time jobs at the end of the 1970s that part-time work really took off. Encouraged by the new regulations introduced in the early 1980s, which made it easier and financially more worthwhile for employers to recruit part-timers,[13] part-time work gradually found support from some trade unions, which saw it as a means of redistributing work in such a way as to reduce unemployment. In this respect, the development of part-time work in the 1980s was essentially a response to the need for both functional and numerical flexibility. It has tended to split the female labour market: on the one hand, there are relatively highly skilled jobs for women, with genuine career prospects, including voluntary part-time work for established civil servants, with the option of reverting to full-time at some later date and, on the other, a supply of flexible jobs (particularly in the distributive trades and services to individuals[14]) which, for women, are largely part-time[15] but which offer many of those least able to compete in the labour market (in terms of skills but also, undoubtedly, in terms of work history) a means of entering or remaining in the labour market. For this category of workers, part-time work is still a predominantly female phenomenon and one that reflects a change in the organisation of work rather than a reorganisation of working time (Nicole-Drancourt 1990).

The traditional relatively low employability of French women should be seen against this background of high average skill levels and the long tradition of female economic activity. The flexibilisation of employment essentially affects a single form of the female labour supply and should not, a priori, modify this tendency, although there is every reason to suppose that the divide within the female labour market will continue to widen.

Sweden remained an agricultural country for a long time. Industrialisation took place later, against a background of serious economic crises, poverty and unemployment leading to waves of mass emigration in the late nineteenth and early twentieth centuries, which lasted until the 1930s (Thirriot 1990). This explains why stable and continuous wage work for women is a relatively recent phenomenon in Sweden; it did not begin to develop until the mid-1930s and only really took off in the early 1960s, mainly in the service sector.

As in the UK, the development of part-time work is closely linked to the entry of married women into the labour market. However, the way it evolved and its social meaning are totally different. Instead of being correlated with the flexibility of the female labour supply in total (as in the UK) or in part (as in France), part-time work in Sweden does not seem to be linked to precarious employment.[16] It would appear to represent a historical form of 'transition' between the tradition of non-participation on the part of mothers and their entry into the labour market, which is widely supported, indeed encouraged, by Swedish political and economic institutions. This transitional form of employment seems to have been intended to establish a tradition of paid work among women with children. The decrease in the share of part-time work in total female employment (which fell from 46 per cent to 41 per cent between 1979 and 1994: see Table 11.2) and the increase in the hours worked by part-timers (21 hours per week in 1979, 24.4 hours in 1995) (OECD 1990 and Eurostat 1995) support this hypothesis. In any event, although French women continue to work the highest average number of hours (34 hours a week), Swedish women are catching up (32.8 hours), with British women lagging some distance behind (30.7 hours) (Eurostat 1995).

Thus there is a typical pattern of female employment in Sweden: women work full-time, make maximum use of the parental leave provisions when their children are born and return to work part-time (secure in the knowledge that they can take leave if their children fall ill). All this can be achieved without 'interrupting' their careers.[17] They then gradually increase their working hours, eventually returning more or less to full-time work.

The economic conditions of the 1970s and 1980s (a period of strong economic growth and high demand for labour from firms and the Welfare State) partly explain the ease with which this new model of female labour market participation became established. It might be concluded that the 'Swedish model', based as it is on solidarity and negotiation, was tending to work in the same direction: employment for all, flexible working hours, a solidaristic pay policy and social, family (parental leave) and fiscal policies have tended to reduce inequalities, including those between men and women, and have encouraged more women to enter the labour market. For some observers, however, it was the strong involvement of women in politics (parties and trade unions) that enabled Swedish women to extend the debate on equality to women on the one hand, and to the private household on the other (Jenson 1991); hence the participation of men, albeit at a low level,[18] in parental leave, the more equal sharing of tasks within the family[19] and the development of different forms of child care. Jenson (1991) sees a difference in this respect from France where, because of a lack of any real links between the feminist movement and the political sphere (or even the trade unions), demands for equality between the sexes have remained confined to the economic sphere, where labour legislation has traditionally been relatively neutral, and has not really influenced the important political debates. With the development of the employment crisis in France, this political weakness appears to have contributed to the development of specifically female forms of flexible employment. Indeed, assessments (Doniol-Shaw et al. 1989; Jobert 1995) of the implementation of the 1983 French law on equality at work conclude that the law has not been a success.

CONCLUSIONS

In this chapter we have outlined the major 'societal configurations' specific to each of the three countries in question, focusing on female labour market participation in order to reveal the interaction between the labour market, state policies and the family.

The UK appears to be following a long-established model, in which family responsibilities are the subject of private arrangements, made within the family and implemented largely by women. Thus women's economic activity tends to be discontinuous, but is now characterised in particular by part-time work, which enables them to reconcile what is, viewed over the life cycle, a high level of activity (Dex et al. 1993) with their family responsibilities. The growth in female employment has been accompanied by a significant reduction in the number of women withdrawing from the labour market but also by an ever growing tendency towards part-time work, which is particularly deskilled in the UK relative to full-time work. Thus, in the UK, it would seem that women's mode of entry into the public world of wage work, particularly if they have children, is still based on a notion of gendered roles that emphasises difference and 'complementarity'. Finally, the absence of any programme to expand the public provision of child care has encouraged the development over the past few years of private facilities, and generally speaking the cost of child care has increased (Finlayson *et al.* 1996); this will tend to widen the gap between well-off families (those with two adults in well-paid jobs) and poor families (Brannen 1995). In sum, rather than constituting a way out of unemployment (Mósesdóttir 1995), part-time jobs in the UK tend to be held by women whose partners are in employment and who work relatively short hours (24 per cent work fewer than 10 hours; 66 per cent work fewer than 20 hours in the UK, in comparison with 50 per cent in France and 35 per cent in Sweden (Eurostat 1995)).

The French paradigm of interaction between the labour market and the family has a tendency to be more conflictual than in the other two countries. Commaille (1993) has described French society as characterised by a structural tension between a 'pro-family tendency', which seeks to 'defend and promote the institution of the family', and a 'feminism', which seeks to gain recognition for women 'as individuals with rights of their own'. This contradictory tension exerts a profound influence on both individual behaviour and state policies affecting the interaction between the labour market and the family. On the one hand, there is little sharing of household tasks between men and women, and women devote a considerable amount of time to domestic tasks and child care, demonstrating the importance of their role in the family in that respect. On the other hand, despite working longer hours than their counterparts in the other two countries, Frenchwomen are very involved in the labour market, even when they have young children, and are much less likely to work part-time than British and Swedish women. Public policies also reflect this ambivalence: on the one hand, there is a high level of publicly funded child care, making it easier for women to work, while on the other, the child-raiser's allowance (APE) acts as an incentive for women to leave the labour market. The contradiction between these logics has led to the emergence of two groups of women: the majority who remain in the labour market, preferably in full-time jobs, and the minority who withdraw, initially temporarily but often permanently. This split corresponds to divisions in the social hierarchy: those who leave the job market are the most vulnerable in terms of both skills and work history. The development of part-time work, which is a key element in employers' attempts to increase flexibility, tends to divide female part-timers along a similar social division: for those in skilled and/or permanent jobs, part-time work represents a voluntary and reversible reorganisation of working time, while for the least skilled and/or most vulnerable, it is usually imposed and often precarious.

In France, in any event, part-time work is not a model favoured by wives and mothers. Having emerged against a background of increasing flexibility in work organisation and high structural unemployment, it mainly involves the most vulnerable members of the labour force: new entrants or returners to the labour market and those with low skill levels. Thus 53 per cent of male and 36 per cent of female part-timers said they were working part-time because they had failed to find a full-time job, compared with 26 per cent and 10 per cent respectively in the UK and 28 per cent and 27 per cent in Sweden (Eurostat 1995).

In Sweden, the position of women in society has evolved in a spectacular fashion, particularly in the labour market, due largely to the development of the 'Swedish model'. Broad agreement between the social partners has led to a more even distribution of family responsibilities between, on the one hand, the community and families and, on the other, between men and women. Working time has been reorganised, paid parental leave introduced, inequality reduced and a public debate held with the purpose of encouraging men to play a greater part in the family: the whole of Swedish society, including the legislature, has helped to rethink the relationship between men and women, particularly as far as the interaction between the employment market and the family is concerned. In this respect, it will be interesting to observe how women's participation in the labour market evolves and how they react to the consequences of a possible break up of the 'Swedish model', of which they could well be the first casualties (Anxo 1993), as both employees and clients of the welfare state. Thus, for example, the decentralisation of wage bargaining may well cause wage inequalities between men and women to widen again (Delsen and van Veen 1992; Wise 1993). At the moment, however, the crisis that has been affecting Sweden since the 1980s (job shortages, crisis in the welfare state, breakdown of the redistributive mechanisms) does not seem to be affecting women any more than men. The high profile of women within the political parties and the trade unions could explain the persistence of a model based on equality, albeit relative equality, between men and women which has been gradually put in place since the 1970s (Daune-Richard and Mahon 1997).

Overall, there are good grounds for thinking that the societal configurations which give shape and meaning to women's employment are rooted as much in specific historical constructions of the relationship between the public and private spheres and of individuality and citizenship (Daune-Richard 1997) as in the relationship between men and women. In other words, although it is absolutely essential and fruitful to study how each society defines its 'gender system' (Mathieu 1991) or its 'gender contract' (Hirdman 1994) or even its 'gender culture' (Pfau-Effinger, Chapter 9, this volume), it is equally important to identify how, in any given society, each (re)definition of social frameworks and actors simultaneously (re)defines the relative position of men and women. The gender system enjoys only limited autonomy from the social and economic framework in which it is deeply embedded, but with which it interacts and reforms.

NOTES

1 Before this reform, a couple's taxes were calculated by adding the woman's salary to the man's which, given the progressive nature of the Swedish tax system, heavily penalised married women's income.

2 For the last three months this is paid at a rate of 60 krone per day. It is also possible to spread this leave over a longer period (until the child is 8) by decreasing one's working time. Eighty-five per cent of the cost of parental leave is financed by contributions paid by employers and self-employed workers, with the remaining 15 per cent paid for by the state (Pauti 1992).

3 Five days if the child is under 1 year of age or if the wage-earner has three or more dependent children.

4 Leave for sick children is generally, but not always, available to men and women alike. In the public sector, workers can take a week plus one day for each child under 16, but this leave is granted to the family whatever the number of children, and 'operational requirements' at the workplace have to be taken into account before it is permitted.

5 The amount of which is not linked to pay as in the Swedish system: it is a basic allowance equal to about half of the minimum wage.

6 Since 1994, prior to this, the allowance was only available for the third or subsequent child.

7 After a long campaign led by women's organisations against employers and unions (see Hakim 1987: 555).

8 One-third of the working population was employed in agriculture at the end of the Second World War.

9 Only in 1982 did the wives of self-employed workers acquire an occupational status defined in law, and even now it is little used (see Zarka 1993).

10 A tradition dating back to the nineteenth century, which should be viewed in the context of the secularisation of the French state and its desire to reduce if not eradicate the Church's stranglehold over education.

11 A part-time worker 'cost' an employer as much as a full-time worker in terms of contributions.

12 Only 11 per cent of economically active French women worked part-time in 1973 and 17 per cent in 1979, compared with 39 per cent in the UK for the same years (OECD Labour Force Statistics). In 1995 this had risen to 44 per cent in the UK compared with 29 per cent in France (European Commission 1996: 153 and 162).

13 Employers' social security contributions were now calculated on the basis of hours worked.

14 The increasing availability of part-time jobs coincided with the decline of employment in manufacturing industry, which used to absorb a substantial proportion of the unskilled female labour force.

15 Flexible jobs for men are more likely to be temporary.

16 Until very recently, temporary work was closely linked with the tradition of combining employment and education at the beginning of the working life and with the replacement of workers on leave (the level of leave is very high in Sweden, but should tend to fall with the reduction of allowance rates: 90 per cent of previous salary until 1994, 75 per cent today).

17 People on leave are counted as members of the working population. Hence there is a wide gap between measured employment levels and the number of Swedish women actually in work (Jonung and Persson 1993).

18 By 1991, 8 per cent of parental leave days had been taken by men (Vielle 1994).

19 The involvement of men in domestic tasks is by far the highest in the three countries studied (see Daune-Richard 1993).

BIBLIOGRAPHY

Anxo, D. (1993) 'Les années 90 ou la fin du modèle suédois?' in B. Gazier (ed.) *Emploi, nouvelles donnes*, Paris: Economica.

Anxo, D. and Johansson, M. (1995) 'Les discriminations salariales en Suède', *Les Cahiers du MAGE*, 2, Paris: CNRS-IRESCO.

Barbier, J.-Cl. (1995) 'Relations emploi-famille: à propos de la comparaison européenne des catégories de chômeurs et de congés parentaux' in M.-Th. Letablier and L. Hantrais (eds) *La relation famille-emploi. Une comparaison des modes d'ajustement en Europe*. Paris: Dossier no. 6, Centre d'Etudes de l'Emploi.

Barrère-Maurisson, M.-A., Daune-Richard, A.-M. and Letablier, M.-Th. (1989) 'Le travail à temps partiel plus développé au Royaume-Uni qu'en France', Paris: *Economie et Statistique*, 220, April: 47–56.

Beechey, V. and Perkins, T. (1987) *A Matter of Hours: Women, Part-time Work and the Labour Market*, Cambridge: Polity Press.

Bloch-London, C., Bue, J. and Coutrot, Th. (1996) 'Politiques de l'emploi: masculin pluriel ou féminin singulier?' in H. Hirata and D. Senotier (eds) *Femmes et partage du travail*, Paris: Syros.

Boisard P., Bouillaguet, P. and Letablier, M.-Th. (1986), 'Le partage du travail: une politique asexuée', Paris: *Nouvelles questions féministes*: 14–15.

Bouillaguet-Bernard, P. and Germe, J.-F. (1981) 'Salarisation et travail féminin en France', Paris: *Critiques de l'Economie politique*, nouvelle série, 17, July to September: 83–117.

Bourguignon, F. (1985) 'Fiscalité, transferts et activité féminine', Paris: Centre d'Economie Quantitative et Comparative. Tiré à part no. 8304.

Brannen, J. (1995) 'Concilier vie professionnelle et vie familiale pour les ménages avec enfants: approches conceptuelles à partir de la situation au Royaume-Uni' in M.-Th. Letablier and L. Hantrais (eds) *La relation famille-emploi. Une comparaison des modes d'ajustement en Europe*. Dossier no. 6, Paris: Centre d'Etudes de l'Emploi.

Bulletin sur l'emploi des femmes dans la CEE (1992) 1 and (1994) 5.

CEE (1993 and 1995) *L'emploi en Europe*.

Centre d'Etudes des Revenus et des Coûts (CERC) (1989) *Les Français et leurs revenus: le tournant des années 1980*, Paris: La Découverte – La Documentation Française.

Commaille, J. (1993) *Les stratégies des femmes. Travail, famille et politique*. Paris: La Découverte.

Daune-Richard, A.-M. (1988) 'Gender relation and female labor – a consideration of sociological categories' in J. Jenson, E. Hagen and C. Reddy (eds) *Feminization of the Labour Force. Paradoxes and Promises*, Cambridge: Polity Press.

Daune-Richard, A.-M. (1993) 'Activité et emploi des femmes: des constructions sociétales différentes en France, au Royaume-Uni et en Suède', Paris: *Sociétés contemporaines*, 4: 25–43.

Daune-Richard, A.-M. (1997) 'Travail et citoyenneté: un enjeu sexué ... hier et aujourd'hui' in P. Bouffartigue and H. Eckert (eds) *Le travail au delà du salariat*, Paris: Harmattan.

Daune-Richard, A.-M. and Mahon, R. (1997) 'Suède: le modèle egalitaire en danger?' in J. Jenson and M. Sineau (eds) *Qui doit garder le jeune enfant?*, Paris: LGDJ.

Delsen, L. and van Veen, T. (1992) 'The Swedish model: relevant for other European countries?', *British Journal of Industrial Relations* 30, 1:83–106.

Desplanques, G. (1993) 'Garder les petits: organisation collective ou solidarité familiale', *Données sociales*, Paris : INSEE.

Dex, S., Walters, P. and Alden, D. (1993) *French and British Mothers at Work*, London: Macmillan.

Doniol-Shaw, G., Junter-Loiseau, A., Geneste, V., Gouzien, A. and Lerolle, A. (1989) *Les plans d'égalité professionnelle*, Paris : La Documentation Française.

Eurostat (1995) *Labour Force Survey*, Paris: Eurostat.

Finlayson, L., Ford, R. and Marsh, A. (1996) 'Paying more for child care', *Labour Market Trends*, July.

Hakim, C. (1987) 'Trends in flexible workforce', *Employment Gazette*, November: 549–55.

Hantrais, L. (1990) *Managing Professional and Family Life*, Hants and Vermont: Dartmouth Publishing.

Hirdman, Y. (1994) 'Women. From possibility to problem?', *Research Report* 3, Stockholm: Arbetslivcentrum.

INSEE (1995) *Les femmes*, Paris: INSEE.

Jenson, J. (1991) 'Making claims: social policy and gender relations in postwar Sweden and France'. Annual Meeting of the Canadian Sociology and Anthropology Association, 29 June.

Jobert, A. (1995) 'L'égalité professionnelle dans la négociation collective en France', Paris: *Travail et emploi*, 63: 77–88.

Jonung, C. and Persson, I. (1993) 'Women & market work: the misleading tale of participation rate in international comparisons, *Work, Employment and Society* 7, 2: 259–74.

King, S. and Murray, K. (1996), 'Family and working life survey: preliminary results', *Labour Market Trends*, May.

Le sexe du travail (1984) ouvrage collectif, Paris: Presses Universitaires de Grenoble.

Lutz, B. (1989) 'Effet sociétal ou effet historique? Quelques remarques sur le bon usage de la comparaison internationale'. Le lien social, actes du IIIe Colloque de l'AISLF, Université de Genève, tome I: 53–66.

Martin, J. and Roberts, C. (1984) *Women and Employment, a Lifetime Perspective*, London: HMSO.

Mathieu, N.-Cl. (1991) 'Notes pour une définition sociologique des catégories de sexe' (1st edn 1971) in N.-Cl. Mathieu, *L'anatomie politique*, Paris: Côté-femmes.

Maurice, M., Sellier, F. and Silvestre, J.-J. (1982) *Politique d'éducation et organisation industrielle en France et en Allemagne*, Paris: PUF.

Mósesdóttir, L. (1995) 'The state and the egalitarian, ecclesiastical and liberal regimes of gender relations', *British Journal of Sociology* 46, 4.

Moss, P. (1991) 'Day care for young children in the United Kingdom' in E. Melhuish and P. Moss (eds) *Day Care for Young Children*, London: Routledge.

Nicole-Drancourt, Ch. (1990) 'Organisation du travail des femmes et flexibilité de l'emploi', Paris: *Sociologie du travail* 2.

OECD (1990, 1995) *Perspectives de l'emploi*, Paris: OECD.

OECD (various years) *Labour Force Statistics*.

O'Reilly, J. (1994) *Banking on Flexibility*, Aldershot: Avebury.

Osborne, K. (1996) 'Earnings of part-time workers: data from the 1995 New Earnings Survey', *Labour Market Trends*, May.

Pauti, A. (1992) 'La politique familiale en Suède', Paris: *Population* 4: 961–84.

Premières informations (1992) 334, Paris: Ministère du Travail.

Roy, C. (1990) 'Les emplois du temps dans quelques pays occidentaux', Données sociales, Paris: INSEE.

Rubery, J. (1988) 'Women and recession : a comparative perspective' in J. Rubery (ed.) *Women and Recession*, London and New York: Routledge & Kegan Paul.

Rubery, J. and Tarling, R. (1988) 'Women's employment in declining Britain', in J. Rubery (ed.) *Women and Recession*, London and New York: Routledge & Kegan Paul.

Sly, F. (1996) 'Women in the labour market: results from the Spring 1995 Labour Force Survey', *Labour Market Trends*, March: 91–114.

Thirriot, L. (1990) 'Le plein emploi en Suède', *Economies et Sociétés, Economie du Travail* 16: 163–7.

Tilly, L. A. and Scott, J. W. (1978) *Women, Work and Family*, New York and London: Holt, Rinehard & Winston.

UNESCO (1993) *Rapport mondial sur l'education*, Paris: UNESCO.

Vielle, P. (1994) 'Les politiques publiques en faveur d'une meilleure conciliation de la vie professionnelle et de la vie familiale en Europe', rapport pour l'Association Internationale de la Sécurité Sociale, Geneva.

Wise, L. R. (1993) 'Wither solidarity? Transitions in Swedish public sector pay policy', *British Journal of Industrial Relations* 31, 1: 75–95.

Zarka, B. (1993) 'Indépendance professionnelle, relations entre les sexes et mobilisations collectives', Paris: *Sociétés contemporaines*, 16.

12

WHAT IS THE NATURE OF PART-TIME WORK IN THE UNITED STATES AND JAPAN?

Susan Houseman and Machiko Osawa

INTRODUCTION

Part-time employment represents a large and growing share of employment in most industrialised countries. One view holds that the amount of part-time employment simply reflects the efficient outcome of supply and demand forces in the labour market. Some workers seek part-time positions to accommodate child care and household responsibilities, school, or other activities. Firms demand part-time workers to increase staffing during peak business hours or to solve other scheduling problems. The relative wages of part-time workers adjust until the supply of part-time workers equals the demand for part-time workers. Another view treats labour markets as segmented, with part-time jobs falling in the secondary sector. Detractors of part-time employment argue that these jobs typically pay low wages, offer few fringe benefits, and have little job security. Moreover, labour markets may not clear in the neo-classical economic sense and many workers desiring regular, full-time jobs work part-time involuntarily.

In this chapter we examine the extent to which these competing views characterise part-time employment in two countries with markedly different industrial relations systems: the United States and Japan. Although Japanese industrial relations practices have received much attention in the United States and other industrialised countries, most studies have focused on 'core' workers, who are typically full-time men, and the industrial relations practices, such as seniority-based wages and promotions and lifetime employment, applying to them. Relatively little attention has been paid to the sizeable non-standard workforce, which includes part-time workers, for whom these traditional industrial relations practices do not apply.

We begin the chapter by describing the two quite different concepts of part-time employment in the United States and Japan. We then provide background information on the characteristics of part-time workers, the industries in which they work, and trends in part-time employment in the two countries. Although the overall levels of part-time employment are similar in the two countries, we show that the demographic and industrial patterns are quite different. We review evidence on differences between the wages, benefits and job security of part-time workers and full-time workers in the United States and Japan and examine competing explanations for these differences. In addition, we analyse the supply- and demand- side forces behind recent increases in part-time employment in the United States and Japan, and discuss evidence on whether or not the growth in part-time employment in each country has contributed to segmentation. We also offer explanations for the much greater growth of part-time employment in Japan than in the United States. We conclude with a review of evidence on the extent of labour market segmentation in part-time employment and a discussion of the policy debate on part-time employment in each country.

WHAT IS PART-TIME EMPLOYMENT?

The concept of part-time employment differs in important ways between the United States and Japan. In US official statistics a part-time worker is one who works fewer than 35 hours per week. Although there has been some academic debate over whether the 35-hour per week cut-off is set too high (Stratton 1994), the concept of part-time employment is tied to the number of hours worked. In contrast, according to common notions of part-time work in Japan, a 'part-time' worker does not necessarily work fewer hours than a full-time worker. Indeed, recent Japanese surveys show that between 20 and 30 per cent of workers classified as part-time by their employers work the same number of hours per week as regular, full-time workers.[1] The Japanese concept of part-time employment is explicitly related to status within the firm. The Japanese industrial relations system is often characterised as two-tiered, with 'core' full-time workers and 'peripheral' part-time and temporary workers. The personnel practices that apply to regular full-time workers are different from those that apply to part-time workers. For example, seniority-based wages and promotions and commitments of lifetime employment, which are common in medium and large firms, are rarely offered to part-time workers. Part-time workers are also much less likely than regular workers to be eligible to receive bonuses, fringe benefits and workplace training.

Although industrial relations practices such as seniority-based wages and promotions may increase employee commitment, they also make the wage and employment structure in Japanese firms extremely rigid. Japanese employers use part-time and other non-standard workers to increase wage and employment flexibility. In this industrial relations context it is understandable why the concept of part-time employment is so closely tied to status, and not just hours of work.

In working with statistics on part-time employment in the two countries, one must be careful not only about cross-country differences in the definition of part-time employment, but also about inconsistencies in the statistics on part-time employment within countries. US part-time employment statistics come from the Current Population Survey (CPS), a monthly household survey. A subtle, but important, change in the definition of part-time employment in the CPS renders part-time statistics incomparable before and after 1994.[2]

Statistics on part-time employment have been collected only in recent years in Japan. Several periodic and special one-time surveys have been conducted by various agencies to shed light on the phenomenon of part-time employment but, unfortunately, definitions are not consistent across surveys. In most surveys conducted by the Ministry of Labour, part-time workers are defined as those who work fewer hours per day or days per week than do regular workers. Although this definition is based on working-time, unlike the US definition, an hours cut-off is not specified. In surveys conducted by the Bureau of Statistics and the Japan Institute of Labour and in some surveys conducted by the Ministry of Labour, a part-time worker is simply defined as someone whose position is classified as part-time by the employer. These surveys capture the more common notion of part-time employment in Japan in which part-time workers have a lower status but may not work fewer hours than regular workers. Most of the Japanese data reported in this chapter come from surveys by the Bureau of Statistics and the Japan Institute of Labour. The Bureau of Statistics' Employment Status Survey, a household survey which has been conducted at five-year intervals in recent years, provides the most comprehensive periodic data on part-time employment in Japan.[3]

AN OVERVIEW OF PART-TIME EMPLOYMENT

Bearing in mind cross-country differences in definition, the aggregate rate of part-time employment is quite similar, although the distribution of part-time employment by age and gender group is quite different in the United States and Japan. Table 12.1 reports the distribution of part-time employment by age and gender group in the first set of columns and the incidence of part-time employment within age and gender groups in the second set of columns for the United States and Japan. Although the majority of part-time workers in both countries are women, the female share of part-time employment in Japan (81 per cent) is much higher than in the United States (68 per cent). This fact reflects a much higher incidence of part-time employment among men and a much lower incidence of part-time employment among women in the United States than in Japan (see Delsen, Chapter 3, this volume).

There are also interesting differences in the incidence of part-time employment by age group. Although younger working men have a much higher incidence of part-time employment than do prime-age working men in both countries, in part because many students take part-time jobs, the incidence of part-time employ-

Table 12.1 Distribution and incidence of part-time employment in Japan and the United States

	Distribution of part-time employment (%)		Incidence of part-time employment (%)	
	US	Japan	US	Japan
Both sexes				
Total	100.0	100.0	18.6	16.1
Male				
Total	32.0	19.0	11.0	5.0
15–19	8.9	3.3	62.7	32.5
20–24	6.0	6.3	20.9	15.7
25–54	9.7	4.0	4.6	1.5
55+	7.4	5.3	20.6	8.0
Female				
Total	68.0	81.0	27.4	33.5
15–19	10.0	3.4	74.4	36.9
20–24	8.3	5.8	33.5	14.8
25–54	38.9	59.3	21.6	37.0
55+	10.7	12.4	37.0	37.9

Sources: Japanese Bureau of Statistics, Employment Status Survey (1992); US Bureau of Labor Statistics, *Employment and Earnings*, (1995)
Note: The Japanese data exclude the self-employed and family workers, while the US data include these workers.

ment among male teenage workers in the United States is almost double that in Japan. The incidence of part-time employment among American female teenage workers is more than double that of Japanese female teenage workers, whereas the rate of part-time employment among working women aged between 20 and 24 and 25 and 54 is considerably lower in the United States than in Japan. This pattern reflects the fact that working women with small children are much more likely to work full-time in the United States than in Japan.

In general, the patterns of part-time employment across industrial sectors are similar in the two countries (Table 12. 2). Retail and wholesale trade and the service industries have relatively high rates of part-time employment in both countries. The most striking difference between the two countries is in the manufacturing sector which has a relatively low incidence of part-time employment in the United States, but a relatively high incidence of part-time employment in Japan. It is also noteworthy that a large percentage (31.2 per cent) of part-time workers in Japanese manufacturing, who are predominantly married Japanese women, report working the same number of hours as full-time regular workers (Ministry of Labour 1990). Thus, the differences in industrial patterns of part-time employment are partly related to the different concepts of part-time employment in the two countries.

Table 12.2 Incidence of part-time employment by sector (%)

	US	Japan
Mining	3.8	3.6
Construction	10.5	7.5
Manufacturing	5.6	14.3
Trade	29.3	28.1
Finance, insurance and real estate	11.2	7.3
Transportation, utilities and communications	8.9	7.7
Services	22.9	16.5
Public administration	5.8	4.6

Source: Japanese Bureau of Statistics, Employment Status Survey (1992) and US Bureau of Labor Statistics, *Employment and Earnings* (1995)

Table 12.3 shows recent trends in the rate of part-time working in the United States and Japan. We report data for the United States for the years 1969, 1979 and 1989, which represent business cycle peaks. Because the rate of part-time employment in the United States is counter-cyclical, rising during recessions and falling during booms, it is important to control for business cycle in evaluating trends. In the decade from 1969 to 1979 part-time employment expanded fairly rapidly, increasing its share of employment by 2.1 percentage points. Growth in part-time employment slowed during the subsequent decade, and the share of employment that was part-time increased by just a 0.5 percentage point. Although there was a 0.7 percentage point increase from 1989 to 1993, much of this increase probably reflects the lingering effects of the 1991–2 recession. Because of the change in the survey instrument, one cannot evaluate trends in part-time employment after 1993.

Table 12.3 Trends in part-time employment

United States[1]		
	1969	15.5
	1979	17.6
	1989	18.1
	1993	18.8
Japan[2]		
	1982	11.0
	1987	14.2
	1992	16.1

1 *Source:* US Bureau of Labor Statistics, *Employment and Earnings* (1995). Part-time rates are expressed as a percentage of employment in non-agricultural industries.
2 *Source:* Bureau of Statistics, Management Coordination Agency, Employment Status Survey (1992). Part-time rates are expressed as a percentage of payroll employment; family workers and self-employed workers are excluded.

Data on part-time employment in Japan have only been collected as part of the Bureau of Statistics' Employment Status Survey, is conducted every five years, since 1982.[4] Unfortunately, both 1982 and 1992 were recession years in Japan, the latter being more serious than the former. However, as is discussed further below, part-time employment in Japan appears to fall relative to trend during a recession, in contrast to the situation in the United States. Thus, if anything, these figures understate trend growth in part-time employment in Japan. Even so, the growth in part-time employment over the 1982–92 period in Japan was spectacular. Over this period overall employment in the country increased by 28 per cent, but 38 per cent of that growth was accounted for by the growth in part-time employment, and the share of employment in part-time jobs increased by 5.1 percentage points.

THE WAGES, BENEFITS AND JOB SECURITY OF PART-TIME WORKERS

Wages

The average hourly wage of part-time workers is considerably lower than the average hourly wage of full-time workers in both countries. Part-time workers, however, tend to be less well educated, less skilled and less experienced than full-time workers. Several studies have used multivariate regression analysis to examine whether differences in individual and job characteristics that would be expected to affect labour productivity can fully explain part-time/full-time wage differentials in the United States and Japan. Such studies of the United States have generally found that even after controlling for differences in individual characteristics and, in some cases, for differences in job characteristics and for possible selection bias in the decision to work part-time, part-time workers earn significantly less than full-time workers (Owen, 1978; Long and Jones, 1981; Nakamura and Nakamura, 1983; Ehrenberg et al., 1988; Rubery, Chapter 7, this volume). A notable exception is Blank (1990), who found that after controlling for selection into the labour market as well as selection into part-time work female part-time workers earn significantly more than female full-time workers, whereas male part-time workers earn significantly less than male full-time workers.

The results of multivariate regression analyses of wage differentials between female full-time and part-time workers show that part-time workers earn significantly less than full-time workers in Japan (Houseman and Osawa, 1996; Nagase, 1997). In our study (Houseman and Osawa, 1996), which uses micro data to control for differences in individual and job characteristics and possible selection bias in the decision to work part-time, we find that wage differentials between female part-time and full-time workers widen greatly with tenure on the job. This finding is consistent with the observation that part-time

237

workers are not part of the seniority-based system in which wages rise sharply with tenure.

Non-wage labour costs

Wages represent only part of an employer's labour costs. Non-wage labour costs include various payroll taxes to fund social insurance programmes and fringe benefits. Part-time workers in the United States earning above some minimal amount are subject to various social insurance taxes. Because the taxable earnings limits make the effective tax rate higher for part-time than for many full-time workers, these taxes, if anything, are believed to discourage the use of part-time workers.

In Japan, in contrast, many part-time workers are exempt from social insurance taxes. Japanese employers must pay disability insurance and unemployment insurance taxes only for part-time workers working more than 20 hours per week. Part-time workers whose hours are less than three-fourths of regular workers' hours and who earn less than 1.3 million yen annually are exempt from government-mandated pension and health insurance payroll taxes, which are shared equally by employers and employees. These exemptions are likely to provide a strong incentive to employers to hire part-time workers working short hours (see Doudeijns, Chapter 6, this volume). Although part-time workers may also benefit from tax savings, they are much less likely to enjoy basic social protections, such as disability insurance, unemployment insurance, company pension and employer-provided health insurance, than are full-time, regular workers. According to a survey by Japan's Ministry of Labour, only 37 per cent of part-time workers are covered by unemployment insurance, 37 per cent are covered by health insurance provided by their employer, and 36 per cent are covered by the government-mandated pension plan.[5]

Part-time workers in both countries are much less likely than full-time workers to receive various fringe benefits from their employers. Although US tax laws inhibit employers from discriminating among full-time employees in the provision of benefits such as pensions and health insurance, employers generally are not required to provide part-time workers with the same fringe benefits they provide for full-time workers.[6] Thus, while US payroll taxes provide a disincentive to employers to hire part-time workers, the tax treatment of benefits provides Japanese employers with an incentive to hire part-time workers in order to avoid providing costly benefits to certain groups of workers.

According to figures from the 1995 Current Population Survey, whereas 63 per cent of full-time workers receive health insurance coverage from their employer, just 19.5 per cent of part-time workers do. Although part-time workers are often covered under a family member's policy or purchase their own insurance, it is noteworthy that part-time workers are much less likely than full-time workers to be covered by health insurance from any source: 70.9 per cent of part-time workers compared to 80.9 per cent of full-time workers have health insurance. Part-time workers are also much less likely than full-time workers to be covered by a company pension plan. While about half of all full-time workers are covered by an employer pension plan, only about 13 per cent of part-time workers receive this benefit. Blank (1990) has found that even after controlling for differences in individual and job characteristics and possible selection bias in the decision to work part-time, part-time workers receive fewer benefits than full-time workers (see also Ginn and Arber, Chapter 8, and Rubery, Chapter 7, this volume).

Part-time workers in Japan are much less likely than regular workers to receive fringe benefits such as free health check-ups or access to recreational facilities. Moreover, they rarely receive company loans or supplemental private pension plans, which are common benefits for regular, full-time workers.[7]

Job security

Although evidence suggests that part-time workers generally earn lower wages and receive fewer benefits than comparable full-time workers in the United States, there is no evidence to suggest that part-time workers are more vulnerable to lay-off than full-time workers. In fact, in the aggregate statistics the share of employment that is part-time moves counter-cyclically, rising during recessions and falling during upturns. This phenomenon probably reflects two underlying factors. First, part-time workers are concentrated in less cyclically sensitive sectors like trade and services. Second, because part-time work is defined as working fewer than 35 hours per week, the aggregate data pick up the relatively greater number of individuals who are put on short-time work during recessions or the relatively smaller number of workers who usually work part-time but who work more than 35 hours during the survey week.[8]

To determine whether part-time workers are more vulnerable to lay-off by virtue of their status of employment would require analysis of the probability of lay-off of part-time and full-time workers using panel data on individuals. To our knowledge such an exercise has not been done for the United States. However, because there are few legal restrictions on dismissals and lay-offs and workforce reductions are the norm in the United States, there is no compelling institutional reason to believe that part-time workers would be more vulnerable to lay-off than full-time workers.

In contrast, private sector norms and legal restrictions make it difficult to dismiss regular workers in Japan. Company personnel policies and court rulings have not afforded part-time workers the same sort of employment protections as full-time, regular workers. In Houseman and Osawa (1996), we show that the rate of part-time employment relative to trend is highly cyclical, a finding which is consistent with widespread reports that Japanese companies use part-time workers to buffer their core workers from lay-off.

Explanations for differences in wages, benefits and job security

Why do part-time workers in both countries generally receive lower wages and fewer benefits and in Japan less job security than full-time workers? Three types of explanation have been offered. The first emphasises the role of worker characteristics. The wages, benefits and job security of part-time jobs may be inferior to those of full-time jobs because workers in part-time jobs have less skill, less experience and otherwise less human capital than workers in full-time jobs. As noted above, even after controlling for differences in individual and job characteristics and, in some studies, possible selection bias in the decision to work part-time, studies of the United States and Japan generally show that part-time workers still earn significantly lower wages than full-time workers. Studies of benefits in the United States similarly show that part-time workers are less likely to be offered key benefits from their employer, even after controlling for human capital in part-time and full-time workers. Thus, differences in human capital cannot explain all of the differences in wages and benefits.

The second explanation emphasises the role of worker choice. Some workers prefer the shorter hours or more flexible employment arrangements often associated with part-time employment, and may be willing to accept lower wages and benefits and less job security in return for shorter hours. If part-time and full-time workers are not perfect substitutes and if the supply of workers desiring part-time work exceeds the demand for part-time workers at compensation levels equal to those of full-time workers, then the equilibrium compensation of part-time workers will be below that of full-time workers.

The third explanation posits that differences in the conditions of employment between part-time and full-time workers reflect a form of segmentation in labour markets. With efficient labour markets, the wages and benefits paid to part-time workers relative to full-time workers will adjust so that demand equals supply. However, prices may not completely adjust, and some workers, who want full-time work, may be 'involuntarily' employed part-time. If labour markets are not perfectly competitive, the lower wages, benefits and levels of job security among part-time workers may reflect weaker bargaining power or social norms. With regard to the latter, it may be socially acceptable for part-time workers, who are predominantly women, to earn lower wages, receive fewer benefits and have less job security if women's welfare is believed to depend primarily on family income and men are expected to be the primary breadwinners. Government regulations or policies, such as those which exempt part-time workers from certain social protections, may effectively weaken their bargaining power or reinforce social norms.

Although simply looking at why workers say they choose part-time employment and why employers say they demand part-time workers cannot definitively tell us the relative importance of the second and third explanations, it is nevertheless informative. If worker choice explains wage, benefits and job security differentials, it must be the case that workers who highly value shorter hours or more flexible arrangements sort themselves into part-time jobs. If labour market segmentation explains the differentials, it must be the case that these wage, benefits and job security differences are important to employers in deciding to use part-time workers.

A number of researchers have examined why people in the United States and Japan choose part-time work. In both countries researchers have found that the younger a woman's children and the more children she has, the greater the probability she will choose part-time over full-time employment. In Japan, the presence of a grandmother in the household increases the likelihood that a woman will choose full-time over part-time work. This fact suggests that the lack of adequate child care covering full-time hours constrains Japanese women's choice between full-time and part-time work.[9]

Tax laws also provide an incentive for Japanese women to work part-time. Individuals who work part-time and earn less than 1.3 million yen per year do not have to pay income tax on their earnings. In addition, they retain their 'dependent' status and are eligible for health insurance coverage under their spouse's plan and are entitled to receive some pension from the government. The household head also receives a dependent deduction from his taxable income and receives a family allowance from his employer. According to a 1992 survey of part-time workers by the Ministry of Labour, about 40 per cent of women working part-time adjust their hours of work so as not to exceed the threshold income. Thus, tax laws tend to reinforce the traditional division of labour in Japanese households with the man as the primary breadwinner.

Evidence from employer surveys in the United States and Japan show that although the reasons employers give for using part-time workers are quite similar in the two countries, their relative ranking is quite different. In the United States, employers most commonly cite scheduling issues (such as providing assistance during peak hours of the day or week or providing assistance during hours not covered by full-time shifts) and the desire to accommodate employees' desires for shorter hours. In contrast, by far the most common reason Japanese employers cite for hiring part-time workers is to save on labour costs.[10]

To distinguish between the worker choice and the labour segmentation hypotheses, one needs some information on whether workers' choices of part-time and full-time work are constrained. The worker choice hypothesis implies that part-time work is entirely voluntary, while the labour market segmentation hypothesis assumes it is constrained. Worker surveys in the United States and Japan sometimes include questions about the voluntary nature of part-time employment. These data should be interpreted cautiously, however. As is demonstrated below with Japanese survey data, answers can be quite sensitive to the question's wording. More fundamentally, there is considerable debate over precisely what constitutes voluntary choice. For example, many Japanese women may choose part-time work because of the absence of day care covering full-time hours. Social expectations about women's roles at home and at work may also influence women's 'choices' about staying at home, working part-time and working full-time. In Japan, women with full-time positions in large companies come under considerable pressure to quit when they marry. Typically only part-time positions or positions at small companies are available to married women. Surveys take the preferences workers express for part-time or full-time jobs as given, and do not address any underlying constraints that may have shaped their preferences or choices.

Given these caveats, survey data can still provide evidence of the most explicit forms of involuntary part-time employment. According to the Current Population Survey, in the United States in 1995, 14.4 per cent of all non-agricultural part-time workers worked part-time for economic reasons, such as slack work and inability to find full-time work, and thus in US statistics are counted as involuntary part-time workers. Among all non-agricultural workers, 3.7 per cent worked part-time for economic reasons. Thus, while the majority of part-time workers in the United States want part-time work, a significant minority work part-time involuntarily in the sense that they indicate a preference for full-time hours and an ability to work those hours.[11] To put these numbers in some perspective, in 1995 the unemployment rate in the United States was 5.6 per cent. Figures on involuntary part-time employment suggest that an additional 3.3 per cent of the labour force was under-employed.

Although regular statistics on the voluntary or involuntary nature of part-time employment in Japan are not collected, special surveys of part-time workers do include questions on the reasons individuals work part-time. In the Japan Institute of Labour's Survey on the status of part-time workers, a survey of over 3,400 female part-time workers, respondents were asked to cite the two most important reasons for working part-time. Their answers suggest that, as is the case in the United States, the vast majority work part-time for non-economic reasons (i.e. the part-time job is near their home, it fits their schedule, they like the job, or it requires shorter hours). However, also as in the United States, a significant minority indicate economic reasons for working part-time. In this survey, 12.2 per cent answered that they work part-time because they are unable to find a regular job.

When asked more directly about their employment preferences, a much larger percentage of the part-time women in the Japan Institute of Labour survey expressed a preference for regular work: 27.3 per cent said they would prefer to be a regular, full-time worker and another 14.4 per cent said they would prefer to be a regular worker if they could keep their short hours. The response to this question suggests a deeper dissatisfaction with their status as part-time workers, even if these women are not actively looking for regular employment.

In sum, differences in workers' human capital cannot explain all the differences in the wages and benefits which part-time and full-time workers receive. If it is more costly in some instances for employers to hire part-time workers than full-time workers and if the supply of part-time workers exceeds the demand at levels of compensation equal to that of full-time workers, then we would expect part-time workers' wages, benefits and possibly other attributes like job security to be inferior to those of full-time workers. In this case, the explanation for part-time/full-time differentials would be a supply-side one: worker choice. The fact that the great majority of part-time workers in both the United States and Japan say they want part-time work suggests that most of the part-time/full-time differentials may be attributed worker choice.[12] This is particularly plausible in the United States, where a majority of employers report that an important reason for hiring part-time workers is to accommodate employees' desires for shorter hours. However, the fact that a substantial minority of part-time workers in each country desire regular, full-time jobs suggests that at least for some portion of the labour market, segmentation theories accurately describe part-time jobs.

GROWTH IN PART-TIME EMPLOYMENT: A RESULT OF SUPPLY OR DEMAND?

It is important to look not only at the supply and demand for part-time work at a point in time, but also at why part-time jobs have been increasing. Some have seen the increase as largely reflecting an increase in the supply of workers desiring part-time employment, and hence effectively mirroring worker choice. Others view the increase as largely coming from employer demand, and believe the trend is resulting in increased labour market segmentation.

Those who believe that the growth in part-time employment reflects an increase in the supply of workers desiring part-time jobs point, in particular, to the increase in female labour force participation. Working women have a much higher incidence of part-time employment than men, and therefore we would expect that as the female share of employment increases, the rate of part-time employment would also increase.

Two factors may have resulted in an increase in employer demand for part-time workers. One is that changes in the industrial composition of employment have increased employer demand for part-time workers. If the employment share of industries with a high rate of part-time employment increases, the demand for part-time workers will increase, all else being equal. Some also hypothesise that employers have increased their demand for part-time workers because they face greater competition than in the past, and thus have come under greater pressure to lower labour costs. Employers may increase productivity and lower labour costs by using part-time workers to accommodate fluctuations in the workload over the day or week. Moreover, employers may save on wages, benefits and other non-wage labour costs by hiring part-time workers. If markets are perfectly competitive, an increase in employer demand for part-time workers will simply drive up part-time workers' wage and non-wage costs and all part-time work will be voluntary. If labour markets are not perfectly competitive, an increase in employer demand for part-time workers may result in an increase in involuntary part-time employment and further labour market segmentation.

Turning first to the United States, we look at the plausibility of the supply-side hypothesis – that the rise in part-time employment was caused by an increase in the female share of employment – through a simple decomposition of the increase in part-time employment.[13] As can be seen in Table 12.3, the rate of part-time employment in the United States grew most rapidly from 1969 to 1979, increasing by over 2 percentage points. While the increase in female labour force participation, as reflected in the female share of employment, certainly contributed to the increase in the rate of part-time employment, it accounted for only 36 per cent of that increase. More important was the increase in the rate at which both women and men were working part-time. The rate of part-time employment increased from 8.9 per cent to 10.1 per cent among men and from 26.3 per cent to 27.8 per cent among women from 1969 to 1979; together these accounted for 63 per cent of the increase. Interestingly, over the period, part-time employment for economic reasons (i.e. involuntary part-time employment) rose dramatically and accounted for over half (52 per cent) of the increase in the rate of part-time employment between 1969 and 1979. This fact also strongly suggests that the increase was not simply caused by an increase in the supply of women seeking part-time employment, but rather was due in large part to an increase in employer demand for part-time workers.

Between 1979 and 1989 the rate of part-time employment increased by about half a percentage point. While the female share of employment continued to grow, the rate at which women worked part-time fell over the period. These two effects almost cancel each other out, and consequently most of the increase in part-time employment may be attributed to the increase in part-time employment among men. Moreover, all the increase in part-time employment over the period came from an increase in the rate of involuntary part-time employment; the rate of voluntary part-time employment remained the same. Thus, many have concluded that demand-side forces accounted for the increase in part-time employment in the United States in the 1980s (Blank, 1990; Callaghan and Hartman, 1991; Tilly, 1991).

One theory for the increase in the demand for part-time workers is that employment in industries with high rates of part-time employment was growing faster than employment in industries with low rates of part-time employment. Data provide considerable support for this hypothesis for the United States over the 1979–89 period.[14] The sectors with the highest rates of part-time employment – wholesale and retail trade and services – expanded their share of employment. A formal decomposition reveals that the increase in part-time employment may be attributed to a shift in the industrial mix of employment away from sectors with low rates of part-time employment and into sectors with high rates of part-time employment, such as trade and services.[15] In aggregate, as noted above, all of the increase in the rate of part-time employment comes from an increase in the rate of involuntary part-time employment; the rate of voluntary part-time employment remained the same over the period.

Within the trade and services sector the rate of involuntary part-time employment increased, while the rate of voluntary part-time employment fell sharply over the 1979–89 period. These figures strongly suggest that the demand for part-time workers outpaced supply in these rapidly expanding sectors.

In Japan, the rapid increase in part-time employment has generally been attributed to an increase in the number of women seeking part-time employment. Indeed, over the period the female share of employment rose from about 35 per cent to 39 per cent. At the same time, however, the rate of part-time employment among both men and women soared. The rate nearly doubled from 2.8 per cent to 5.0 per cent among men, and jumped from 26.0 per cent to 33.5 per cent among women. The increase in the female share of employment accounted for just 17 per cent of the increase in part-time employment, while the rise in the rate of part-time employment among men accounted for 28 per cent of the increase and the rise in the rate of part-time employment among women accounted for 52 per cent of the increase. Clearly, the explanation for the rise in part-time employment in Japan lies not with the increase in female labour force participation, as is often assumed, but rather with the increase in the rates at which both men and women are working part-time.

Nagase (1997) offers an interesting explanation for why the rate of part-time employment increased among women that is consistent with a supply-side story. She points out that the dramatic increase in part-time employment paralleled a sharp decline in family and self-employment. Asserting that both types of employment afford women greater flexibility to accommodate child care and household responsibilities, she argues that when opportunities for family and self-employment dried up, women increasingly sought part-time jobs. Arguably, part-time jobs, which are generally associated with higher wages and shorter hours than family and self-employment, were even more attractive to these women.

Nagase's argument does not address the large rise in male part-time employment, however. Moreover, in Houseman and Osawa (1996) we point out that during the 1980s the number of employers seeking part-time workers grew much more rapidly than the number of workers seeking part-time jobs, while the number of employers seeking full-time workers and the number of workers seeking full-time jobs grew at a similar pace. Thus, demand-side factors played a dominant role in the recent growth of part-time employment in Japan.

As with the United States, then, the growth in part-time employment in Japan appears to have been in large part demand driven. Unlike the United States, however, the increase in demand for part-time workers may not simply be attributed to a shift in the industrial composition of employment away from sectors with low rates of part-time employment and towards sectors with high rates of part-time employment.[16] Although employment has shifted somewhat towards the trade and services sectors, which have relatively high rates of part-time employment, the rate of part-time employment has increased dramatically in virtually all sectors. Formal decomposition of the increase in part-time employment in Japan over the 1982–92 period shows that only 6 per cent of the increase may be attributed to changes in the industrial composition of employment, while 92 per cent may be attributed to increases in the rate of part-time employment within industries.[17] In addition, the rate of part-time employment increased across establishments of all sizes.

What caused this dramatic increase in the demand for part-time workers across firms in all industries and of all sizes? The answer, we argue, has to do with the structure of Japanese industrial relations and recent pressures to lower labour costs and increase employment flexibility. Key features of Japanese industrial relations, such as seniority-based wages and promotions and lifetime employment commitments, are designed to increase employee loyalty. They also make workforce levels and labour costs extremely rigid. Japanese companies have always hired some peripheral workers, including part-timers, who are not given seniority-based wage increases and promotions and commitments of lifetime employment, to lower labour costs, increase wage flexibility and buffer core workers from fluctuations in demand.

Several factors have caused many Japanese companies to increase the relative size of their part-time workforce and shrink the size of their core workforce. In general, the increase in international competition has placed downward cost pressure on Japanese employers. Since the 1970s, the yen has appreciated dramatically against foreign currencies, placing particularly strong downward pressure on labour costs in export industries. In addition, the Japanese economy has been more volatile in recent years than in the immediate post-war period. Another widely cited factor is the ageing of the Japanese workforce. Under the Japanese seniority-based wage and promotion system prevalent in large and medium-sized Japanese companies, wages and promotions depend more on age and tenure with the company and less on performance than is the case in the United States. This system is viable when the economy is growing rapidly and the population is pyramid-shaped. However, as economic growth has slowed and the population has aged, Japanese companies have found themselves saddled with disproportionately large numbers of older, highly paid workers who are hard to lay off. In the face of downward pressures on labour costs, increased volatility and an ageing workforce, Japanese companies, arguably, have pursued a strategy to reduce labour costs and increase employment flexibility by substituting part-time workers for full-time workers.[18]

Although the increase in the rate of part-time employment in both the United States and Japan appears to have been driven, in large part, by demand, the magnitude of the increase in the two countries has been quite different. It is interesting to ask why the rate of part-time employment has increased only modestly in the United States, while it has soared in Japan in recent years. Although we cannot definitively answer that question, our analysis suggests a couple of reasons. On the supply side, working women in the United States have increasingly favoured full-time employment over part-time employment. The push for greater workplace equality has resulted in more career possibilities and higher wages for women, thus encouraging longer hours. In addition, the increase in divorce and the decline in real wages among many men have pushed many women into full-time jobs in order to maintain family income.[19] Thus, the growth in the supply of workers seeking part-time jobs was probably relatively less in the United States than in Japan.

On the demand side, it is also plausible that the increase in demand for part-time workers relative to full-time workers has been greater in Japan than in the United States. We have argued that a broad spectrum of Japanese employers has sought to hire more part-time workers in order to lower labour costs and increase employment flexibility. Although some of the pressures to reduce labour costs and increase employment flexibility – such as the appreciation of the yen and the ageing of the workforce – are unique to Japan, American employers have also been under considerable pressure to lower labour costs. However, Japanese industrial relations practices make the labour costs for regular workers extremely rigid in Japan. The hiring of more part-time workers allows employers to lower labour costs and increase employment flexibility without dismantling the basic industrial relations system for core workers, which might have quite adverse consequences for employee morale and productivity. Because there is less of a distinction both in American industrial relations practices and in US law between full-time and part-time workers, American employers have not turned to part-time workers to reduce costs and increase flexibility to the same degree that Japanese employers have. In fact, full-time workers have borne much of the brunt of cost-cutting measures in recent years, as is evidenced by widespread reductions in real wages and massive lay-offs of both blue- and white-collar workers.

CONCLUSION

In this chapter we set out to examine how similar part-time work is in Japan and the United States. We began by presenting two contrasting views of part-time employment. One holds that part-time employment is the consequence of optimal choices by employees and their employers. The other is that labour markets are segmented; part-time jobs fall into the secondary sector with many part-time workers desiring full-time jobs. Supporting the first view is the fact that the vast majority of part-time workers in both the United States and Japan desire part-time work to accommodate household responsibilities, school or other activities. However, statistical studies show that part-time workers in both countries earn less and receive fewer benefits than do comparable full-time workers. In Japan, part-time workers also enjoy considerably less job security. The lower pay, benefits and job security, coupled with the fact that a significant minority is working part-time involuntarily supports the second view, at least for some portion of the part-time workforce. The labour market segmentation view of part-time employment is particularly appropriate for Japan, where the very concept of part-time work is wedded not to hours of work, as it is in the United States, but rather to the industrial relations practices applying to part-time workers and hence their status in the firm.

Evidence suggests that the growth in part-time employment has resulted in further labour market segmentation, particularly in Japan. All the increase in part-time employment in the United States may be attributed to the growth in involuntary part-time employment, although the growth has been quite small in recent years. Japanese employers have always followed a core-peripheral model of employment, using part-time and temporary workers to increase employment and labour cost flexibility. Japanese employers, we have argued, have reduced the share of regular workers and increased the share of part-time workers in order to lower labour costs and buffer core workers from demand fluctuations, resulting in an explosive growth in part-time employment.

Serious debate over policies related to part-time workers has been limited in both countries. Debate in the United States over part-time work has been largely subsumed in a more general debate over the quality of jobs. Although the United States has experienced healthy job growth and relatively low unemployment over the last decade, there is widespread concern that the quality of jobs in terms of wages, benefits and job security has declined; part-time work is typically associated with low-quality jobs. Figures on involuntary part-time employment suggest that, even with low unemployment, in 1995 over 3 per cent of the labour force was effectively under-employed. Moreover, many Americans work full-time by piecing together two or more part-time jobs, which typically do not come with fringe benefits. Much of the recent policy interest in job quality has focused on benefits, particularly health insurance. The principal way to obtain affordable health insurance in the United States is as a benefit of a full-time job. The fact that so many workers, particularly part-time workers, have no health insurance has raised serious questions about the desirability of the current system of health insurance provision in the United States.

The lack of debate over part-time employment in Japan is particularly surprising given its rapid growth in that country. The lower status and buffer role played by the predominantly female part-time workforce in the Japanese economy reinforces rigid gender roles in a society in which men are seen as the primary breadwinners of the family and women as the homemakers. Business, unions and government place highest priority on protecting the core male workforce. The absence of any strong opposition to the growth of part-time employment and indeed the explicit or tacit support of this growth by business, unions and government may be better understood in this context.

Nikkeiren, the Association of Japanese Employers, has specifically advocated an employment system in which a significant proportion of the labour force is employed on a part-time basis. Rengo, the umbrella union organisation, has not made the growth of part-time work a major issue. Affiliated unions have made little effort or headway in recruiting either women or part-time workers. Given that full-time pay is generally deemed adequate, the focal issue for unions has become job security for core workers. To the extent that union leaders appreciate that part-time workers buffer the core labour force, it makes little sense for them to espouse the cause of part-time workers. The government has also failed to make the growth of part-time employment a high-profile issue. By providing numerous tax breaks for part-time workers, the Japanese government, perhaps unintentionally, has encouraged the expansion of part-time employment. In 1996 the government initiated a plan targeting small businesses to subsidise seminars on improving the working conditions of part-time workers and to subsidise the costs of equalising the benefits of part-time and regular employees. However, it has taken no major legislative or administrative action to regulate or provide more protection for part-time workers. Like Nikkeiren and Rengo, the government appears to be convinced that the benefits of employment stability for full-time workers outweigh the problems encountered by the part-time workforce.

ACKNOWLEDGEMENTS

We thank Jacqueline O'Reilly, Colette Fagan and participants in the Workshop on Part-time Paradoxes for many helpful comments on an earlier draft of this chapter. We are indebted to Carolyn Zinn for research assistance and Claire Black for assistance in preparing the document.

NOTES

1 According to the 1990 Ministry of Labour *Report on the Status of Part-time Workers* 20.6 per cent of part-time workers reported working the same number of hours as regular workers. In a separate survey of part-time workers conducted by the Japan Institute of Labour in 1989, 28.7 per cent of respondents reported working the same schedule as full-time workers.
2 Prior to 1994, workers were classified as part-time if (1) they worked fewer than 35 hours during the survey week and (2) they usually worked fewer than 35 hours; those who worked more than 35 hours during the survey week but who usually worked fewer than 35 hours were still counted as full-time. Since 1994, part-time employment is officially based on 'usual' status. Thus, someone who usually works part-time but happened to work full-time during the survey week will be counted as a part-time worker. Other changes in the employment statistics in the CPS also affect the comparability of part-time statistics before and after 1994.
3 Wakisaka and Bae (Chapter 13, this volume) generally cite data from surveys in which the definition of Japanese part-time employment is based on hours of work.
4 Data on part-time employment have been available on an annual basis since 1978 in the Ministry of Labour's Survey of Employment Trend. However, the industry coverage and the definition of part-time employment are more limited in this survey than in the Bureau of Statistics' survey.
5 Ministry of Labour, Survey on the Diversification of Employment, 1987. The data in this survey exclude part-time workers whose hours are the same as those of regular employees. Assuming that about 25 per cent of workers classified as 'part-time' by

their employers work the same schedule as regular workers and that these high-hours part-time workers are covered by social insurance programmes, about 50 per cent of part-time workers are not covered by Japan's social insurance programmes.

6 Specifically, tax laws treat fringe benefits such as pension plans and health insurance as non-taxable income. However, if an employer offers these benefits to some full-time workers but not others, the value of the fringe benefit is subject to income tax. In the case of pensions, if an employer offers pension benefits to any employees, it must offer them to all employees working 1,000 or more hours per year. In the case of health insurance and other benefits, the employer may determine who is a part-time employee.

7 The micro data necessary to test whether Japanese part-time workers are still less likely to receive benefits after controlling for individual and job characteristics are not available.

8 Because of the change in the definition of part-time employment in 1994, this latter group is no longer counted as full-time in US data.

9 Studies of the labour supply of part-time workers in the United States include Morgenstern and Hamovitch (1976); Long and Jones (1981); Nakamura and Nakamura (1983); and Blank (1988); and in Japan include Nagase (1997).

10 We report the results of Japanese employer surveys in Houseman and Osawa (1996). The results of the US employer survey are reported in Houseman (1996, 1997).

11 The proportion of part-time workers classified as involuntarily working part-time fell with the redesign of the CPS in 1994. One reason is that those indicating a preference for full-time work now also have to state that they are available for full-time work.

12 Again, this conclusion is subject to the caveat that workers may be subject to other economic or social constraints in forming their choices.

13 The aggregate rate of part-time employment may be written as follows:

$$P = P_m (1-S_f) + P_f S_f$$

The rate of part-time employment in the economy is simply the rate of part-time employment among men, P_m, multiplied by the share of male employment $(1-S_f)$, plus the rate of part-time employment among women, P_f, multiplied by the female share of employment, S_f. The change in the aggregate rate of employment may be decomposed into the part due to changes in the rate of part-time employment among men and women, the part due to the shift in the share of employment accounted for by men and women, and the interaction of these effects.

$$\Delta P = \Delta P_m(1-S_f) + \Delta P_f S_f + (P_f - P_m)\Delta S_f + (\Delta P_f - \Delta P_m)\Delta S_f$$

14 The data necessary to do this analysis are not available for the 1969–79 period.

15 Specifically, we decomposed the change in part-time employment into the part due to the change in the rate of part-time employment within industries and the part due to the shift in the industrial composition of employment:

$$\Delta P = \Sigma \Delta P_i S_i + \Sigma P_i \Delta S_i + \Sigma \Delta P_i \Delta S_i$$

where P_i is the rate of part-time employment in industry i and Si is the share of employment in industry i.

16 Smith et al. (Chapter 2, this volume) and Walwei (Chapter 5, this volume) also show that shifts in the industrial composition of employment account for little of the growth in part-time employment in most European countries.

17 The remaining 2 per cent is attributable to the interaction of these two effects. We present this analysis in Houseman and Osawa (1996).

18 We develop this point further in Osawa (1993) and Houseman and Osawa (1994, 1996).

19 For a review of the evidence on the decline in men's wages in the United States and a discussion of their effects on female labour force participation, see Houseman (1995).

BIBLIOGRAPHY

Blank, R. M. (1990) 'Are Part-time Jobs Bad Jobs?' in G. Burtless (ed.) *A Future of Lousy Jobs?*, Washington, DC: Brookings Institution.

—— (1988) 'Simultaneously Modelling the Supply of Weeks and Hours of Work among Female Household Heads', *Journal of Labour Economics* 6, April: 177–204.

Callaghan, P. and Hartmann, H. (1991) *Contingent Work: A Chart Book on Part-time and Temporary Employment*, Washington, DC: Economic Policy Institute.

Ehrenberg, R. G., Rosenberg, P. and Li, J. (1988) 'Part-time Employment in the United States' in R. A. Hart. (ed.) *Employment, Unemployment, and Labour Utilization*, London: George Allen & Unwin.

Houseman, S. (1995) 'Job Growth and the Quality of Jobs in the US Economy', *Labour*: 93–124.

—— (1996) *Temporary, Part-time, and Contract Employment in the United States: A Report on the W.E. Upjohn Institute's Employer Survey on Flexible Staffing Policies*. Report prepared for the US Department of Labor, Office of the Assistance Secretary for Policy.

—— (1997) 'Temporary, Part-time, and Contract Employment in the United States: New Evidence from an Employer Survey', presented at Labour Market Inequality Conference, Madison, Wisconsin, 28 February to 1 March.

Houseman, S. and Osawa, M. (1994) 'Part-time and Temporary Employment in Japan: A Comparison with the United States', project report to US Department of Labor, Bureau of International Labour Affairs.

—— (1996) 'The Growth of Part-time Employment in Japan', Working Paper, June.

Long, J.E. and Jones, E.B. (1981) 'Married Women in Part-time Employment', *Industrial and Labour Relations Review* 34, April: 413–25.

Ministry of Labour (1990) 'Report on the Status of Part-time Workers' (Rodosha, 'Parto-Time Rōdōshō Sogo Jittai Chôsa Hokoku).

Morgenstern, R. D. and Hamovitch, W. (1976) 'Labour Supply of Married Women in Part-time and Full-time Occupations', *Industrial and Labour Relations Review* 30, October: 59–67.

Nagase, N. (1997) 'Wage Differentials and Labour Supply of Married Women in Japan: Part-time and Informal Sector Work Opportunities', *Japanese Economic Review* 48, 1: 29–42.

Nakamura, A. and Nakamura, M. (1983) 'Part-time and Full-time Work Behaviour of Married Women: A Model with a Doubly Truncated Dependent Variable', *Canadian Journal of Economics* 14, May: 229–57.

Osawa, M. (1993) *Economic Change and Women Workers: a US–Japan Comparison*, ('*Keizai Henka to Joshi Rodo'*), Tokyo: Nihon Keizai Hyôronsha.

Owen, J. D. (1978) 'Part-time Workers and Low-wage Jobs', *Monthly Labour Review* June: 11–14.

Stratton, L. S. (1994) 'Reexamining Involuntary Part-time Employment', *Journal of Economic and Social Measurement* 20, 2: 95–115.

Tilly, C. (1991) 'Reasons for the Continuing Growth of Part-time Employment', *Monthly Labour Review*, March: 10–18.

13

WHY IS THE PART-TIME RATE HIGHER IN JAPAN THAN IN SOUTH KOREA?

Akira Wakisaka and Haesun Bae

INTRODUCTION

Much of the research published in English on Japan and the newly industrialised countries (NICs) of the Pacific Rim has tried to explain the success of these economies relative to those in North America and Europe. This research has, however, tended to focus on the attractive conditions offered to 'core' nenko employees but to neglect atypical workers and the role of women in these employment systems (however, see Lam 1992; Honda 1993). The aim of this chapter is to focus on this neglected area by comparing the conditions of part-time workers in Japan and South Korea. The rationale for this comparison is the expectation that there will be several similarities in the way women are integrated into paid employment in two societies; although Japan is currently a wealthier society than South Korea, they share not only an 'Asian culture' but also the experience of rapid industrialisation. However, a closer look at the way women are involved in paid employment reveals striking differences between the two societies in this respect. Although the levels of female labour force participation are fairly similar, at 50 per cent in Japan and 47 per cent in South Korea, part-time rates are very different: 31 per cent of women work part-time in Japan compared to only 8 per cent in South Korea in 1993. These differences raise the question of why the part-time rate is higher in Japan than in South Korea. The aim of this chapter is to explore these differences by looking at the characteristics of the demand for and supply and regulation of part-time employment in each society.

THE PROBLEMS OF DEFINING AND COMPARING PART-TIME WORK

One of the initial problems encountered in any such comparison is that of the definition of part-time workers. There are essentially two ways of conceptualising and defining part-time work in Japan and South Korea. One is based on weekly working hours and the other on the actual status of employees in firms. Since the South Korean data do not give a definition of status, this chapter defines part-timers as those employees working fewer than 35 hours per week.[1] However, this is also problematic, because the Japanese Labour Force Survey defines part-timers as those working fewer than 35 hours per week, while a South Korean government guideline on working conditions adopts a 32-hour cut-off point.

In Japan, the status of part-time workers, or 'paato' workers as they are called, is the standard term for married female employees, while the term 'arubaito' denotes student part-timers. This definition of 'paato' is often based not on working-time but on status within the firm, and these part-timers usually work more than 35 hours a week. The most recent data available from the Special Labour Force Survey (SLFS) for 1996, which asks about actual hours in the survey week, shows that 29 per cent of female 'paato' worked 35 hours or more a week. Data from the 1992 Employment Structure Survey, based on usual working hours, indicates much higher figures: 38.8 per cent of female 'paato' worked 35 hours or more a week and 21.9 per cent worked 43 hours or more. Among those who worked fewer than 35 hours a week in 1993, 60 per cent were female 'paato', 4 per cent were executives, 18 per cent were sei-shain (regular full-time workers) and 14 per cent were 'arubaito'. Houseman and Osawa (Chapter 12, this volume) use the status definition in their analysis of Japan, whereas we use the hours threshold. These statistical definitions are important reflections of the differences in part-time work in Japan and South Korea which are investigated in the following comparison.

In the early post-war period, female labour force participation was much higher in Japan. During the period until 1975, female participation rates appeared to be converging as levels declined in Japan and rose in South Korea (Figure 13.1). Since 1975, they have continued to rise in both countries, so that by 1993 the gap had nearly closed, with women accounting for 50.3 per cent of the labour force in Japan and 47.2 per cent in South Korea. Nevertheless, the share of part-time employment in this growth was greater in Japan, where it increased from 8.2 per cent in 1959 to 31.2 per cent in 1993, than in South Korea, where it grew from 5.2 per cent in 1980 to only 8.4 per cent in 1993,[2] which suggests that the integration of women into paid employment takes different forms in the two countries. As earlier chapters in this book have shown, explanations for these differences can be analysed in terms of demand, supply or regulatory factors.

DEMAND FOR PART-TIME WORKERS

Comparison of the sectoral distribution of part-timers in each country reveals a trend towards convergence but, at the same time, the persistence of differences. First, during the early 1980s, the proportion of female part-timers in agriculture,

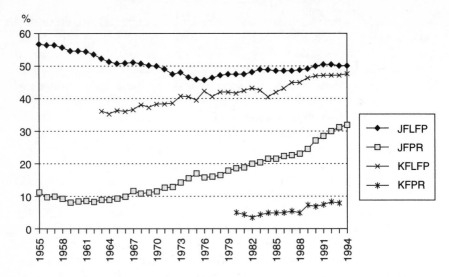

Figure 13.1 Female labour force participation and part-time rates in Japan and South
Korea
  Sources: Korea National Statistical Office, *Economically Active Population Survey*; Korea
  Women's Development Institute, *Analysis of Part-time and Fixed-term Employment and
  Policy Implications in Korea* (1993)
  Japan: Statistics Bureau, Management and Coordination Agency, Labour Force Survey
  (1994)
  Notes:
  JFLFP: Female labour force participation rates in Japan
  JFPR: Female part-time workers as the percentage of female employees in Japan
  KFLFP: Female labour force participation rates in Korea
  KFPR: Female part-time workers as the percentage of female employees in Korea

fishing and mining in South Korea was much higher than in Japan. For example, in 1980 in South Korea, 40 per cent of part-timers worked in these primary
industries, compared to less than 1 per cent in Japan. By 1993, only 4.1 per cent
of South Korean part-timers were working in these industries, compared to 1 per
cent in Japan. The proportion of part-timers in manufacturing has also declined
in both countries. In South Korea, it fell from 32 per cent in 1980 to 21 per cent
in 1993, while the fall in Japan over the same period was smaller, from 25 to
20 per cent. The service sector accounts for the growing numbers of part-time
employees. In South Korea, the proportion of part-timers in services went
from 18 per cent in 1980 to 34 per cent in 1993; in Japan, the increase was from
26 per cent to nearly 30 per cent by 1993.

Nevertheless, there are notable differences between the types of service
employment in which part-timers are found. Banking and market services
accounted for 39.6 per cent of Japanese part-timers in 1993, compared with
26.2 per cent in South Korea. The difference between the two countries was
even greater in 1980, with only 10.5 per cent of South Korean part-timers
working in these industries, compared with 37 per cent in Japan. In South

Korea, 19.4 per cent of part-timers are found in domestic services, while 10.7 per cent of all female part-time workers in 1992 were in educational services. Although it is difficult to obtain comparable data for part-timers in Japan, these two sectors have only a minimal share of female employees: 0.14 per cent for domestic services and 5 per cent in education.[3]

Part-timers in South Korea tend to be concentrated in small firms, whereas in Japan they are more likely to work for larger organisations. Over half of the part-timers in South Korea (56.5 per cent) work in firms employing fewer than five people, compared with only 13.7 per cent of Japanese part-timers. Very few part-timers in South Korea are employed in large corporations with 1,000 or more employees – 1.9 per cent – compared with 16.8 per cent in Japan. Part-timers in Japan are more likely to work for medium-sized to large firms:[4] 48.8 per cent in Japan compared with 28.8 per cent in South Korea. This distribution may in fact reflect the industrial composition of firms in each country, but it also shows that part-time workers in South Korea are more likely to be found in small firms.

It is difficult to find comparable data on employers' policies with regard to their use of part-timers, which reflects the relative neglect of this issue in South Korea. The first survey of employers' use of part-timers in South Korea was conducted in November 1992. From a sample of 1,050 firms with a hundred or more employees, 237 firms responded. Part-timers were defined as those working 30 or fewer hours per week. Clearly, this data can provide only a very limited picture of the use of part-timers, given that the survey only concentrated on larger firms and a high percentage of part-timers tends to be employed in firms with fewer than five employees. Japanese data are available from the general survey of part-time workers conducted by the Ministry of Labour in October 1990. This covered 15,000 establishments with five or more employees. Although comparisons based on these surveys must be treated with a great deal of caution, some interesting observations can be drawn from the results.

More than half of the Japanese firms reported using part-timers, compared with less than 20 per cent of South Korean firms. The use of part-time work was more common in non-manufacturing companies in each country, which supports what we already know about the differences in part-time rates in each country from labour force surveys. More significantly, when asked why they used part-timers, employers in both countries cited 'simplicity of job content' as one of the most important reasons, although this was more significant in Japan than in South Korea. Using part-timers as a temporary measure to meet fluctuating demand was also important, and especially in Japan employers were also more likely to say they used part-timers to reduce personnel costs. Japanese employers found it relatively easy to recruit part-timers, although it was not part of a personnel strategy to retain or reintegrate former female employees returning to work after a period of child-rearing. Only a minority of firms, approximately 14 per cent in Japan and 6.5 per cent in South Korea, said they used part-timers as a source of specific skills.

In the case of Japan, Nakamura (1990) distinguishes between core part-timers (kikan-gata paato) and supplementary part-timers (hokan-gata paato). The latter do monotonous and repetitive jobs with no possibility of a wage increase, irrespective of job tenure or effort. Their jobs basically supplement those of full-time workers. The former group, on the other hand, perform highly skilled tasks. These part-time workers acquire their skills through on-the-job training, starting with easier tasks and gradually moving to more difficult ones. Research by Mitsuyama (1991) and Honda (1993) also demonstrates that core part-timers are important and essential in retail companies. Wakisaka (1995) suggests that part-time workers are to some extent integrated into internal labour markets. Although this distinction between supplementary and core part-timers has parallels with the typology used by Tilly (1992 and 1996) between marginal and retention part-time jobs, our contention here is that quasi-internal labour markets can operate in such a way as to allow part-timers to move from peripheral to core status.

This potential change of status is a significant reason for the stability seen among part-time workers in Japan. The average length of service for women part-timers, of all ages and in all industries, increased from two years in 1970 to 4.9 years in 1994. In 1990, 12.5 per cent of female part-timers had been working with the same company for over ten years, and 33.4 per cent for over five years. This stability among part-timers is also seen in other countries such as the UK, Germany and Australia (Gallie and White 1994; Wakisaka 1997b). This would suggest that part-time work is a stable form of employment. The longer tenure a part-time worker has, the more likely they are to become a core part-time worker. Although it is difficult to estimate the number of core and supplementary part-timers, earlier calculations suggested that at least 20 per cent of all part-timers are core part-timers (Wakisaka 1995). However, according to a more recent unpublished survey in 1996, this indicates a much higher proportion of more than half of female part-time workers doing a similar job with comparable length of tenure as full-timers. It is not yet possible to make similar calculations for part-timers in South Korea, partly because part-time work seems to play a different role in the employment system, which becomes evident when we look more closely at the differences in labour supply between the two countries.

THE SUPPLY OF FEMALE PART-TIMERS

In both Japan and South Korea, the highest proportion of part-timers used to be in the 30–39 age group. Although this has remained fairly stable in South Korea, in Japan the share of this group has declined since the mid-1980s and older workers in the 40 and 50+ age groups now dominate the part-time category. Unfortunately, without panel data, it is impossible to judge whether this change is due to the 30-year-old cohort entering part-time work and remaining there or to the increased recruitment of older female workers. It would appear that Japanese firms prefer to offer part-time rather than full-time jobs to married women seeking to return to work after raising children, which would suggest that this trend is related to firms' recruitment strategies. We have also seen in the previous section how there is a tendency for the job tenure of part-timers to increase, which suggests that once these workers have a 'paato' job they are unlikely to change their status.

Part-time work in South Korea is dominated by the 30–39 age group, although over the course of the 1980s the 20–29 age group accounted for an increasing share of such employment. According to a report on the Employment Structure Survey (ESS) published by the Economic Planning Board of the National

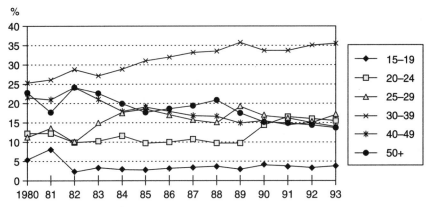

Figure 13.2a Age distribution of part-timers in South Korea
Source: Korean Women's Development Institute, *Analysis of Part-time and Fixed-term Employment and Policy Implications in Korea* (1994)

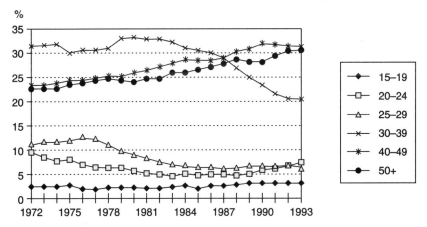

Figure 13.2b Age distribution of part-timers in Japan
Source: Statistics Bureau, Management and Coordination Agency, Labour Force Survey (1993).

257

Bureau of Statistics, about 40 per cent of part-time workers in their thirties give domestic responsibilities as a reason for working part-time. The increase in this younger cohort of part-time workers is due largely to university graduates using temporary, part-time jobs as a point of entry into the labour market and a stepping stone to regular, full-time employment. Overall, the age distribution of younger (20–29) and older workers (40–50+) has been converging. In Japan, in contrast, the distribution of part-timers between younger and older age groups is more skewed, with the growth of part-time employment concentrated in the older cohorts (Figure 13.2b).

INVOLUNTARY PART-TIMERS

One of the key issues around part-time employment, which has also been discussed in other chapters in this book, is the extent to which this corresponds to employees' preferences or whether it is taken up *faute de mieux*. According to the OECD (1990, 1993, 1995), involuntary part-time workers are defined as workers who 'are usually full-time workers but are working part-time for economic reasons' or who 'could not find full-time jobs'. All other part-timers are considered voluntary part-timers. The data that can be used to estimate the number of involuntary part-time workers are contained in the ESS in South Korea and the Special Labour Force Survey (SLFS) in Japan. The former is conducted every three years and is now available for 1983, 1986, 1989 and 1992; the latter is conducted annually. Both sets of statistics include data on 'current status'. The items in the questionnaires are not the same in the two sets of statistics, so some items have to be adjusted for the purposes of comparison.[5]

Involuntary part-time work is twice as high in South Korea as in Japan: 21 per cent of part-timers in South Korea compared with 10.1 per cent in Japan in 1992. Among female part-timers 14.2 per cent were involuntary in South Korea compared to 9.3 per cent in Japan, which is particularly significant among the 45–54 age group. The rate for men is even higher with 32.1 per cent compared with 11.5 per cent respectively. These figures for 1992 represent a significant fall in the number of involuntary part-timers in South Korea compared with overall rates of approximately 35–40 per cent during the 1980s. This change was related to the economic upturn whereby those working reduced hours because of 'slack' returned to their normal hours. Although the number of involuntary part-time workers in Japan gradually increased from the late 1980s to the early 1990s, the proportion of involuntary part-time workers to total part-time workers remained relatively stable.

As Fagan and O'Reilly point out in the introduction to this volume the conceptualisation of voluntary and 'involuntary' part-time employment from national statistics can often hide more than it reveals, as it fails to take account of the way choices are socially constructed. Given the limits of this chapter we can only explore the potential to examine this issue in more detail here through survey data. Another indicator that can be used to measure the involuntariness of part-time work is the share of part-timers seeking to change their jobs or wishing to work longer hours. Data from the Korean Women's Development Institute for 1993 show that more part-timers than full-timers in South Korea wish to change jobs and/or work longer hours. In Japan, on the other hand, there is no difference in this respect between part-timers and full-timers (Japanese SLFS 1993). Thus the level of dissatisfaction with part-time work still appears to be higher in South Korea than in Japan.

The most important reason cited for people wanting to change jobs in South Korea is because their current job is only temporary or has poor prospects (44.7 per cent of female part-timers cited this reason). The comparable response in Japan of wanting a more stable job was cited by only 11.1 per cent of part-timers. This would suggest that while female part-time employment in Japan is seen as fairly stable, in South Korea it is viewed as a more precarious employment relationship by part-time employees according to these surveys. Nevertheless, survey work conducted by Wakisaka in Japan found that there was a notable demand among 'paato' to have the 'sei-shain' status and benefits, while not increasing their hours. These differences reflect the different role and status of part-time employment in each society.

The major reason for wanting to change jobs in Japan was because employees wanted more income (32.8 per cent of all female employees); a similar proportion also cited this reason in South Korea (31.9 per cent), although this was second to wanting to leave precarious employment. In Japan, in 1976 the earnings of female part-timers was 80 per cent of female full-timers. The wage gap widened during the 1980s when female part-timers earned 70 per cent of the full-time female wage, but has remained stable in the 1990s. The widening of the wage gap during the1980s could be accounted for by the disparity in wage increases between part-timers and full-timers (responsible for 61.9 per cent of the gap) and by a job tenure effect (38.1 per cent) (MOL 1989). Regrettably, data on part-timers' earnings are not available for South Korea.

EDUCATIONAL LEVELS

Part of the explanation for levels of dissatisfaction and wage differentials may be attributable to educational differences among the part-time workforce in each country. Although there has been a general increase in educational attainment in both countries, part-timers in South Korea tend to be more highly educated than in Japan. Overall, the number of female workers in Japan with only a junior high school level of education decreased from 37.9 per cent in 1975 to 16 per cent in 1992, while those with a university education increased from 3.5 per cent to 6.2 per cent. The change has been even more dramatic in South Korea, where the percentage with only a junior high school education fell from 82.5 per cent in 1975 to 33.7 per cent in 1992, while those with university qualifications increased from 1.8 per cent to 5 per cent of the female population.

There are noticeable differences in the distribution of educational qualifications among part-timers in the two countries, as can be seen from Figure 13.3.

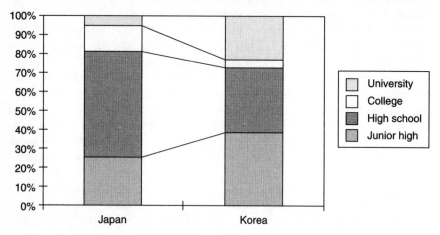

Figure 13.3 Educational distribution of female part-timers
　　　　Source: Korea: Korea Women's Development Institute, *Analysis of Part-time and Fixed-term Employment and Policy Implications in Korea* (1994)
　　　　Japan: Statistics Bureau Management and Coordination Agency, *The Employment Survey of Structure* (1993)
　　　　Note: Data for Japan are for 1992 and for South Korea for 1993

While the vast majority of part-timers in Japan are high school graduates, in South Korea there is greater polarisation between very high- and relatively low-skilled workers. Changes in the educational levels of Japanese part-timers are difficult to assess because there are data available up to only 1992. For South Korea, however, there has been a decline in the share of part-timers with a junior high school level of education from 86.3 per cent in 1980 to 37.4 per cent in 1993, while the share of high school graduates has increased from 8.8 per cent to 34.1 per cent and that of university graduates from 3.8 per cent to 24.3 per cent. However, although these figures are not directly comparable, they do at least provide a general impression of the differences between the two countries, and suggest that part-time workers in South Korea tend to be better educated than those in Japan.

The impact of the tax system on the part-time labour market

The tax and social security systems also influence the behaviour of part-time workers, particularly insofar as they risk falling into the poverty trap (see Doudeijns, Chapter 6, this volume). It is clear that the Japanese tax system encourages married female part-timers to adjust their working hours so that their income does not exceed a certain threshold. In the current Japanese income tax system, the married man's allowance (380,000 yen) and the supplementary married man's allowance (0–380,000 yen) can be offset against the husband's annual income tax liability provided his wife's income does not exceed 1,030,000 yen. If her income exceeds that level, she has to pay income tax and the husband loses his married man's allowance. If her income is between 1,030,000 and 1,410,000 yen, only the supplementary allowance (0–380,000 yen) can be offset against the husband's tax liability. If her income exceeds 1,410,000 yen, the allowances are forfeited altogether. In addition, social insurance contribution (health and old-age insurance) are payable on incomes above 1,300,000 yen. Moreover, the married man's allowance paid to husbands by their employers may not be paid if a wife's income exceeds 1,030,000 yen.

According to a survey conducted by the Ministry of Labour in 1990, one-third of married female part-timers whose husbands are the main family breadwinners adjust their working hours in order to take account of the taxation system, and firms are willing to facilitate this adaptation of hours. In particular, 63 per cent of those whose income is between 800,000 and 1,000,000 yen adjust their working hours for this reason. This has an adverse effect on the part-time labour market. Not only does the tax system keep the wages of part-time workers low, but it also prevents competent part-time workers from becoming core part-timers.

The decision as to whether or not the wife works is a neutral one, as is the choice of working time in the South Korean tax system. In 1993, the special deduction programme for working couples came into force. A total of 540,000 won is deducted from the annual income of working wives, irrespective of their husbands' incomes.

CONCLUSION

This chapter set out to examine why the rate of part-time work in Japan is so much higher than in South Korea, despite similar levels of female labour force participation in both countries. We have seen how part-timers are largely found in service sector employment, although significantly more part-timers in South Korea are in domestic and educational services than in Japan. In South Korea part-timers also tend to be found in small firms, whereas in Japan they are more likely to be used by large firms as a means of reducing labour costs. The significance of this can be seen from the growing wage gap between full- and part-time female employees in Japan.

Dissatisfaction with the income from part-time employment is a major cause for these employees wanting to change their job, in both countries. While there are significantly higher levels of dissatisfaction with part-time jobs in South Korea this could, in part, be linked to the fact that part-timers tend to be better qualified than their counterparts in Japan. A noticeable feature to emerge from the analysis of involuntary part-timers was the degree to which South Korean employees perceived this to be a temporary secondary form of employment. In Japan there are clear distinctions in the status of part-timers; while this does not suggest that it is a precarious form of employment, 'paato' often miss out on the benefits awarded to full-time employees. The social construction of 'paato' jobs for married women is reinforced by the tax system which creates significant incentives for married women to curtail their hours and income over the year, while no comparable incentives exist in South Korea. 'Paato' in Japan is largely concentrated on employment for married women with inferior conditions to full-time sei-shain; in South Korea there is a greater polarisation among part-timers, with younger highly qualified women accepting this as a temporary transitional entry point into paid work.

The expectation is that part-time jobs will continue to increase; however, whether Korean women and Korean firms will adopt a Japanese model of part-time work remains to be seen as economic structures, tax regulation and educational attainment indicate significant differences between the two countries. The role of part-time work in these societies has been a largely neglected issue in debates and research around the 'Asian miracle'. What is clear from this chapter is that future comparative research could benefit from the availability of more systematic data; it could examine the role of transitions between different employment statuses in these societies in order to assess how the differentiated structure of employment contributes to accounting for the success of these economies and the rapid changes they are going through.

NOTES

1   We draw on Japanese data from the Labour Force Survey (LFS), the Special Labour Force Survey (SLFS) and the Employment Structure Survey (ESS). For South Korea, the data sources are the Economically Active Population Survey (EAP) and the Employment Structure Survey (ESS). We have also used data from the South Korean Women's Development Institute (KWDI).

2   These figures are slightly lower than those reported by the OECD because our figures only include employees, whereas the OECD include self-employed, unpaid family workers and employees.

3   The Japanese industry data are based on the 1990 Population Survey, which does not differentiate between full- and part-time employees; detailed industry data are not available in the Japanese Labour Force Survey.

4   Medium-sized to large firms with between 10 and 499 employees. South Korean data do not allow for a differentiation of firms within this category, although it is possible to distinguish more between Japanese firms.

5   In the 1992 South Korean ESS, employed people were asked: 'How many hours did you work last week?' If they answered 'fewer than 36 hours', they were asked whether or not they usually worked fewer than 36 hours a week in their current job. Depending on whether they answered 'yes' or 'no', they were asked why they worked fewer than 36 hours. Those answering 'yes' were offered the following answers to choose from:

(Y1) Poor health (Y2) Slack work (Y3) Too busy with housework (Y4) Too busy with child care (Y5) Too busy with school (Y6) Want less work (Y7) Nature of work (Y8) Other.

Those answering 'no' were offered the following possible answers:

(N1) Slack work (N2) Strike or closed (N3) Company affairs (N4) Bad weather (N5) Private affairs (N6) Other.

(Y7) Nature of work was included only in the 1992 survey. In 1986 and 1989, 'Shortage of materials' and 'Plant or establishment closed for repair' replace (N2) Strike/closed and (N3) Company affairs.

In the SLFS in Japan, employed people who answered 'fewer than 35 hours in the last week of February' were asked why they worked fewer than 35 hours during the reference week. They were offered the following answers to choose from:

Normal work time is less than 35 hours:
  Wish to work 35 hours or more (A)
  Wish to work less than 35 hours (B)
Economic reasons:
  Due to slack in business (C)
  Other (D)
Personal or family reasons (E) (e.g. illness, vacation, etc.)
Bad weather (F)
Other (G)

In our estimates we adopted the OECD definition of involuntary part-timers, defining involuntary part-timers in Japan as the sum of (A) and (C) and in South Korea as the sum of (Y2) and (N1). We used the 1992 ESS and 1993 SFLS as the basis for comparison of the two countries. Calculations were based on persons working rather than employees because the relevant figures were not available.

BIBLIOGRAPHY

Clark, K., Dunlop, J. T., Harbinson, F. H. and Myers, C. A. (1960) *Industrialism and Industrial Man*, London: Heinemann.

Deutermann Jr., W. and Brown, S. C. (1978) 'Voluntary Part-time Workers: A Growing Part of the Labor Force', *Monthly Labor Review*, June: 3–10.

Doeringer, P. and Piore, M. (1971) *Internal Labor Markets and Manpower Policy*, Lexington, MA: D.C. Heath and Co.

Gallie, D. and White, M. (1994) 'Employer Policies, Employee Contracts, and Labour Market Structure' in J. Rubery and F. Wilkinson (eds) *Employer Strategy and the Labour Market*, Oxford: Oxford University Press.

Honda, K. (1993) 'Utilization of Part-time Workers and Their Compensation Programs (Paatotaimu rodosha no kikan rodoryoku-ka to shogu seido)', *Studies of the Japan Institute of Labour* 6: 1–24.

Ichino, S. (1985) 'Employment and Wage Structure of Female Part-time Workers (Joshi Paatotaimu Rodosha no Koyo/Chingin Kozo)', *Monthly Bulletin of Labour Statistics* 37, 1: 7–20.

—— (1989) 'Transformation Process of Part-time Workers (Paatotaimu Rodosha no Henbo Katei)', *Monthly Journal of the Japan Institute of Labour* 31, 5: 16–30.

Japanese SLFS (1993) *Rodoryoku Chousa Tokubetsu Chosa* (Special Labour Force Survey), Tokyo: Sourifu Tokeikyoku.

Koike, K. (1985) 'Workers in Small Firms and Women in Industry' in Taishiro, S. (ed.) *Contemporary Industrial Relations in Japan*, Madison, WI: University of Wisconsin.

—— (1988) *Understanding Industrial Relations in Modern Japan*, London: Macmillan.

Kumazawa, M. and Yamada, J. (1989) 'Jobs and Skills under the Lifelong Nenko Employment Practice' in Stephen Wood (ed.) *The Transformation of Work*, London: Unwin Hyman.

Lam, A. (1992) *Women and Japanese Management*, London: Routledge.

Ministry of Labour, Japan (MOL) (1989) White Paper on Labour (Rodo Hokusho), Ministry of Labour (Rodosho).

Mitsuyama, M. (1991) 'Utilization of Part-time Workers and Training within Firms (Paatotaima senryoku-ka to Kigyo-nai Kyoiku)', *Monthly Journal of the Japan Institute of Labour* 33, 3: 28–36.

Nakamura, M. (1990) 'Part-time Labour (paatotaimu rodo)', *Monthly Journal of the Japan Institute of Labour* 32, 1: 40–1.

OECD (1990, 1993 and 1995) *Employment Outlook*, Paris: OECD.

Tilly, C. (1991), 'Reasons for the Continuing Growth of Part-time Employment', *Monthly Labor Review* 114, 3: 10–18.

—— (1992), 'Dualism in Part-time Employment', *Industrial Relations* 31, 2: 330–47.

—— (1996) *Half a Job: Bad and Good Part-time jobs in a Changing Labor Market*, Philadelphia: Temple University Press.

Wakisaka, A. (1990) *Women in the Workplace* (Kaisha-gata Josei), Tokyo: Dobunkan.

—— (1995), 'Typology of Part-time workers (II)' (in Japanese), *Okayama Economic Review* 27, 4: 545–73.

—— (1997a) 'Women at Work', in M. Sako and H. Sato (eds) *Japanese Labour and Management in Transition*, London: Routledge.

—— (1997b) 'A Comparison of Part-time Workers between Japan and Germany' (in Japanese), *Okayama Economic Review* 29, 1.

14

WILL THE EMPLOYMENT CONDITIONS OF PART-TIMERS IN AUSTRALIA AND NEW ZEALAND WORSEN?

Janeen Baxter

INTRODUCTION

In Australia and New Zealand between a quarter and one-fifth of the workforce work part-time. Part-time jobs rose from 12 per cent in 1973 to 17 per cent in 1983 and to 24 per cent of the Australian workforce in 1993. Similar patterns are evident in New Zealand: in 1973 part-time work comprised 11.2 per cent of total employment, compared to 15 per cent in 1983 and 21 per cent by 1993 (OECD 1983, 1994). This growth mirrors trends in other OECD countries over this period: first, it has occurred in a limited number of occupations and industries, primarily service-related, and second, the majority of part-time workers are women (see Smith *et al.*, Chapter 2, and Delsen, Chapter 3, this volume). Of course, the gendered nature of part-time employment and its concentration in particular industries and occupations are related, as increased female participation in paid employment has not led to a diminishing of their responsibility for unpaid work.

Where Australia and New Zealand differ from patterns found in other OECD countries is in terms of the relatively favourable pay and conditions of part-time work. Both countries have long histories of centralised wage bargaining, high levels of union membership and relatively strong feminist bureaucracies. These factors have combined to produce comparatively favourable conditions for part-time workers compared to countries such as the United States and the United Kingdom. However, recent changes in government policies, including moves towards deregulation of the labour market, the emergence of enterprise bargaining, declining support for the trade union movement and cuts to the public sector, may lead to a gradual worsening of the conditions of part-time work. In particular, the trend towards casualisation of part-time work is a significant factor threatening to undermine many of the positive aspects of part-time work in these two countries.

This chapter examines these issues for Australia and New Zealand, focusing on the way in which the economic, political and social features of each country impinge on the availability and desirability of part-time work. Specifically, the aim is to map the growth of part-time work in each country and then to examine the characteristics of part-time work. More broadly, the chapter discusses the implications of recent changes in the economic and political climate in both countries for the conditions of part-time work. One possible outcome will be a polarisation of part-time work. For some this will provide a means of reducing work hours to accommodate varying demands on time at different stages of the life cycle and career. For others it may represent a form of ghettoisation in inferior and precarious forms of employment for certain groups, such as women, leading to greater divisions within the labour market.

AUSTRALIA AND NEW ZEALAND: COUNTRY CONTEXTS

Australia and New Zealand share many social and political features. Both are former British settler colonies with broadly similar economic, social and political structures. Both have been broadly classified as dominion capitalist countries (Ehrensaft and Armstrong 1978) with liberal welfare regimes (Esping-Andersen 1990). But there are also some significant differences, particularly in relation to recent political initiatives and industrial relations policy which have important implications for employment conditions in recent years. This section briefly discusses some of the main economic, political and social welfare features of each country which relate to part-time employment patterns.

Employment

In both Australia and New Zealand women's labour force participation rates have increased markedly since the Second World War. In 1973 the labour force participation rate of women in Australia was 42 per cent. By 1983 it had increased to 45 per cent and in 1993 it was 52 per cent (ABS 1994a). In New Zealand, women's labour force participation rate rose from 25 per cent in 1951 to 39 per cent in 1981 and then to 54 per cent in 1991 (Statistics New Zealand 1993a). Much of this growth is due to women's increased involvement in part-time work. In Australia, for example, over 90 per cent of the increase in female labour force participation between 1973 and 1993 was due to an increase in participation in the part-time labour market, resulting in 75 per cent of part-time positions in 1993 being filled by women. The pattern in New Zealand is remarkably similar with 74 per cent of part-time jobs in 1993 done by women. In contrast, men's employment participation rates have declined slightly in both countries as a result of increased involvement in education, earlier retirement ages and declining employment opportunities.

Australia and New Zealand are very similar in terms of women's overall labour force participation rates. In comparison to other OECD countries women's labour force participation rates in Australia and New Zealand are significantly lower than those of women in Scandinavia, but significantly higher than those of women in countries such as the Netherlands, Italy and Spain (Statistics New Zealand 1993a). These differences are most likely due to country variations in overall employment growth and employment opportunities for women, differences in the availability of child care and parental leave and differences in ideologies relating to gender roles (see Pfau-Effinger, Chapter 9, and Daune-Richard, Chapter 11, this volume).

Despite the overall increase in women's levels of participation, fuelled by the removal of formal barriers to married women's involvement in paid work, the increasing need of two incomes to maintain household standards, and changes in social values regarding women's position in society, women's access to employment in Australia and New Zealand is restricted to a small range of industries and occupations. In Australia 55 per cent of women's jobs are in clerical, sales and personal service occupations. Men, on the other hand, are distributed more evenly across the occupational range with 54 per cent in three groups: trades, labourers and managers/administrators (ABS 1995). In terms of industry segregation, the largest proportion of female employees is located in retail trade (17.2 per cent) followed by health and community services (16 per cent) and education (11 per cent). Men dominate in manufacturing, outnumbering women in this industry by three to one.

A similar pattern of sex segregation in industry and occupation is evident in New Zealand. Almost a quarter of all employed New Zealand women work in clerical occupations with a further 21 per cent in service or sales occupations. The smallest occupational group for women is trades, accounting for only 1.6 per cent of female employment. In contrast this is the largest occupational group for men (17.6 per cent) followed by legislators, administrators and managers (14.6 per cent). The smallest occupational group for men is clerical work (5.1 per cent). In terms of industry, women are mainly concentrated in two industrial groups, community, social and personal services (38.7 per cent) and wholesale, retail, restaurants and hotels (23.9 per cent). Men are distributed more evenly with the three largest divisions being manufacturing (22.7 per cent), wholesale, retail, restaurants and hotels (18.9 per cent) and community, social and personal services (18 per cent) (Statistics New Zealand 1996).

In addition to restricting women's access to specific occupational and industrial groups, sex segregation of the workforce is a major factor lowering women's earnings relative to men's (Hyman 1994; Mitchell 1995; Pocock 1995; Rubery, Chapter 7, this volume). Despite the introduction of equal pay legislation in Australia in 1972, the Sex Discrimination Act in 1984 and the Affirmative Action Act in 1986, women in Australia still earn considerably less than men. In 1994 the ratio of the average weekly earnings of females and males was

0.67 for all employees and 0.81 for full-time employees. In other words, among full-time employees women earn about 19 per cent less than men (ABS 1995). In New Zealand a similar situation exists despite the introduction of the Equal Pay Act in 1972. Women's average ordinary time hourly earnings, as a percentage of men's, increased from 74 per cent in 1974 to 80 per cent in 1983. Since then there has been little change. In 1993 the ratio of women's to men's earnings was just over 0.81 (Statistics New Zealand 1993a). There are a number of reasons for the persistence of the gender gap in earnings, including women's discontinuous work histories, women's concentration in a limited number of occupations which are female-dominated and low paid, women's concentration at the bottom of organisational hierarchies and the fact that women in the workforce are on average younger than men.

By comparison, men's and women's rates of unemployment in Australia and New Zealand are roughly comparable, particularly among the young. Both Australia and New Zealand have registered comparatively high levels of unemployment over the last decade. In 1989 New Zealand's unemployment rate climbed above the OECD average and continued to increase. New Zealand's highest unemployment rate was in 1992 when 10.4 per cent of the population was recorded unemployed; this dropped to 8.1 per cent in 1994. Australia's highest rate was in 1993 with 10.8 per cent of the population unemployed; this fell to 9.7 per cent in 1994.

Both countries also have relatively high levels of under-employment; that is, part-time employees who would prefer to work more hours, but are unable to obtain the work (ABS 1994b; Statistics New Zealand 1993b). Since women outnumber men among those employed part-time, it might be expected that this will be more of a problem for women than for men. However, this does not appear to be the case. In New Zealand in 1990, 12 per cent of all women employed part-time would have preferred a job in which they worked more hours, compared to 17 per cent of men (New Zealand Statistics 1990: 68). In Australia in 1993, 44 per cent of male part-time workers were under-employed compared to only 23 per cent of women. The highest rate of under-employment among male part-time workers was in the 25–34 year age group, while for women the highest rate of under-employment was in the 20–24 year age group (ABS 1994b: 108). These figures suggest that most women who work part-time do so out of choice as a result of child-bearing and child-rearing considerations, while most men do so because of the difficulty of finding full-time jobs.

Political and industrial relations systems

Both Australia and New Zealand have occupied peripheral positions in the international capitalist economy with, at least until the 1960s, a strong dependence on primary production and the export of primary products to a narrow range of markets, primarily Britain (Castles et al. 1996). Since the 1970s this dependence on Britain has waned as globalisation, greater international competition and the increasing dominance of the United States forced the Australasian governments to diversify export products and trading partners with a greater emphasis on the Asia-Pacific region (Easton and Gerritsen 1996). In contrast to their relative affluence during the first half of the twentieth century, by the 1980s both countries were in economic crisis as a result of falling commodity prices, little foreign investment in domestic manufacturing and agricultural protectionism in Europe and North America weakening their natural advantages in primary production (Castles et al. 1996: 9).

These factors created considerable challenges for the Labour governments elected in both countries in the early 1980s. Both governments launched rapid programmes of deregulation. In New Zealand, the Labour government elected in 1984 pursued an economic strategy of reducing inflation, overseas debt and the budget deficit. It was committed to increasing the productivity and competitiveness of both the public and private sectors through monetary, fiscal and regulatory reforms with a focus on a market-driven economy with diminished intervention by the state. This was combined with the reform of the public sector in the form of cut-backs to some government departments and the privatisation of certain state assets. During the late 1980s New Zealand experienced a severe recession, low investment and rising levels of unemployment with consequent implications for women's attempts to increase access to paid work and improve the wages and conditions of employment (NACEW 1990: 20).

On the other hand, the Labour government did take some steps in pursuit of greater equity for women and other minority groups. The Employment Equity Act which was passed in July 1990 required all public and private sector employers with more than fifty employees to develop and implement Equal Employment Opportunity programmes. Its aims were to identify areas of inequality of opportunity or remuneration; the promotion of equal employment opportunities; and to redress the inequitable impact of any current or historical remuneration discrimination. There was also provision for comparable worth assessments and a procedure for pay equity claims (NACEW 1990: 135). Unfortunately, the Act was only in existence for six months. The National government elected in 1990 repealed the Act and introduced the Employment Contracts Act which abolished the Arbitration Commission, outlawed compulsory unionism and emphasised a contractual model based on enterprise bargaining between individuals and their employers rather than collective wage bargaining based on centralised wage fixing. The government has since rejected calls for equal employment opportunity legislation but has established an Equal Employment Opportunities Trust to promote EEO on a voluntary basis (Du Plessis 1995: 247–50).

The Employment Contracts Act has significant implications for women workers and generally increases their precarious position in the labour market (Hill and Du Plessis 1993).

National awards, backed by arbitration, bridged problems of logistics, personal vulnerability and consequent industrial weakness by enabling unions to negotiate rates for scattered workers across the whole labour market for their particular kind of work. Women's concentration in a narrow range of low paid traditionally female occupations, dispersed over a large number of work sites, with few opportunities to collec- tively exercise industrial muscle, contributes to their general vulnerability in the labour market.

(Du Plessis 1995: 251).

There is some indication that the gender gap in earnings has widened since the introduction of the Act (Hammond and Harbridge 1995). In addition, the Employment Contracts Act has had considerable ramifications for union representation of women. The loss of union bargaining power left little incen- tive for membership. The clerical unions lost about 45 per cent of their membership as a result of the Act, and the Distribution Workers' Union covering the retail trade lost about one-third of its membership in the year following the Act. As Du Plessis has argued, this constitutes a significant loss of autonomous action for predominantly female unions which led the way in pay equity battles, sexual harassment and industrial health and safety issues (Du Plessis 1995: 254).

In Australia the Labour government elected in 1983 pursued a similar programme of decentralisation and deregulation in an attempt to control infla- tion and the effects of periodic recessions. But in contrast to New Zealand's 'commercialist' economic strategies, the Australian Labor Party adopted a more 'consensual-corporatist' approach (Easton and Gerritsen 1996). The Australian Labor Party negotiated closely with unions and key interest groups in setting wages and industrial policies while the New Zealand Labour Party tended to operate more unilaterally (Bray and Neilson 1995; Easton and Gerritsen 1996). Key components of the Australian reforms were successive Accords (the first in 1983) which involved wage policy agreements between the Labor Party, the Australian Conciliation and Arbitration Commission and employers. A key premise underlying the consultative approach of the Australian government was the view that rapid growth was sustainable only if there was a degree of wage restraint by unions who in return would receive an increase in the social wage and a say in the direction of economic policy (Easton and Gerritsen 1995: 37). In general, most commentators have suggested that this approach was more successful than the strategies adopted by New Zealand, especially in terms of economic and employment growth (O'Donnell and Hall 1988; Easton and Gerritsen 1996; Bray and Neilson 1996). Moreover, much of the employment growth in the early 1980s went to women. 'Of the 670,000 jobs created under the Hawke government, 50 per cent went to women and three-quarters of the increase was in full-time jobs' (O'Donnell and Hall 1988: 16).

Nevertheless, the Australian industrial relations system remains male-dominated and the trend towards enterprise bargaining has serious consequences for women's employment similar to those outlined above for New Zealand. In Australia, women are under-represented in the trade union movement, comprising less than 29 per cent of union officials, making it difficult for women's interests to be placed on the agenda (Hammond and Harbridge 1995: 373). Moreover, some studies report that women are faring worse than men in enterprise bargaining and the rate of growth of male earnings is twice that of female earnings (ibid.: 374).

In 1996 the Australian Federal Labor Party lost government to a conservative Liberal–National coalition. It is likely that the reforms introduced by the new government, including a radical plan of industrial deregulation, increased enterprise bargaining on an individual basis between employee and employer, the removal of the safety award net and decreased power to unions will have significant negative consequences for women and other groups in the Australian labour market. As Mitchell has argued: 'One of the reasons why Australian women's hourly wage rates, relative to men's, compares favourably on an international basis has been the enshrinement of equal pay legislation in the award and minimum pay system' (Mitchell 1995: 92). As these regulations are gradually eroded under a conservative government it is likely that women's wages and conditions of employment will suffer.

The feminist movement and family policies

New Zealand and Australia both led the way in granting women the right to vote. In 1893 New Zealand was the first country to give women the vote, while in Australia women's suffrage was achieved in 1902. This is much earlier than in most other OECD countries (Statistics New Zealand 1993a). But until the 1970s the influence of women's groups on state legislation and government policies in both countries was minimal (Sawer 1991: 258). Sawer argues that since the 1970s Australia has led the way 'in the creation of a wide range of government-funded services run by women, for women, usually in accordance with collectivist principles' (ibid.). For example, she notes that there is no equivalent in the United States, the United Kingdom, Canada or New Zealand of the women's information referral services funded by government and run by women. The Australian women's movement has operated largely through government rather than from outside, as in the United States, and has been extremely successful in the creation of specialised bureaucratic machinery (ibid.). The factors contributing to this success include the Australian political tradition of seeking reform through government, the election of a reformist government at a time when the women's movement was at its peak, the lack of effective anti-feminist opposition and the existence of a centralised wage-fixing system (ibid.: 260). In contrast, although the New Zealand women's policy machinery made some early attempts to model itself on the Australian system through the establishment of the Ministry of Women's Affairs in 1985 (similar to Australia's Office of the Status of Women), its effectiveness has been limited by the New Zealand government's move away from collectivism and solidarity to hierarchical management structures and individualist performance norms (ibid.: 266). According to Sawer, the success of the Australian system has been largely dependent on the co-operation of the Australian Labor government, compared to New Zealand, where Labour's policies provided a less favourable political environment for feminist reforms. Nevertheless, both Australia and New Zealand have more in common in terms of integration into the state bureaucracy than they do with the strategies adopted by feminists in other countries. Sawer, for example, argues that the women's movement in the United States has concentrated on lobbying from the outside, while neither the United Kingdom nor Scandinavia has been successful in developing distinctively feminist bureaucratic structures (ibid.: 268) (see Daune-Richard, Chapter 11, this volume for a comparison of the French and Swedish feminist movements).

Despite the success of the Australian femocrats, Australia has not reached the level of social welfare achieved by social democratic governments in Scandinavian countries such as Sweden and Norway (Castles 1996). For example, the majority of women in the Australian labour force do not have access to paid maternity leave. This was first introduced into the Australian Public Service in 1973. At this time, female employees with twelve months' continuous service became entitled to twelve weeks' paid leave at the rate of their normal salary. This included temporary staff and part-time staff who worked more than 24 hours per week on four or more days. In addition, all female employees gained entitlement to up to fifty-two weeks of unpaid maternity leave. Following leave, employees were entitled to resume their previous position or be appointed to another as near as possible in salary and status (NWCC 1993).

In 1990 a significant advance was made when the Australian Industrial Relations Commission handed down the Parental Leave Test Case which extended provisions to the case of paternity leave. This provided for twelve months' unpaid leave to be shared between the parents and one week's paternity leave. It also included provision for permanent part-time work for parents up to the child's second birthday and during pregnancy, subject to employer agreement (NWCC 1993). These entitlements are not generally available in the public sector. While many private sector workers have access to unpaid maternity leave, often up to fifty-two weeks, paid maternity leave and parental leave are not usually available.

The situation for women in New Zealand is less favourable. Women in New Zealand are entitled to fourteen weeks' unpaid maternity leave and to reinstatement in their previous job if the employer can show that it is a 'key position'. Two weeks' paternity leave is available at the time of birth. Twelve months' parental leave may be taken by either parent, but, like Australia, is subject to twelve months' service with the same employer and is unpaid (NWCC 1993: 10). In contrast to Australia and New Zealand, many Western European countries provide employees with 14–16 weeks on at least 80 per cent of pay with Sweden providing the most generous benefits where either parent is entitled to fifteen months' leave on 90 per cent of previous earnings for the first twelve months. Moreover, neither Australia nor New Zealand currently conforms to the International Labour Organisation's specifications in relation to maternity leave.

THE GROWTH OF PART-TIME WORK IN AUSTRALIA AND NEW ZEALAND

How do these institutional features of Australia and New Zealand contribute to the patterning of part-time work in these countries? Part-time work (defined in Australia as less than 35 hours of paid work per week and in New Zealand as less than 30 hours of paid work per week) has grown at a phenomenal rate in Australia and New Zealand over the last two decades. Most of the increase has gone to women. In Australia 43 per cent of women workers were employed part-time in 1993 compared to 28 per cent in 1973. This is very close to Swedish patterns, albeit that part-time work has actually declined over the period from 1973 to 1993 in Sweden. In New Zealand the number of women employed part-time in 1993 is somewhat smaller than in Australia (36 per cent) but, like Australia, this represents a substantial increase of 11 per cent since 1973.

In most OECD countries women's share of part-time employment has remained about the same, or even decreased slightly over the last two decades. But in all countries most part-time workers are women. In Australia in 1993, 75 per cent of part-time work was done by women while in New Zealand for the same year the figure is 74 per cent. But there have also been large increases in the proportion of men working part-time, a pattern which appears to be fairly uniform across the OECD countries (see Delsen, Chapter 3, this volume). In Australia, 4 per cent of male workers were employed part-time in 1973 compared to 10 per cent in 1993, and in New Zealand the figures went from 5 to 10 per cent. These patterns are probably a reflection of the increase in education among 15–24-year-olds, during which many students are forced to rely on part-time work to supplement their income. In addition, for some men part-time work may increasingly be used as a means of easing into retirement.

One way of investigating this is to examine part-time employment rates in relation to age and family status. We would expect to see quite different distributions for men and women since, for many women, part-time employment is a means of combining employment with child-rearing, while for men we would expect to see peaks in part-time employment towards the beginning and end of their working lives. The Australian Bureau of Statistics reports that there are large differences in the reasons given by parents for working part-time, with mothers almost nine times more likely than fathers to work part-time for family reasons (ABS 1994). This pattern is borne out by the data presented in Figures 14.1 and 14.2. The pattern for male participation is U-shaped while the pattern for women is the reverse.

These patterns reflect the differing impact of family responsibilities on men's and women's labour force attachment. Male part-time workers are less likely to be married and less likely to have children compared to male full-time workers. On the other hand, female part-time workers are much more likely to be married with dependent children than women working full-time. Moreover, female part-time workers with dependent children work fewer hours than those without dependent children, while the reverse is the case for men (Clark 1986: 6–10; Lewis 1990: 9). There is some indication however that over time women's patterns of part-time employment may be moving closer to men's.

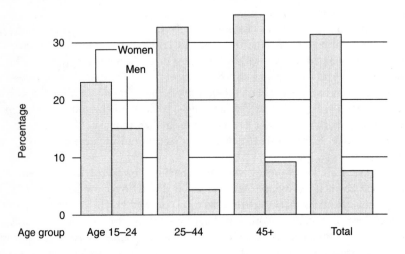

Figure 14.1   Employed women and men working part-time in New Zealand, 1991
Source: Census of Population and Dwellings (Statistics New Zealand 1993a)

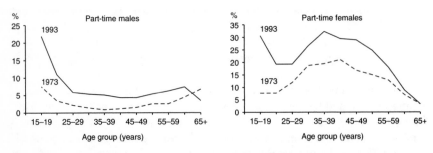

Figure 14.2   Labour force participation rate profiles in Australia
Source: Labour Force Survey (ABS 1994b)

In New Zealand during the 1980s, young employed women became more likely to work part-time and older employed women less likely to work part-time. This suggests something of a convergence towards male labour force patterns.

There are very clear trends in terms of the occupational and industrial location of part-time work. In Australia in 1993, 79 per cent of all part-time workers were employed in four of the major industry categories, all of which were service industries. Twenty-eight per cent of part-time workers were located in wholesale and retail trade, 26 per cent in community services, 14 per cent in recreation and personal services and 10 per cent in finance, property and business. These industries have experienced the fastest growth over this period. The New Zealand experience is much the same. In 1991, 63 per cent of all part-time employment was located in wholesale and retail trade and community social and personal services. Interestingly, in New Zealand, unlike Australia, the proportion of part-time employment in community services has declined slightly over the last decade, from 38 per cent to 35 per cent. A number of factors have probably contributed to the selective growth of part-time work in specific industries, including the introduction of extended working hours, particularly in the retail and recreation groups, the introduction of new technologies which has led to a reorganisation of work in areas such as finance, business, banking and clerical occupations and the increasing demand by employers for a more flexible workforce (ABS 1994b: 105).

Part-time workers are also concentrated in a limited range of occupations. In Australia in 1993, cleaners had the highest proportion of people working part-time (63 per cent). This was followed by miscellaneous salespersons (bar attendants, waiters and waitresses) with 60 per cent, tellers, cashiers and ticket salespersons with 59 per cent and sales assistants with 51 per cent. The occupation group with the largest percentage of part-time workers was sales assistants, comprising 14 per cent of all part-time workers (ABS 1994b: 106). The same pattern is evident in New Zealand with the majority of part-time workers concentrated in clerical, cleaning, cooking, waitressing and bartending occupations (Statistics New Zealand 1993b). These patterns reinforce the view that part-time work tends to be concentrated in lower-paid jobs with fewer opportunities for training, skills development and promotion.

A further characteristic of part-time employment in Australia and New Zealand is the lack of award coverage and employment benefits. The percentage of full-time employees in Australia receiving employment benefits far outweighs those in the part-time workforce. There are significant differences here between those employed on a casual basis, the majority of whom are women, and those employed on a permanent part-time basis, with the latter usually receiving the same benefits and award coverage as full-time workers. The key difference between casual employment and permanent employment is that permanent employees have an ongoing contract of employment of unspecified duration, while casuals do not. Casuals can be employed on a part-time or full-time basis, but most part-time work is casual and as such receives little in the way of employment benefits. As Romeyn has shown, the lack of a permanent contract has important implications in terms of the conditions of employment. Casual employees have no legal entitlements to benefits generally associated with continuity of employment, such as sick leave or annual leave, no legal entitlement to prior notification of retrenchment and no case for either reinstatement or damages for arbitrary dismissal (Romeyn 1992: 2).

In Australia casual employment has increased steadily over the last decade. In 1986, 17.2 per cent of the workforce was employed on a casual basis, compared to 18.9 per cent in 1988 and 19.4 per cent in 1990. At the same time, permanent part-time work has also increased, from 6.1 per cent of the workforce in 1986 to 7.1 per cent in 1990, but comprises a significantly smaller proportion of the workforce.

Despite the relatively poor conditions of part-time work in terms of award coverage, the earnings of Australian and New Zealand women in part-time work compare very favourably to the earnings of women in full-time work. Even though female part-time employees earn less per hour than their male counterparts, the average hourly earnings of part-time female workers in Australia and New Zealand is generally comparable to, or even greater than, the average hourly earnings of women employed full-time. As Table 14.1 shows, in 1985 women in part-time work in Australia earned $9.30 per hour compared to $9.10 per hour for women in full-time employment. Men in part-time work, on the other hand, earned less per hour than their full-time counterparts. By 1993 the relatively favourable position of women in part-time work compared to their full-time counterparts had declined, but women in part-time work still earned about the same per hour as women in full-time work. The patterns for Australian women are quite different to the patterns observed in other OECD countries where the

Table 14.1 Average hourly earnings of full-time adult non-managerial employees and part-time non-managerial employees in Australia and New Zealand

	Full-time			Part-time		
	Male	Female	Total	Male	Female	Total
Australia						
1985	10.50	9.10	9.80	10.20	9.30	9.50
1993	15.71	14.14	15.15	14.70	14.10	14.20
New Zealand						
1988	12.18	9.79	11.33	9.25	9.42	9.39
1996	15.91	12.88	14.74	13.75	13.08	13.24

Sources: Average Earnings and Hours of Employees, Australia, November 1985 (ABS Cat No. 6304.0) and *Distribution and Composition of Employee Earnings and Hours, Australia* (ABS Cat No. 6306.0). Statistics New Zealand Household Economic Survey
Note: The data for Australia are based on a sample of non-managerial employees, while the data for New Zealand are based on all employees.

average hourly earnings of male and female part-time employees are considerably lower than those of full-time employees (Gornick and Jacobs 1996). The reason for Australian women's relatively favourable position in this respect lies partly with the active role played by trade unions in safeguarding rates for part-time employment and the availability of penalty rates. For men, on the other hand, a greater proportion of those employed part-time may be in second jobs which are more marginal in terms of access to union coverage, award coverage and penalty rates. But it is likely that the conditions for women in part-time work will continue to deteriorate as a result of labour market deregulation, declining union membership and the introduction of enterprise bargaining.

A DIVIDED LABOUR MARKET?

It seems clear that both labour demand and labour supply have contributed to the patterning of part-time work in Australia and New Zealand. In terms of labour demand, the growth in particular industries is instructive. Part-time work has grown in specific industries, primarily in the service sector, and it is precisely these industries which have experienced the most growth overall during the last two decades. In addition, there has been a growing demand by employers for a more flexible workforce to meet changing production schedules and growing consumer demand for more flexible trading hours.

At the same time, the patterning of part-time labour and, in particular, the large numbers of married women in part-time work cannot be fully explained without reference to the gender division of labour within households. Women in both Australia and New Zealand spend considerably more time on domestic work than men (Baxter 1993; Statistics New Zealand 1993b; ABS 1994a). The unequal division of child care and housework duties, combined with the lack of adequate parental leave and child care provisions and prevailing gender ideologies which continue to define women as primarily responsible for unpaid caring work, lead to a far greater concentration of married women in part-time work than either single women or men. These patterns of a combination of labour supply and labour demand tend to follow fairly closely those observed in other countries. In terms of the occupational and industrial segregation of part-time work, as well as the over-representation of women in their child-bearing years in part-time work, the patterns reported here for Australia and New Zealand tend to mirror those reported for most European countries in this volume.

Differences seem to appear, however, when we consider the conditions of part-time work in Australasia. Some of the data presented above suggest that the conditions of part-time work in Australia and New Zealand, at least until the early 1990s, may have been better than those experienced by part-time workers in other countries. For example, centralised bargaining of wages, strong national unions and relatively high levels of unionisation have all combined to keep the wages of part-time workers, especially women in Australia, at comparatively high levels compared to their full-time counterparts. In both Australia and New Zealand, part-time workers have been covered by awards and unionised to a greater extent than in most other countries (Lewis 1990; Hyman 1994). Whether this adequately compensates for a low level of employee benefits, concentration in selected occupations and industries, and a lack of access to further training and promotion prospects is a more complex question and its answer will no doubt vary by gender and age. But the rapid growth in part-time employment in Australia and New Zealand has been accompanied by relatively favourable conditions compared to those experienced in other countries.

Of course, the situation varies dramatically between permanent part-time work and casual part-time work with casual employment enjoying far fewer benefits than other forms of part-time work. Even for those employed on a permanent basis, it is unlikely that the relatively favourable conditions in Australia and New Zealand will continue throughout the 1990s. In both countries moves towards a system of decentralised bargaining may have serious consequences and create a potential polarisation of women's employment opportunities. For example, Hammond and Harbridge report findings from a number of workplace studies which show that women fare worse than men under enterprise bargaining in terms of receiving 'lower and later pay increases, reduced access to employment, reduced job security and poorer conditions, increased management control of working time and job flexibility, and less representation and participation in bargaining' (1995: 374). In both countries case study evidence suggests that part-time employees are seen as more marginal to the workforce than full-time employees and as such tend to be confined to the lowest levels of organisational structures, have fewer opportunities for promotion, less established career paths, fewer opportunities for career training, and low skill utilisation (Clark 1986; DEET 1989; Lewis 1990; Romeyn 1992; Probert 1995). Moreover, the situation for female part-time employees in New Zealand, where the introduction of the Employment Contracts Act in 1991 effectively ended a century of centralised bargaining between employers and unions, may well be worse than in Australia.

If the conditions of part-time work in Australia and New Zealand have been supported in the past by the existence of employment regulation, centralised wage bargaining, high levels of unionisation and the integration of the feminist movement into state bureaucracy, it seems likely that conditions will worsen in the coming years as we move away from these institutional features. The factors that we might expect to contribute further to the undermining of 'good' part-time jobs include increased occupational segregation associated with the growth of part-time work in the service sector, increased moves towards casual part-time work as a result of deregulation and decentralised wage bargaining, and continuing unequal gender divisions of labour in the home which encourage women to seek more marginal forms of employment. All these factors make it increasingly likely that part-time work will become further marginalised rather than providing a means of moving between different forms of employment over the life course.

The challenge for governments, unions, employer groups and feminists is how to reverse these trends. This will mean monitoring the conditions of part-time employees, particularly those in casual employment, implementing strategies which expand the opportunity for permanent part-time employment, as opposed to casual employment, and facilitating ease of movement between full-time and part-time positions. It is clear that part-time work is a desirable option for men and women at different stages of the life cycle. What must be guarded against is the possibility that those in part-time employment become trapped in segregated, low-paid, low-unionised sections of the labour force. In Australia and New Zealand this is of particular concern over the next few years as we move towards greater deregulation of the labour market and away from centralised bargaining.

ACKNOWLEDGEMENTS

A number of people helped me to locate the material for this chapter. Thanks to Nicola Armstrong, Celia Briar, Frank Castles, Jennifer Curtin, Margrit Davies, Chris Eichbaum, Deborah Mitchell, Michele Robertson and Mark Western. And thanks to Vasa Stoyanoff for preparing the tables and graphs.

REFERENCES

Anderson, Gordon, Brosnan, Peter and Walsh, Pat (1994) 'Flexibility, Casualization and Externalisation in the New Zealand Workforce', *Journal of Industrial Relations* 36 (4): 491–518.

Australian Bureau of Statistics (ABS) (1994a) *Focus on Families. Work and Family Responsibilities*. Catalogue No. 4422.0, Canberra.

ABS (1994b) *Australian Social Trends*. Catalogue No. 4102.0, Canberra.

ABS (1995) *Australian Women's Year Book*. Catalogue No. 4124.0, Canberra.

ABS (1996) *Year Book Australia*. Canberra.

Baxter, Janeen (1993) *Work at Home. The Domestic Division of Labour*. St Lucia: University of Queensland Press.

Bray, Mark and Neilson, David (1996) 'Industrial Relations Reform and the Relative Autonomy of the State' in Frances Castles, Rolf Gerritsen and Jack Vowles (eds) *The Great Experiment. Labour Parties and Public Policy Transformation in Australia and New Zealand*. Sydney: Allen & Unwin.

Castles, Francis. G. (1996) 'Needs-based Strategies of Social Protection in Australia and New Zealand' in Gøsta Esping-Andersen (ed.) *Social Welfare States in Transition*. London: Sage.

Castles, Francis, Gerritsen, Rolf and Vowles, Jack (1996) *The Great Experiment. Labour Parties and Public Policy Transformation in Australia and New Zealand*. Sydney: Allen & Unwin.

Clark, Alison (1986) *Part-time Work in New Zealand*. New Zealand Planning Council, Planning Paper No. 25, Wellington.

Department of Employment Education and Training, Women's Bureau (DEET) (1989) *New Brooms: Restructuring and Training Issues for Women in the Service Sector*. Canberra: AGPS.

Du Plessis, Rosemary (1995) 'Women in a Restructured New Zealand' in Anne Edwards and Susan Magarey (eds) *Women in a Restructuring Australia. Work and Welfare*. Sydney: Allen & Unwin.

Easton, Brian and Gerritsen, Rolf (1996) 'Economic Reform: Parallels and Divergences' in Frances Castles, Rolf Gerritsen and Jack Vowles (eds) *The Great Experiment. Labour Parties and Public Policy Transformation in Australia and New Zealand*. Sydney: Allen & Unwin.

Ehrensaft, Philip and Armstrong, Warwick (1978) 'Dominion Capitalism: A First Statement', *Australian and New Zealand Journal of Sociology* 14 (3), October: 352–63.

Esping-Andersen, Gøsta (1990) *The Three Worlds of Welfare Capitalism*. New Jersey: Princeton University Press.

Gornick, Janet C. and Jacobs, Jerry A. (1996) 'A Cross-national Analysis of the Wages of Part-time Workers: Evidence from the United States, the United Kingdom, Canada and Australia', *Work, Employment and Society* 10 (1): 1–27.

Hammond, Suzanne and Harbridge, Raymond (1995) 'Women and Enterprise Bargaining: The New Zealand Experience of Labour Market Deregulation', *Journal of Industrial Relations* 37, September: 359–76.

Hill, Linda and Du Plessis, Rosemary (1993) 'Tracing the Similarities, Identifying the Differences: Women and the Employment Contract Acts', *New Zealand Journal of Industrial Relations* 18 (1): 31–43.

Hyman, Prue (1994) *Women and Economics. A New Zealand Feminist Perspective*. Wellington: Bridget William Books.

Lever-Tracy, Constance (1988) 'The Flexibility Debate: Part Time Work', *Labour and Industry* 1 (2), June: 210–41.

Lewis, Helen (1990) *Part-time Work. Trends and Issues*. Department of Employment Education and Training. Canberra: AGPS.

Mitchell, Deborah (1995) 'Women's Incomes' in Anne Edwards and Susan Magarey (eds) *Women in a Restructuring Australia. Work and Welfare*. Sydney: Allen & Unwin.

National Advisory Council on the Employment of Women (NACEW) (1990) *Beyond the Barriers. The State, the Economy and Women's Employment 1984–1990*. Wellington: Department of Labour.

National Women's Consultative Council (NWCC) (1993) *Paid Maternity Leave: A Discussion Paper on Paid Maternity Leave in Australia*. Canberra: AGPS.

O'Donnell, Carol and Hall, Philippa (1988) *Getting Equal*. Sydney: Allen & Unwin.

OECD (1983) *Employment Outlook*. Paris: OECD.

OECD (1994) *Employment Outlook*. Paris: OECD.

Pocock, Barbara (1995) 'Women's Work and Wages' in Anne Edwards and Susan Magarey (eds) *Women in a Restructuring Australia. Work and Welfare*. Sydney: Allen & Unwin.

Romeyn, Jane (1992) *Flexible Working Time: Part-time and Casual Employment*. Industrial Relations Research Monograph No. 1, June.

Rosenfeld, Rachel and Birkelund, Gunn Elisabeth (1995) 'Women's Part-time Work: A Cross-national Comparison', *European Sociological Review* 11 (2), September: 111–34.

Probert, Belinda (1995) *Part-time Work and Managerial Strategy. 'Flexibility' in the New Industrial Relations Framework*. Canberra: Department of Employment Education and Training.

Sawer, Marian (1991) 'Why Has the Women's Movement Had More Influence on Government in Australia than Elsewhere?' in Francis G. Castles (ed.) *Australia Compared. People, Policies and Politics*. Sydney: Allen & Unwin.

Statistics New Zealand (1993a) *All about Women in New Zealand*. Catologue No. 01.021.0093, Wellington.

Statistics New Zealand (1993b) *New Zealand Social Trends. Work*. Catalogue No. 01.053.0093, Wellington.

Statistics New Zealand (1996) *New Zealand Official Yearbook*. Canberra: AGPS.

INDEX